I AM FREUD!

Psychoanalysis Is the Only Method of Cure: It's Too Bad No One Knows How to Do One!!!

Karmic Law- Natural Law- Civil Law

DR. LEN BERGANTINO, ED.D., PH.D.

WORKBOOK PRESS LLC
187 E Warm Springs Rd,
Suite B285, Las Vegas, NV 89119, USA

Website: https://workbookpress.com/
Hotline: 1-888-818-4856
Email: admin@workbookpress.com

Ordering Information:
Quantity sales. Special discounts are available on quantity purchases by corporations, associations, and others.
For details, contact the publisher at the address above.

Library of Congress Control Number:

ISBN-13: 000-0-000000-00-0 (Paperback Version)
000-0-000000-00-0 (Digital Version)

REV. DATE: 10/05/2022

I AM FREUD!

Psychoanalysis Is the Only

Method of Cure:

It's Too Bad No One

Knows How to Do One!!!

I AM FREUD!

I AM CAESAR! I AM THE WORLD'S GREATEST PSYCHOANALYST!!!

PSYCHOANALYSIS-DEVELOPMENT OF EXTRA SENSORY PERCEPTION-REINCARNATION

Dr. Len Bergantino, Ed.D., Ph.D.

ACKNOWLEDGEMENTS

Karen Grant, Senior Publishing Consultant at Workbook Press Publishing Company was at the core of evoking the thoughts in me of publishing all four books that would evoke future clinicians as well as people for the next two hundred years to utilize these books to encourage the freedom of thought from the culture bind to continue to extend both psychoanalytic methodology and ways of Being in the world that will facilitate mankind's pursuit of showing up on a daily basis to answer Shakespeare's question "TO BE OR NOT BE!", and view the question as life's work. In other words, I knew I had the goods but it remained for Karen Grant to know how to market those goods in the service of mankind!

As these books are part of a karmic mission in a pledge made to God to send me back the souls of Drs. Milton H. Erickson and Dr. Wilfred Bion to teach me what to do with paranormal gifts within the confines of what I was later to find out what may be described as "the psychoanalysis frame", I can only say that both children were instrumental in their own unique and unexpected ways in fulfilling their part of their karmic mission in their willingness to seek me out as a parent under the auspices of such pre-determined hardships. Their names are Lisa Francesca Bergantino and Alexander Leonard Bergantino, aka Lisa and Alex!!!

Thus, Karen Grant is to me what Helena Deutsch, aka Hilda Doolittle, aka HD is to FREUD!

-Dr. Len Bergantino, Ed.D., Ph.D.

Dr. LEN BERGANTINO, Ed.D.(USC), Ph.D., A.B.P.P.

Psychoanalysis

(424) 293-9511

June 3, 2021

Dr. Len Bergantino is the most gifted psychoanalyst who ever lived. Admittedly, he had a direct connection with God and the full body of his writings are intended to be "The-Thing-In-Itself" and over the next couple of hundred years evoke an upward spiraling society as opposed to the downward spiraling society from which men suffered. These books provide the tools which is to carry on the work of attending closer and closer approximations of pure being, while at the same time giving psychoanalysis and the world at large the fools with which to carry on The Work. In direct revelation, God informed me that the tools which to carry on The Work is 12 out of 100,000,000 people cross the pearly gates of Heaven. Doubting Thomases go straight to hell!!!

1215 Brockton Ave., Ste. 104, W. Los Angeles, CA 9000-25-U.S.A

Dr. LEN BERGANTINO, Ed.D.(USC), Ph.D., A.B.P.P.

Psychoanalysis

(424) 293-9511

David Welsh

June 3, 2021

In addition to being trained by many world renown psychoanalysts, psychiatrists and clinical psychologists, God helped me utilize paranormal extrasensory abilities by my children as well as myself. These skill sets were imperative that if you can't do politics, you can't do Analysis!!!
Dr. Bergantino and his two children were sent back on a karmic mission to complete the work. Dr. Bergantino is the reincarnated soul of Sigmund Freud and Julius Caesar, his daughter, Lisa Francesca Bergantino is the reincarnated soul of Dr. Wilfred R. Bion. (The great British psychoanalyst) and Cleopatra. His son, Alexander Leonardo Bergantino is the reincarnated soul of Milton H. Erickson, M.D. and guided by the reincarnated soul of Brutus.

1215 Brockton Ave., Ste. 104, W. Los Angeles, CA 9000-25-U.S.A

Dr. LEN BERGANTINO, Ed.D.(USC), Ph.D., A.B.P.P.

Psychoanalysis

(424) 293-9511

June 3, 2021

Dr. Len Bergantino practiced psychoanalysis in Beverly Hills, California from 1979-1993. He has personally trained psychoanalysts, psychiatrists and clinical psychologists at the International level at Wentworth Castle in Sheffield, England, The Royal College of Medicine in London, England, The Bion Conference in Torino Italy and at workshops in Brisbane Sydney, Newcastle and Melbourne Australia.

Dr. Len Bergantino was trained in psychoanalysis including the paranormal and ordinary methods of training by Dr. Wilfred R. Bion, MRCS (Medical Royal College of Surgeons), many of Bions MD Analysis in Beverly Hills, CA, Dr. Morton Grotjohn, M.D., and Dr. Bruno Bettelheim, Ph.D. (who was in the original training group of the world famous Australians and founder of psychoanalysis, Sigmund Freud. It was Freud's mission that I was sent back to clean up. For example, in 1903, Freud gave a presentation on the Oedipal Complex and one of his MD Colleague was yelled out, "This is not a matter for a scientific meeting! It is a matter for the police!". I was trained either to overcome or to bypass such resistance!!!

Dr. Bergantino's work and training included "Developing The Use of Extrasensory Perception in the Practice of Psychoanalysis, Psychotherapy and Clinical Hypnosis. "His work has been described as, "the most gifted clinic of his time, and as a "kind of mental precision that electrified the Australian Therapeutic Community and had lasting therapeutic impact!!

He is an expert in his field, a prominent musician, former radio show personality, a trainer and author. He has written over ten books and is recognized by his poems and Pope Francis himself! His peers hold him in high regards as an extremely brilliant and talented psychotherapist. Below are just a few of the many glowing reviews he has deservingly received.

1215 Brockton Ave., Ste. 104, W. Los Angeles, CA 9000-25-U.S.A

1215 Brockton Ave., Ste. 104, W. Los Angeles, CA 9000-25-U.S.A

Dr. LEN BERGANTINO, Ed.D.(USC), Ph.D., A.B.P.P.

Psychoanalysis

(424) 293-9511

Dr. Bergantino has a mental precision that electrified the Australian Therapeutic Community and had a lasting therapeutic impact!!-Professor Yaro Starale, Director of International Gestalt Therapy Training in Brisbane Australia.

Dr. Wilfred R. Bion, MRCS (Medical Royal College of Surgeons) wrote to Dr. Bergantino. "Your work is evocative and stimulating." I am happy to recommend Dr. Len Bergantino as an excellent workshop leader, trainer and psychotherapist.. "I RECOMMEND HIS WORK, BOTH CLINICAL AND TEACHING, IN ANY SITUATION." Dr. Barry Blicharski, Psychiatrist, Dr. Dinald Rinsley, M.D., Fellow-American College of Psychoanalysts, wrote of Dr. Bergantino, "There is no doubt that some possess a healing capacity... I knew at once of your outsiderism .. as well as your talent".
Dr. James S. Simkin, Ph.D, A.B.P.P, Diplomate American Board of Professional Psychology wrote, " Among all the other therapistsVB V8G, I have ever seen or trained including Fritz Perks, Bergantino, Him I think about. Him I consider. a man of depth. He is a man of substance. "Dr. Bergantino is obviously a gifted therapist. The great advantage of his work is the openness and frankness with which the author reveals his experiences when treating patients."
Dr. Martin Grotjahn, M.D (Training and Supervising Analyst). Dr. James S. Simkin quote should read "Among all the other therapists I have ever seen or trained, including Fritz Per's Bergantino, Him I think about! Him I consider! He is a man of depth, a man of substance. He is a man of substance."

1215 Brockton Ave., Ste. 104, W. Los Angeles, CA 9000-25-U.S.A

Dr. LEN BERGANTINO, Ed.D.(USC), Ph.D., A.B.P.P.

Psychoanalysis
(424) 293-9511

Psychoanalysis
Los Angeles, CA

About the author

Dr. Len Bergantino is the most gifted psychoanalyst who ever lived. Admittedly, he had a direct connection with God and the full body of his writings and intended to be "The-Thing-In-Itself" and over the next couple of hundred years evoke an upward spiraling society as opposed to the downward spiraling society from which men suffered. These books provide the tools which is to carry on the work of attending closer and closer approximations of pure being, while at the same time giving psychonalysis and the world at large. In direct revelation, God informed me that the tools which to carry on The Work is 12 out of 100,000,000 people cross the pearly gates of Heaven. Doubting Thomases go straight to hell!!!

In addition to being trained by many would renowned psychoanalysts, psychiatrists and clinical psychologists, God helped me utilize paranormal extrasensory abilities by my children as well as myself. These skill sets were imperative that if you can't do politics, you can't do analysis!!!

Dr. Bergantino and his two children were sent back on a karmic mission to complete the work. Dr. Bergantino is the reincarnated soul of Sigmund Freud and Julius Caesar. His daughter, Lisa Francesca Bergantino is the reincarnated soul of Dr. Wilfred R. Bion (The great British psychoanalyst) and Cleopatra. His son, Alexander Leonardo Bergantino is the reincarnated soul of Milton H. Erickson, M.D and guided by the reincarnated soul of Brutus.

1215 Brockton Ave., Ste. 104, W. Los Angeles, CA 9000-25-U.S.A

Dr. LEN BERGANTINO, Ed.D.(USC), Ph.D., A.B.P.P.

Psychoanalysis

(424) 293-9511

Dr. Len Bergantino was trained in psychoanalysis including the paranormal and ordinary methods of training by Dr. Wilfred R.Bion, MRCS,(Medical Royal College of Surgeons),many of Bion M.D Analysists in Beverly Hills, CA, Dr. Martin Grotjahn, M.D. ,and Dr. Bruno Bettelheim, Ph.D. (who was in the original training group of the world famous Austrians and founder of psychoanalysts, Sigmund Freud. It was Freud's missions that I was sent back to clean up. For example, in 1903 Freud gave a presentation on the Oedipal Complex, and one of his MD colleagues yelled out, "This is not a matter for scientific meeting! It is a matter for the police!" I was trained either to overcome as to bypass such resistance!!!

Dr. Bergantino's work and training included "Developing The Use of Extrasensory Perception in the Practice of Psychoanalysis, Psychotherapy and Clinical Hypnosis." His work has been described as, "The most gifted clinician of his time", and as "a kind of mental precision_that electrified the Australian Therapeutic Community and had lasting therapeutic impact!!

He is an expert in his field, a prominent musician, former radio show personality, a trainer and author. He has written over ten books and is recognized by his peers and Pope Francis himself! His peers hold him in high regards as an extremely brilliant and talented psychotherapist.

Peer Reviews of Dr. Len Bergantino

Dr. Bergantino has a mental precision that electrified the Australian Therapeutic Community and has a lasting therapeutic impact." - Professor Yaro Starale, Director of International Gestalt Therapy Training in Brisbane, Australia.
Dr. Wilfred R. Bion, MRCS (Medical Royal College of Surgeons) wrote to Dr. Bergantino "Your work is evocative and stimulating. ". I am happy to

1215 Brockton Ave., Ste. 104, W. Los Angeles, CA 9000-25-U.S.A

Dr. LEN BERGANTINO, Ed.D.(USC), Ph.D., A.B.P.P.

Psychoanalysis

(424) 293-9511

recommend Dr. Len Bergantino as an excellent workshop leader, trainer and psychotherapist.. " Dr. Barry Blicharski Psychiatrist. - Sydney, Australia.

"I RECOMMEND HIS WORK, BOTH CLINICAL AND TEACHING, IN ANY SITUATION." --Dr. Barry Blicharski, Psychiatrist.
Dr. Donald Rinsley, M.D., Fellow-American College of Psychoanalysts, wrote of Dr. Bergantino, "There is no doubt that some possess a healing capacity.. I knew at once of your outsiderism.. as well as your talent".
Dr. James S. Simkin, Ph.D, A.B.P.P, Diplomate American Board of Professional Psychology wrote, " Among all the other therapists I have ever seen or trained, Bergantino, He is A man of depth. He is a man of substance. Him I think about. Him I consider."
"Dr. Bergantino is obviously a gifted therapist…the great advantage of his work is the openness and frankness with which the author reveals his experiences when treating patients..." -Dr. Martin Grotjahn, M.D (Training and Supervising Analyst).

Reviews of Dr. Len Bergantino's Music

What an honor to receive your CD of Instrumental classics, it will play of this CD often! Thank you for sharing it. I find your lists of books most interesting-all subjects I enjoy psychology, music and the paranormal. Someday, I'd love to have you on the show to tell our audience about your CT Roots then subsequent migration to Sunny California. - Joe Costa, Host of "Carosello Italiano" radio show. WATR plays 2 songs per week at 11:15 PST on Carosello Italiano. – Milton H. Brickson, M.D. "I respect Dr. Bergantino's dedication to THE WORK."

1215 Brockton Ave., Ste. 104, W. Los Angeles, CA 9000-25-U.S.A

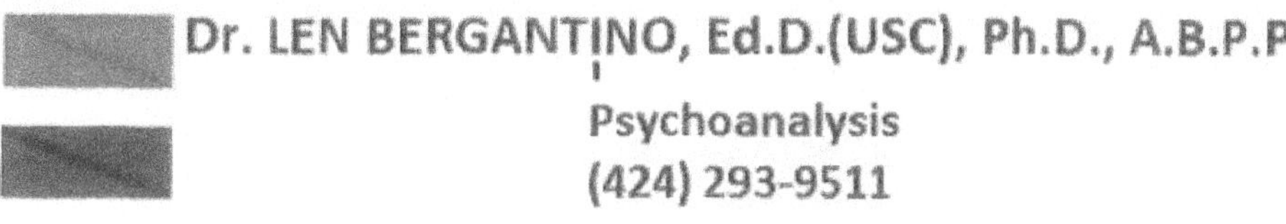

Dr. Bergantino's MP3 on Amazon Digital has the correct pacing from which to make international and tell stories.

1215 Brockton Ave., Ste. 104, W. Los Angeles, CA 9000-25-U.S.A

JAMES S. GROTSTEIN, M.D.
INCORPORATED
522 DALEHERST AVENUE
LOS ANGELES CALIFORNIA 900024
(213) 276-3456
PSYCHOANALYSIS

Len Bergantino, Ph.D.
450 N. Bedford Drive, Suite 300
Beverly Hills, CA 90210

December 30, 1989

Dear Len,

I finally had a pleasure of viewing your tape. I found it very impressive. It helped to understand better where you are coming from and to be able to observe first hand your intuitive way of approaching people. <u>Your technique reminded me of an elegant sophistication, of Gestalt along with Erikson and Bion.</u>

My intimate knowledge of the members of y study group (Interdisciplinary Group for Advanced Studies in Physics – (IGASP) suggests to me that this tape, unfortunately, is not for them. They are not like me nor like you. They are more conservative in their attitudes and tastes and are especially defensive about Bion. Many of them have been analyzed and/or supervised by him, and I believe, to quote Bion, "it would produce more heat than." I think there would be such debate over "beta elements" that the beta elements encountering contrary beta elements would create a beta element cacophony.

On the other hand, let me gently broach the subject to them at the next meeting and see what they say. I will let you know in either case.

Thank you very much for letting me see the tape. It was really educational for me to watch the way you work. You are truly talented.

I hope this year brings you more happiness than any preceding.

Warmest regards,

James S. Grotstein, M.D.

P.S. while this letter was being typed, I learned that Don Rinsley had just passed away!

Letter from Pope Francis

Dr. LEN BERGANTINO, Ed.D.(USC), Ph.D., A.B.P.P.

Psychoanalysis
(424) 293-9511

Dear Billionaire,

I WANT YOU TO GIVE A GIFT OF ABOUT TWO MILLION DOLLARS AS A <u>TAX WRITEOFF</u> MUCH AS STIPENDS WERE GIVEN TO MICHAEL ANGELO FOR PAINTING THE CISTENE CHAPEL! ALONG WITH THIS GIFT AS MY BENEFACTOR IT IS PARAMOUNT THAT YOU FIND THE BEST SYSTEM THAT MARKETS AND DISTRIBUTES BOOKS AND GIVE THEM WHATEVER THEY WANT TO PUT IN BOOKSTORES ON DISPLAY SIX BOOKS I HAVE PUBLISHED BETWEEN NOVEMBER, 2016 AND DECEMBER, 2019.

While is tantamount to PROVING THE EXISTENCE OF GOD ANY AND ALL BOOKS WILL NE SHIPPED TO YOU UPON REQUEST FOR THIS <u>TAX WRITEOFF!!!</u> (UP TO SIX BOOKS FOR DONOR EVALUATION PURPOSES)

MY BOOKS ARE A PUBLIC SERVICE IN THAT THEY WILL TURN A DOWNWARD SPIRALING SOCIETY INTO AN UPWARD SPIRALING SOCIETY WHEN READ AN INGESTED EN TOTO!

The pages that follow give the billionaire of front and <u>back book covers of how one can develop and utilize "HIGHER SENSE PERCEPTION" IN THE DEVELOPMENT OF LIFE PURSUITS TO AN ART FORM!!!</u>

BEST THREE REMAIN A DEARTH OF QUALITY AND EXCELLENCE THE TAX WRITEOFF OF THE BILLIONAIRE KILL PROVIDE A DEVELOPMENT IN THE HIGHEST CALIBRE OF PERSONS AND CITIZENS FOR AT LEAST THE NEXT TWO HUNDRED YEARS!!! PLEASE ON AND CALL BY LETTING 424-293-9511 RING TEN TIMES TO LEAVE A MESSAGE WITH A CALL BACK #.

Sincerely,

Dr. Len Bergantino

To order a copy of the CD Falling in Love send a check for $25 made out to Dr. Len Bergantino and mail to 1215 Brockton Avenue, #104, Los Angeles, CA 900025-1366

Falling In Love
by Dr. Len Bergantino
MP3 Music
Listen with Music Unlimited Or $9.49 to buy MP3
Or $9.49 to buy MP3

At the time this cd was made Joe Diorio, my guitar accompanist, was the foremost jazz guitar player in the world, known primarily to jazz guitar players. I am the only one that got him to play songs for the general public, all of whom agree this cd is magnificent!!!!!!!!!!!!!!!!!!
Dr. Len Bergantino

Currently available from https://tinyurl.com/2p8e3saw

Dr. LEN BERGANTINO, Ed.D.(USC), Ph.D., A.B.P.P.

Psychoanalysis

(424) 293-9511

November 21, 2019

Dear Psychoanalyst,

I want you to be on the lookout for a book recently sent by my publisher entitled I AM FREUD! PSYCHOANALYSIS IS THE ONLY METHOD OF CURE! IT'S TOO BAD NO ONE KNOWS HOW TO DO ONE!!!

THIS BOOK AND OTHERS I HAVE WRITTEN WILL HELP PSYCHOANALYSTS BECOME "HIGHER SENSITIVES" (as written about in a book in 1967 by Shaffica Karagulla, DeVorss Press). This will make all the difference in successfully working through transferences.

My first book, PSYCHOTHERAPY, INSIGHT AND STYLE: THE EXISTENTIAL MOMENT, 1981 Allyn & Bacon, 1994 retitled MAKING AN IMPACT IN THERAPY: HOW MASTER CLINICIANS INTERVEWNE, Jason Aronson, Inc. is an important preface in that the psychoanalytic chapter actually has interviews with the best of Wilfred Bion's Analysands-Supervising and Training Analysts - M.D.'s as well as the order in which Bion's books must be read to develop the level of attention required for psychoanalysis to, in "good faith" continue to grow as a profession! Analysts thought Bion's work was brilliant conceptually and theoretically but not relevant to the practice of psychoanalysis. This IS NOT TRUE AND I AM FREUD, THE BOOK IT TOOK ME FORTY YEARS TO WRITE, DEMONSTRATES MANY OF HIS UNIQUE TECHNICAL APPROACHES TIED TO THE QUALITY OF BEING OF THE PSYCHOANALYST.

FURTHUR, BION SAID "THE ENTIRE PSYCHOANALYTIC LIBRARY IS GOOD for about the first hour and one half of an Analysis! After that YOU HAVE TO KNOW WHAT TO SAY TO THE PATIENT!" Martin Grotjahn,MD told me "Psychoanalysis is a great method of education, but it is ineffective as a method of treatment!"

My also new book "The Art of Psychotherapy And The Liberation of The Therapist" remedies both the concerns of Bion and Grotjahn! As I was trained by 17 or more world renown psychiatrists, psychoanalysts and clinical psychologists THIS UPDATED VERSION OF FORTY YEARS OF THE EXISTENTIAL MOMENT PROVIDES BOTH OPTIONS OF WHAT YOU SAY TO A PATIENT THAT MUST BE INCORPORATED INTO PSYCHOANALYTIC EDUCATION IN WAYS THAT PROVIDE EFFECTIVE TREATMENT! LOOK AT IT THIS WAY! FOR $300,000 OVER A 7 YEAR PERIOD OF FIVE DAY A WEEK ANALYSIS THE PATIENT HAS A RIGHT TO COME OUT OF THE ANALYSIS NOT AS CRAZY AS THE DAY THEY WENT IN!

Sincerely,

P.S. I AM THE ONLY ONW WHO COULD ACTUALLY DO ALL OF WHAT WILFRED BION WROTE!

Dr. Len Bergantino, Ed.D. (USC), Ph.D,A.B.P.P.

1215 Brockton Ave., Ste. 104, W. Los Angeles, CA 90025-U.S.A.

LEN BERGANTINO, Ed.D., Ph.D., A.B.P.P.

Psychoanalysis

(310) 207-9397

Clinical Psychologist

A.B.P.P. – Diplomate in Family Psychology
American Board of Professional Psychology

DO YOU THINK THAT SOME SLUG WHO LOOKS VERY PROFESSIONAL WHO "WHISPERS" AN OCCASIONAL INTERPRETATION TO YOU FIVE TIMES A WEEK FOR 7 YEARS CAN MAKE ONE BIT OF DIFFERENCE IN YOUR LIFE OR DOES SUCH A PSYCHOTOXIC SLUG CALLED A PSYCHOANALYST MERELY STICK YOU IN AN EMOTIONAL TOILET BOWL FOR SEVEN YEARS HAVING THE CUMULATIVE RESULT OF TURNING YOU INTO A HOPELESS BASTARD WHO WILL NEVER TURN THE TRAGIC CORNER IN HIS OR HER LIFE?

CAN YOUR ANALYST ANALYZE AN ARCHAIC LIQUID SYMBIOTIC OR AN OSMOTIC TRANSFERENCE, OR CAN THEY EVEN RECOGNIZE THIS PHENOMENA IN ORDER TO ANALYZE IT ?! IF THE PSYCHOANALYST CANNOT ANALYZE THESE TRANSFERENCES THEY CAN'T DO AN ANALYSIS!!!

I USED TO GET "GOOD FAITH" PATIENTS WHO HAD THE BALLS TO WORK ON THE CUTTING EDGE AT THE SAME TIME I DID BECAUSE THEY HAD HAD COMBINATIONS OF TWENTY YEARS OF TWO SEVEN YEAR ANALYSES PLUS SEVERAL BRIEFER PSYCHOTHERAPIES, ONLY TO BE AS CRAZY AS THE DAY THEY WALKED IN!!! (-$200,000.00)

AS DR. DONALD RINSLEY, M.D., FELLOW-AMERICAN COLLEGE OF PSYCHOANALYSTS WROTE ABOUT ME, MY WORK HAS BOTH A HEALING EFFECT AND AFFECT. PATIENTS USED TO PAY ME SIX MONTHS IN ADVANCE TO HOLD THE TIME OPEN BECAUSE I WAS IRREPLACEABLE: I WAS THE ONLY ONE WHO COULD ANALYZE THE PSYCHOTIC CORE OF THE PERSONALITY AND I WAS THE ONLY ONE WHO COULD ACTUALLY DO WHAT DR. WILFRED R. BION, MRCS (MEDICAL ROYAL COLLEGE OF SURGEONS) WROTE ABOUT ANALYZING THE PSYCHOTIC CORE OF THE PERSONALITY.

AS I AM SEVENTY SIX YEARS OLD, I HAVE WRITTEN FIVE BOOKS THAT MUST BE READ AND DIGESTED IN THEIR ENTIRETY. AS THESE BOOKS ARE THE THING-IN-ITSELF THEY WILL TRANSFORM THE READER INTO THE KINDS OF ANALYST, PATIENT AND PSYCHOTHERAPIST WHO CAN MAKE A DIFFERENCE IN HELPING PEOPLE TURN THE TRAGIC CORNER IN THEIR LIVES! IN OTHER WORDS, THESE FIVE BOOKS ARE ANALYSIS!

THESE BOOKS WERE WRITTEN TO BE AROUND FOR A FEW HUNDRED YEARS AND WERE DIRECTLY GUIDED BY THE ALMIGHTY!!

Letter from Pope Francis

Dr. LEN BERGANTINO, Ed.D.(USC), Ph.D., A.B.P.P.

Psychoanalysis
(424) 293-9511

Dear Billionaire,

I WANT YOU TO GIVE A GIFT OF ABOUT TWO MILLION DOLLARS AS A TAX WRITEOFF MUCH AS STIPENDS WERE GIVEN TO MICHAELANGELO FOR PAINTING THE CISTENE CHAPEL!

ALONG WITH THIS GIFT AS MY BENEFACTOR IT IS PARAMOUNT THAT YOU FIND THE BEST SYSTEM THAT MARKETS AND DISTRIBUTES BOOKS AND GIVE THEM WHATEVER THEY WANT TO PUT IN BOOKSTORES ON DISPLAY SIX BOOKS I HAVE PUBLISHED BETWEEN NOVEMBER, 2018 AND DECEMBER, 2019.

While it is tantamount to PROVING THE EXISTENCE OF GOD ANY AND ALL BOOKS WILL BE SHIPPED TO YOU UPON REQUEST FOR THIS TAX WRITEOFF!!! (UP TO SIX BOOKS FOR DONOR EVALUATION PURPOSES)

MY BOOKS ARE A PUBLIC SERVICE IN THAT THEY WILL TURN A DOWNWARD SPIRALING SOCIETY INTO AN U PWARD SPIRALING SOCIETY WHEN READ AN INGESTED EN TOTO!

The pages that follow give the billionaire of front and back book covers of how one can develop and utilize "HIGHER SENSE PERCEPTION" IN THE DEVELOPMENT OF LIFE PURSUITS TO AN ART FORM!!!

LEST THERE REMAIN A DEARTH OF QUALITY AND EXCELLENCE THE TAX WRITEOFF OF THE BILLIONAIRE WILL PROVIDE A DEVELOPMENT IN THE HIGHEST CALIBRE OF PERSONS AND CITIZENS FOR AT LEAST THE NEXT TWO HUNDRED YEARS!!! PLEASE READ ON AND CALL BY LETTING 424-293-9511 RING TEN TIMES TO LEAVE A MESSAGE WITH A CALL BACK #!

Sincerely,

Dr. Len Bergantino, Ed.D., Ph.D.

1215 Brockton Ave., Ste. 104, W. Los Angeles, CA 90025-U.S.A.

SECRETARIAT OF STATE

From the Vatican, 17 June 2019

Dear Mr Bergantino,

His Holiness Pope Francis has received your letter, and he has asked me to thank you.

The Holy Father will remember you in his prayers, and he invokes upon you God's blessings of joy and peace.

Yours sincerely,

Monsignor Paolo Borgia
Assessor

Mr Len Bergantino
1215 Brockton Avenue
Suite 104
Los Angeles, CA 90025
USA

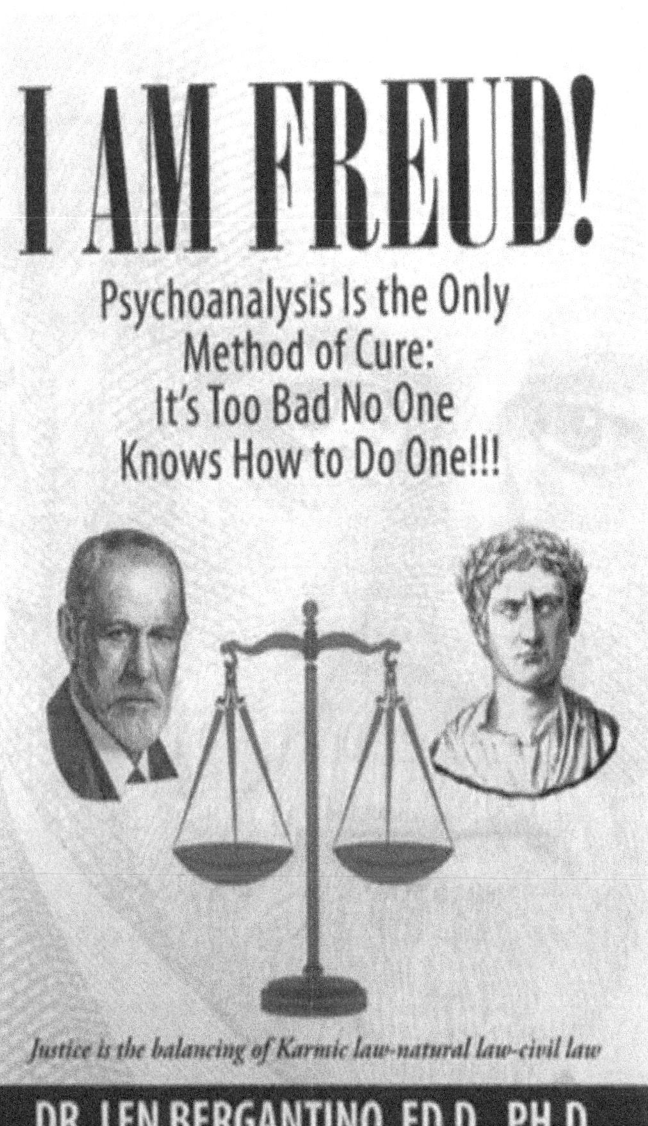
I AM FREUD!
Psychoanalysis Is the Only Method of Cure: It's Too Bad No One Knows How to Do One!!!
Justice is the balancing of Karmic law-natural law-civil law
DR. LEN BERGANTINO, ED.D., PH.D.

This is a book for all time. As I had extrasensory perception to help me find out things on a primitive level and depth with an ability to pick up split-off, severe pathological projective identifications moment to moment in an era when psychologists were only permitted to be research psychoanalysts by the American Psychoanalytic Association (but tightly controlled where that research was going that in many ways nullified it as true psychoanalytic research), I present to you a book that might at that time have been considered wild psychoanalysis. And I will show you how extrasensory perception can be developed and utilized by the therapeutic use of self within the psychoanalytic frame in ways that can enhance the treatment of borderline, narcissistic, obsessive-compulsive, and schizophrenic disorders and other diagnoses, as well as help pinpoint psychophysiological awareness, which through the repetition compulsion, can prevent disease and will circumvent disease in later life. This kind of psychoanalysis will go a long way in preventing the next holocaust!

Dr. Bergantino and his two children were sent back on a karmic mission to complete the work. Dr. Bergantino is the reincarnated soul of Sigmund Freud and Julius Caesar. Those skill sets were required to complete this project. His children are Wilfred Bion and Milton Erickson. They taught Dr. Bergantino how to use paranormal abilities. We are all off the karmic wheel and WE WIL NOT BE BACK!!! GOODBYE!!!

page 17

THE QUALITY OF BEING: PSYCHOANALYSIS - STATE OF THE ART

A REVOLUTIONARY Approach by Len Bergantino, Ed.D., Ph.D
"The Discipline of Being IN THE PRACTICE OF PSYCHOANALYSIS

Beta Elements: An Expansion of the conceptual work of Wilfred R. Bion, M.R.C.S. into Psychoanalytic Technique.

- VHS VIDEO TAPE - ONE HOUR - $45

Seminar by Len Bergantino, Ed.D., Ph.D: Working with a professional audience.

MAKING AN IMPACT IN THERAPY: HOW MASTER CLINICIANS INTERVENE, Jason Aronson Publ., Northvale, N.J.,1993. 288 pages. Author: Bergantino, L.

- For Physicians who want their patients to get better psychologically and for Training Analysts and Psychiatrists who want to learn to succeed at doing these jobs in paragraph 1.

This kind of work permits psychoanalysts to develop techniques to do jobs that have either never or rarely been done:

1. Form a solid nuclear self in a patient who never had one - a job Kohut wrote couldn't be done.
2. Work successfully with the kind of archaic liquid symbiotic transferences that Searles wrote about treating with limited success over 13 and 18 year cases;
3. Detect and work with underlying psychotic thinking disorders - such as Bion wrote about even in narcissistic, borderline and neurotic patients;
4. Detoxify psychotoxic states of being (Kernberg's work stops here) and return patients to natural states of being where affect is connected and life force and the fight for that life force is sustained;
5. Help psychoanalysts' quality of being (Becoming 'O'-Bion) become enhanced so they may be curative of primitive mental states at deep emotional levels, even in patients thought not to be in treatment for that problem. Otherwise, patients will respond to the primitive mental states of the analyst even though the analyst does not act out. The end result would be an analysis whereby the analyst's blocked quality of being would leave patients in prematurely stuck places with self and a significant other whereby that patient's life would remain tragic even after a long analysis.

The Job

- Beta elements that Bion wrote about from a conceptual frame of reference actually exist. The question then becomes how can one do an analysis if they do not perceive with their senses these beta elements because they would not know what needed to be contained, therefore the underlying psychotic thinking disorder aspects of patients personalities, even those thought to be neurotic, narcissistic or borderline, could not be dealt with authentically beyond the point with which a psychoanalyst could 'detect', 'detoxify' and 'interpret' these beta elements.

- Donald Rinsley, M.D., Fellow, American College of Psychoanalysts, in a review of Dr. Bergantino's book, Psychotherapy, Insight and Style: The Existential Moment, Jason Aronson Publishers, 1986, made reference to Dr. Bergantino and his work in the following way: "There is no doubt that some people possess a healing capacity and that others do not. Nor is there any doubt that a Zulu witch doctor, a Puerto Rican curendero, a Navaho Medicine man, or a voodoo spiritist may remit symptoms more effectively than the best trained psychotherapist or psychoanalyst." Bulletin of the Menninger Clinic, Vol. 47, No. 5.

- Len Bergantino, Ed.D., Ph.D is was in the private practice of psychoanalysis in Beverly Hills, CA.

For book send $100 to Len Bergantino, Ed.D, Ph.D
1215 Brockton Avenue, Suite 104
Los Angeles, California 90025 USA

For Training Analysis or psychoanalysis Call (310) 207-9397

DR. LEN BERGANTINO
I AM THE REINCARNATED SOUL
OF SIGMUND FREUD + JULIUS CAESAR
GOD SENT ME BACK
ON A KARMIC MISSION!

"RETIRED CLINICAL PSYCHOLOGIST

drlenbergantino.com

HOME THE AUTHOR THE BOOKS EXCERPT REVIEWS ORDER NOW

DR. LEN BERGANTINO, ED.D., PH.D.

BOOK COLLECTIONS

Books that are either published or will be published authored by **Dr. Len Bergantino** as these books were written as the thing-in itself and were divinely inspired by the Holy Spirit to at the very least give men and women an opportunity to be more fully themselves and more in touch with their own nature. It is strongly recommended that the readers develop their level of attention to read all ten books and permit them to become part parcel of how each individual answers the question "TO BE OR NOT TO BE". As The Reverend Dr. Len Bergantino is seventy five years old, he will not be around personally to do psychoanalysis or psychotherapy with you, therefore these books were written on the basis of them being around for at least TWO HUNDRED YEARS!!!

1. I AM FREUD! Psychoanalysis Is the Only Method of Cure: It's Too Bad No One Knows How to Do One!!!
2. Reverse Analysis, the Existential Shift, Gestalt Family Therapy and the Prevention of the Next Holocaust
3. The Art of Psychotherapy and the Liberation of the Therapist
4. The Essence of Music
5. When Baseball was King The New York Yankees were King of Baseball
6. Germans – Jews – Holocausts and the Collective Unconscious
7. Political Psychology Invasions
8. The Sanctimonious Psychoproctological Invasions: The Handbook for Political Analysis
9. The Denial of Reverse Racism in America
10. The Greatest Basketball Player I Ever Saw

The Author

Dr. Len Bergantino, Ed.D., Ph.D.

Dr. Len Bergantino was trained in psychoanalysis including the paranormal and ordinary methods of training by. Dr. Wilfred R. Bion. MRCS-Medical Royal College of Surgeons. Many of Bion's M.D. Analysands in Beverly Hills, CA, Dr. Martin Grotjahn, M.D. and Dr. Bruno Bettelheim, Ph.D. who was in Freud's original training group. They were all Training Analyst. Dr. Michael Paul M./D. is one of the best of Bion's Training Analysands.

Dr. Ronald Rinsley M.D. Fellow American College of Psychoanalysts wrote about me, "There is no doubt that some people possess a healing capacity and that others do not." "Envies---- jealousies ---- outsiderism."

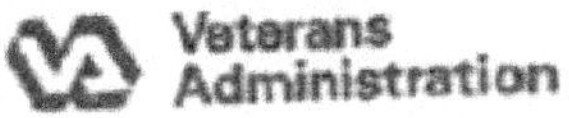
Veterans Administration

1 July 1985

In Reply Refer To

Len Bergantino, Ed.D., Ph.D.
10266 Kilrenney Avenue
Los Angeles, California 90064

Dear Len:

How nice to receive yours of June 24th, and to learn of your upward spiral! I'm very pleased indeed to believe that my little review of your book has contributed to your success!

Frankly, Len, I have long been eructatively fed up with the sort of territorial cupidities and other evidences of narcissistic nonsensicality so many of the colleagues display. Such antics reveal the essentially limbic nature of people as it comes to be expressed in envies and jealousies to which you allude in your letter. When I read your book I knew at once of your outsider-ism (cf. Colin Wilson's seminal book of the same name—The Outsider) as well as your talent; since I know I am good also, I do not need to do the Big-Daddy-in-Cat-On-A-Hot-Tin-Roof bit, viz., to shit on one's sons out of envy and fear that they will appropriate my penis-cum-wife-cum-everything-else!

I trust your family are in good health. Keep in touch.

Most sincerely,

Donald B. Rinsley, M.D., F.R.S.H. (Lond.)
Associate Chief for Education
Psychiatry Service

Clinical Professor of Psychiatry
University of Kansas School of Medicine
Kansas City

DBR:mtf

A Review

By **DONALD B. RINSLEY, M.D., F.R.S.H.,**
Fellow, American College of Psychoanalysis;
Fellow, American psychiatric Association

Psychotherapy, Insight and Style,
By Lea Bergantino, Ed.D., Ph.D.

Boston: Allyn and Bacon, 1981, 288 pp.
Published in Bulletin of the Menninger Clinic,
Vol. 47, No. 5, September 1983.

There is no doubt that some people possess a healing capacity and that others do not; nor is there any doubt that a Zulu witch doctor, a Puerto Rican curandero, a Navacho medicine man or a voodoo spiritist may remit symptoms more effectively than the best trained psychotherapist or psychoanalyst. The differences between healing and therapy are not inconspicuous even as both may readily dissolve into quackery in the hands of the exploitive and the unscrupulous. A wise Freud once commented that the function of psychoanalysis is to convert neurotic misery into ordinary human suffering, a point of view to be dismissed only at one's peril even though it doubtless reflected the essence of Freud's depressive personality. From such few considerations as these emerge questions concerning the difference separating healing and therapy, the features that unite them and the goals and objectives they may be noted to share. And whatever answers to these questions may satisfy those who propound them will reflect whether one's Wellanschauug considers the world to be a vale of tears or, after the fashion of the Gallic optimist, Coué, a place where everything keeps getting better and better.

Dr. Bergantino's book in scholarly and even entertaining fashion out to address issues such as these. The blurb on its bookjacket states that it "integrates 17 prominent therapists' styles and problem solving techniques…" Its more accurate subtitle, The

Existential Moment reflects the authors searching awareness that effective psychological healing, or psychotherapy, or whatever one chooses to call such interpersonal transactional processed ultimately expands one's awareness, hence one's knowledge of one's self, one's surround and the relationship between them; and further, that such awareness and knowledge develops in salutatory fashion, deriving from unheralded and even momentary experiences of insight illumination ("aha!") or unconscious internal change. So far so good, but there is after all nothing new in that, so why read yet another book devoted to arresting human experiences that many believe to be inexplicable and unteachable?

There are at least two answers to that question. To begin, with the book reflects the personal odyssey of a trained, disciplined yet open minded professional psychologist who has deeply drunk at the wells of a number of acknowledged healer-therapists whose work he has carefully studied and evaluated, among them, Viktor Frankl, Wilfred Bion, the Gouldings, Frederick Perls, Milton Erickson and Carl Whitaker. A unique feature of Dr. Bergantino's presentation is his detailed accounts of these therapists' hour-to-hour work, drawn form his own personal experience and from verbatim descriptions provided by their students and analysands, offering fascinating and instructive insights into the therapeutic labors of admittedly gifted treaters. The book is thus replete with clinical materials, excerpts from therapeutic encounters and direct reports of those precious "aha"-type moments, conveyed within a disciplined epistemic context that presents each example in terms of ethical professionalism rather than exemplary amateurishness.

Again, the book reflects its author's ongoing growth and development as both thinker and therapist. Dr. Bergantino has gone to great length to converse and consult with both primary and secondary sources, delving into the what and the how, ferreting out illustrative clinical situations and indicating how he has preceded to synthesize and integrate what he has learned from them and from his own therapeutic work. His book is indeed a literate statement of how one clinician has made of himself a therapist and his statement is both informative and poignant.

As I read this book my thoughts returned to a little-known 1962 Psychiatric Quarterly paper by Ernst Federn, the son of psychoanalyst Paul Federn entitled, "The Therapeutic Personality, As Illustrated by Paul Federn and August Aichorn." It described in some detail the uniquely intuitive therapeutic work of these two outstanding clinicians, drawn from the author's experience from knowing them both; Federn and Aichorn brought disciplined artistry to their respective therapeutic tasks in working psychoanalytically with "difficult" cases, Federn with psychotics, Aichorn with disturbed adolescents; both readily sensed suffering and never flinched from addressing it; both could occupy honored places in Dr. Bergantino's book. I learned much from that paper and I have learned much from Dr. Bergantino's book as well.

Psychotherapy, Insight and Style is an absorbing work, to be returned to time and again after one has read it through, to be

Clinical Psychology (PL3837)

10266 Kilrenney Ave.

Los Angeles, CA 90064

1/12/81

Carl Whitaker, M.D.
Professor of Psychiatry
U. of Wisconsin Medical School
Center for Health Sciences
600 Highland Avenue
Madison, Wisconsin 53792

Dear Carl,

The following is material that you dictated to me over the telephone regarding material that may be used in any advertising capacity that Allyn & Bacon, Inc., chooses to do in the promotion of my book, "Psychotherapy Insight And Style: The Existential Moment."

"The author as a therapist is a student of creativity and he offers a metaphorical elaboration that is both impressionistic, artistic and a stimulus for thinking. He is a professional reporter of interpersonal change models in the family therapy set and even intrapsychic change process in itw twentieth century face. The book rouses powerful feelings and stimulates growth in its readers."

"Reading this book is an active experience in the use of self in the field of psychotherapy, and as such, it both expands and enriches the community standards of practice of professional psychotherapists. That self is really our only tool. It's use is critical and evolving through each practitioner's professional lifetime."

Please sign below acknowledging your permission to quote.

Sincerely,

Len

Carl Whitaker, M.D.

Len Bergantino, Ed.D., Ph.D.

P.S. Please return one copy to me, keep one for your records and send one to Allyn & Bacon, Inc. Thank you.

The Books

I AM FREUD! Psychoanalysis Is the Only Method of Cure:
It's Too Bad No One Knows How to Do One!!!

This is a book for all time. As I had extrasensory perception to help me find out things on a primitive level and depth with an ability to pick up split-off, severe pathological projective identifications moment to moment in an era when psychologists were only permitted to be research psychoanalysts by the American Psychoanalytic Association (but tightly controlled where that research was going that in many ways nullified it as true psychoanalytic research), I present to you a book that might at that time have been considered wild psychoanalysis. And I will show you how extrasensory perception can be developed and utilized by the therapeutic use of self within the psychoanalytic frame in ways that can enhance the treatment of borderline, narcissistic, obsessive-compulsive, and schizophrenic disorders and other diagnoses, as well as help pinpoint psychophysiological awareness, which through the repetition compulsion, can prevent disease and will circumvent disease in later life. This kind of psychoanalysis will go a long way in preventing the next holocoust!

ORDER A COPY NOW

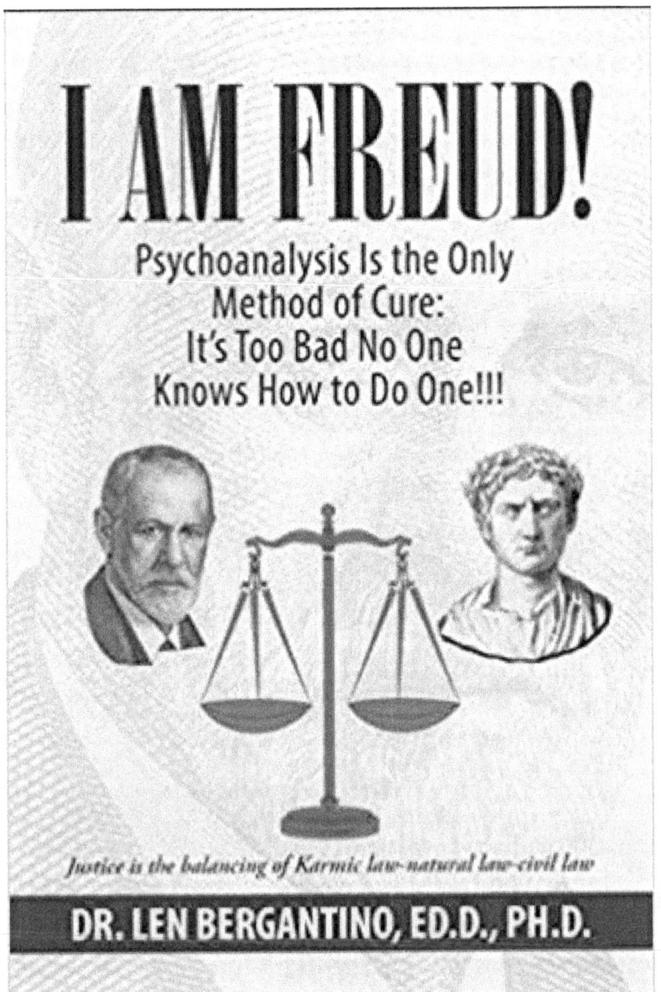
I AM FREUD!
Psychoanalysis Is the Only
Method of Cure:
It's Too Bad No One
Knows How to Do One!!!
Justice is the balancing of Karmic law-natural law-civil law
DR. LEN BERGANTINO, ED.D., PH.D.

This is a book for all time. As I had extrasensory perception to help me find out things on a primitive level and depth with an ability to pick up split-off, severe pathological projective identifications moment to moment in an era when psychologists were only permitted to be research psychoanalysts by the American Psychoanalytic Association (but tightly controlled where that research was going that in many ways nullified it as true psychoanalytic research), I present to you a book that might at that time have been considered wild psychoanalysis. And I will show you how extrasensory perception can be developed and utilized by the therapeutic use of self within the psychoanalytic frame in ways that can enhance the treatment of borderline, narcissistic, obsessive-compulsive, and schizophrenic disorders and other diagnoses, as well as help pinpoint psychophysiological awareness, which through the repetition compulsion, can prevent disease and will circumvent disease in later life. This kind of psychoanalysis will go a long way in preventing the next holocaust!

Dr. Bergantino and his two children were sent back on a karmic mission to complete the work. Dr. Bergantino is the reincarnated soul of Sigmund Freud and Julius Caesar. Those skill sets were required to complete this project. His children are Wilfred Bion and Milton Erickson. They taught Dr. Bergantino how to use paranormal abilities. We are all off the karmic wheel and WE WIL NOT BE BACK!!! GOODBYE!!!

ISBN 978-1-9845-5729-2
52399
9 781984 557292

Press Release

I DARED TO DISTURB THE UNIVERSE

Dr. Len Bergantino Ed. D., Ph.D., releases "I AM Freud! Psychoanalysis Is the Only Method of Cure: It's Too Bad No One Knows How to Do One!!!"

BEVERLY HILLS, Calif.- Dr. Len Bergantino, Ed.D., is the reincarnated soul of Sigmund Freud and Julius Caesar and his children Lisa Francesca is the reincarnated soul of the great British psychoanalyst Wilfred R. Bion and Cleopatra while his developmentally delayed son Alexander Leonardo is the reincarnated soul of Milton H. Erickson, M.D. (known as the father of Modern Medical hypnosis and for Uncommon Therapy) and Brutus. All of those skills sets were necessary in the writing of "I Am Freud! Psychoanalysis Is the Only method of Cure; It's Too Bad no One Knows How To Do One!!!" (published by Xlibris) and the issues it is meant to deal with at both conscious and unconscious levels.

Further, Bergantino in 1980, made a direct contact with God to have Bion and Erickson sent back as the reincarnated souls of his children to teach him what to do with the paranormal gifts that were given to him and unleashed by Erickson. Through this development, he, with god's tutelage became the best psychoanalyst that ever lived and began to implement Freud's plan that both psychoanalysis and subsequently developed psychotherapies would create the kind of patients who would and could then go out and create an upward spiraling society.

Wilhelm Reich, M.D. – Freud's most gifted training analyst said "if you can't do politics, you can't do analysis!" the book shows how to develop extrasensory perception so that analysts and the therapists have an opportunity to develop the tools necessary to do the jobs at hand if they are so inclined. In this way, people will not pay for a five day a week, seven-year analysis and come out as crazy as the day they began with few if any tools to carry on the work.

"When I did an analysis with the crème de la crème of society, they customarily tripled their income and the quality of their life! (Don't waste $50,000 per year or 350,000 per analysis)."

The book is not based on anything Bergantino may or may not believe. It is based on his attaining a level of "pure being" that Jean Paul Sartre wrote about as the thig it-self. And it is at that level that this book was written as the thing-in-itself to effect change in the reader.

"I Am Freud! Psychoanalysis Is the Only Method of Cure: It's Too Bad no One Knows how to Do One!!!"

By Dr. Len Bergantino, Ed.D., Ph.D.

Hardcover | 6 x 9 in | 504 pages | ISBN 9781984557308

Softcover | 6 x 9 in | 504 pages | ISBN 9781984557292

E-book | 504 pages | ISBN 9781984557285

Available at www.amazon.com and www.barnesandnoble.com

About the Author

Dr. Len Bergantino, Ed.D.,Ph.D. practiced psychoanalysis in Beverly Hills, California from 1979-1991. He saw seven patients five days a week for between five and seven years totaling 49 hours a week and saw an occasional family therapy or clinical hypnosis case totaling 52 hours a week at $125 per hour; $625 per week; 4240,000 per year. In addition, he trained psychiatrists and clinical psychologists at the international level delivering on his workshop promise "The Therapeutic Wizardry of Dr. Len Bergantino" at Wentworth Castle in Sheffield, England and training the British at the Royal College of Medicine in London in "developing the Use of Extrasensory Perception in the practice of psychoanalysis, Psychotherapy and Clinical Hypnosis." In Brisbane, Australia, his work described as "a kind of mental precision that electrified the Australian Therapeutic Community and had lasting therapeutic impact." Furthermore, he was an affiliate of the Italian American Lawyers Association for seven years. He became an expert witness in both severe parental Alienation Syndrome in criminal cases. He was the only clinician to plea a bargain a man for release who was on death row. He was President of the Southern California Society of Clinical Hypnosis when they were compassed of exclusively MD's PHD's and DDS'. The year he was president he turned it into a psychoanalytic institute.

Reverse Analysis, the Existential Shift, Gestalt Family Therapy and the Prevention of the Next Holocaust

The purpose of this book is to tell stories that both entertain and bring value to people's lives. The order of the stories told will have no rhyme or reason other than they went through my unconscious mind when I sat down at the typewriter along with the notion they may have value and reach the unconscious mind is the readers in a way that has a better that average chance of entertaining the reader. As I am seventy-five years old when beginning this book, I have worn many hats during my lifetime, and the stories run the gamut.

This book focuses on the lifelong effects that Milton H. Erickson, M.D., Carl Whitaker, M.D., and James Simkin, PhD. Had upon me. It gives the reader a firsthand experience at a ONE THERAPY SESSION EXISTENTIAL SHIFT OF A LIFELONG PERSONALITY CHARACTERISTICS, AS WELL AS THE BOOK ITSELF EVOKING A ONE SESSION EXISTENTIAL SHIFT OF THE COLLECTIVE UNCONSCIOUS MINDS OF SOCIETY AS A WHOLE IN EFFECTING AND AFFECTING "THE PREVENTION OF THE NEXT HOLOCAUST." FURTHER, IN TERMS OF FAMILY THERAPY IT BOTH

DEMONSTRATE HOW TO MAKE DEEP PRIMITIVE AND SUBSTANTIVE CONTACT WITH FAMILY MEMBERS HELPFUL IN SUSTAINING A DEEP PRIMITIVE AND SUBSTANTIVE RELATIONSHIP WITH FAMILY MEMBERS. Dr. James S. Simkin was a Diplomate in Clinical Psychology of The American Board of Professional Psychology.

And then there was DR. WALTER KEMPLER M.D. – A FIRE BREATHING DRAGON THAT LOOKED LIKE ZEUS!!!

REVERSE ANALYSIS, THE EXISTENTIAL SHIFT, GESTALT FAMILY THERAPY AND THE PREVENTION OF THE NEXT HOLOCAUST

Dr. Len Bergantino, Ed.D., Ph.D.

The purpose of this book is to open up the space so that the reader – society at large, psychotherapists and patients might start contributing to LIFE FORCE AND THE THERAPEUTIC USE OF SELF IN CREATING A SOCIETY THAT IS UPWARD SPIRALING INSTEAD OF ONE DOMINATED BY INCURABLE DEATH FORCE! FOR THIS TO HAPPEN SOCIETY AT LARGE MUST LEARN TO THINK AND PAY ATTENTION TO THE FACTS IN THIS BOOK THAT WILL PERMIT THE CREATION OF NEW THOUGHT TO MEET NEW PROBLEMS, SO THAT WE DO NOT HAVE SITUATIONS LIKE 122 VETERANS A DAY COMMITTING SUICIDE WITHOUT HOPE THAT THERE ARE ANY TREATMENTS FOR THEM NOW OR THAT CAN BE CREATED! IT IS RECOMMENDED THAT THIS BOOK BE READ AS ONE OF A SERIES OF FOUR WRITTEN BY DR. LEN BERGANTINO TO CREATE THIS NEW SOCIETY! WHILE PSYCHOTHERAPY IS THE MEDIUM OF CHOICE IN TH THIS BOOK, THE FOURTH BOOK UTILIZES MUSIC AS THE MEDIUM TO ANSWER SHAKESPEARE'S QUESTIONS "TO BE OR NOT TO BE!!!!!!!!!!!!!!!!!!!!!!!!!!!!!!!"

My Children and I were sent back on a karmic mission to PREVENT THE APOCALYPSE AND WE HAVE DONE OUR PART IN WRITING FOUR BOOKS. NOW IT IS UP TO YOU TO READ AND UTILIZE THEM! GOD HAS MYSTERIOUSLY MURDERED THREE PERSONS WHO COULD HAVE STOPPED ME FROM FULFILLING THIS MISSION! WE HAVE SUCCEEDED! THE REST IS UP TO YOU OR YOUR ROOMS WILL BE RESERVED IN HELL! Twelve out of 100 million make it into Heaven!

"This book is a one-sessions existential….

THE ART of Psychotherapy an dthe Liberation of the Therapist

This is a book for professional psychotherapists, psychoanaysts and counselors, students in those areas of specialty and laypersons whoa re interested in the essence of effective therapy and how some of the people who do it best practice their art. Ffor professionals, the book presents a personal way os viewing therapy that can add pleasurable options. Each of the therapists with whom Bergantino worked, and himself, all had a feeling of enjoyment that they hope will carry over to the office and practices of the readers. For students of therapy, the book offers a search for a professional stature and working posture that may be of value in the development of each studen't unique personal style. For laypersons, the book speaks of therapy that can make an impact aand speaks of how some of the most potent therapists practice.

"This book contains Dr. Bergantino's seminal work "Psychotherapy Insight & Style: The Existential moment", Alltyn & Bacon., 1981 Boston (SOLD SIX TTHOUSAND COPIES)!!! PLUS REQUIREMENTS FOR THE DEVELOPMENT AND PRACTICE OF THE ART OF PSYCHOTHERAPY INCLUDING THE UTILIZATION AND DEVELOPENT OF CRETIVE AGGRESSION AS BOTH A THERAPEUTIC TOOL AND THE GROUNDWORK FOR PSYCHOPOLITICAL INTERVENTIONS. IF YOU CAN'T DO POLITICS YOU CAN'T DO PSYCHOTHERAPY, AS THERE WILL BE THOSE THAT INTERVENE WITH THE INTENTION OF AMKING PSYCHOTHERAPY SAFE FOR THE GENERAL PUBLIC WHILE IN FACT GROUPS SUCH AS BOARDS OF PSYCHOLOGY ONLY CREATE THE ILLUSION OF SAFETY, WHILE GUARANTEEING THE DEATH AND DESTRUCTION OF THE ART OF PSYCHOTHERAPY!!!!!!!!!!!!!!

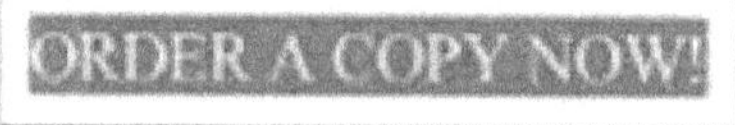

The Art *of*
Psychotherapy
And the Liberation
of the Therapist

Give me
LIBERTY
or give me
DEATH

Much has been written about the Science of Psychotherapy, but it has remained for Dr. Bergantino to write about the Art of Psychotherapy with such elegant impact.

Dr. Len Bergantino, Ed.D., Ph.D.

This is a book for professional psychotherapists, psychoanalysts, and counselors; students in those areas of specialty; and lay persons who are interested in the essence of effective therapy and how some of the people who do it best practice their art. For professionals, the book presents a personal way of viewing therapy that can add pleasurable options. Each of the therapists with whom I worked, and myself, all had a feeling of enjoyment that we hope will carry over to the office and practices of the readers. For students of therapy, the book offers a search for a professional stature and working posture that may be of value in the development of each student's unique personal style. For lay persons, the book speaks of therapy that can make an impact and speaks of how some of the most potent therapists practice. For Psychoanalysts interested in the work of the Great British Psychoanalyst, Dr. Wilfred R. Bion MRCS (Medical Royal College of Surgeons), This is the only book that demonstrates exactly what he did.

I wrote the book with the intention of having it be both an experience and an explanation. I have presented it according to my developmental needs while maturing personally and professionally. This was done so the book might be informative at the conscious level, entertaining at the child level, and persuasive at the unconscious level.

The existential moment is the thread that ties the book together; it is a moment of therapeutic potency. While all moments are existential by definition, there are certain moments that are more powerful in helping patients live happier and healthier lives. Positive results, whether they be from one session or over the long haul, are partially, if not fully, a result of existential moments.

The Essence of Music

This multi-purpose book serves as a natural model for how musicians, as human beings, deal with each other. It provides a baseline for humans in answering Shakespeare's question, "To be or not to be."

Furthermore, the book is substantive and full of depth, enough to be used in music schools no matter what musical genre since it focuses on musicality, pure sound, the art of musicality and peace. It can be utilized in the psychotherapeutic arts, and its content is healing in nature.3

The Essence of Music will teach you the ingredients required to "TURN NOTES INTO MUSIC!"

"ALL YOU HAVE TO SELL IS SOUND!!!"

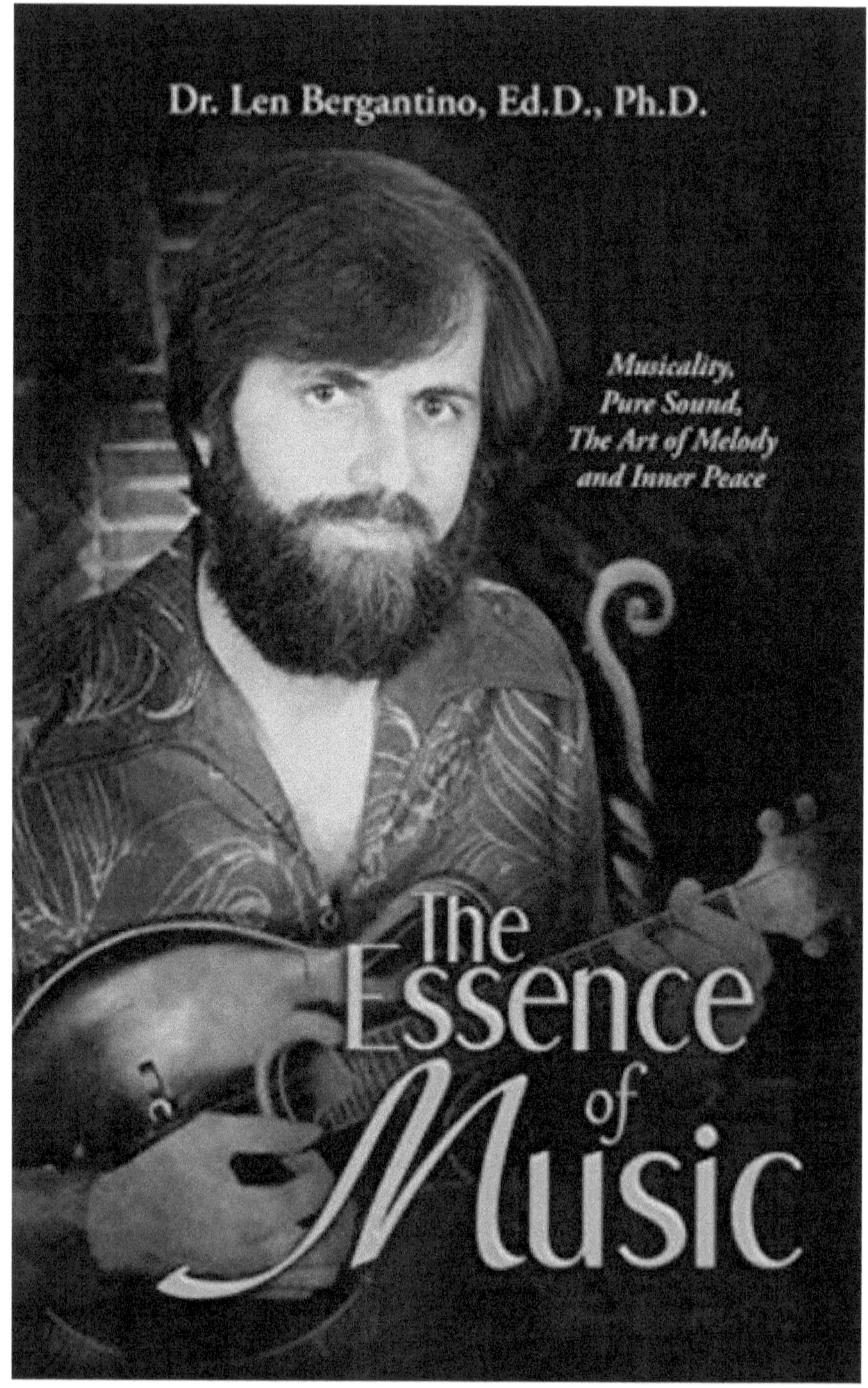
Dr. Len Bergantino, Ed.D., Ph.D.
Musicality, Pure Sound, The Art of Melody and Inner Peace
The Essence of Music

Music is the international language, but what is music!?!!?

For The Bergantino-Bredice Family Music was the FAMILY BUSINESS!
My father, Dan Bergantino, always told me, (in terms of what kind of music you listen to) "IF YOU PUT SHIT IN, SHIT WILL COME OUT! (WHEN YOU PLAY MUSIC)

My cousin Louis Bredice told me, "When I first started playing Jazz, I played a lot of notes! Then I realized, all I needed were the right ones!"

My cousin Freddie Bredice had the fastest technique on guitar I had ever seen! The first time I met him was on a gig in 1967. His speed was blinding, faster than a speeding bullet! I was leaning against a wooden beam next to him and when he finished I said, "You must be cousin Fred!" He said, "Yeah, I don't play chords! It fucks up your hands! "Freddie was one of Joe Diorio's guitar teachers and Joe said he still has nightmares about Freddie's speed! Joe was known as the best jazz guitar playerin the world among guitar players. I got him to play songs again in a cd entitled "FALLING IN LOVE" where I am playing mandolin and Joe is accompanying me on guitar. This cd can be purchased from orchard records.com and amazon.com . On the top picture: LISA BERGANTINO (left), DR. LEN BERGANTINO (middle), and ALEX BERGANTINO (right).

This is a multi-purpose book in that much as a previously published book entitled "ZEN AND THE ART OF MOTORCYCLE MAINTENANCE" had more to do with human growth than motorcycle maintenance; this book is a natural model of how musicians as human beings deal with each other thereby providing a baseline for humans in answering Shakespeare's question, "TO BE OR NOT TO BE!" FURTHER, THIS BOOK IS SUBSTANTIVE AND DEPTHFUL ENOUGH TO BE USED IN MUSIC SCHOOLS, NO MATTER WHAT MUSIC GENRE, IN THAT IT FOCUSES ON MUSICALITY, PURE SOUND, THE ART OF MELODY AND PEACE' AND IT CAN BE UTILIZED IN THE PSYCHOTHERAPEUTIC ARTS AND ITS CONTENTS ARE HEALING IN NATURE!

THE REVEREND DR. LEN BERGANTINO
PROFESSIONAL MUSICIAN FROM 1996-2012
(AGE 56-70) MUSICIAN'S LOCAL 47
AMERICAN FEDERATION OF MUSICIAN'S

On the bottom picture:
HARRY JAMES - 1942

Trained by Carl Whitaker, M.D. in Telephonic Family Therapy

page 37

DR. LEN BERGANTINO
TELEPHONIC FAMILY THERAPY

Dr. of Divinity - (Univ. Life Church) No. 12,656 — Tel. (424) 293-9611
A.B.P.P. - Diplomate in Family Psychology — To Leave Message 7 Rings

TO ORDER HEALING CD SEND $25 TO "THE REVEREND DR. LEN BERGANTINO" AT 1215 BROCKTON AVENUE, #104, LOS ANGELES, CA 90025-1366

HELPS TO FIGHT OFF CORONA VIRUS

RESTORES ENERGY PLAYING AS NEEDED WHEN DEPLETED OF ENERGY

STRENGTHENS IMMUNE SYSTEM TO HELP FIGHT OFF CORONA VIRUS AS WELL AS OTHER FLUS AND ILLNESSES.

This cd combines my musical studies with my best shot at putting together a pacing or slowed down timing I was exposed to when trained by Milton H. Erickson, M.D.- The Father of Modern Medical Hypnosis.

THE COMBINATION OF BEAUTIFUL MUSIC WITH A SLOWER PACING HELPS PEOPLE DEVELOP AN INTERNAL CLOCK THAT IS MUCH SLOWER AND THEREFORE "RELATIVELY FREE OF DISEASE!"

Sincerely,

The Reverend Dr. Len Bergantino

The Reverend Dr. Len Bergantino, Ed.D. (USC), Ph.D. and Doctor of Divinity -No. 12656 registered with The State of California in 1975.

To order a copy of the CD Falling in Love send a check for $25 made out to Dr. Len Bergantino and mail to 1215 Brockton Avenue, #104, Los Angeles, CA 900025-1366

Falling In Love
by Dr. Len Bergantino
MP3 Music
Listen with Music Unlimited Or $9.49 to buy MP3
Or $9.49 to buy MP3

At the time this cd was made Joe Diorio, my guitar accompanist, was the foremost jazz guitar player in the world, known primarily to jazz guitar players. I am the only one that got him to play songs for the general public, all of whom agree this cd is magnificent!!!!!!!!!!!!!!!!!!

Dr. Len Bergantino

Currently available from https://tinyurl.com/2p8e3saw

page 40

When Baseball was King The New York Yankees were King of Baseball

Dr. Len Bergantino's most intense love affair with baseball was between the years 1951 – 1961. Then he went to college and his attentions went elsewhere. Yet, he returned to baseball by reading baseball books on overseas flights and noticed that every time he read about baseball, it brought peace and tranquility to his life. This prompted him to pen ***When Baseball was King The New York Yankees were King of Baseball****.*

**THE MINIMUM CONDITIONS REQUIRED TO ACHIEVE THE COMPLETE DEVELOPMENT OF YOUR OWN BEING REQUIRES THAT YOU READ EACH OF THE BOOKS IN A MANNER WHERE THE WORK IS INTEGRATED AT A DEEP AND SUBSTANTIVE LEVEL. THE BASEBALL BOOK ROUNDS OUT THE CHILDHOOD FUN ASPECTS OF YOUR PERSONAL DEVELOPMENT.*

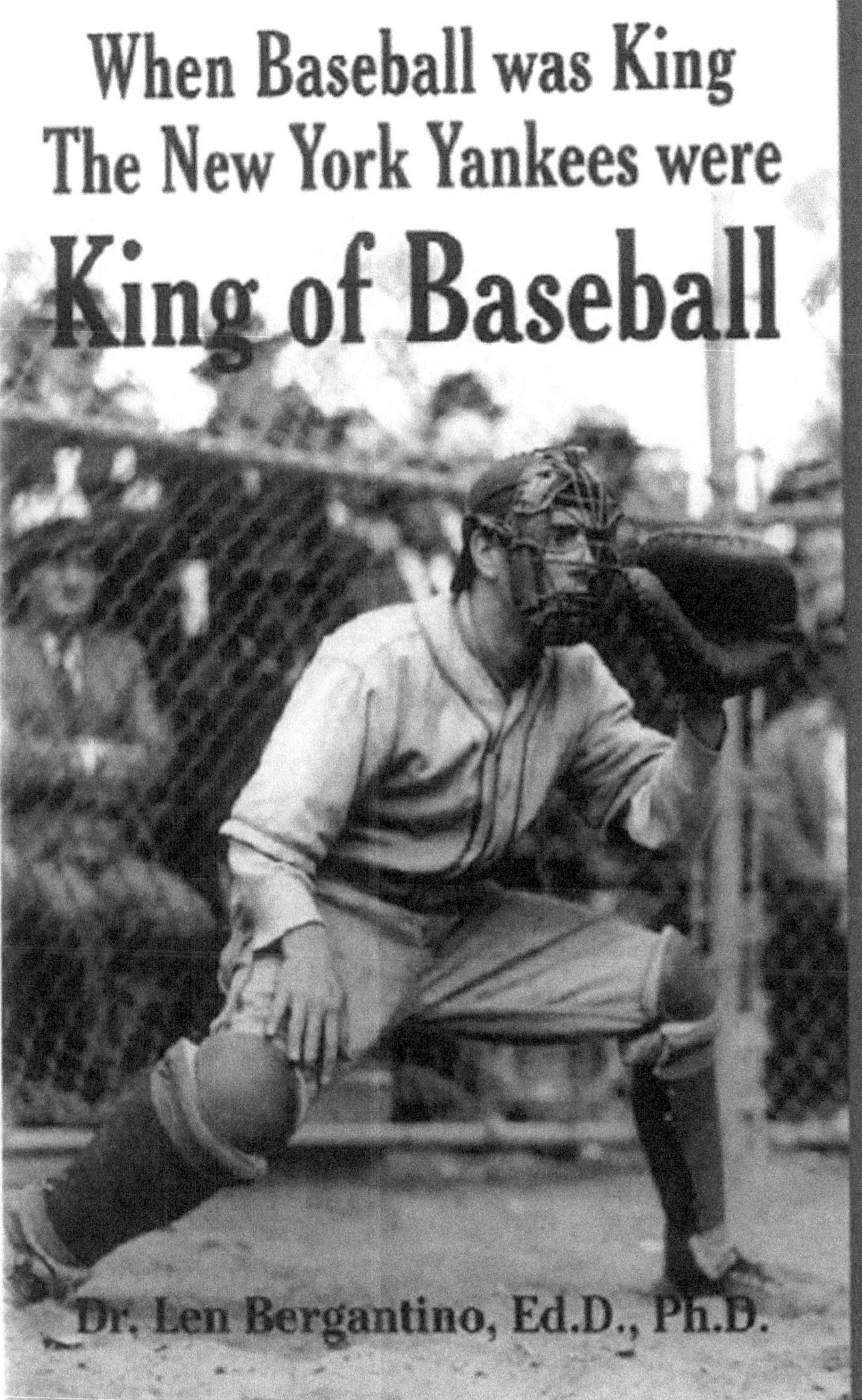
When Baseball was King
The New York Yankees were
King of Baseball
Dr. Len Bergantino, Ed.D., Ph.D.

This photo was given to me by the Mick himself. (Courtesy of Mickey Mantle)

The Reverend Dr. Len Bergantino is a multi-faceted individual who achieved international prominence in the areas of psychoanalysis, psychotherapy, clinical psychology, and music. His other fields include education and religion, with a precursory knowledge of medicine and law. He is a weathervane in terms of knowing the right thing to do and has the temperament of Che Guevarra in getting it done!

When the Reverend Dr. Len Bergantino grew up, the first thing he had in mind was to wear number 22 and take over for Allie Reynolds, the Super Chief, as the Mainstay of the Mound Staff of the NEW YORK YANKEES!!! The New York Yankees won 5-world series in a row. (1949-1953) !!!

CARL ERSKINE

This photo was given to me by Mick himself. (Courtesy of Mickey Mantle)

Unsolicited Review

February 24, 2022

Len…
I just want to let you know how much I enjoyed your book. The stories about the players, managers and owners of our youth were great.

What made the book so enjoyable was that some stories brought out wonderful memories and some events that I didn't know about.

It's a bit of history from a time when, Baseball was the "only sport."

It was a great read.

Thank You and take care,

F.

"WHEN BASEBALL WAS KING THE NEW YORK YANKEES WERE KING OF BASEBALL"

Perhaps Allie Reynolds best summed it up when the New York Yankees bought him from the Cleveland Indians and he was asked "What is the difference pitching for Cleveland as opposed to The New York Yankees?" He said, "I am a Cherokee Indian from Oklahoma. In Cleveland they call me copperhead and old blanket ass! In New York they call me The Super Chief!

That's the difference" The New York Yankees won five world series in a row! (1949-1953)

This book contains the folklore of baseball in an era that not only achieved EXCELLENCE but produced a quality of athlete that became part of your family at the dinner table!

It is an era the spirit of place of which should be remembered; even those who played against the Yankees and provided a good deal of torture to Yankee fans! For example, one of the highlights for me in writing this book was in getting to know and talk with Carl Erskine, the Brooklyn Dodger who in the third game of the 1953 world series pitched the most dominant game I ever saw pitched against what many consider to be the best baseball team in the history of baseball. He struck out 14 Yankees, and Mickey Mantle four times on that day!

thought about, mulled over and placed on one's bedside table if not under one's pillow. It is a book that the experienced clinician will read with knowledgeable satisfaction and that the nascent therapist will read with excitement. And both will profit from what it has to tell.

Donald Rinsley, M.D., F.R.S.H.
Senior Faculty Member in Adult and Child Psychiatry, Karl Menninger School of Psychiatry

Associate Chief for Education, Psychiatry Service, Colmery-O'Neil Veterans Administration Medical Center

Dr. Donald Rinsley, MD was a Fellow of The American College of Psychoanalysts

A Review

By DONALD B. RINSLEY, M.D., F.R.S.H.,
Fellow, American College of Psychoanalysts;
Fellow, American Psychiatric Association

Psychotherapy, Insight and Style.
By Len Bergantino, Ed.D., Ph.D.
Boston: Allyn and Bacon, 1981, 288 pp.
Published in Bulletin of the Menninger Clinic, Vol. 47, No. 5, September 1983.

There is no doubt that some people possess a healing capacity and that others do not; nor is there any doubt that a Zulu witch doctor, a Puerto Rican *curandero*, a Navaho medicine man or a voodoo spiritist may remit symptoms more effectively than the best trained psychotherapist or psychoanalyst. The differences between healing and therapy are not inconspicuous even as both may readily dissolve into quackery in the hands of the exploitive and the unscrupulous. A wise Freud once commented that the function of psychoanalysis is to convert neurotic misery into ordinary human suffering, a point of view to be dismissed only at one's peril even though it doubtless reflected the essence of Freud's depressive personality. From such few considerations as these emerge questions concerning the differences separating healing and therapy, the features that unite them and the goals and objectives they may be noted to share. And whatever answers to these questions may satisfy those who propound them will reflect whether one's *Weltanschauung* considers the world to be a vale of tears or, after the fashion of the Gallic optimist, Coué, a place where everything keeps getting better and better.

A Review

By **DONALD B. RINSLEY, M.D., F.R.S.H.,**
Fellow, American College of Psychoanalysis;
Fellow, American psychiatric Association

Psychotherapy, Insight and Style,
By Lea Bergantino, Ed.D., Ph.D.

Boston: Allyn and Bacon, 1981, 288 pp.
Published in Bulletin of the Menninger Clinic,
Vol. 47, No. 5, September 1983.

There is no doubt that some people possess a healing capacity and that others do not; nor is there any doubt that a Zulu witch doctor, a Puerto Rican curandero, a Navacho medicine man or a voodoo spiritist may remit symptoms more effectively than the best trained psychotherapist or psychoanalyst. The differences between healing and therapy are not inconspicuous even as both may readily dissolve into quackery in the hands of the exploitive and the unscrupulous. A wise Freud once commented that the function of psychoanalysis is to convert neurotic misery into ordinary human suffering, a point of view to be dismissed only at one's peril even though it doubtless reflected the essence of Freud's depressive personality. From such few considerations as these emerge questions concerning the difference separating healing and therapy, the features that unite them and the goals and objectives they may be noted to share. And whatever answers to these questions may satisfy those who propound them will reflect whether one's Wellanschauug considers the world to be a vale of tears or, after the fashion of the Gallic optimist, Coué, a place where everything keeps getting better and better.

Dr. Bergantino's book in scholarly and even entertaining fashion out to address issues such as these. The blurb on its bookjacket states that it "integrates 17 prominent therapists' styles and problem solving techniques…" Its more accurate subtitle, The

Existential Moment reflects the authors searching awareness that effective psychological healing, or psychotherapy, or whatever one chooses to call such interpersonal transactional processed ultimately expands one's awareness, hence one's knowledge of one's self, one's surround and the relationship between them; and further, that such awareness and knowledge develops in salutatory fashion, deriving from unheralded and even momentary experiences of insight illumination ("aha!") or unconscious internal change. So far so good, but there is after all nothing new in that, so why read yet another book devoted to arresting human experiences that many believe to be inexplicable and unteachable?

There are at least two answers to that question. To begin, with the book reflects the personal odyssey of a trained, disciplined yet open minded professional psychologist who has deeply drunk at the wells of a number of acknowledged healer-therapists whose work he has carefully studied and evaluated, among them, Viktor Frankl, Wilfred Bion, the Gouldings, Frederick Perls, Milton Erickson and Carl Whitaker. A unique feature of Dr. Bergantino's presentation is his detailed accounts of these therapists' hour-to-hour work, drawn form his own personal experience and from verbatim descriptions provided by their students and analysands, offering fascinating and instructive insights into the therapeutic labors of admittedly gifted treaters. The book is thus replete with clinical materials, excerpts from therapeutic encounters and direct reports of those precious "aha"-type moments, conveyed within a disciplined epistemic context that presents each example in terms of ethical professionalism rather than exemplary amateurishness.

Again, the book reflects its author's ongoing growth and development as both thinker and therapist. Dr. Bergantino has gone to great length to converse and consult with both primary and secondary sources, delving into the what and the how, ferreting out illustrative clinical situations and indicating how he has preceded to synthesize and integrate what he has learned from them and from his own therapeutic work. His book is indeed a literate statement of how one clinician has made of himself a therapist and his statement is both informative and poignant.

As I read this book my thoughts returned to a little-known 1962 Psychiatric Quarterly paper by Ernst Federn, the son of psychoanalyst Paul Federn entitled, "The Therapeutic Personality, As Illustrated by Paul Federn and August Aichorn." It described in some detail the uniquely intuitive therapeutic work of these two outstanding clinicians, drawn from the author's experience from knowing them both; Federn and Aichorn brought disciplined artistry to their respective therapeutic tasks in working psychoanalytically with "difficult" cases, Federn with psychotics, Aichorn with disturbed adolescents; both readily sensed suffering and never flinched from addressing it; both could occupy honored places in Dr. Bergantino's book. I learned much from that paper and I have learned much from Dr. Bergantino's book as well.

Psychotherapy, Insight and Style is an absorbing work, to be returned to time and again after one has read it through, to be

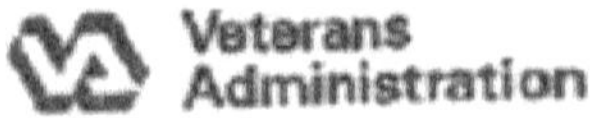
Veterans Administration

1 July 1985

In Reply Refer To:

Len Bergantino, Ed.D., Ph.D.
10266 Kilrenney Avenue
Los Angeles, California 90064

Dear Len:

How nice to receive yours of June 24th, and to learn of your upward spiral! I'm very pleased indeed to believe that my little review of your book has contributed to your success!

Frankly, Len, I have long been eructatively fed up with the sort of territorial cupidities and other evidences of narcissistic nonsensicality so many of the colleagues display. Such antics reveal the essentially limbic nature of people as it comes to be expressed in envies and jealousies to which you allude in your letter. When I read your book I knew at once of your outsider-ism (cf. Colin Wilson's seminal book of the same name—The Outsider) as well as your talent; since I know I am good also, I do not need to do the Big-Daddy-in-Cat-On-A-Hot-Tin-Roof bit, viz., to shit on one's sons out of envy and fear that they will appropriate my penis-cum-wife-cum-everything-else!

I trust your family are in good health. Keep in touch.

Most sincerely,

Donald B. Rinsley, M.D., F.R.S.H. (Lond.)
Associate Chief for Education
Psychiatry Service

Clinical Professor of Psychiatry
University of Kansas School of Medicine
Kansas City

DBR:mtf

Clinical Psychology (PL3837)

10266 Kilrenney Ave.

Los Angeles, CA 90064

1/12/81

Carl Whitaker, M.D.
Professor of Psychiatry
U. of Wisconsin Medical School
Center for Health Sciences
600 Highland Avenue
Madison, Wisconsin 53792

Dear Carl,

The following is material that you dictated to me over the telephone regarding material that may be used in any advertising capacity that Allyn & Bacon, Inc., chooses to do in the promotion of my book, "Psychotherapy Insight And Style: The Existential Moment."

"The author as a therapist is a student of creativity and he offers a metaphorical elaboration that is both impressionistic, artistic and a stimulus for thinking. He is a professional reporter of interpersonal change models in the family therapy set and even intrapsychic change process in itw twentieth century face. The book rouses powerful feelings and stimulates growth in its readers."

"Reading this book is an active experience in the use of self in the field of psychotherapy, and as such, it both expands and enriches the community standards of practice of professional psychotherapists. That self is really our only tool. It's use is critical and evolving through each practitioner's professional lifetime."

Please sign below acknowledging your permission to quote.

Sincerely,

Len

Carl Whitaker, M.D.

Len Bergantino, Ed.D., Ph.D.

P.S. Please return one copy to me, keep one for your records and send one to Allyn & Bacon, Inc. Thank you.

page 17

THE QUALITY OF BEING: PSYCHOANALYSIS - STATE OF THE ART

A REVOLUTIONARY Approach by Len Bergantino, Ed.D., Ph.D

"The Discipline of Being IN THE PRACTICE OF PSYCHOANALYSIS

Beta Elements: An Expansion of the conceptual work of Wilfred R. Bion, M.R.C.S. into Psychoanalytic Technique.

- VHS VIDEO TAPE - ONE HOUR - $45

Seminar by Len Bergantino, Ed.D., Ph.D: Working with a professional audience.

MAKING AN IMPACT IN THERAPY: HOW MASTER CLINICIANS INTERVENE, Jason Aronson Publ., Northvale, N.J.,1993. 288 pages. Author: Bergantino, L.

- For Physicians who want their patients to get better psychologically and for Training Analysts and Psychiatrists who want to learn to succeed at doing these jobs in paragraph 1.

This kind of work permits psychoanalysts to develop techniques to do jobs that have either never or rarely been done:

1. Form a solid nuclear self in a patient who never had one - a job Kohut wrote couldn't be done.
2. Work successfully with the kind of archaic liquid symbiotic transferences that Searles wrote about treating with limited success over 13 and 18 year cases;
3. Detect and work with underlying psychotic thinking disorders - such as Bion wrote about even in narcissistic, borderline and neurotic patients;
4. Detoxify psychotoxic states of being (Kernberg's work stops here) and return patients to natural states of being where affect is connected and life force and the fight for that life force is sustained;
5. Help psychoanalysts' quality of being (Becoming 'O'-Bion) become enhanced so they may be curative of primitive mental states at deep emotional levels, even in patients thought not to be in treatment for that problem. Otherwise, patients will respond to the primitive mental states of the analyst even though the analyst does not act out. The end result would be an analysis whereby the analyst's blocked quality of being would leave patients in prematurely stuck places with self and a significant other whereby that patient's life would remain tragic even after a long analysis.

- Beta elements that Bion wrote about from a conceptual frame of reference actually exist. The question then becomes how can one do an analysis if they do not perceive with their senses these beta elements because they would not know what needed to be contained, therefore the underlying psychotic thinking disorder aspects of patients personalities, even those thought to be neurotic, narcissistic or borderline, could not be dealt with authentically beyond the point with which a psychoanalyst could 'detect', 'detoxify' and 'interpret' these beta elements.

- Donald Rinsley, M.D., Fellow, American College of Psychoanalysts, in a review of Dr. Bergantino's book, Psychotherapy, Insight and Style: The Existential Moment, Jason Aronson Publishers, 1986, made reference to Dr. Bergantino and his work in the following way: "There is no doubt that some people possess a healing capacity and that others do not. Nor is there any doubt that a Zulu witch doctor, a Puerto Rican curendero, a Navaho Medicine man, or a voodoo spiritist may remit symptoms more effectively than the best trained psychotherapist or psychoanalyst." Bulletin of the Menninger Clinic, Vol. 47, No. 5.

- Len Bergantino, Ed.D., Ph.D was is in the private practice of psychoanalysis in Beverly Hills, CA.

For book send $100 to Len Bergantino, Ed.D, Ph.D

1215 Brockton Avenue, Suite 104
Los Angeles, California 90025 USA

For Training Analysis or psychoanalysis Call (310) 207-9397

*RETIRED CLINICAL PSYCHOLOGIST

DR. LEN BERGANTINO
I AM THE REINCARNATED SOUL
OF SIGMUND FREUD + JULIUS CAESAR
GOD SENT ME BACK
ON A KARMIC MISSION!

Page 11

JAMES S. GROTSTEIN, M.D.
INCORPORATED
522 DALEHURST AVENUE
LOS ANGELES, CALIFORNIA 90024
(213) 276-3456
PSYCHOANALYSIS

December 30, 1989

Len Bergantino, Ph.D.
450 N. Bedford Drive, Suite 300
Beverly Hills, CA 90210

Dear Len,

I finally had the pleasure of viewing your tape. I found it very impressive. It helped me to understand better where you are coming from and to be able to observe first hand your intuitive way of approaching people. Your technique reminded me of an elegant sophistication of Gestalt along with Erikson and Bion.

My intimate knowledge of the members of my study group (Interdisciplinary Group for Advanced Studies in Psychosis -- "IGASP") suggests to me that this tape, unfortunately, is not for them. They are not like me nor like you. They are more conservative in their attitudes and tastes and are especially defensive about Bion. Many of them have been analyzed and/or supervised by him, and I believe, to quote Bion, "it would produce more heat than light!" I think there would be such debate over "beta elements" that the beta elements encountering contrary beta elements would create a beta element cacophony.

On the other hand, let me gently broach the subject to them at the next meeting and see what they say. I will let you know in either case.

Thank you very much for letting me see the tape. It was really educational for me to watch the way you work. You are truly talented.

I hope this year brings you more happiness than any preceeding.

Warmest regards,

James S. Grotstein, M.D.

JSG/sf

P.S. While this letter was being typed, I learned that Don Rinsley had just passed away!

FOREWORD

The purpose of this book is multifaceted. It is offered as a proof beyond a reasonable doubt that the energy work of Anton Mesmer, the character armor energy work of Wilhelm Reich, the cutting away the character disorder work of John Rosen as well as my integration of all my works must be combined with the disease free pacing work of Milton H. Erickson and Wilfred R. Bion to actually put the work of Bion into psychoanalytic practice in a manner that will leave patients psychosexually connected ala the working through of Freud's Oedipus and Electra complexes at not only the neurotic and psychotic levels, and by doing so psychoanalysis will truly both become the only method of cure as well as set the frame for all other psychotherapies that may impact differing aspects of the psychoanalytic puzzle. But make no mistake about it. Psychoanalysis is the only method that has the opportunity to work as effectively as a Rolls Royce engine.

A second purpose is the doing away with licensing boards to regulate both psychoanalysis and psychotherapies as they guarantee that the creative cannot use what they know to experiment with the courageous patient in successfully doing the unknowable! A simple example is the taking of notes in a psycho-litigious environment that has legally created the need for such notes. SIMPLY STATED, THOSE TAKING NOTES ARE NOT ABLE TO PAY ATTENTION TO THE NUANCES OF PRIMITIVE DETAIL TO CREATE SUCH A PSYCHOANALYSIS. THE RESULTS OF KEEPING CHECKS AND BALANCES ON PSYCHOANALYSTS AND

PSYCHOTHERAPISTS IS THAT YOU HAVE PATIENTS WHO HAVE HAD TWO SEVEN YEAR ANALYSES AND ABOUT ANOTHER SEVEN OF PSYCHOTHERAPY AND STILL CANNOT TURN THE TRAGIC CORNER IN THEIR LIVES. AND THEN THERE ARE THE 122 VETERANS THAT COMMIT SUICIDE EVERY DAY WITHOUT A PRAYER IN THE WORLD OF FINDING A PSYCHOTHERAPY THAT WILL REVERSE THIS CATASTROPHIC TREND IN SUICIDES!

A third purpose is the unification of psychoanalysis as the method of treatment at the top being unified with religion so the spirit of place of Analysis will be in accord with Freud's original purpose of Analysis-SAVING MAN'S SOUL! This spirit of place will transcend down through the other psychotherapies and we will no longer have a soulless, Godless environment from which to pursue mental health. It is in this manner that Freud's objective of turning society into an UPWARD SPIRALING SOCIETY AS OPPOSED TO A DOWNWARD SPIRALING SOCIETY MAY ACTUALLY BE WORKED UPON!

A fourth purpose is about as easy as proving the existence of God, that reincarnation actually exists. This also calls for a reckoning with the Roman Catholic Church. I was born a Roman Catholic and so God has given me both the gifts to carry on the work, and to do so as the reincarnated soul of Sigmund Freud and Julius Caesar, having inherited their skill sets in doing a job that goes against all the psychoanalytic, psychiatric and psychological guilds that guarantee MEDIOCRITY!

The Hindus have written the most near my experiences regarding reincarnation, the only difference being that when God sent me back on a karmic mission to clean up the messes I made as Freud and Caesar, God, upon my continued prayers over a year and one half without result sent back Wilfred Bion and Milton Erickson as my children to help me figure out what to do with the "gift". In 1978 energy used to shoot out of my hands. UCLA Kurlian Photography was sending me cancer patients, and colleagues were complaining to the Board of Psychology. I prayed to God that Milton Erickson and Wilfred Bion would be sent back karmically to help me KNOW WHAT TO DO WITH MY HEALING CAPACITY AND STILL EARN A LIVING AT THE

BEGINNING OF MY CAREER. THIS WAS DONE AND WITH THE ADDITIONAL HELP OF OLGA WORRALL, THE GREAT AND LEGITIMATE PSYCHIC HEALER WHOM UCLA TOOK PICTURES OF IN THEIR KURLIAN PHOTOGRAPHY LAB WITH FLAMES COMING OUT OF HER HANDS (ENERGY), I WAS ABLE TO DUMB DOWN AND APPLY MY GIFTS TO PSYCHOANALYSIS FOR THE NEXT FORTY YEARS. MUCH OF WHAT I HAVE WRITTEN CAME FROM THE HOLY SPIRIT, IN THAT I DO NOT KNOW WHAT I AM GOING TO WRITE IN ADVANCE. I JUST FEEL COMPELLED TO SIT AT THE TYPEWRITER AND IT COMES OUT.

While God sent me back Bion and Erickson as my children God also tipped me off that one soul can have more than one reincarnation in that I was sent back as both Freud and Caesar with their accompanying skill sets to accomplish the tasks I have written about and my daughter, Lisa Francesca was sent back as both Bion and Cleopatra and my son Alexander Leonardo was sent back as both Milton Erickson and Decimus Brutus. They indeed helped me achieve the reasons God sent me back, only not at all in the way I had envisioned such a task from a temporal perspective. Yet, there was no way neither I nor YOU THE READER could KNOW what you were in store for. That is I was not able to discern the way in which God planned for me and my children to accomplish the KARMIC MISSION I ASKED FOR!

ERGO, THE SAYING, "YOU BETTER WATCH WHAT YOU ASK FOR BECAUSE YOU MIGHT GET IT!"

This was a book intended to be of value to psychoanalysts who will work directly on the problem using their own gifts in developing what is meant to be EVOCATIVE AND STIMULATING TO BOTH PSYCHOANALYSTS AND ALL OTHER MENTAL HEALTH PROFESSIONS FOR AT LEAST THE NEXT TWO HUNDRED YEARS AND MAYBE FOR ALL ETERNITY IN THAT IT IS UNLIKELY THE READERS WILL DEVELOP THEIR PSYCHOANALYTIC AND THERAPEUTIC USE OF SELVES TO THE DEGREE WRITTEN ABOUT IN THIS BOOK. This discipline of self was one of the reasons I was chosen, as unlikely a candidate as I might be even to myself.

This presents a big problem for the Catholic Church. They do not believe in reincarnation. I have written to the Pope many times as well as some of his most powerful Cardinals in the United States. I have presented them with a person that is in "Good Faith", who is a lifelong Roman Catholic, who insists that God chose me to reunify the Catholic Church with psychoanalysis and other psychotherapies as a means of cleaning up the karmic mess that exists in that Freud's purpose of Analysis was to save Man's Soul and to create an upward spiraling society. Further, at this point in time I call cleaner and more infallible shots than the Pope in matters of faith and morals in that I have a direct connection to God and The Pope does not! In other words THE CATHOLIC CHURCH HAS TO STRETCH TO CONTAIN WHAT THE HOLY SPIRIT SENT ME BACK TO DO! (READ BION'S WORK ON THE CONTAINER AND THE CONTAINED)

I am seventy five years old now. The first book I wrote became a master classic in the field for 20 years. I was 37 years old. However, a rereading of Psychotherapy, Insight and Style: The Existential Moment (written when I was 37 years old) will help psychoanalysts and psychotherapists to do what Bion actually said, "The entire psychoanalytic library is good for about the first hour and one half of an Analysis; After that you have to know what to say to the patient!" This book will provide a springboard for creative approaches to make contact with the unreachable in actually knowing what to say to the patient; as well in many cases to turn the tragic corner in patients' lives! This book is expected to be published by Workbook Press Publishing Company soon.

A third and fourth book are expected to be published soon by Workbook Press. One is Reverse Analysis. Gestalt Family Therapy, The Existential Shift, and PREVENTING THE NEXT HOLOCAUST!. This book shows you the kinds of therapies I did since the first book and THE KIND OF THINKING THAT WILL LEAD TO A HEALING THERAPEUTIC PROCESS.

The fourth book is written about Music as a Way of Being in The World, which is also instrumental not only for music, but in becoming the kind of persons who create music from the inside out, so they are not playing a bunch of practiced notes that sound more like noise than touching one's soul! The title of this book is "All I have to sell is sound!" I may add "The Essence of Music to the title.

It is not only recommended that you read all of my books as they will evoke the development of psychoanalysis and psychotherapies to an art form, but to read the music book in that it demonstrates a way of being in the world that both touches man's soul and teaches man to live and procreate at that soulful level despite the societal opposition you will get in doing so. THESE BOOKS WILL GIVE YOU COURAGE!!!

I enjoyed each and every aspect of doing and writing what The Holy Spirit intended for me to present to you to clean up my own karma and as Bion said, "I make it a point to do what I enjoy doing!"

In 1981 Harold Greenwald, Ph.D., Diplomate in Clinical Psychology wrote, "Much has been written about the science of psychotherapy, but it has remained for Dr. Bergantino to write about the art of psychotherapy!"

*** Postscript-After you read all of my books, (everything I have ever written as this was the Holy Spirit's intention in giving me the skill sets to develop and deliver the gifts), go back to my first book and read each of the books in the exact order presented of Wilfred Bion's books, with the notion that he did not write theory, but actually wrote about psychoanalytic methodology from the perspective of a "higher sensitive" and that when you pay that kind of attention you may develop ways to work from an elevated level of Being, as in To Be Or Not To Be!

The importance of the sophisticated patient populations of psychoanalysts is to determine whether or not a psychoanalyst is pursuing the development of his own being during the work and thereby providing an environment whereby the patient can pursue his or her own being, or whether that analyst blocks such pursuit of being all that you can and is primarily interested in making money! Making money is
important in that the psychoanalyst has to make a living doing Analysis but Money is not at the heart of the matter! That is "The Saving of Man's Soul" and providing Patient's with the tools to pursue such a journey!

READ THE TWELVE HOURS OF BION
SUPERVISING ON AUDIO TAPE!
(PSYCHOTHERAPY INSIGHT &
STYLE: THE EXISTENTIAL MOMENT)

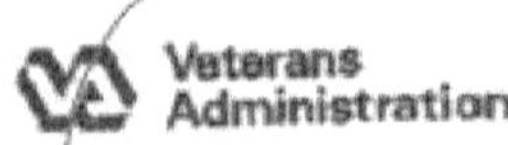

1 July 1985

In Reply Refer To:

Len Bergantino, Ed.D., Ph.D.
10266 Kilrenney Avenue
Los Angeles, California 90064

Dear Len:

How nice to receive yours of June 24th., and to learn of your upward spiral! I'm very pleased indeed to believe that my little review of your book has contributed to your success!

Frankly, Len, I have long been eructatively fed up with the sort of territorial cupidities and other evidences of narcissistic nonsensicality so many of the colleagues display. Such antics reveal the essentially limbic nature of people as it comes to be expressed in envies and jealousies to which you allude in your letter. When I read your book I knew at once of your outsider-ism (cf. Colin Wilson's seminal book of the same name—The Outsider) as well as your talent; since I know I am good also, I do not need to do the Big-Daddy-in-Cat-On-A-Hot-Tin-Roof bit, viz., to shit on one's sons out of envy and fear that they will appropriate my penis-cum-wife-cum-everything-else!

I trust your family are in good health. Keep in touch.

Most sincerely,

Donald B. Rinsley, M.D., F.R.S.H. (Lond.)
Associate Chief for Education
Psychiatry Service

Clinical Professor of Psychiatry
University of Kansas School of Medicine
Kansas City

DBR:mtf

To order a copy of the CD Falling in Love send a check for $25 made out to Dr. Len Bergantino and mail to 1215 Brockton Avenue, #104, Los Angeles, CA 900025-1366

Falling In Love
by Dr. Len Bergantino
MP3 Music
Listen with Music Unlimited Or $9.49 to buy MP3
Or $9.49 to buy MP3

At the time this cd was made Joe Diorio, my guitar accompanist, was the foremost jazz guitar player in the world, known primarily to jazz guitar players. I am the only one that got him to play songs for the general public, all of whom agree this cd is magnificent!!!!!!!!!!!!!!!!!!
Dr. Len Bergantino

Currently available from https://tinyurl.com/2p8e3saw

Germans – Jews – Holocausts and the Collective Unconscious

This book is comprised of methods and stories that are intended to evoke a one session existential shift in the reader's grasp of the entire situation in a way that supplants the word "appropriate" with the words "finer and finer discriminations of pure being" and the addition of the words "creative aggression" as an authentic working tool!

Sincerely,

Dr. Len Bergantino, Ed.D., Ph.D.

The Art of Psychotherapy and the Liberation of the Therapist

This is a book for professional psychotherapists, psychoanalysts and counselors, students in those areas of specialty and laypersons who are interested in the essence of effective therapy an how some of the people who do it best practice their art.

www.xlibris.com

ISBN 13 (SOFT): 978-1-7960-2422-7
ISBN 13 (HARD): 978-1-7960-2423-4
ISBN 13 (eBook): 978-1-7960-2421-0

ORDER A COPY NOW!

The Essence of Music

This multi-purpose book serves as a natural model for how musicians, as human beings, deal with each other.

www.xlibris.com

ISBN 13 (SOFT): 978-1-7960-2916-1
ISBN 13 (HARD): 978-1-7960-2917-8
ISBN 13 (eBook): 978-1-7960-2915-4

ORDER A COPY NOW!

Order Now

I Am Freud! Psychoanalysis Is the Only Method of Cure: It's Too Bad No One Knows How to Do One!!!

This book shows how extrasensory perception can be developed, utilized by the therapeutic use of self, and help pinpoint psychophysiological awareness, which can prevent disease and circumvent disease in later life.

www.xlibris.com

ISBN 13 (SOFT): 978-1-9845-5729-2
ISBN 13 (HARD): 978-1-9845-5730-8
ISBN 13 (eBook): 978-1-9845-5728-5

ORDER A COPY NOW!

REVERSE ANALYSIS, THE EXISTENTIAL SHIFT, GESTALT FAMILY THERAPY AND THE PREVENTION OF THE NEXT HOLOCAUST

Reverse Analysis, the Existential Shift, Gestalt Family Therapy and the Prevention of the Next Holocaust

This is a clinical example of a one-session existential shift in a lifelong personality characteristic of a patient. This is for hypnosis or training in hypnosis contact.

www.xlibris.com

ISBN 13 (SOFT): 978-1-7960-2117-2
ISBN 13 (HARD): 978-1-7960-2118-9
ISBN 13 (eBook): 978-1-7960-2116-5

ORDER A COPY NOW!

LEN BERGANTINO, Ed.D., Ph.D., A.B.P.P.

Psychoanalysis

(310) 207-9397

Clinical Psychologist
Psychology
of professional Psychology

A.B.P.P.Diplomate in Family
American Board

REVIEWS

WHEN I first started to build my private practice in Beverly Hills, California. "I think psychoanalysts, psychiatrists and clinical psychologists have a hard time understanding each other. It is like the tower of babel. I think you are the one who can write it in a way whereby they can both understand and talk to each other. Dr. Dorn wasn't in it for the money. He left Beverly Hills to become Dean of Dept. of Psychiatry at Eastern Virginia Medical School.

I have always loved the BRITS! I gave a workshop in Sheffield, England at Wentworth Castle entitled "THE THERAPEUTIC WIZARDRY OF DR. LEN BERGANTINO!" and one at the Royal College of Medicine entitled "THE DEVELOPMENT AND USE OF EXTRA SENSORY PERCEPTION IN THE PRACTICE OF PSYCHOANALYSIS, PSYCHOTHERAPY AND CLINICAL HYPNOSIS" I DELIVERED THE GOODS EACH AND EVERY TIME OUT!

Dr. Len Bergantino, Ed.D., Ph.D.

IN OTHER WORDS, WHEN GOD USED THE KARMIC WHEEL TO SEND ME BACK AS THE REINCARNATED SOUL OF SIGMUND FREUD AND JULIUS CAESAR AND MY CHILDREN LIS, BACK AS THE REINCARNATED SOULS OF DR. MILTON H. ERICKSON AND BRUTUS, ASSESSING THAT ALL OF THOSE SKILL SETS WERE NECESSARY TO DO THE JOB. HOW CAN MY OWN EVALUATION OF ME, MY CLINICAL SKILLS, AND MY WRITINGS OF ALL YOUR BOOKS BE ANYTHING LESS THAN.

1215 Brockton Ave., Ste. 104, W. Los Angeles, CA 90025 U.S.A.

I AM THE BEST PSYCHOANALYST OF ALL TIME AND IN ACCORD WITH MY ORIGINAL IDEA (FREUD-THE LAST TIME AROUND), THE SLOW READING AND INTEGRATION OF ALL FOUR BOOKS WILL EVOKE AN UPWARD SPIRALING SOCIETY AND PREVENT BOTH THE NEXT HOLOCAUST AND THE APOCALYPSE AND FREE FROM THE DESTRUCTION OF THE LINKS TO KNOWLEDGE AT THE HANDS OF ENVIOUS AND HATEFUL HUMAN MORTAL COLLEAGUES!

IN OTHER WORDS, GOD HAS REVIEWED ME AND MY WORK AND ANYONE ELSE PALES IN COMPARISON!

1215 Brockton Ave., Ste. 104, W. Los Angeles, CA 90025 U.S.A.

1215 Brockton Ave., Ste 104, W. Los Angeles, CA 90025 U.S.A.

LEN BERGANTINO, Ed.D., Ph.D., A.B.P.P.

Psychoanalysis

(310) 207-9397

Clinical Psychologist A.B.P.P.Diplomate in Family
Psychology American Board of
professional Psychology

REVIEWS

"When thinking of all the therapist, I have ever trained or seen (including Fritz Perls, M.D. Ph.D.) Bergantino! Him I think about! Him I consider! He is a man of substance!"
Dr. Donald Winsley, M.D. (particularly helpful for the Art of Psychotherapy and the Liberation of the Therapist) wrote. "A unique texture of Dr. Bergantino's presentation –offering, FASCINATING AND INSTRUCTIVE INSIGHTS INTO THERAPEUTIC LABORS OF ADMITTEDLY GIFTED THEATERS."
Dr. Carl Whitaker, M.D. wrote, "The approach to his own craziness, the freedom from the culture bind, and the discipline of self each emerged as attainable goals of that professional parent we call the psychotherapist."
Psychiatrist Barry Blicharski wrote "I am happy to recommend Len Bergantino as an excellent workshop leader, trainer and psychotherapist.... We will be

inviting Len Bergantino to return to AUSTRALIA AND RECOMMEND HIS WORK, BOTH CLINICAL AND TEACHING, IN ANY SITUATION."

Betty Erickson, wife of Milton Erickson, M.D. dictated, "The mutual respect that Dr. Erickson and Dr. Bergantino held for each other was reflected in the friendship that continued until; Dr. Erickson's death… and has continued with Dr. Erickson's wife, Elizabeth Erickson, now 92 years old."

Yaro Stark, Gestalt Therapy trainer and Director of International Gestalt Therapy Training Institute in Brisbane, Australia, "Dr." Bergantino has a mental precision that electrified the Australian therapeutic community and had lasting therapeutic impact."

Clinical Psychologist whose name I cannot locate, "DR. BERGANTINO IS THE MOST GIFTED CLINICIAN OF HIS TIME!"

MY OWN REVIEW

THE MOST GIFTED CLINICIAN OF ALL TIME! THE BEST THAT EVER LIVED! IN ADDITION TO WHAT THE MORTALS HAVE SAID ABOUT ME I HAVE FULFILLED MY KARMIC MISSION AS AGREED UPON AT THE BEGINNING OF MY CAREER OVER A FIFTY-TWO YEAR PERIOD AND AS CONTINUALLY INTERVENDED UPON BY THE HOLY SPIRIT TO ACCOMPLISH THE TASK ONLY EXPANDED UPON TI INFINITY AS STATED BY Dr. Robert Dorn, M.D., Training and Supervising Analyst, who state

LEN BERGANTINO, Ed.D., Ph.D., A.B.P.P.

Psychoanalysis

(310) 207-9397

Clinical Psychologist A.B.P.P.Diplomate in Family Psychology American Board of professional Psychology

REVIEWS

Dr. Wilfred R. Bion, MRCS (Medical Royal College of Surgeons) the great British psychoanalyst wrote to Dr. Bergantino, "Your work is evocative and stimulating."

Dr. Milton H. Erickson M.D. –the Father of Modern Medical Hypnosis told Dr. Bergantino" I am just an old man who tells stories. It's your unconscious mind that has the pinpoint accuracy." I respect your dedication to the work." And so Reverse Analysis has born along with a working knowledge of the Existential Shift.

Dr. Donald Rinsley, M.D., Fellow of the American College of Psychoanalysts wrote of Dr. Bergantino and his work, "There is no doubt that some people presents a healing capacity and that others do not"; "I know at once of your outsiderism….as well as your talent."

Dr. Carl Whitaker, M.D. – the foremost family therapist at the international level wrote of Dr. Bergantino and his work, "He is an international reporter of international change, models in the family, therapy act and even interpsychic change process." Reading his work "is an active experience in the use of self in the field of psychotherapy and as such, it both expands and enriches the country's standard of practice of professional psychotherapists."

Dr. James Grotstein, M.D., Training and Supervising Analyst wrote of me. "I finally had the pleasure of viewing your tape. I found it very impressive. It helped me to understand better where you are coming from and to be able to observe first hand your intuitive way of approaching people. Your technique reminded me of an elegant sophistication of Gestalt, along with Erickson and Bion."

1215 Brockton Ave., Ste. 104, W. Los Angeles, CA 90025 U.S.A.

LEN BERGANTINO, Ed.D., Ph.D., A.B.P.P.

Psychoanalysis

(310) 207-9397

Clinical Psychologist A.B.P.P.Diplomate in Family Psychology American Board of professional Psychology

Dr. Martin Grotjahn, m.D., Training and Supervising Analyst wrote, "Dr. Bergantino is obviously a gifted therapist…Most cases as reported in the literature describe the patient's hidden in the mystery of darkness unrevealed. Dr. B is an exception; the great of his work is the openness ad frankness with which the reveals his experiences when treating patients or accepting himself as a patient of another therapist.

1215 Brockton Ave., Ste. 104, W. Los Angeles, CA 90025 U.S.A.

The Greatest Basketball Player I Ever Saw

PRES RELEASE FOR "THE GREATEST BASKETBALL PLAYER I EVER SAW"

To Notice greatness ad not deny greatness in others you have to notice that ordinary people often claim do not exist. As ordinary people would much rather blame the victim rather than do their own personal work of self-development. They often deny greatness in others to protect themselves from looking at their own shortcomings often through "hatred and deceptive manipulation (malevolent omnipotence!) Such was the case with Billy Finn, who were he not surrounded by assholes would have averaged fifty two points a game instead of merely holding the state record of fifty two points in one game! It is not the fact he had 52 points, it was the way he got them that transcended human experience.

***When Billy Finn played there was no such option! Bob Cousy, famed guard told him he had nothing to teach him in the seventh grade!

*** "BILLY FINN WAS TO BASKETBALL WHAT WILLIE MAYS WAS TO BASEBALL – THE MOST EXCITING BALLPLAYER THAT EVER LIVED DESPITE GREATNESS IN OTHERS." For example, Ted Williams was the greatest hitter I ever saw, I saw him take batting practice. He hit consecutive line drives so hard they nearly bounced back to 2nd base. This book lays out the details of what made Billy Finn the greatest basketball player who ever lived!

PRESS RELEASE FOR "THE DENIAL OF REVERSE RACISM IN AMERICA"

THIS BOOK IS INTENDED TO HELP BLACK PEOPLE – PARTICULARLY THOSE IN ADMINISTRATIVE POSITIONS AT THE TOP FOR TREATING WHITE PEOPLE AT THE BOTTOM OF THE TOTEM POLE WHILE DOING IN THE BEST AND BRIGHTEST OF THEIR OWN BLACK CHILDREN AND FALSELY BLAMING IT ON WHITES so as to provide a psychotic PROTECTION GAME OF BLACKS THAT BOTH DO IN THEIR OWN YOUTH AND NEVER ROLL OVER ON ANY BLACK BROTHER OR SISTER THAT REMINDS THEM OF TWO HUNDRED YEARS OF SLAVERY WHILE AT THE SAME TIME PRETENDING TO BE FAIR BY USING "GUILT" AS A MANIPULATION TO JUSTIFY KEEPING "WHITE BOY" AT THE BOTTOM OF THE SOLUTION IS SIMPLE BUT NOT EASY! "BLACK BOY" THE TOTEM POLE! HAS TO STOP BLAMING AND LAYING "GUILT TRIPS" ON MODERNS "WHITE BOY" FOR HIS FOREFATHERS' SINS!"

THIS NEEDS IMMEDIATE CORRECTION IF "WHITE BOY" IS NOT TO BUILD SUCH PRIMITIVE RESENTMENT AT THE UNCONSCIOUS LEVEL THAT YOU GET ONE NEWSLINE AFTER THE OTHER THAT "WHITE BOY" COP SHOOTS BLACK TWELVE YEAR OLD KID RUNNING AWAY IN THE BACK! THIS BOOK PROVIDES AN INTERIM STEP FOR BOTH BLACKS AND WHITES TO EXAMINE THEIR OWN UNDERLYING RACIAL THOUGHTS AND FEELINGS IN A MANNER THAT BRINGS THE SUBCONSCIOUS AND UNCONSCIOUS MORE TO THE SURFACE IN A WAY THAT HELPS THOSE WHO SO ENDEAVOR TO FIND ONGOING SOLUTIONS TO DEAL WITH THE PRIMITIVE REMNANTS OF CRIMES COMMITTED THROUGH TWO HUNDRED YEARS OF SLAVERY! FOR EXAMPLE, I WAS GETTING DONE IN BY A WAITER IN KOLN, GERMANY OF ITALIAN DESCENT in 1990 IN AN ITALIAN RESTAURANT AND THE OWNER SAID HE HATED AMERICANS BECAUSE GENERAL PATTON KILLED HIS ENTIRE FAMILY WHEN COMING THROUGH ITALY IN 1944!

I have reason to believe that the sum total of characteristics that make up my personality and the variety of occupations, athletics and musical endeavors in which I have engaged provide me with some unique primitive viewpoints regarding racial relations between Blacks and Whites that are and will be worthy of consideration in RACE RELATIONS FOR CENTURIES TO COME.

What makes these comments valuable is the candor with which I report them at the deepest primitive levels, no matter whom they offend, including myself, my parents, my neighbors and in particular not only the Northeast section of the United States but also the West Coast, primarily Los Angeles.

IN OTHER WORDS, IF YOU ARE BORN IN THE UNITED STATES, YOU ARE A RACIST AND IF YOU SAY YOU ARE NOT, YOU ARE A RACIST AND DO NOT KNOW YOU ARE A RACIST! Just as I studied macro-economics in college as opposed to micro-economics, IF ONE EXAMINES THE MINUTIA OF OUR EXPERIENCES IN THE ORDER IN WHICH THEY OCCURRED, WE ARE ALL RACISTS IN AMERICA, TO SOME DEGREE OR OTHER AND WOULD BE BETTER OFF PLANNING OUR COURSE OF ACTION BASED ON WHAT ACTUALLY EXISTS AS OPPOSED TO THE NONSENSE WE CLAIM EXISTS. THAT IS WHY WHEN I HEAR A POLITICIAN SAY THEY ARE NOT A RACIST I TURN THE CHANNEL IMMEDIATELY!

I had the good fortune to speak with Carl Erskine who pitched the most dominant game I ever saw pitched when he struck out 14 New York Yankees (including Mickey Mantle 4 times 1953 World Series) and Carl Erskine was most proud of having been Jackie Robinson's teammate when Jackie broke the color barrier. That is "good faith" no matter how you were born or raised!

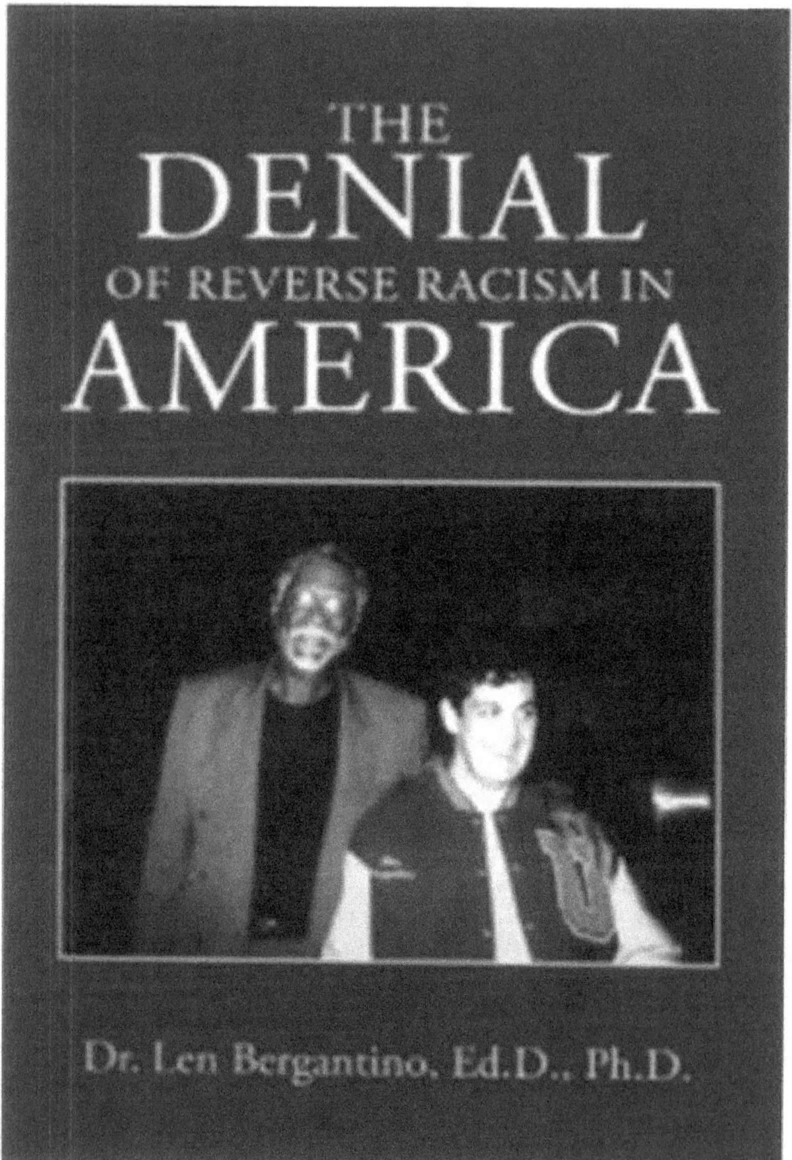
THE
DENIAL
OF REVERSE RACISM IN
AMERICA
Dr. Len Bergantino, Ed.D., Ph.D.

DECLARATION OF DR. LEN BERGANTINO

I, DR. LEN BERGANTINO, DECLARE:

Bill Russell personally gave me permission to take his picture with my developmentally delayed son Alex Bergantino around the year 2003 when he was making an appearance supporting an orthopaedic pain relief Medical doctor whereby Bill Russell discussed the wear and tear from running up and down hardwood floors on the joints of his body. This meeting and this picture were taken at the Sports Club Los Angeles at 7p.m. in the evening on Westwood Blvd. just south of Santa Monica Blvd.

I declare under penalty of perjury that the foregoing is true and correct and I would and could testify as such in a court of law if called upon to do so.

This declaration was written in Los Angeles, California on March 5, 2020.

Publisher:
To Order a copy of The Sanctimonious Psychoproctological Invasions (ISBN 978-1-6461-0238-9)
Email: bookorders@rosedogbooks.com
Or call 1-800-788-7654 (Mon-Fri) 9AM-4PM

The Denial of Reverse Racism in America

Do you think that some slug who looks very professional who "whispers" an occasional interpretation to you five times a week for 7 years can make one bit of difference in your life or does such a psychotoxic slug called a psychoanalyst merely stick you in an emotional toilet bowl for seven years having the cumulative result of turning you into a hopeless bastard who will never turn the tragic comer in his or her life?
Can your analyst analyze an ARCHAIC LIQUID SYMBIOTIC OR AN OSMOTIC TRANSFERENCE, or can they even recognize this phenomena in order to analyze it? If the psychoanalyst cannot analyze these transferences they can't do an analysis!

I used to get "good faith" patients who had the balls to work on the cutting edge at the same time I did because they had had combinations of twenty years of two seven year analyses plus several briefer psychotheraphies, only to be as crazy as the day they walked in! (-$200,000.00)

As Dr. Donald Rinsley, M.D., fellow-American College of Psychoanalysts wrote about me, my work has both a healing effect and affect. Patients used to pay me six months in advance to hold the time open because I was

irreplaceable; I was the only one who could analyze the psychotic core of the personality and I was the only who could actually do what Dr. Wilfred R. Bion, MRCS (Medical Royal College of Surgeons) wrote about analyzing the psychotic core of the personality/

As I am seventy-six years old, I have written five books that must be read and digested in their entirety. As these books are the thing-in-itself they will transform the reader into the kinds of analyst, patient and psychotherapist who can make a difference in helping people turn the tragic corner in their lives! In other words, these five books are analysis!

These books were written to be around for a few hundred years and were directly guided by the Almighty!

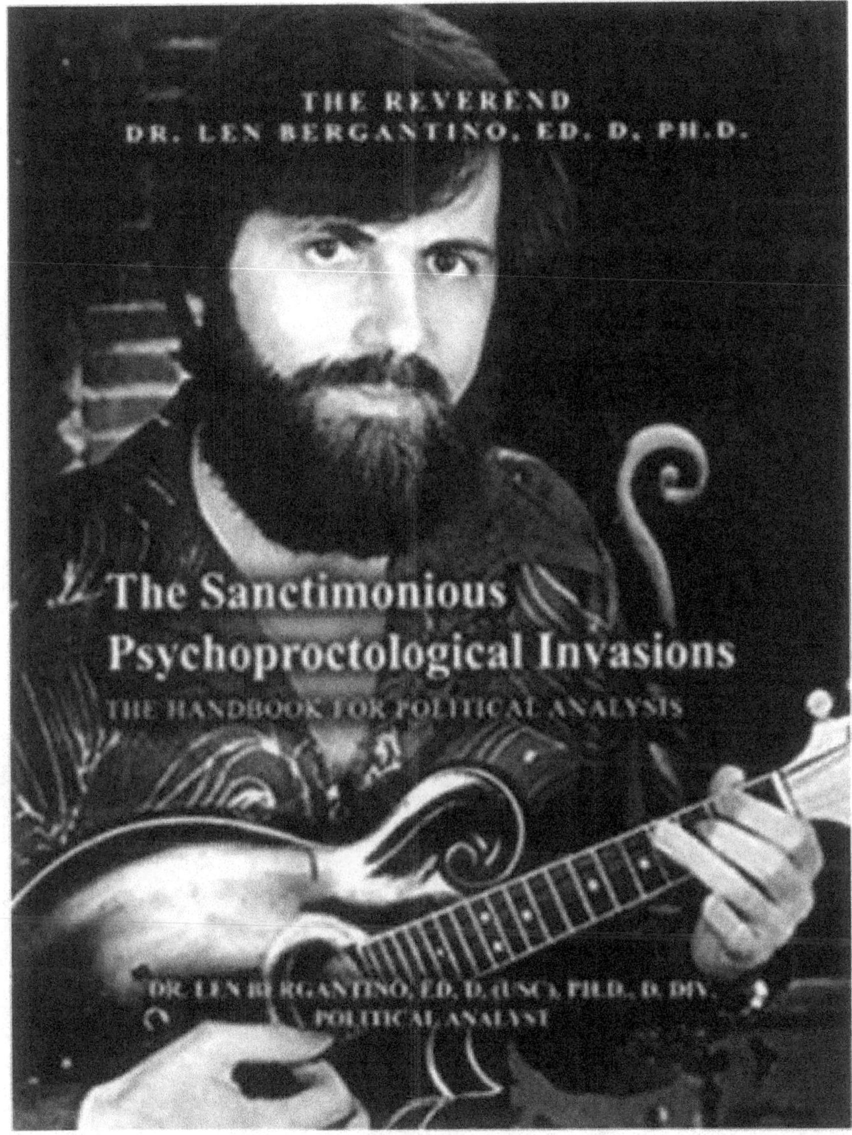
THE REVEREND
DR. LEN BERGANTINO, ED. D, PH.D.
The Sanctimonious
Psychoproctological Invasions
THE HANDBOOK FOR POLITICAL ANALYSIS
POLITICAL ANALYST

From 2012 through 2018, Len Bergantino began each day with pro bono writings and invasive interventions that insist and expand upon the first amendment rights of United States citizens. In all areas, he is both knowledgeable and feels national, state, and local governments are stuck in socially immobile positions. He created ways to invade entire cultures and governments to move those stuck in quicksand off the dime and into a society that spirals upward. He refers to the creation of these methods as sanctimonious psychoproctological invasions in the creation of a political psychology that should be studies by all human beings who want to make a difference and give meaning to their lives.

About the Author

Len Bergantino is a multi-faceted individual who achieved international prominence in the areas of psychoanalysis, psychotherapy, clinical psychology, and music. His other fields include education and religion, with a precursory knowledge of medicine and law. He is a weathervane in terms of knowing the *right* thing to do and has the temperament of Che Guevara in getting it done!

ROSEDOG BOOKS
585 Alpha Dr, Pittsburgh, PA 15238

The Sanctimonious Psychoproctological Invasions: The Handbook for Political Analysis

From 2012 through 2018, Len Bergantino began each day with pro bono writings and invasive interventions that insist and expand upon the first amendment rights of United States citizens. In all areas, he is both knowledgeable and feels national, state, and local governments are stuck in socially immobile positions. He created ways to invade entire cultures and governments to move those stuck in quicksand off the dime and into a society that spirals upward. He refers to the creation of these methods as sanctimonious psychoproctological invasions in the creation of a political psychology that should be studies by all human beings who want to make a difference and give meaning to their lives.

ORDER A COPY NOW!

To Order a copy of The Sanctimonious Psychoproctological Invasions (ISBN 978-1-6461-0238-9)

Email: bookorders@rosedogbooks.com

Or call 1-800-788-7654 (Mon-Fri) 9AM-4PM

irreplaceable; I was the only one who could analyze the psychotic core of the personality and I was the only who could actually do what Dr. Wilfred R. Bion, MRCS (Medical Royal College of Surgeons) wrote about analyzing the psychotic core of the personality/

As I am seventy-six years old, I have written five books that must be read and digested in their entirety. As these books are the thing-in-itself they will transform the reader into the kinds of analyst, patient and psychotherapist who can make a difference in helping people turn the tragic corner in their lives! In other words, these five books are analysis!

These books were written to be around for a few hundred years and were directly guided by the Almighty!

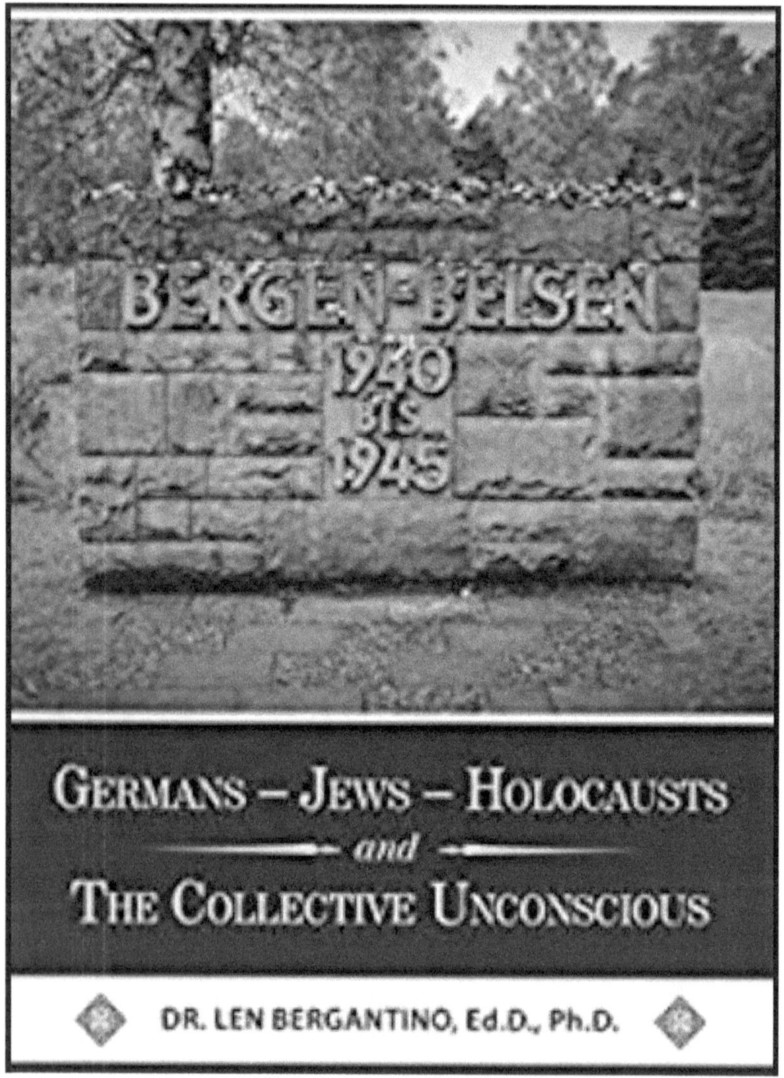
BERGEN-BELSEN
1940
BIS
1945
GERMANS – JEWS – HOLOCAUSTS
and
THE COLLECTIVE UNCONSCIOUS
DR. LEN BERGANTINO, Ed.D., Ph.D.

CIPRIANI
ISBN 978-1-7960-8445-0
51999
9 781796 084450

Dr. Bergantino and his two children were sent back on a karmic mission to complete the work. Dr. Bergantino is the reincarnated soul of Sigmund Freud and Julius Caesar. Those skill sets were required to complete this project. His children are Wilfred Bion and Milton Erickson. They taught Dr. Bergantino how to use paranormal abilities. We are all off the karmic wheel and WE WILL NOT BE BACK!!! GOODBYE!!!

Political Psychology Invasions

Using the principles of "authenticity, congruence and empathic understanding along with the principles of CREATIVE AGGRESSION has reached and influenced not only those at state and Local Government, but both national and International levels at the highest levels.

For example I have received a letter from Queen Elizabeth, Pope Francis transcribed into English by Paulo Borgia, sec of State of the Vatican and member of the Borgia Family of the 1500's ABOUT 20 letters and a Christmas card from President Donald Trump, 3 letters from President Obama, a few from Senator Rand Paul, one from Senator John McKain, and 3 from Congressman Henry Waxman.

Once The Powers That Be Decide you are Reliable, Informative and Spot On, YOU OFTEN SEE THE CHANGES YOU RECOMMEND ON THE NEWS THE FOLLOWING DAY.

Excerpt taken from the conclusion section of the book:

This book has nothing to do with the politics of the word "appropriate" and how those that read it may try to spin it. This book has everything to do with the primitive nature of man and what is actually required to educate peoples of all countries from all walks of life, no matter what caste system they knowingly or unknowingly are stuck in! Along the way to my training family therapists at the international level, Dr. Carl Whitaker, M.D., my teacher and mentor from 1979- 1994, in his last verbal communication to me said, "The work is easy! It's the justification that is hard!" So I will merely present you the facts as they occurred. I will provide no justification for any of it, other than to tell you that is what really occurred.

"I DID ALL THIS SPEAKING AND WRITING ORDINARY CONVERSATIONAL ENGLISH!!!"

This book focuses upon the initial psycho-political assessments of the Democratic candidates who were among the sixteen original characters that threw their "hats in the ring!" so to speak! Further, it shows those interested in the current political climate and all other historical political climates HOW TO DIFFERENTIATE REAL NEWS FROM FAKE NEW THROUGH THE DEVELOPMENT AND UTILIZATION OF HIGHER SENSE PERCEPTION.

THE BOOK FURTHER INVADES SEVERAL POLITICAL AND RELIGIOUS TERRITORIES N DEMONSTRATING "HOW TO ASSESS AND DO THE RIGHT THING" AS A WAY OF LIFE. THEREBY AS CITIZENS HELPING TO CREATE AN UPWARD AS OPPOSED TO A DOWNWARD SPIRALING SOCIETY.

IN ADDITION TO ASSESSING AND MAKING DIRECT RECOMMENDATIONS TO THE POPE, AS WELL AS POLITICIANS DIRECT RECOMMENDATIONS ARE MADE SUCH AS THE DOING AWAY WITH LICENSING BOARDS IN THE FIELDS OF PSYCHOANALYSIS, CLINICAL PSYCHOLOGY, PSYCHOTHERAPY, MARITAL AND FAMILY THERAPY AND CLINICAL SOCIAL WORK SO AS NOT TO PROVIDE:

THE GENERAL PUBLIC A FALSE SENSE OF SECURITY WHILE ACTUALLY DESTROYING CLINICIANS" ABILITY TO DO THE WORK THAT CAN ONLY COME WITH THE EVER GROWING THERAPEUTIC USE OF SELF -OR AS SHAKESPEARE PUT IT, "TO BE OR NOT TO BE!"

Submitted by Dr. Len Bergantino, Ed.D., Ph.D.

"POLITICAL PSYCHOLOGY INVASIONS"

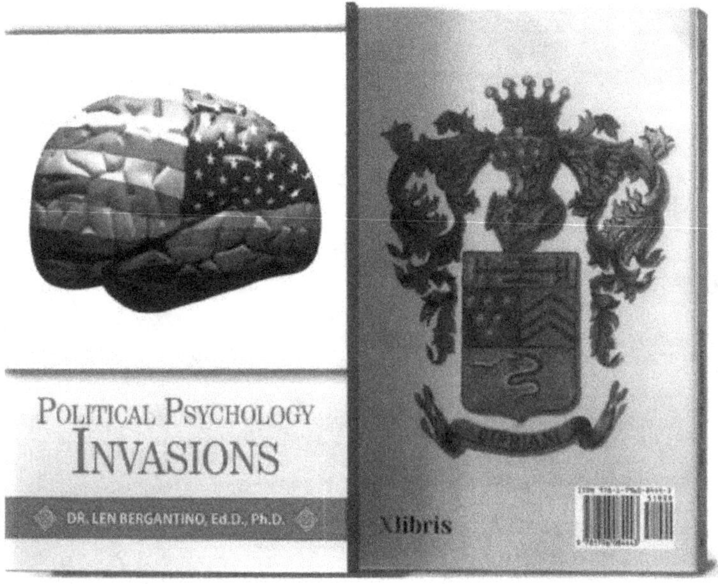

page 50

The Sanctimonious Psychoproctological Invasions: The Handbook for Political Analysis

From 2012 through 2018, Len Bergantino began each day with pro bono writings and invasive interventions that insist and expand upon the first amendment rights of United States citizens. In all areas, he is both knowledgeable and feels national, state, and local governments are stuck in socially immobile positions. He created ways to invade entire cultures and governments to move those stuck in quicksand off the dime and into a society that spirals upward. He refers to the creation of these methods as sanctimonious psychoproctological invasions in the creation of a political psychology that should be studies by all human beings who want to make a difference and give meaning to their lives.

ORDER A COPY NOW!

To Order a copy of The Sanctimonious Psychoproctological Invasions (ISBN 978-1-6461-0238-9)

Email: bookorders@rosedogbooks.com

Or call 1-800-788-7654 (Mon-Fri) 9AM-4PM

The Sanctimonious Psychoproctological Invasions: The Handbook for Political Analysis

From 2012 through 2018, Len Bergantino began each day with pro bono writings and invasive interventions that insist and expand upon the first amendment rights of United States citizens. In all areas, he is both knowledgeable and feels national, state, and local governments are stuck in socially immobile positions. He created ways to invade entire cultures and governments to move those stuck in quicksand off the dime and into a society that spirals upward. He refers to the creation of these methods as sanctimonious psychoproctological invasions in the creation of a political psychology that should be studies by all human beings who want to make a difference and give meaning to their lives.

The Greatest Basketball Player I Ever Saw

Dr. Len Bergantino, Ed.D., Ph.D.

The Greatest Basketball Player I Ever Saw

Dr. Len Bergantino, Ed.D., Ph.D.

Excerpt

SANCTIMONIOUS PSYCHOPROCTOLOGICAL INVASIONIST

MY LAST SUPERVISOR, DR. BRUNO BETTELHEIM, WAS TRAINED IN FREUD'S ORIGINAL TRAINING GROUP. FREUD TOLD HIM THAT "WILHELM REICH, M.D. WAS FREUD'S MOST GIFTED TRAINING ANALYST."

DR. WILHELM REICH SAID, "IF YOU CAN'T DO POLITICS, YOU CAN'T DO ANALYSIS!" DR. BERGANTINO SAYS, "THAT IS THE KIND OF ANALYSIS THAT REACHES AND TRANSFORMS THE UNDERLYING PSYCHOTIC THINKING DISORDERS, PRIMITIVE MENTAL STATES AND PSYCHOTIC CORE OF THE PERSONALITIES OF WHAT ARE THOUGHT TO BE YOUR EVERYDAY NARCISSISTIC, BORDERLINE AND OBSESSIVE COMPULSIVE PERSONALITY DISORDERS!"

Come and join Dr. Len Bergantino as he recounts and celebrates the glory of The New York Yankees.

www.xlibris.com

ISBN 13 (SOFT): 978-1-7960-7891-6
ISBN 13 (eBook): 978-1-7960-8028-5

ORDER A COPY NOW!

Germans – Jews – Holocausts and the Collective Unconscious

There is no available information at this time. Author will provide once available.

www.xlibris.com

ISBN 13 (SOFT): 978-1-7960-8445-0
ISBN 13 (eBook): 978-1-7960-8446-7

ORDER A COPY NOW!

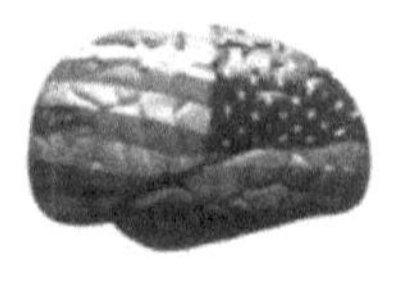

Political Psychology Invasions

See how Dr. Len Bergantino, Ed.D., Ph.D. assess the Democratic candidates in POLITICAL PSYCHOLOGY INVASIONS.

www.xlibris.com

ISBN 13 (SOFT): 978-1-7960-2916-1
ISBN 13 (HARD): 978-1-7960-2917-8
ISBN 13 (eBook): 978-1-7960-2915-4

ORDER A COPY NOW!

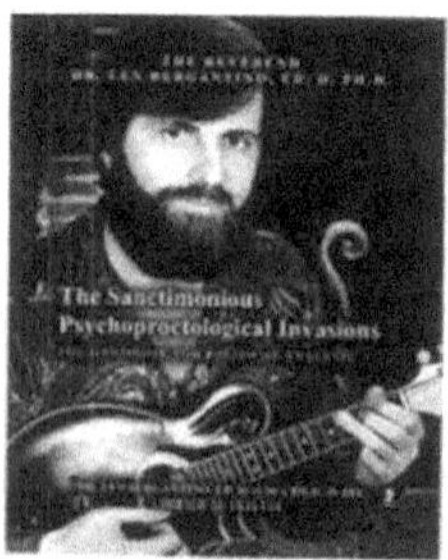

The Sanctimonious Psychoproctological Invasions: The Handbook for Political Analysis

ISBN: 978-1-6461-0238-9
EI: 978-1-6461-0880-0

To order a copy of

The Sanctimonious Psychoproctological Invasions (ISBN 978-1-6461-0238-9)

Email bookorders@rosedogbooks.com

or call 1-800-788-7654 (Monday-Friday -am-4pm)

The book is also available on Amazon.com or Barnesandnoble.com

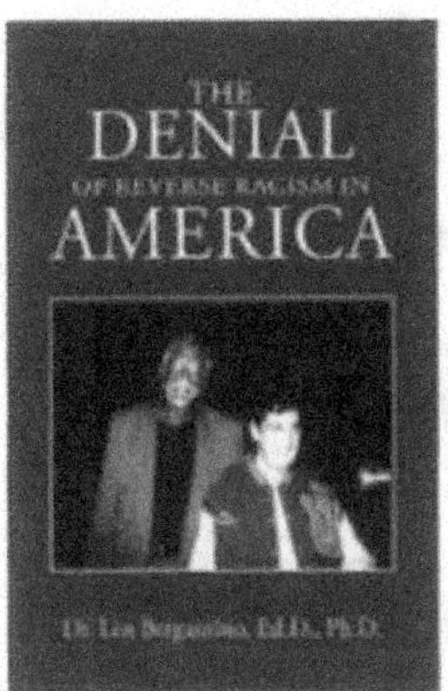

The Denial of Reverse Racism in America

ISBN 13 (SOFT): 9781-7960-9390-2
ISBN 13 (eBook): 978-1-7960-9389-6

ORDER A COPY NOW!

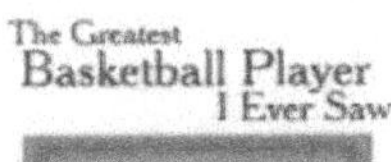

Dr. Len Bergantino, Ed.D., Ph.D.

The Greatest Basketball Player I Ever Saw

ISBN 13 (SOFT): 978-1-7960-9392-6
ISBN 13 (eBook): 978-1-7960-9391-9

ORDER A COPY NOW!

SANCTIMONIOUS PSYCHOPROCTOLOGICAL INVASIONIST

MY LAST SUPERVISOR, DR. BRUNO BETTELHEIM, WAS TRAINED IN FREUD'S ORIGINAL TRAINING GROUP. FREUD TOLD HIM THAT "WILHELM REICH, M.D. WAS FREUD'S MOST GIFTED TRAINING ANALYST."

DR. WILHELM REICH SAID, "IF YOU CAN'T DO POLITICS, YOU CAN'T DO ANALYSIS!" DR. BERGANTINO SAYS, "THAT IS THE KIND OF ANALYSIS THAT REACHES AND TRANSFORMS THE UNDERLYING PSYCHOTIC THINKING DISORDERS, PRIMITIVE MENTAL STATES AND PSYCHOTIC CORE OF THE PERSONALITIES OF WHAT ARE THOUGHT TO BE YOUR EVERYDAY NARCISSISTIC, BORDERLINE AND OBSESSIVE COMPULSIVE PERSONALITY DISORDERS!!

TRAINED IN PSYCHOANALYSIS BY THE BEST OF DR. WILFRED BION'S MD ANALYSANDS, AND MARTIN GROTJAHN, M.D. & DR. BRUNO BETTELHEIM, PH.D.

LEN BERGANTINO, Ed.D., Ph.D., A.B.P.P.

Psychoanalysis

(310) 207-9397

I AM THE MORAL AUTHORITY FOR THE UNITED STATES GOVERNMENT SELF ANNOINTED - PRO BONO

DR. LEN BERGANTINO I AM THE REINCARNATED SOUL OF SIGMUND FREUD • JULIUS CAESAR GOD SENT ME BACK ON A KARMIC MISSION

Clinical Psychologist
License Number 3837

A.B.P.P. - Diplomate in Family Psychology
American Board of Professional Psychology

January 12, 2018

"RETIRED CLINICAL PSYCHOLOGIST PRO BONO CONTRIBUTION"

Attn: Assessment Desk

DEAR PRESIDENT TRUMP,

HOW REFRESHING THAT YOU STATED WHAT I NOTICED AROUND THE TIME I STOPPED DOING PSYCHOANALYSIS! YOU STATED "WHY ARE ALL THESE PEOPLE FROM "SHITHOLE COUNTRIES" COMING HERE!

TO DO PSYCHOANALYSIS AN INTELLECTUAL ELITE WITH MENTAL SOPHISTICATION IS REQUIRED. THE NUANCES MAKE THE WORK FASCINATING!

AS I WAS TRAINED IN FAMILY THERAPY BY WORLD RENOWN PIONEERS CARL WHITAKER, M.D. AND WALTER KEMPLER, M.D. I NOTICED THAT THE WORK ITSELF BEGAN TO MOVE IN THE DIRECTION OF FAMILY THERAPY WITH MORE "ORDINARY" PELPLE DUE TO THE IMMIGRATION POLLCIES THAT LET IN PEOPLE FROM "SHITHOLE COUNTRIES" ON SOME SAVIOR MISSION THAT HAS DESTROYED NOT ONLY THE PSYCHOANALYTIC POPULATION THAT MIGHT SEND IT'S GRADUATES OFF TO CREATE AN UPWARD SPIRALING SOCIETY BY THE LOWERING OF ABILITIES OF THE COMMUNITY STANDARDS OF PRACTICE OF EVEN OUR MEDICAL SCHOOLS. I FIND THE MOST MEDICAL BRAINS THESE DAYS ARE IN THE HEADS OF THOSE FROM CHINESE HERITAGE WHO CHOOSE TO REMAIN HERE!. THEY ARE FAR SUPERIOR TO PHYSICIANS EDUCATED IN THE UNITED STATES!

YOUR STATEMENT HAS NOTHING AT ALL TO DO WITH RACIAL PREJUDICE OR RACIAL HATRED. IT HAS TO DO WITH THE BEGINNING OF WHEN A PRESIDENT I LOVED, JFK, MADE A SERIOUS MISTAKE AND CUT BACK THE ENTRANCE OF BRITS, ITALIANS, POLES, GERMANS, et. al and DEVOTED HIS EFFORTS TO "SHITHOLE COUNTRIES" COMING HERE TURNING THE UNITED STATES INTO A THIRD WORLD COUNTRY!.

THE PROBLEM FOR ME IS THAT I WORKED MY ASS OFF TO DEVELOP A SKILL SET THAT WORKED IN THE HIGHEST LEVEL OF SUPERSTARS! IF I WANTED TO WORK IN A THIRD WORLD COUNTRY I WOULD HAVE MOVED TO BELIZE. I CAN DO BOTH KINDS OF WORK! Norway loves Americans! They were one of two countries that appreciated the contribution of the United States from World War II! You might also try Denmark! They are not a shithole country!

You are refreshing in what you say. Don't let them twist your words and intentions! YOU ARE JUST CALLING EM LIKE YOU SEE EM!

Respectfully,

Dr. Len Bergantino

Dr. Len Bergantino

P.S. The problem is that THE SLUGS THAT WE LET IN ARE MUCH MORE LIKELY TO DRAG US INTO THIRD WORLD STATUS THAN WE ARE TO LIFT THEM UP INTO BEING A CITIZEN IN THE GREATEST COUNTRY IN THE HISTORY OF MANKIND!

P.S. 2 TRUMP UNDERSTANDS WHAT IS REQUIRED TO PLAY IN HIGH ROLLER CIRCUIT!

1215 Brockton Ave., Ste. 104, W. Los Angeles, CA 90025 - U.S.A.

JANUARY 7, 2018

WHAT IS GENIUS?

1.\ From 1979-1993 I did PSYCHOANALYSIS with patients at differing Beverly Hills-90210 addresses-the primary being 450 N. Bedford Drive, Ste. 300. I saw them five times a week; for fifty minutes a session for between three and seven years.

2.\ Wilfred Bion, M.R.C.S. stated "The minimum conditions of an Analysis are five times a week, at a certain hour at a certain fee. My fee at that time was $125 per hour, or thirty thousand per patient per year, or about $150,000 per patient per Analysis! BION SAID THAT "KNOWING HOW TO DEAL WITH THOSE MINIMUM CONDITIONS IS THE ONLY BLOODY ANALYSIS ANYONE WILL EVER NEED TO KNOW!"

3.\ Bion also said "THE ENTIRE PSYCHOANALYTIC LIBRARY IS GOOD FOR ABOUT THE FIRST HOUR AND ONE HALF OF AN ANALYSIS! AFTER THAT YOU HAVE TO KNOW WHAT TO SAY TO THE PATIENT!"

4.\ Most of these patients came in making $125,000 per year and left making $750,000 per year. MOST WERE GENIUSES!

5.\ My first psychoanalytic patient made $22,000 per year. He was as slippery as an eel! I didn't have a chance at doing the job with him at less than four times a week, so I said, "Well, if you want to see me I am going to take 18 of that 22 thousand!" I thought he would get up and walk out-preferable to taking a job you do not have the conditions to be successful at doing. To my amazement he said “Alright!” Through the first three months he kept pointing out that he was indispensable to his employers; that they could not function without him, and they were spending $8,000 a week on cocaine! I said, “So you are a $50,000 a year man working for $22,000! Ask them for a $30,000 raise!” This self devaluation was a theme during the Analysis. After three months he walked in and said “I got a thirty thousand dollar a year raise!” I said, “Good, now the Analysis is free!”

A.\ Most geniuses are thought to have an IQ measured by the Stanford-Binet Intelligence test of 140 or over; perhaps be a member of Mensa or have achieved something of great value to the world that might win them a Nobel Prize.

B.\ I have found that true genius involves the strength of personality to do what has never been done before and have the courage to see it through to the end! With this criteria one would have to define President Trump as a genius-from the moment he said, “Build a Wall!”

MAY 21, 2016

DONALD TRUMP AND THE CLAIMS OF "CERTAINTY"

1.\ Donald Trump's claims of "certainty" bring up the epistemological question of "HOW DOES ONE KNOW".

2.\ In my professional lifetime Wilfred R. Bion, the great British psychoanalyst lived his entire life in a manner that would give him "primitive certainty". His best analysand, Mike Paul, M.D. trained me in a way to live my life to do what Bion referred to as "The Language of Achievement." The method is for the psychoanalyst to tell the patient, "IT IS MY JOB TO TELL YOU WHAT I THINK AND FEEL ABOUT YOU AND IT IS YOUR JOB TO TELL ME WHAT YOU THINK AND KNOW AND FEEL AND KNOW ABOUT WHAT I THINK AND FEEL ABOUT YOU!" THIS TAKES PLACE ABOUT FIVE DAYS A WEEK, FIFTY MINUTES PER HOUR FOR ABOUT SEVEN YEARS. AT THE END OF THAT TIME YOU WILL ACHIEVE HIGH DEGREES OF "PRIMITIVE CERTAINTY" WHICH WILL MAKE YOU AT ODDS WITH THE REST OF SOCIETY WHO CLAIM IT IS IMPOSSIBLE TO KNOW WITH "CERTAINTY.

3.\ As I ring in at about the 97th% of "authenticity" and "primitive certainty" I know that THERE IS NO MISTAKE THAT DONALD TRUMP POSSESSES THE QUALITY I REFER TO

AS PRIMITIVE CERTAINTY. I JUST DON'T KNOW HOW HE GOT THERE OTHER THAN BEING BORN AS SMART AND AS GIFTED AS HE IS. HE WILL BE RIGHT MOST OF THE TIME AND WAY AHEAD OF PUBLIC RECOGNITION THAT HE IS RIGHT!!! EVEN ON THE RARE OCCASION HE IS WRONG HE WILL LEAD YOU IN THE RIGHT DIRECTION.

***ASSIGNMENT DESK FOR NEWS MEDIA & MAKE COPIES FOR ALL M.D'S, J.D.'S & CLINICAL PSYCHOLOGISTS IN YOUR OFFICE!!!+ PROFESSIONAL MUSICIANS!

16 YEAR PROFESSIONAL
MUSICIAN-RETIRED
MEMBER IN GOOD
STANDING-LOCAL 47
LOS ANGELES, CA

I AM FREUD!!!

UNDER OATH, EYEBALL TO EYEBALL, HON. MICHAEL LEVANAS (2008) SAID "CAN YOU PROVE YOU ARE FREUD!" I SAID, "CAN YOU PROVE I AM NOT!"

Around 1979 energy used to shoot out of my hands, as did Olga Worrall who was filmed in the Kurlian photography lab at UCLA. I had a gift that was outlawed by the Board of Psychology, so Olga Worrall gave direction to my gift having to dumb down. This is why I told three boards of psychology that even at 72 years old if they put their best psychologist or psychiatrist up against me working with the same patient in a public demonstration I would waste them!!! No one took me up on the challenge. (BOARDS OF PSYCHOLOGY INHIBIT SKILL SET OF PSYCHOLOGISTS THAT UNLESS THEY ARE DONE AWAY WITH PSYCHOLOGY CAN ONLY REGRESS!!!) In 1979 I was first touched by the hand of God and Wilfred Bion M.R.C.S.-the great British psychoanalyst and Milton H. Erickson, M.D. were sent back as reincarnated souls to help me, the reincarnated soul of Sigmund Freud clean up the mess I created the last time around the Karmic Wheel.

WITHOUT THIS WORK FAMILIES AND COUNTRIES WILL NEVER TURN THE TRAGIC CORNER=WAR & DIVORCE!!! In 1981 Allyn & Bacon, Boston published my book Psychotherapy, Insight & Style: The Existential Moment. To successfully work with the psychotic core of the personality all that is in that book must be available within the psychoanalytic frame. ALL PEOPLE HAVE UNDERLYING PSYCHOTIC THINKING DISORDERS & A PSYCHOTIC CORE!!! Most of the Master Clinicians of that era wrote reviews indicating they thought I was the most gifted clinician alive. In 1984 my work was described in Australia as "a kind of mental precision that electrified the Australian therapeutic community and had lasting therapeutic impact." In Sheffield England I delivered the goods in 1986 in a workshop entitled "The Therapeutic Wizardry of Dr. Len Bergantino". In 1990 I gave a workshop at the Royal College of Medicine in London entitled "The Development and Use of Extrasensory Perception in the Practice of Psychoanalysis, psychotherapy and clinical hypnosis." My personal training with Carl Whitaker, M.D., Milton Erickson, M.D. and Wilfred Bion, M.R.C.S. & his best M.D. analysands were critical in my being able to get an entire audience at a higher level of Being to work with what Bion wrote about as Beta Elements (my unpublished manuscript entitled "FROM PSYCHOANALYSIS TO INFINITY!!!") (THIS BOOK IS CRUCIAL TO PSYCHOSEXUAL CONNECTION WITH SELF & SIGNIFICANT OTHER) While The Hindus most closely write about what I directly experienced in that the skill sets necessary to do the job-my daughter Lisa Francesca Bergantino is the reincarnated soul of Bion and Cleopatra; my son Alexander Bergantino is the reincarnated soul of Milton H. Erickson, M.D. and Decimus Brutus; and I am the reincarnated soul of Sigmund Freud and Julius Caesar.

Reincarnation is not new. God's gift was in revealing who two reincarnations per person were that had to be cleaned up in unison. Without the knowledge in this book there will be no balance among karmic law, natural law and civil law!!!

Dr. Len Bergantino

***This work is 100 years ahead of the way psychoanalysis is being taught and trained today!!!

THE QUALITY OF BEING: PSYCHOANALYSIS - STATE OF THE ART

A Revolutionary Approach by Dr. Len Bergantino, Ed.D, Ph.D

"The Discipline of Being in the Practice of Psychoanalysis"

Beta Elements: An Expansion of the conceptual work of Wilfred R. Bion, M.R.C.S. into Psychoanalytic Technique.

- VHS VIDEO TAPE - ONE HOUR - $45 MAKING AN IMPACT IN THERAPY: HOW

Seminar by Dr. Len Bergantino, Ed.D., Ph.D. MASTER CLINICIANS INTERVENE, Jason

Working with a professional audience. Aronson Publ., Northvale, N.J., 1993.

288 pages. Author: Bergantino, L.

- For Physicians who want their patients to get better psychologically and for Training Analysts and Psychiatrists who want to learn to succeed at doing these jobs in paragraph 1.

This kind of work permits psychoanalysts to develop techniques to do jobs that have either never or rarely been done:

1. Form a solid nuclear self in a patient who never had one - a job Kohut wrote couldn't be done.
2. Work successfully with the kind of archaic liquid symbiotic transferences that Searles wrote about treating with limited success over 13 and 18 year cases;
3. Detect and work with underlying psychotic thinking disorders – such as Bion wrote about even in narcissistic, borderline and neurotic patients;
4. Detoxify psychotoxic states of being (Kernberg's work stops here) and return patients to natural states of being where affect is connected and life force and the fight for that life force is sustained;
5. Help psychoanalysts' quality of being (Becoming 'O' -Bion) become enhanced so they may be curative of primitive mental states at deep emotional levels, even in patients thought not to be in treatment for that problem. Otherwise, patients will respond to the primitive mental states of the analyst even though the analyst does not act out. The end result would be an analysis whereby the analyst's blocked quality of being would leave patients in prematurely stuck places with self and a significant other whereby that patient's life would remain tragic even after a long analysis.

- Beta elements that Bion wrote about from a conceptual frame of reference actually exist. The question then becomes how can one do an analysis if they do not perceive with their senses these beta elements because they would not know what needed to be contained, therefore the underlying psychotic thinking disorder aspects of patients personalities, even those thought to be neurotic, narcissistic or borderline, could not be dealt with authentically beyond the point with which a psychoanalysis could 'detect', 'detoxify' and 'interpret' these beta elements.
- Donald Rinsley, M.D., Fellow, American College of Psychoanalysts, in a review of Dr. Bergantino's book, Psychotherapy, Insight and Style: The Existential Moment, Jason Aronson Publishers, 1986, made reference to Dr. Bergantino and his work in the following way: "There is no doubt that some people possess a healing capacity and that others do not. Nor is there any doubt that a Zulu witch doctor, a Puerto Rican curendero, a Navaho Medicine man, or a voodoo spiritist may remit symptoms more effectively than the best trained psychotherapist or psychoanalyst." Bulletin of the Menninger Clinic, Vol. 47, No. 5.
- Dr. Len Bergantino, Ed.D., Ph.D was in the private practice of psychoanalysis was in Beverly Hills, CA 90210

FOR (469 pp. UNPUBLISHED MANUSCRIPT: FROM PSYCHOANALYSIS TO INFINITY send $100 to:

Dr. Len Bergantino, Ed.D., Ph.D

1235 Brockton Avenue, Suite 104

Los Angeles, California 90025 USA

FOR PSYCHOANALYTIC STUDY GROUP (MDs ONLY) CALL (424) 293-9511 (7 RINGS).

LEN BERGANTINO
Ed.D., Ph.D., A.B.P.P.

(Clinical Psychologist - License Number 3837)

A.B.P.P. - Diplomate in Family Psychology
American Board of Professional Psychology

Author: Making An Impact in Therapy, How Master Clinicians Intervene (master classic series). Jason Aronson, publishers, Northvale, NJ.

PSYCHOANALYSIS

Heavily Influenced by Wilfred R. Bion, M.R.C.S. (Medical Royal College of Surgeons). Trained by Wilfred Bion's Analysands M.D. Training Analysts, Martin Grotjahn, M.D. (Training Analyst), and Bruno Bettelheim, Ph.D. (Training Analyst).

Pursuit of finer and finer discriminations of PURE BEING evocative of the capacity to think to infinity in the emotional line of fire! (ala Toscanini! Paganini!)

Treatment of the psychotic core of the personality even in normal neurotic, narcissistic, obsessive compulsive, and borderline personalities. The treatment for those who are willing to go the distance and have not been able to develop the tools to do the job at the highest levels of personal achievement and emotional development.

When I do an analysis with people they customarily triple their income and the quality of their life!

CALL: (310) 207-9397

1215 Brockton Ave., Ste. 104, W. Los Angeles

WILFRED R. BION, M.R.C.S. the great British psychoanalyst stated "The entire psychoanalytic library is good for about the first hour and one half of an analysis. After that you have to know what to say to the patient."

Wilhelm Reich, M.D., Freud's most gifted training analyst wrote that "The Little Man" became "very very nervous" when the work involved THE SENSES! (Moving about).

Harold Searles, M.D., the best American Psychoanalyst I saw during my lifetime wrote on page 6 of his book entitled "THE BORDERLINE PERSONALITY" that he had treated cases with archaic liquid symbiotic transferences unsuccessfully for 13 and 18 years. Also, that borderline patients experienced verbal aggression as if it were physical aggression.

Heinz Kohut wrote that a solid nuclear self cannot be built on patients who have lost their self because they cannot stand the chaos and anxiety of not knowing that would be required to put Humpty Dumpty back together again, as in the work of Bion, Melanie Klein and others working with the underlying psychotic core of the personality even in neurotics, as well as your next door neighbors who may be narcissistic, borderline and obsessive compulsive personality disorders. So he recommended analytic interpretations that are "near" the patient's experience, so as not to rattle the patient's guts. THE PROBLEM IS THIS NEVER BRINGS THE PATIENT ANY CLOSER TO BEING HIS OR HER AUTHENTIC SELF!

Wilhelm Reich said "IF YOU CAN'T DO POLITICS, YOU CAN'T DO ANALYSIS!" The problem here is that those who have vested interests in protecting the status quo, do all in their power to see to it that those who can make a difference in creating a psychoanalysis, a psychotherapy and a clinical hypnosis that will significantly add to the psychoanalytic armantarium in CREATING A SOCIETY WHERE ANALYSANDS WHO HAVE A SOLID NUCLEAR SELF WILL HELP TO CREATE AN "UPWARD SPIRALING SOCIETY-BERGANTINO" as opposed to Freud's fear as stated in "Civilization and It's Discontents" of a downward spiraling society."

Dr. Bruno Bettelheim, trained in Freud's original training group along with Dr. Wilhelm Reich told me in personal communications that Freud said "The Americans will never understand ANALYSIS BECAUSE THEY DO NOT UNDERSTAND THAT IT IS A FIGHT FOR MAN'S SOUL AND THEY DO NOT UNDERSTAND THE RELATIONSHIP BETWEEN SEX AND DEATH!"

Carl Whitaker, M.D. in a review of my book "Psychotherapy, Insight and Style: The Existential Moment", Allyn & Bacon, Boston, 1981, 288 pp. wrote that the only tool the psychotherapist had was the evolving development of the therapeutic use of self." It is my experience that FROM PSYCHOANALYSIS DOWNWARD THROUGH THE PSYCHOTHERAPIES AND CLINICAL HYPNOSIS THAT THE PROFESSIONALS AND PROFESSIONAL GUILDS AND MOST OF ALL LICENSING BOARDS SUCH AS THE BOARDS OF MEDICAL QUALITY ASSURANCE AND PSYCHOLOGY LICENSING BOARD HAVE MADE TRAINING OF PSYCHOANALYSTS, PSYCHOTHERAPISTS AND CLINICAL HYPNOTISTS SUCH THAT THEY LEARN BY STUDYING ABOUT PATIENTS INSTEAD OF HAVING THE DIRECT EXPERIENCE DONE TO THEM AND THEM WITH PATIENTS OF WHAT HAS BEEN DONE TO THEM IN A LIFELONG PURSUIT OF WHAT SHAKESPEARE CALLED "TO BE OR NOT TO BE", OR WHAT JEAN PAUL SARTRE WROTE ABOUT AS "THE THING IN ITSELF" OR WHAT DR. WILFRED R. BION WROTE ABOUT AS THE TOOLS OF AN ANALYSIS GIVING THE PATIENT THE ABILITY TO PURSUE FINER AND FINER DISCRIMINATIONS OF BECOMING "O", PURE BEING!

Freud wrote that the most an ANALYSIS COULD DO WAS GIVE PATIENTS THE OPPORTUNITY TO CARRY ON THE WORK! BION WROTE THAT THE PURPOSE OF AN ANALYSIS WAS TO GIVE A PATIENT THE TOOLS TO THINK AND FUNCTION IN THE LINE OF EMOTIONAL FIRE! BERGANTINO AGREES WITH FREUD, BION AND BETTELHEIM BUT ADDS TO THEIR WORK BY STATING THE GIVING THE PATIENT THE TOOLS TO TURN THE TRAGIC CORNER IN THEIR PERSONAL LIVES IS A NECESSARY ADDITION TO THE

PSYCHOANALYST ARMANTARIUM; and to do so one must both be willing to go through the gates of hell in the development of the analytic use of self as well as have patients who are willing to go for broke and are willing to walk on a tightrope without a net. It is only when both the ANALYST AND THE PATIENT ENTER INTO SUCH A CONTRACT THAT BOTH WILL FEEL GRATEFUL ENOUGH FOR THE WORK TO BEGIN! ONE CAN EITHER DO THIS WORK OR THEY CANNOT! THIS APPLIES TO BOTH ANALYST AND PATIENT! SUPPLY AND DEMAND WILL CONTROL THE MARKETPLACE AND ALL LICENSING BOARDS ARE A MERE INTERRUPTION INTO THE ACTUAL DOING OF AN ANALYSIS! THEY MUST BE DONE AWAY WITH AS IT APPLIES TO PSYCHOANALYSIS AND ALL THE SUBSEQUENT PSYCHOTHERAPIES AND METHODS OF HYPNOSIS IF PSYCHOANALYSIS IS TO DEVELOP IT's true capacity as an <u>Art Form!</u>

Wilfred R. Bion, M.R.C.S. (Medical Royal College of Surgeons) stated "About all you can tell anyone is that you will see them five times per week for fifty minute sessions at a specified hour. These are the minimum conditions required to be able to do an ANALYSIS! KNOWING HOW TO DEAL WITH THESE MINIMUM CONDITIONS ON A DAILY BASIS IS ALL THE BLOODY ANALYSIS ANYONE WILL EVER NEED TO KNOW!" PATIENTS USED TO PAY ME $125 per hour totaling $625 per week and thirty thousand per year per patient during 1979 through 1992 whereby I used to see patients for between 3 and 7 years for an ANALYSIS. Further, when they understood I WAS BOTH GIVING THEM THE TOOLS TO SAVE THEIR SOULS AS WELL AS FUNCTION AT NEAR PARANORMAL LEVELS IN THE LINE OF EMOTIONAL FIRE THEY WOULD PAY ME $625 A WEEK JUST TO HOLD THE TIME OPEN EVEN IF IT WAS SIX MONTH PERIODS WHERE THEY WERE ON LOCATION OR WORKING ON MOVIES. THEY MADE A LOT OF MONEY AND I WAS CERTAINLY NOT GOING TO DEPRIVE MY FAMILY OF MAKING A LIVING WITH SOME

HALF BAKED ARRANGEMENT THAT HAD NO CHANCE OF SUCCESS. BION STATED "SO MANY LIES A MINUTE SO MANY DOLLARS AN HOUR" AND OFTEN DEALT WITH WHETHER OR NOT HE COULD AFFORD TO SPEND ANY TIME AT ALL WITH SUCH A PERSON. IN OTHER WORDS IT WAS NOT A MATTER OF MAKING MONEY. IT WAS A MATTER OF BECOMING 'O'-finer and finer discriminations of PURE BEING, OR AS SARTRE PUT IT, THE-THING-IN-ITSELF!" Mrs. Francesca Bion, Dr. Bion's widow, was instrumental in my developing and UNDERSTANDING ALL OF BION'S WORK AND BEING ABLE TO UTILIZE IT CLINICALLY!

I LOVED HER DEARLY! I JUST DID NOT WANT TO MARRY HER! Francesca Bion told me that when Dr. Bion decided he had done what he could do in Sao Paulo Brazil and decided to move to Beverly Hills, California many of the training analysts of The Southern California Psychoanalytic Institute and Society as well as The Los Angeles Psychoanalytic Institute and Society who had promised to seek a second training analysis with Bion did not show up, AND OF THOSE THAT DID BION TOLD THEM HE COULD NOT FIND THE TIME TO SEE THEM!" He took only the cream of the crop with the highest level of personal integrity. Of those was Richard Alexander, M.D. who told me about his first interview with Bion. Bion said "I will see you Monday through Friday at 10 a.m. (The minimum conditions are non-negotiable if one is to do what John Rosen was able to do in cutting away character disorders (Rosen's book THE DIRECT ANALYSIS OF SCHIZOPHRENIA-1956) was brilliant. The American Psychoanalytic threw out the baby with the bathwater as Rosen himself was a character disordered bastard who both fucked his patients and on occasion beat them up). His work needs to be brought back! It is brilliant! Nobody cuts away character disorders better than John Rosen, M.D.

So Dr. Alexander said to Dr. Bion, "Well, Wednesdays I take the day off and I play golf! Bion said, Fine, come four, pay me for five! So much for the day off. Dr. Alexander "chucked up enough to make the game work!" and went for five days of Analysis. You may think these little tidbits don't or won't amount to much, BUT IF YOU DON'T CALL THE MINIMUM CONDITIONS CORRECTLY IN THE FIRST MEETING YOU HAVE BLOWN THE ENTIRE ANALYSIS IN THAT YOU HAVE TAKEN ON A PATIENT WITH CONDITIONS THAT DO NOT GIVE YOU WHAT YOU NEED TO DO THE JOB. And in Analysis, the job is analyzing the underlying psychotic core of the personality experientially in narcissistic, borderline and obsessive compulsive personality disorders while they manifest archaic liquid symbiotic transferences that most ANALYSTS AND PSYCHOTHERAPISTS DO NOT EVEN RECOGNIZE, THEREFORE MISSING THE SEVERE PATHOLOGICAL PROJECTIVE IDENTIFICATIONS THAT ARE SPLIT OFF FROM PATIENTS WHO CANNOT STAND THE EXPERIENTIAL PAIN THEREFORE MAKING IT IMPOSSIBLE FOR THE ANALYST TO HELP THE PATIENT TURN "THE TRAGIC PRIMITIVE CORNER" IN THEIR LIVES WHICH IS PLAYED OUT OVER AND OVER IN THE "TRANSFERENCE RELATIONSHIP BETWEEN PSYCHOANALYST AND PATIENT! FREUD'S IDEA WAS THAT ONE ANALYSAND COULD INFLUENCE THOUSANDS OF THE GENERAL PUBLIC IN CREATING "AN UPWARD SPIRALING SOCIETY!"

THE QUALITY OF BEING: PSYCHOANALYSIS - STATE OF THE ART

A REVOLUTIONARY Approach by Len Bergantino, Ed.D., Ph.D

"The Discipline of Being IN THE PRACTICE OF PSYCHOANALYSIS

Beta Elements: An Expansion of the conceptual work of Wilfred R. Bion, M.R.C.S. into Psychoanalytic Technique

- VHS VIDEO TAPE - ONE HOUR - $45
Seminar by Len Bergantino, Ed.D., Ph.D.
Working with a professional audience.

MAKING AN IMPACT IN THERAPY: HOW MASTER CLINICIANS INTERVENE, Jason Aronson Publ., Northvale, N.J., 1993. 288 pages. Author: Bergantino, L.

- For Physicians who want their patients to get better psychologically and for Training Analysts and Psychiatrists who want to learn to succeed at doing these jobs in paragraph 1.

This kind of work permits psychoanalysts to develop techniques to do jobs that have either never or rarely been done:

1. Form a solid nuclear self in a patient who never had one - a job Kohut wrote couldn't be done.
2. Work successfully with the kind of archaic liquid symbiotic transferences that Searles wrote about treating with limited success over 13 and 18 year cases;
3. Detect and work with underlying psychotic thinking disorders - such as Bion wrote about even in narcissistic, borderline and neurotic patients;
4. Detoxify psychotoxic states of being (Kernberg's work stops here) and return patients to natural states of being where affect is connected and life force and the fight for that life force is sustained;
5. Help psychoanalysts' quality of being (Becoming 'O'-Bion) become enhanced so they may be curative of primitive mental states at deep emotional levels, even in patients thought not to be in treatment for that problem. Otherwise, patients will respond to the primitive mental states of the analyst even though the analyst does not act out. The end result would be an analysis whereby the analyst's blocked quality of being would leave patients in prematurely stuck places with self and a significant other whereby that patient's life would remain tragic even after a long analysis.

- Beta elements that Bion wrote about from a conceptual frame of reference actually exist. The question then becomes how can one do an analysis if they do not perceive with their senses these beta elements because they would not know what needed to be contained, therefore the underlying psychotic thinking disorder aspects of patients personalities, even those thought to be neurotic, narcissistic or borderline, could not be dealt with authentically beyond the point with which a psychoanalyst could 'detect', 'detoxify' and 'interpret' these beta elements.

- Donald Rinsley, M.D., Fellow, American College of Psychoanalysts, in a review of Dr. Bergantino's book, Psychotherapy, Insight and Style: The Existential Moment, Jason Aronson Publishers, 1986, made reference to Dr. Bergantino and his work in the following way: "There is no doubt that some people possess a healing capacity and that others do not. Nor is there any doubt that a Zulu witch doctor, a Puerto Rican curandero, a Navaho Medicine man, or a voodoo spiritist may remit symptoms more effectively than the best trained psychotherapist or psychoanalyst." Bulletin of the Menninger Clinic, Vol. 47, No. 5.

- Len Bergantino, Ed.D., Ph.D is was in the private practice of psychoanalysis in Beverly Hills, CA.

For book send $100 to Len Bergantino, Ed.D, Ph.D
1215 Brockton Avenue, Suite 104
Los Angeles, California 90025 USA

For Training Analysis or psychoanalysis Call (310) 207-9397

DR. LEN BERGANTINO
I AM THE REINCARNATED SOUL
OF SIGMUND FREUD + JULIUS CAESAR
GOD SENT ME BACK
ON A KARMIC MISSION

*RETIRED CLINICAL PSYCHOLOGIST

THE WHITE HOUSE

WASHINGTON

November 20, 2017

Dr. Len Bergantino
Los Angeles, California

Dear Dr. Bergantino:

Thank you for your kind letter and generous words of support. Working together, we will unify and strengthen our great Nation, honor our Government's sacred duty to the people, and fulfill the promise of America for all of its citizens. United, we will achieve lasting change, peace through strength, and prosperity like never before.

Melania and I are forever grateful for your support. Your encouragement, and that of millions around the world, sustains us every step of the way. Thank you for taking the time to share your thoughts.

With very best wishes,

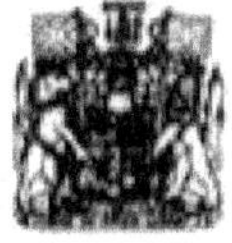

BALMORAL CASTLE

6th October 2017

Dear Dr. Bergantino,

The Queen wishes me to thank you for your letter in which you told Her Majesty a little about yourself and your career and of your musical achievements.

It was also kind of you to share your memories of watching The Queen's Coronation in 1952 and Her Majesty was touched by the sentiments you expressed.

The Queen greatly appreciates the support she has received, from across the world, throughout her long reign and I am to thank you, very much, for your thoughtfulness in writing as you did.

Yours sincerely,

Susan Hussey

Lady-in-Waiting

Dr L Bergantino

BY AIR MAIL
par avion

LOS ANGELES
CA 900
11 OCT '17
PM 12 L

Royal Mail
Postage Paid Great Britain
- 6 OCT 2017
Balmoral Castle
Aberdeenshire AB35 5TB

Dr L Bergantino
1215 Brockton Avenue, Ste 104
W Los Angeles
CA 90025
USA

90025-136629

U.S. Department of Justice

Civil Rights Division

JS:RJF
WH 05172012-103
DJ 168-12C-0

Special Litigation Section - PHB
950 Pennsylvania Ave, NW
Washington DC 20530

MAY 3 1 2012

NEWSFLASH! SALINAS VALLEY STATE PRISON SOLEDAD, CA WARDEN ANTHONY HEDGEPETH AND DEPUTY CHIEF WARDEN ARLENE SOLIS HAVE VACATED THE PREMISES!!!!!!!!!!!!!!!!

Len Bergantino, Ed.D., ABPP
1215 Brockton Avenue
Suite 104
Los Angeles, CA 90025-1366

Dear Dr. Bergantino:

The White House has referred your letter addressed to President Barack Obama to the Department of Justice. We apologize for our delay in responding. In your letter, you expressed serious concerns about what you characterize as "murders" at an unnamed facility in the California state prison system. You allege that certain state correctional officials, including the warden, may be complicit in inmate activities that may lead to the death of another inmate. You also allege that there is a culture of silence there that chills persons with knowledge from speaking out about improper practices. You call for action "to prevent additional murders in the prison system."

In your letter, you make vague reference to a case in federal district court involving Judge Lawrence Karlton and Special Master Matthew Lopes. We understand this to be the longstanding *Coleman* case where the Court is addressing conditions and practices throughout the state prison system. You indicate that you sent a copy of your letter to Judge Karlton and Master Lopes.

Although the United States is not involved in the *Coleman* matter as a party, in general, a Special Master is well-positioned to most immediately address serious allegations such as those contained in your letter. We see that you included your contact information, so the Master is already in a position to approach you if he needs additional information.

In addition, you may want to contact counsel for the Plaintiffs in the *Coleman* case, who likely would be interested in learning more and could pursue remedial relief, if appropriate. Specifically, you may want to provide your information to the Prison Law Office in San Quentin (www.prisonlaw.com).

-2-

Thank you for writing to President Obama regarding this matter. We hope the information we have set forth above is helpful. Please do not hesitate to contact this office if we may be of assistance regarding this or any other matter.

Sincerely,

Richard J. Farano
Senior Trial Attorney
Special Litigation Section

THE WHITE HOUSE
WASHINGTON

April 11, 2013

Dr. Len Bergantino
Apartment 104
1215 Brockton Avenue
Los Angeles, California 90025

Dear Dr. Bergantino:

Thank you for taking the time to write. I have heard from many Americans regarding firearms policy and gun violence in our Nation, and I appreciate your perspective. From Aurora to Newtown to the streets of Chicago, we have seen the devastating effects gun violence has on our American family. I join countless others in grieving for all those whose lives have been taken too soon by gun violence.

Like the majority of Americans, I believe the Second Amendment guarantees an individual right to bear arms. In this country, we have a strong tradition of gun ownership that has been handed down from generation to generation. Hunting and sport shooting are part of our national heritage. Yet, even as we acknowledge that almost all gun owners in America are responsible, when we look at the devastation caused by gun violence—whether in high-profile tragedies or the daily heartbreak that plagues our cities—we must ask ourselves whether we are doing enough.

While reducing gun violence is a complicated challenge, protecting our children from harm should not be a divisive one. Most gun owners agree that we can respect the Second Amendment while keeping an irresponsible, law-breaking few from inflicting harm on a massive scale. Most also agree that if we took commonsense steps to curtail gun violence, there would be fewer atrocities like the one that occurred in Newtown. We will not be able to stop every violent act, but if there is even one thing we can do to reduce gun violence—if even one life can be saved—then we have an obligation to try.

That is why I asked Vice President Joe Biden to identify concrete steps we can take to keep our children safe, help prevent mass shootings, and reduce the broader epidemic of gun violence in this country. He met with over 200 groups representing a broad cross-section of Americans and heard their best ideas. I have put forward a specific set of proposals based off of his efforts, and in the days ahead, I intend to use whatever weight this office holds to make them a reality.

My plan gives law enforcement, schools, mental health professionals, and the public health community some of the tools they need to help reduce gun violence. These tools include strengthening the background check system, helping schools hire more resource officers and counselors and develop emergency preparedness plans, and ensuring mental health professionals know their options for reporting threats of violence. And I directed the Centers for Disease Control to study the best ways to reduce gun violence—because it is critical that we understand the science behind this public health crisis. From improving mental health services to looking more closely at a culture that too often glorifies violence, we must leave no stone unturned when working to keep Americans safe.

As important as these steps are, they are not a substitute for action from Congress. To make a real and lasting difference, members of Congress must also act. As part of my comprehensive plan, I have called on them to pass some specific proposals right away. First, it is time to require a universal background check for anyone trying to buy a gun. Second, Congress should renew the 10-round limit on magazines and reinstate and strengthen the assault weapons ban. We should get tougher on those who buy guns with the purpose of selling them to criminals, and we should impose serious punishments on anyone who helps them do this.

These are reasonable, commonsense measures that have the support of the majority of the American people. But change will not come unless the American people demand it from their lawmakers. Now is the time to do the right thing for our children, our communities, and the country we love. We owe the victims of heartbreaking national tragedies and the countless unheralded tragedies each year nothing less than our best effort—to seek consensus in order to save lives and ensure a brighter future for our children.

Thank you, again, for writing. I encourage you to visit www.WhiteHouse.gov/NowIsTheTime to learn more about my Administration's approach.

Sincerely,

Dr. Len Bergantino

Clinical Psychologist - Psychological Consultant (VIA TELEPHONE)

Licensed Psychologist CA (3837), AZ (266), HI (990)

President Obama has sent two letters RE: My Written Consultations

••••• ***If I think I can be of help*** in creating a unique way of dealing with whatever problem you present via my one of a kind gift utilizing extrasensory perception, a $1000 prepaid retainer is required prior to my beginning work. I presented a workshop in the "Development and Use of Extrasensory "Perception" at the Royal College of Medicine in London!

CALL 310-207-9397

THE QUALITY OF BEING: PSYCHOANALYSIS - STATE OF THE ART

A REVOLUTIONARY Approach by Len Bergantino, Ed.D., Ph.D

"The Discipline of Being IN THE PRACTICE OF PSYCHOANALYSIS

Beta Elements: An Expansion of the conceptual work of Wilfred R. Bion, M.R.C.S. into Psychoanalytic Technique

- VHS VIDEO TAPE - ONE HOUR - $45

Seminar by Len Bergantino, Ed.D., Ph.D
Working with a professional audience

MAKING AN IMPACT IN THERAPY: HOW MASTER CLINICIANS INTERVENE, Jason Aronson Publ., Northvale, N.J., 1997. 288 pages. Author: Bergantino, L.

- For Physicians who want their patients to get better psychologically and for Training Analysts and Psychiatrists who want to learn to succeed at doing these jobs in paragraph 1

This kind of work permits psychoanalysts to develop techniques to do jobs that have either never or rarely been done

1. Form a solid nuclear self in a patient who never had one - a job Kohut wrote couldn't be done
2. Work successfully with the kind of archaic liquid symbiotic transferences that Searles wrote about treating with limited success over 13 and 18 year cases.
3. Detect and work with underlying psychotic thinking disorders - such as Bion wrote about even in narcissistic, borderline and neurotic patients.
4. Detoxify psychotoxic states of being (Kernberg's work stops here) and return patients to natural states of being where affect is connected and life force and the fight for that life force is sustained.
5. Help psychoanalysts' quality of being (Becoming 'O'-Bion) become enhanced so they may be curative of primitive mental states at deep emotional levels, even in patients thought not to be in treatment for that problem. Otherwise, patients will respond to the primitive mental states of the analyst even though the analyst does not act out. The end result would be an analysis whereby the analyst's blocked quality of being would leave patients in prematurely stuck places with self and a significant other whereby that patient's life would remain tragic even after a long analysis.

- Beta elements that Bion wrote about from a conceptual frame of reference actually exist. The question then becomes how can one do an analysis if they do not perceive with their senses these beta elements because they would not know what needed to be contained, therefore the underlying psychotic thinking disorder aspects of patients personalities, even those thought to be neurotic, narcissistic or borderline, could not be dealt with authentically beyond the point with which a psychoanalyst could 'detect', 'detoxify' and 'interpret' these beta elements

- Donald Rinsley, M.D., Fellow, American College of Psychoanalysts, in a review of Dr. Bergantino's book, Psychotherapy, Insight and Style: The Existential Moment, Jason Aronson Publishers, 1986, made reference to Dr. Bergantino and his work in the following way: "There is no doubt that some people possess a healing capacity and that others do not. Nor is there any doubt that a Zulu witch doctor, a Puerto Rican curandero, a Navaho Medicine man, or a voodoo spiritist may remit symptoms more effectively than the best trained psychotherapist or psychoanalyst." Bulletin of the Menninger Clinic, Vol 47, No 5

- Len Bergantino, Ed.D., Ph.D is was in the private practice of psychoanalysis in Beverly Hills, CA.

For book send $100 to Len Bergantino, Ed.D., Ph.D

[illegible] Avenue, Suite 104
Los Angeles, California 90025 USA

For Training Analysis or psychoanalysis Call (310) [illegible]

DR. LEN BERGANTINO
I AM THE REINCARNATED SOUL
OF SIGMUND FREUD + JULIUS CAESAR
GOD SENT ME BACK
ON A KARMIC MISSION

RETIRED CLINICAL PSYCHOLOGIST

THE WHITE HOUSE

WASHINGTON

November 20, 2017

Dr. Len Bergantino
Los Angeles, California

Dear Dr. Bergantino:

Thank you for your kind letter and generous words of support. Working together, we will unify and strengthen our great Nation, honor our Government's sacred duty to the people, and fulfill the promise of America for all of its citizens. United, we will achieve lasting change, peace through strength, and prosperity like never before.

Melania and I are forever grateful for your support. Your encouragement, and that of millions around the world, sustains us every step of the way. Thank you for taking the time to share your thoughts.

With very best wishes,

BALMORAL CASTLE

6th October 2017

Dear Dr. Bergantino,

The Queen wishes me to thank you for your letter in which you told Her Majesty a little about yourself and your career and of your musical achievements.

It was also kind of you to share your memories of watching The Queen's Coronation in 1952 and Her Majesty was touched by the sentiments you expressed.

The Queen greatly appreciates the support she has received, from across the world, throughout her long reign and I am to thank you, very much, for your thoughtfulness in writing as you did.

Yours sincerely,

Susan Hussey

Lady-in-Waiting

Dr L. Bergantino

BY AIR MAIL
par avion
Royal Mail

LOS ANGELES
CA 900
11 OCT '17
PM 12 L

Dr L Bergantino
1215 Brockton Avenue, Ste 104
W Los Angeles
CA 90025
USA

90025-136629

FROM PSYCHOANALYSIS TO INFINITY

by LEN BERGANTINO, ED.D., PH.D.
1215 Brockton Avenue, Suite 104
Los Angeles, California 90025

424 293-9511
Let it Ring 7 Times to Leave Message

JAMES S. GROTSTEIN, M.D.
INCORPORATED
522 DALEHURST AVENUE
LOS ANGELES, CALIFORNIA 90024
(213) 276-3456

PSYCHOANALYSIS

December 30, 1989

Len Bergantino, Ph.D.
450 N. Bedford Drive, Suite 300
Beverly Hills, CA 90210

Dear Len,

I finally had the pleasure of viewing your tape. I found it very impressive. It helped me to understand better where you are coming from and to be able to observe first hand your intuitive way of approaching people. Your technique reminded me of an elegant sophistication of Gestalt along with Erikson and Bion.

My intimate knowledge of the members of my study group (Interdisciplinary Group for Advanced Studies in Psychosis -- "IGASP") suggests to me that this tape, unfortunately, is not for them. They are not like me nor like you. They are more conservative in their attitudes and tastes and are especially defensive about Bion. Many of them have been analyzed and/or supervised by him, and I believe, to quote Bion, "it would produce more heat than light". I think there would be such debate over "beta elements" that the beta elements encountering contrary beta elements would create a beta element cacophony.

On the other hand, let me gently broach the subject to them at the next meeting and see what they say. I will let you know in either case.

Thank you very much for letting me see the tape. It was really educational for me to watch the way you work. You are truly talented.

I hope this year brings you more happiness than any preceeding.

Warmest regards,

James S. Grotstein, M.D.

JSG:sf

P.S. While this letter was being typed, I learned that Don Rinsley had just passed away!

A REVIEW

By DONALD B. RINSLEY, M.D., F.R.S.H.,
Fellow, American College of Psychoanalysts;
Fellow, American Psychiatric Association
Psychotherapy, Insight and Style.
By Len Bergantino, Ed.D., Ph.D. Boston:
Allyn and Bacon, 1981, 288 pp. Published in
Bulletin of the Menninger Clinic, Vol. 47,
No. 5, September 1983.

■■ ■

There is no doubt that some people possess a healing capacity and that others do not; nor is there any doubt that a Zulu witch doctor, a Puerto Rican curandero, a Navaho medicine man or a voodoo spiritist may remit symptoms more effectively than the best trained psychotherapist or psychoanalyst. The differences between healing and therapy are not inconspicuous even as both may readily dissolve into quackery in the hands of the exploitive and the unscrupulous. A wise Freud once commented that the function of psychoanalysis is to convert neurotic misery into ordinary human suffering, a point of view to be dismissed only at one's peril even though it doubtless reflected the essence of Freud's depressive personality. From such few considerations as these emerge questions concerning the differences separating healing and therapy, the features that unite them and the goals and objectives they may be noted to share. And whatever answers to these questions may satisfy those who propound them will reflect whether one's Weltanschauung considers the world to be a vale of tears or, after the fashion of the Gallic optimist, Coué, a place where everything keeps getting better and better.

Dr. Bergantino's book in scholarly and even entertaining fashion sets out to address issues such as these. The blurb on its bookjacket states that it "integrates 17 prominent therapists' styles and problem solving techniques..." Its more accurate subtitle, The Existential Moment reflects the author's searching awareness that effective psychological healing, or psychotherapy, or whatever one chooses to call such interpersonal transactional processes ultimately expands one's awareness, hence one's knowledge of one's self, one's surround and the relationship between them; and further, that such awareness and knowledge develops in saltatory fashion, deriving from unheralded and even momentary experiences of insight, illumination ("aha!") or unconscious internal change. So far so good, but there is after all nothing new in that, so why read yet another book devoted to arresting human experiences that many believe to be inexplicable and unteachable?

There are at least two answers to that question. To begin with, the book reflects the personal odyssey of a trained, disciplined yet open-minded professional psychologist who has drunk deeply at the wells of an number of acknowledged healer-therapists whose work he has carefully studied and evaluated, among them, Viktor Frankl, Wilfred Bion, the Gouldings, Frederick Perls, Milton Erickson and Carl Whitaker. A unique feature of Dr. Bergantino's presentation is his detailed accounts of these therapists' hour-to-hour work, drawn from his own personal experience and from verbatim descriptions provided by their students and analysands, offering fascinating and instructive insights into the therapeutic labors of admittedly gifted treaters. The book is thus replete with clinical material, excerpts from therapeutic encounters and direct reports of those precious "aha"-type moments, conveyed within a disciplined epistemic context that presents each example in terms of ethical professionalism rather than exemplary amateurishness.

Again, the book reflects its author's ongoing growth and development as both thinker and therapist. Dr. Bergantino has gone to great length to converse and consult with both primary and secondary sources, delving into the what and the how, ferreting out illustrative clinical situations and indicating how he has proceeded to synthesize and integrate what he has learned from them and from his own therapeutic work. His book is indeed a literate statement of how one clinician has made of himself a therapist and his statement is both informative and poignant.

As I read this book my thoughts returned to a little-known 1962 Psychiatric Quarterly paper by Ernst Federn, the son of the psychoanalyst Paul Federn, entitled "The Therapeutic Personality, As Illustrated by Paul Federn and August Aichorn." It described in some detail the uniquely intuitive therapeutic work of these two outstanding clinicians, drawn from the author's own experience of knowing them both; Federn and Aichorn brought disciplined artistry to their respective therapeutic tasks in working psychoanalytically with "difficult" cases, Federn with psychotics, Aichorn with disturbed adolescents; both readily sensed suffering and never flinched from addressing it; both could occupy honored places in Dr. Bergantino's book. I learned much from that paper and I have learned much from Dr. Bergantino's book as well.

Psychotherapy, Insight and Style is an absorbing work, to be returned to time and again after one has read it through, to be thought about, mulled over and placed on one's bedside table if not under ones pillow. It is a book that the experienced clinician will read with knowledgeable satisfaction and that the nascent therapist will read with excitement. And both will profit from what it has to tell.

LEN BERGANTINO, Ed.D., Ph.D.
Clinical Psychology (PL3837) to Polls

10266 Kilrenney Ave.

Los Angeles, CA 90064

1/12/81

Carl Whitaker, M.D.
Professor of Psychiatry
U. of Wisconsin Medical School
Center for Health Sciences
600 Highland Avenue
Madison, Wisconsin 53792

Dear Carl,

The following is material that you dictated to me over the telephone regarding material that may be used in any advertising capacity that Allyn & Bacon, Inc., chooses to do in the promotion of my book, "Psychotherapy Insight And Style: The Existential Moment."

"The author as a therapist is a student of creativity and he offers a metaphorical elaboration that is both impressionistic, artistic and a stimulus for thinking. He is a professional reporter of interpersonal change models in the family therapy set and even intrapsychic change process in itw twentieth century face. The book rouses powerful feelings and stimulates growth in its readers."

"Reading this book is an active experience in the use of self in the field of psychotherapy, and as such, it both expands and enriches the community standards of practice of professional psychotherapists. That self is really our only tool. It's use is critical and evolving through each practitioner's professional lifetime."

Please sign below acknowledging your permission to quote.

Sincerely,

Len

Carl Whitaker, M.D.

Len Bergantino, Ed.D., Ph.D.

P.S. Please return one copy to me, keep one for your records and send one to Allyn & Bacon, Inc. Thank you.

INTRODUCTION

This book is a declarative and definitive statement about a kind of training that needs to become part of psychoanalytic training, otherwise, at the deepest and most soulful levels of transference, the field cannot progress to any significant degree in its methods of treatment. Psychoanalysis as it stands cannot progress beyond where it is at because it is chained to looking at and dealing with itself from a structure that does not permit psychoanalysis to advance beyond itself in the ways that are necessary to advance human civilization.

So what's new about this statement. You have read it before. You have heard it before, but there has been a problem in that to this point no one has found a remedy to the dilemma.

Not so with this book! I am going to provide the evidence that will show you what needs to be done and how it can be done in order to advance and transform the field of psychoanalysis.

In what I show, and what I demonstrate, and what I write about, it is my intention to in a way that is the experience-itself, take psychoanalysis, in method, concept and technique, to infinity. That is, to make finer and finer discriminations that have been hinted at or written about conceptually, but never put into a working psychoanalytic technique that would help its practitioners to transcend and transform themselves to be able to do what they cannot now do.

STATEMENT OF THE PROBLEM: THE POLITICS OF PSYCHOANALYSIS

> Dr. Bruno Bettelheim told me in a personal communication that "Wilhelm Reich was Freud's most gifted training analyst." Wilhelm Reich said, "If you can't do politics, you can't do analysis!"

This book is an impassioned plea to both a group of professionals that define at its most sophisticated levels the nature of psychotherapeutic treatment at its highest level. The American and International Psychoanalytic Associations and their component training institutes, and the patient populations which the graduates of these institutes practice in performing treatment upon. The problem has been twofold: The Institutes have kept out much of the genius that would have enabled psychoanalysis to successfully treat what I will describe in much greater depth as the psychotic core of the personality; and second; the patient population who in good faith are dedicated to the pursuit of their own being toward finer and finer discriminations, are not touched, have not turned the tragic corner in their lives, as a result of analysis that sometimes take seven years at five days per week or in many instances desperate patients who have in good faith tried twenty years of combinations of analysis and psychotherapies, only to be as tragic in their lives or nearly so as when they began the analysis. I am not talking here about the treatment of psychotic patients. I am talking about the treatment of characterological disorders, normal narcissistic, borderline, neurotic, schizoid patient populations. You know, the kind of people who are your next door neighbors.

WHO AM I AND WHY DO I WRITE TO YOU, THE PSYCHOANALYSTS?

I am a man, who like you, was an 'ordinary' human being with certain kinds of personal gifts and personality traits that motivated me to take things to the far reaches and I am therefore in a place to write experiential dicta that is so far ahead of where the profession not only of psychoanalysis, but the profession of psychotherapy as a whole is in its development, that what I have to write and offer you may be of value for years to come in that it will take the best of mankind to develop that of which I write, and to move beyond what I have written.

Thus, I am not so much concerned about your opinion of what I write because from what I can see you haven't suffered enough along the path of development to have one.

Further, I have low level psychic capacity, a kind of extrasensory perception if you will, and you do not. So without having this gift developed in yourselves any comments about the so called validity of what I write to you is meaningless. You have not and without training as such experienced the kind of nuances in the transference about what I will write.

Robert Langs has written about truth therapy and lie therapy referring to psychoanalysis as a truth therapy. Yet, what I have found is that the most characterological of liars are psychoanalysts. It is a rather complex problem in that they experientially lie to themselves about lying, therefore they do not know that they lie. They are just experientially dead in the ways that would lead to more "primitive certainty" in terms of "knowing".

Then psychoanalysts keep the field primarily decadent to where it currently is and is not able to move beyond by creating theories or picking the theories that fit their own clinical limitations without stating this as such, so they can actually with clear conscience feel they are doing the most they can do in terms of what Bion wrote in terms of "Becoming 'O'", finer and finer discriminations of one's Being.

Bion has written there is an underlying psychotic core even in normal people. The lies of the psychoanalyst have prevented any significant development of treatment at these levels except for Melanie Klein, Bion and Rosenfelt personally in what they have written. When Rosenfelt wrote about "osmotic pressure in the transference" in Impasse & Interpretation you know he knew what the hell he was doing. When Searles wrote that he has unsuccessfully treated liquid symbiotic transferences in cases for thirteen and eighteen years you knew he at least knew enough to know what the problem was and what he was having trouble doing. Most psychoanalysts do not know what the problem is or the job that they are tackling on the deepest and most subtle levels of nuance, so it is no wonder they cannot do it. In other words, after having been trained by many world renowned psychotherapists, and many of Wilfred Bion's analysands, I am convinced that "PSYCHOANALYSIS IS THE ONLY METHOD OF CURE! IT'S TOO BAD NO ONE KNOWS HOW TO DO ONE!"

WHAT HAPPENS ARE THE DESTRUCTION OF THE LINKS TO THE ADVANCEMENT OF THE EXPERIENTIAL KNOW HOW OF DOING A PSYCHOANALYSIS THROUGH "K" (KNOWLEDGE).

Any psychoanalyst who reads what I have written can close down his or her own personal experience without knowing that is happening, and come up with theoretical reasons for "dismissing" in part or in toto of what I have written. Thus, the attempt and the challenge of writing this book in a way that you cannot do that is to write the book as the <u>thing-in-itself</u>, the experience itself, with as fine-tuned levels of pure being that will penetrate your defenses. In other words this book is psychoanalysis and it is supervision. It is not a book about psychoanalysis. It is psychoanalysis.

Wilfred Bion wrote about the destruction of the links to relationship through "K", knowledge. In other words the psychoanalyst's current knowledge is used to "close the space" so that where something can occur it does not occur. In order for the psychoanalyst to devote his or her life to Becoming 'O', at finer and finer discriminations of one's Being in ways that will advance the profession, they have to be dealt with in a way-actually intruded and imposed upon (as one analyst stated to me, through what he felt to be 'contemptuous intrusion'-James Gooch, M.D.-Training Analyst for Adult and Children-Southern California Psychoanalytic Institute and analyzed by Bion for seven years), because the "space has to be kept open for fresh unsaturated experience to not only occur, but continue to occur". Otherwise, one cannot sustain the tools of being able to think in the emotional line of fire of doing an analysis in ways that will keep the space open in the patients throughout the course of an analysis. What you are most likely to have occur in such situations is a psychoanalyst making interpretations while the space is closed in themselves, while not knowing this to be true, thereby facilitating an environment that patients are all too willing to submit to, whereby there is an experiential collusion that something fresh cannot occur. When I heard Bion speak he began by saying, “With all that’s been said about me I can hardly wait to hear what I am going to say.” And he meant it. His personal equipment had been developed to work well enough where he could trust that a way of life would be to see what thoughts occurred to him in that he could enjoy the freshness of a thought that he might never have put together in quite that way before, and might certainly never do again.

In Bion’s own words in a book published posthumously by his wife and my loyal friend, Francesca Bion, whom I really do not have words to describe the magnificence of, Bion wrote(on page 68 of All My Sins Remembered: The Other Side of Genius, Fleetwood Press, Abingdon, 1985-England) in reference to his analysis with Melanie Klein: “I recovered, went back to work and my own analysis, swore ‘never to do it again’, and, as usual, invariably did again whatever it was I had sworn not to do. I was assiduous in my psycho-analytic sessions. When I was given an interpretation I used very occasionally to feel it was correct; more usually I thought it was nonsense but hardly worth arguing about since I did not regard the interpretation as much more than the expression of one of Mrs. Klein’s opinions that was unsupported by any evidence. The interpretations that I ignored or did not understand or made no response to, later seemed to have been correct. But I did not see why I regarded them as any more correct than I had thought they were when I refuted or ignored them. The most convincing were those that appeared to harmonize with what I knew, or what Mrs. Klein said, about my personality. She tried to pass on to me her interpretations of the material <u>of which her senses made her aware</u> (emphasis added by me). But to become efficacious her methods_were dependent on my receptivity. This is in no way different from any other form of human assistance-there must be someone or something willing to receive."

Bion continued with "How banal is this conclusion! How obvious! And how perpetually that fact becomes clear and how frequently ignored. Yet a willing co-operation in teacher and taught is difficult to achieve when the participants are human. This banal observation seemed to be more than usually bitterly resisted when it was I who had to listen to what my senses told me (emphasis added by me), even with the assistance of Melanie Klein. But as time passed I became more reconciled to the fact that not even she could be a substitute for my own senses, interpretations of what my senses told me, and choice between contradictories."

So there we have it! The one place in all the literature Bion has written where he actually says it, exactly how he did it. He used his senses and his interpretation of what his senses told him to make choices between contradictories.

So now we can begin to see the problem as it applies to psychoanalysis in that there has been no training per se to develop the personal equipment necessary to advance the state of the art in psychoanalysis because there has been no training as directly applied to psychoanalysis that has begun with the development of the senses, and acuity of these senses, to be able to perform any better than we are as a profession. In fact, the opposite has occurred, the blocks of attention to the senses and an International Politic if you will, that has either kept out or thrown out anyone of anything that could have openly made a difference in the incorporation of the body and soul of psychoanalysis such training of the senses that could lead to the development thereof what I shall describe as in the realm of the possible.

An interesting paragraph that speaks to the subject was written by Ilse Ollendorff Reich, in a book entitled "Wilhelm Reich: A Personal Biography", St. Martin's Press, NY, 1969. Ilse Ollendorff was Reich's wife. An interesting coincidence is that two of the greatest clinicians, Bion and Reich, married women who wrote to carry on their work after their deaths. In my case it looks like I will have to do it myself while I am still alive. Ilse wrote "There does not seem to be any doubt that concerted efforts were made against Reich and his work by such organizations as the American Medical Association and the American Psychiatric Association. Such strikes were repeatedly reported to Reich by his medical colleagues and co-workers; they also appeared in the professional periodicals, as in the Journal of the AMA (January 1949), or the Bulletin of the Menninger Clinic (March 1948). Reich would attribute these strikes to the deeply imbedded fear human beings have of recognizing the core of moving sensations in the human body. (p._132) (emphasis added by me)

"Reich's approach to any problem was never mechanical, but always functional. One step logically led to the next. Thus the potential connection between emotional block, energy stasis, tissue disintegration, and cancer development was not difficult for him to find. To the reproach that as a psychiatrist he should stay away from the somatic problems, his answer was that the energy concept cannot conceive of a split, but has to consider man as a unified biological function of psyche and soma." (p. 38-39)

Reich is quoted having said "It sometimes seems hopeless and it is no consolation to hear again and again from well-meaning people that this is the way all geniuses have been persecuted all through history." (p. 92)

Now I am not Reich's lawyer and this is not a defense of him or a strike upon him, but merely a paying attention to the functional process of what he could do at that time and the fact that we as a psychoanalytic profession learned nothing from it. Due to politics we have to keep reinventing the wheel except the wheel again gets destroyed just before it is invented, and then we wonder why psychoanalysis has not delivered the goods of its promise. I do not mean that as a cheap shot as others who have written it in that I actually know how and will show you what is required to remedy the problem of function that both Bion's comments and Reich's quotes touch upon. That is, what functions must a psychoanalyst be able to do to do an analysis? That is, at least at the_level Reich or Bion could do one. Remember, Bruno Bettelheim told me that Reich was Freud's most gifted training analyst; and well, Bion's writings are in the psychoanalytic stratosphere. The problem is that few have a notion of what is required to actually function that way so they tend to pass Bion off as a conceptual genius rather than seeing his work as a lead into the actual training and extension of psychoanalytic technique taken into the realm of infinity, which is my intention of showing and demonstrating for you in this book.

Or look at what we have not followed up on when Ilse wrote "Thus, the potential connection between emotional block, energy stasis, tissue disintegration, and cancer development was not difficult for him to find." Would this not be the link between psychoanalysis, psychiatry, the practice of medicine and the finding of "the first cause" as opposed to the treatment and possible surgical removal of the symptom oftentimes when it is far too late.

Reich after being interviewed for the "Psychoanalytic Journal" was written by Brodsky who stated "the whole Orgone theory is a complete schizophrenic idea, and paranoic system." Reich said "if you show it to them who know nothing about it, and they don't understand it, then it is schizophrenic. But they would not take the trouble to study it or even to try to understand the practical results." (p. 92)

The reason I quote that schizophrenic comment is that Martin Grotjahn, M.D. Psychoanalyst, between 1979 and 1980 used to invite me up to his office on 416 N. Bedford Drive in Beverly Hills, California for lunch. Dr. Grotjahn had an elegance and a class that was all his own. He would make both of us lunch, bring out a sandwich, a fruit, and coffee on a little tray, and he would teach me about the history of psychoanalysis as he said he thought one day I would be in a position to be an important link in the transmission of the psychoanalytic culture. Well, on this particular day, Bion having been the best I had ever seen, heard or experienced anytime, anyplace, anywhere, I said, "Martin, What do you think of Bion?" Martin could go from an ordinary conversation to an expression of what he felt with full feeling and meaning in an instant. He responded in a way that shocked me, saying, "Bion was a schizophrenic fool who imposed a method of analysis on a psychoanalytic community that didn't want it! He's better off dead!" I asked another psychiatrist who was undergoing a more traditional Freudian analysis about Grotjahn's comment as I was a novice to the psychoanalytic world and had an inquiring mind, but certainly not in a position at that time "to know". He said, "Bion may have been a schizophrenic! But he was certainly no fool!"

Martin in the days that he trained me had pretty well shifted over to group analysis. After the comment about Bion he looked at me and said, "You wish you could like me better than you do." He was uncanny about some of his comments. I suppose after that one it was clear, I liked him, but not as much as I wish I could have. Yet, it was his candid expression, something I found out psychoanalysts did not hold back on in the least when discussing their fellow colleagues. All in all, I think that is healthier than therapies where colleagues give false emotional protection to each other.

I suppose there is the comment that those who live by the sword die by the sword. A former president of a movie studio said he saw me as "an avenging angel" so I often wondered if I would die by the sword. Nevertheless, there is Grotjahn doing group analysis with what he referred to as five "million dollar babies" in the same group, and myself who was half in training and half in group analysis. One man told the group he made $30,000 that day (1979) and Grotjahn turned to me and said, "Len, that's a half a year's salary for us". There were movie and television stars in there as well as famous novel writers and those that were just very rich. They had a tight knit social group and I often wondered if that was because no one else would talk to them. The novelist turned around in reference to me and said, "And we can bring the baby too!" I had to laugh, she was right. Then there was the famous movie actress and television star who used to wear high leather boots and a lumber jacket to the group. I thought she was sexy as hell and most of what I thought of during the group was having sex with her, although in those days, I was too embarrassed to say it. I remember Grotjahn saying to me in regard to the league which I had recently entered, "And Len actually likes those boots!", with a sense of showing me that my taste was ridiculous! While I am giving you a local color of that group, that is not the reason I am telling you about it. Before I knew what I know now or had developed any of the functional methods and sensitivities I am going to write about, I did notice that each of these million dollar babies would vie to experientially grasp onto Grotjahn and fight as though the very breast milk that would keep them alive were at stake. This had in my experience the effect of five primitive transferences at once all strangling Grotjahn in some way I felt was horrible. When they used to do it the room became colder and devoid of feeling. I said these things to him but his one weakness was that he was "Grotjahn" and that is what he did, and that is what his five million dollar babies expected him to do. I said, "Martin, they are going to give you a heart attack. This is going to kill you." I could feel his heart becoming smaller as if it were being strangled and smothered by all these hungry feeders at once. I later found out that what had experientially happened to Grotjahn, (who was one of the two best in Beverly Hills during his day, the other being Ralph Greenson, M.D.-a day prior to the identification of such subtle phenomena) was not only one transference which would have been unbearable enough, but five that projective identified the "osmotic transference" written about by Rosenfelt and/or the "liquid symbiotic transference" written about by Searles, all at once. It was a short time after that Grotjahn had a major heart attack and retired from the practice of psychoanalysis and group analysis. He was a training analyst emeritus of the Southern California Psychoanalytic Institute and Society. Grotjahn often said to me, "You know Len, psychoanalysis is a good method of education, but it is not a good method of therapy." In this book, I am doing my best to rectify that problem, and I am doing what Grotjahn liked least about Bion. I am imposing it on you because I have found when it comes to such matters there are no volunteers. (By the way Grotjahn never missed the practice of psychoanalysis. Each time I visited or ran into him he said he never realized how happy he could feel without it. I commented on how much lighter he looked. He commented on how much lighter and better I looked since I was divorced. It was as if each time we met we both acknowledged covertly both how dangerous psychoanalysis was a profession and how daring it was to be married.)

Actually, George Bach, Ph.D., co-author of "Creative Aggression", Doubleday & Co, NY, 1974, a book that would be of personal and professional value to every psychoanalyst I ever met except for Otto

Kernberg, (George Bach) referred me to Martin Grotjahn after he was through training me. This reminds me of a story of a conversation that took place between Bach and Grotjahn in front of 450 N. Bedford Drive in 1950, then and always known as the most significant part of "Couch Canyon", and where I was to practice psychoanalysis from 1979 through 1990. There was a beautiful woman walking out of 450 N. Bedford and George, who was like that, said to Martin, "Look Martin, They are all waiting for us!" As Grotjahn told me the story several times it seemed to be the one comment that most impressed him about George Bach.

I remember the first time I met Grotjahn I went to a seminar he gave on group analysis with hospital patients. I always liked to check out the turf of who someone was and what they could do before the introduction. I went up to Martin and said, "Dr. George Bach said I should look you up, that I had something to learn from you." Grotjahn's reply was "You are the first young clinician I have been interested in in years." Then he looked puzzled as if he could not immediately figure out why, and then invited me to his office for lunch.

While you may wonder and I as I write this had not intended to put so much local color, I think it will add to the eventual and overall feeling about psychoanalysis that I am trying to convey. Furthermore, as Grotjahn, a writer of international repute himself, agreed to edit and write a review for my first book, Psychotherapy, Insight and Style: The Existential Moment (Allyn & Bacon, Inc., Boston, 1981 and republished as part of Jason Aronson's Master Classic Series under the new title (1993) "Making An Impact In Therapy: How Master Clinicians Intervene", I am deeply grateful in that his political astuteness as he put it would allow the baby to be born until he became big enough to become the kind of warrior to fight the battle that as Grotjahn said, "Would be on very dangerous turf." He cut the section out of the book showing and demonstrating psychic capacities that I had already developed by that time, although had not refined into psychoanalysis. He said you must cut this or the psychoanalytic community will think you are crazy and you will never get off the ground, regardless of the validity or truth of it. I later published that as an article (Appendix A) entitled: <u>Gestalt Hypnotherapy: An Exploration in the use of Hypnotic</u>

Energy Passes and Kinesthetic Sensory Perception, in "Voices: J. of the American Academy of Psychotherapy, Vol. 17, No. 1, 1981.

While this is a book that involves a proposal regarding the training of psychoanalysts one might ask what are writings of hypnosis doing in such a book. Later on I am going to point out the relationship between what was evoked in me by Milton H. Erickson, M.D. and its relationship to the "transformation" of higher states and/or qualities of Being 'Becoming 'O' necessary to actually do the kind of work Wilfred Bion wrote about. It is only when this relationship is made clear that psychoanalytic technique can become both transformative in working with "higher sensitives" (quote Karagalla, S. Your Higher Sense Perception, De Vorss Press) and can also become curative at the levels of the "psychotic core" of the personality.

We have made the mistake of "throwing out the baby with the bathwater" far too often. It began with the work of Anton Mesmer whose work was discredited, as was he, by a commission headed by Benjamin Franklin. However, the two dissenting opinions were Benjamin Franklin and LaVoisier, the great French scientist. Imagine if at that time rather than discrediting that which we did not know about or were fearful of, we began to incorporate the primitive working knowledge with animal magnetism and the training of psychoanalysts to work with it. Do you not think we would be a lot closer to being able to effectively work with primitive mental states and the psychotic core of the personality as well as the gifted higher sensitive-the Toscanini, the Caruso, The Paganini? What we have insured is an ability to work with the ordinary, the mediocre, and to keep it that way so we can all earn a living in case we personally are not able to make the transition to higher levels of being from which to do higher levels of work.

James Wyckoff, author of "Franz Anton Mesmer: Between God and Devil" (Prentice Hall, Englewood Cliffs, N.J., 1975) made some comments worthy of note. "Actually, intellect is something different from, and higher than the reason. It is capable of understanding knowledge that is beyond the reach of reason. It is in fact a divine quality in man." (p. 9) This is the kind of primitive certainty I only experienced in my exposure to Wilfred Bion and Milton Erickson, among the seventeen world renowned therapists who trained me. Most of the profession claims one would have to be grandiose or omnipotent to claim they have such capacity, yet I have seen it twice in the best I have been exposed to, and was taught how to develop it in myself, and have learned how to teach its development to others.

Along the road to such development as was to tip me off to how Bion did what he did, what if we had considered the precursors written again by Wyckoff: "But Mesmer's Fluidum was quite different. It seems clear now that what he meant by Fluidum corresponds to vibration or universal energy, and we may equate Mesmer's Fluidum with Wilhelm Reich's orgone energy..." (p. 12). "...by impregnating a dying body with vitality it may be made to live again." (p. 13) Prior to the offense on Mesmer, Wyckoff wrote "He had no need to prove himself and so he could afford to be quiet, patient, unambitious and direct. Very likely it was these qualities-as opposed to the accustomed neurotic aggressiveness, so obvious in our century-that helped him to be so much in contact with himself and with nature so that he was able to work with his patients from "inside", as it were, rather than from outside; the opposite of the orthodox approach. In a word, he treated the whole person, not just the symptom, working with the energy or Life Force, rather than concentrating only on the physical structure in which it was housed." (p. 14) Bion and Erickson both worked this way in the most disciplined and fine-tuned ways I had ever experienced, and make these words attain another plateau in what I am attempting to show you in terms of the human condition being treated on a higher plateau instead of playing for the "lowest common denominator".

As with Erickson and Bion, Wyckoff quotes Wilhelm Reich: "The most important tool is sensation, be it inner organ sensation or outer sensory perception...he listens to the gentle warnings of his sensations that tell him whether his thinking is right or wrong, clear or muddied by personal interests, whether he follows his irrational inclinations or any objective process...It has to do...with keeping our sensory apparatus, the tool of our research, in good condition. This condition is not a 'gift', not a special talent, but a continuous effort, a continuous exercise in self-criticism and self-control...Without an invariably clear system of sensation, without the ability to clear if it becomes irrationally distorted, we would not be able to take one step into the depth of human character structure or describe natural processes as they are....." (pp. 103-104)

The problem to the masses of psychoanalysts to this point is even if they considered Reich's description accurate, or that of Wilfred Bion which was almost identical to Reich when discussing his analysis with Melanie Klein and the realization that it was only his paying attention to his senses that allowed him to make choice between contradictories, they have not been shown a way to attain the attunement of the senses required to do what Reich and later Bion and Erickson were to refer to as being the core of their work. Erickson's term was the paying attention to "minimal cues". Easily said, not so easily done. This is particularly true when the minimal cues are "internal" as opposed to "external". Bion referred to "Becoming 'O' as finer and finer discriminations in the pursuit of one's Being. Wyckoff wrote "...that a healer who is in contact with perhaps a finer vibration can heal many people" (p. 142). IT IS THAT FINER VIBRATION THAT I CAME ON BY ACCIDENT IN WORKING WITH ERICKSON AND LEARNED IT WAS THE KEY TO BION'S WORK, AND FOUND OUT IT IS TEACHABLE IN THAT I DISCOVERED THE PROCESS OF HOW IT IS TAUGHT AND WHAT IS REQUIRED TO DO IT, TO BE IT, AND APPLY IT TO PSYCHOANALYSIS!

Yet, I am not unaware, and thus the reason for this lengthy introduction that my colleagues may very well attempt to murder me off as were Mesmer and Wilhelm Reich instead of benefit mankind from what I have learned and can teach. Perhaps these words by Wyckoff are most poignant although not addressed to the particular method I will show you, but to the people themselves. "Reich's orgone accumulator, which triggered his arrest by the United States Government, was clearly similar to Mesmer's banquet-and was treated with the same contempt and derision. It was also similar in effect to the pyramid shape, the cone, as well as certain 'energy spaces' found in sacred structures and places. His books were banned and actually burned by government officials. He was denounced as a quack and charged with being 'insane.' He died in prison in 1957, murdered by the cause he was trying to help. A curious footnote may be seen in the loud enthusiasm for work in the iron curtain countries and, lately, in the United States, that is clearly derivative of Reich, but which gives him little if any credit. But he who coined the term "emotional plague" and ended up its victim would probably not be surprised at seeing his work treated in this fashion..... Reich verified scientifically the work of Mesmer-photographing the life energy and, according to his patients, awakening them to it in their bodies, just as Mesmer had done. The bitter pill, the irony, is that Mesmer had to wait two hundred years for verification, and when it came, he who gave it was treated with equal outrage and slander..... Has anything changed? Has anything been learned?" (p. 140) Not as far as I can see! That is the challenge of my life's work and this book! Further, the problem is how to integrate that of significant value which has been discarded into the mainstream of psychoanalysis. Without this happening you will have splinter groups that do not know the only method of cure, psychoanalysis; and you will have psychoanalysis, the only method of cure, preventing itself from developing the tools necessary to do its job! FURTHER DEVELOPMENTS IN THE SEARCH FOR A PSYCHOANALYSIS THE CURES

Certain psychoanalysts have been monumental in leading me in the directions of being able to synthesize the work of Bion and Erickson, along with the quality of Being I had pursued from the very beginning of my career and the ever present pursuit of technical genius as developed in me by my father-Daniel A. Bergantino, who from boyhood onward had me listening to Heifetz, Caruso, Toscanini and studying the technicality of how to become the best in the world at what I did. Of course, Nicolo Paganini was the legend I most sought to find out about. Once again his technical skills, being and soul were of such oneness that people who could not do so said he must be in league with the devil. While my father had hoped it would be as a musician, and I learned to play mandolin and trumpet from the heart, it was those musical teachings that taught me about the fine tuning of one's instrument, in this case, the therapeutic use of self, or psychoanalytic use of self, as the case may be.

Martin Grotjahn, then Donald Rinsley and later Bruno Bettelheim were all important guides for me in my search. However, as a historian and a political scientist, I am tradition bound to do things in historical order, so I will come back to "Grotjahn!", as he was called.

Martin told me three stories that made a major impact on me given his notion that I would one day help psychoanalysts with the transmission of the psychoanalytic culture, and with his unstated hope, that perhaps I could help move psychoanalysis from what he referred to as "an excellent method of education that didn't cure anyone" to a method of treatment that would live up to the idealistic promise I sensed he wished psychoanalysis had fulfilled-that of being a treatment that cured. Again, one must consider Grotjahn's storytelling in the frame of invading the unconscious mind of the student in a way that would evoke a technical search for a method that would cure.

The first of these stories was about Grotjahn's own analysis which took place in Nazi Germany. As only Grotjahn could tell a story with the feeling and impact of bringing you right into the consulting room with he and his training analyst, Grotjahn said, "I heard the Nazi's footsteps coming up the sidewalk and I said, 'Are you leaving, too, Heir Professor? (very mild affectionate tone). And Heir Professor said, also in a very mellow, sad and loving tone, 'No, Martin. I am going to stay.' At which point Grotjahn's inflection became authoritarian to the point of being Nazi-like and he said, "IN THAT CASE, HEIR PROFESSOR, THE ANALYSIS IS OVER!" (as he speedily got up off the couch and ran out the back window!) From this I learned that if in the analytic technique the analyst cannot save himself or herself, the patient cannot be saved. The analysis must be done in a way the continually preserves the well being and psychoanalytic use of self of the analyst in terms of the quality of the analyst's being. If this is not done the analyst will be killed. Grotjahn got out to prevent being killed and wound up as a training analyst in Chicago prior to becoming a training analyst at the Southern California Psychoanalytic Institute and Society in Los Angeles.

The second story was of Freud and Helene Deutsch. Again the way Grotjahn told this story I almost broke out in tears. "Freud sat behind HD, Helena Deutsch, as she was on the couch. Toward the very end of one session he became enraged, slammed his fist down on the back of the couch, the headpiece, and screamed-'The problem with you is that you think I am too old to love!" He implied that HD was speechless. Then one afternoon she came up the stairs and knocked on the door for her appointment and Freud answered the door. He said, given the Nazi's had occupied Vienna, "You are the only one who has come today" (affect of sadness, from the heart, and of some surprise with concern). And Helena Deutsch thought, but did not say (full heart affect with love) 'And you thought I didn't love you.') From this story I realized Freud had been getting a bad rap as a passive fellow sitting behind the couch thinking to himself most of the time and then making an interpretation once in awhile that was thought to be what was misinterpreted to me throughout the profession as an excuse for not being there, as "technical neutrality". What I saw in this story was a man, a psychoanalyst, Freud the man-psychoanalyst, who was fully present and with full passion in his very "personal yet technically neutral interpretation" reached the bottom of his soul and gave all that he had in the way he was with Helene Deutsch. It was with the same kind of passion some eight or nine years later that Bruno Bettelheim, in almost the same manner, shouted to me in a personal communication that "Freud said the Americans would never understand analysis because they did not understand that the purpose of an analysis was to save man's soul!" That was certainly the level at which Freud reached Helene Deutsch, in that the kind of love that saves one's soul existed to such a degree between them that it was important for her to show that to Freud, even at a time when others whose souls were perhaps in greater danger were frightened off by the Nazi peril.

Those who see patients five days a week over three to seven years will be familiar with the patient who develops a sleepy child ego state where there is a state of inability to overcome the almost drug like sleepy state of mindlessness without a thought or a stir. When this occurred, Freud, who used to have his dog under the couch, did not kick the dog, but often kicked the couch! This was another of Grotjahn's stories about Freud's "passionate involvement", only quitting analysis-that is, the doing of it, when the zeal was no longer there.

Grotjahn told of Freud's treating of a woman patient whose husband he had known was quite fond of Cuban cigars. For Christmas, Freud, from his special collection, gave the woman a box of the kind of Cuban cigars he had known her husband was very fond of. He was very human in the course of an analysis. He apparently did not get caught on one side of the polarization of the transference or the other. There was something about that story that forever affected the way I did psychoanalysis while keeping forever vigilant of technical neutrality in its most antiseptic forms, once I began doing psychoanalysis (1979 throughout 1990, seeing patients five days a week for between three and seven years per patient).

Last but not least the story of all stories that Grotjahn told that made me laugh uncontrollably for the longest time but the consequences of which were of overwhelming importance to psychoanalysis in ways that did not make me laugh at all; only to realize exactly how difficult it was to do an analysis at the levels at which I will later describe.

First, let me paint a little better picture of Grotjahn. He was a pixie; was known as a pixie and referred to himself in this way. There was an elegant air of sophistication that when he said something it didn't make any difference if any of his patients thought it was a correct interpretation or not; of if they made $30,000 in a day or millions in a year and he only made $60,000 in a year. He was "Grotjahn!," and they loved the ayre with which he said it and the way he said it, as if it had been delivered from an oracle himself from a place that might be referred to as the "Sermon on the Mount." It didn't make any difference what he said or did. He could do no wrong whether group analysis was happening or whether it was not happening; and of course, there was a good deal of both. So it is with this picture of Grotjahn through my eyes that I saw and heard of his visit to John Rosen's farm house in Doylestown Pennsylvania. I couldn't believe it when he used to do shit like that. Anyone else would have been knocked on their ass, and all his clients used to say is, "Well, he's Grotjahn!"

Grotjahn told it this way. "I was in Philadelphia. I knew I was near where John Rosen lived and I always wanted to meet him. I took a cab to his farm house in Doylestown, Pennsylvania. I went to the door. I knocked on the door (and here Grotjahn was laughing at himself as he had great self-confidence and was not in the least self-conscious). Rosen opened the door. (Demonstrating the Grotjahn pixie flair at his greatest he said) "I'm Grotjahn!" Rosen said, "You're not Grotjahn! I know Grotjahn! And you're not Grotjahn!" (Grotjahn became indignant as he told the story, showing me just how the indignation escalated in what was to be a twenty minute exchange between Grotjahn and Rosen with exactly the same words. I was laughing so hard I was almost rolling on the floor). I'm Grotjahn! (with ever rising indignation). You're not Grotjahn! I know Grotjahn! And you're not Grotjahn! Well, after twenty minutes of this he finally said, "OK, you're Grotjahn. Come on in. (And I'm thinking to myself, but didn't say, "And these guys are both two world famous therapists and there both as nutty as a fruit cake!" It was the craziest story I ever heard!)

Grotjahn went on. He said, "Then I saw him treating a 13 year old schizophrenic girl in the living room on the first floor of his farm house. There were three floors. The girl kept claiming and stating 'There are Chinese Communists on the third floor!' Rosen said, 'There are no Chinese Communists on the third floor!' The girl said 'There are Chinese Communists on the third floor!' Rosen said 'There are no Chinese Communists on the third floor!' Grotjahn said, 'This conversation went on for twenty minutes'. I thought, but didn't say, 'This sounds like the same thing Rosen did with Grotjahn', and I began to laugh again. Grotjahn went on, 'Then Rosen grabbed her by the arm and said, I'll tell you what. I'm going to drag you up three flights of stairs and if there are no Chinese Communists there I am going to throw you down three flights of stairs and break every fucking bone in your body!' The girl said, 'There are no Chinese Communists on the third floor.' I thought to myself, but didn't say, 'She may be crazy but she was no fool.'

Grotjahn went on. 'Then I saw Rosen treating a schizophrenic man in the living room in the same chair as the girl was in. The man got up off the chair and kicked Rosen in the balls as hard as he could. As Rosen recovered (not stated, but implied, that he was hurt and it took awhile) he leaped to his feet, got the man on the ground, and choked him until he was blue in the face to within an inch of his life.' Grotjahn, then matter of factly turned to me, once again taking on the full characteristics of the pixie, and putting both arms stretched outward nearly as far as they could go, shrugged his shoulders and said, 'What could I do? It was the man's method of treatment." I was on the floor laughing. It was the funniest story I ever heard. I had no idea of the significance this story was to have in my development as a psychoanalyst and the practice thereof. Sometimes fact is stranger than fiction.

Grotjahn told me of Rosen. He said he was a genius. He wrote brilliant work in the fifties and called his work "Direct Analysis" (I have photocopies of his books). However, he got into trouble with the medical board. There was rumor he had sexual relations with a patient or some patients and that he beat up a patient or two and he was thrown out of the American Medical Association, the American Psychiatric Association and the American Psychoanalytic Association and his work was discredited." However, there was also the feeling from Grotjahn that a grave mistake had been made here in throwing out Rosen's work along with Rosen, in that there was a genius to the work that was not yet obvious to me. So the American Psychoanalytic was consistent. It threw out the genius and the work of the genius with the person himself that was thrown out, certainly in the cases of Reich and now Rosen, both of whom could have been instrumental in the development of the treatment of the psychotic core of the personality had their teachings become part and parcel of a psychoanalytic technique that had the only minimum conditions where cure at the level of the psychotic core was possible. As Bion was to point out in his papers, this psychotic core exists in all of us. As I am pointing out, this is why we have a downward spiraling society with ever increasing hatred, corruption and violence-because psychoanalysis has failed to live up to Freud's mission for it. Freud did not think very much of ordinary man, often referring to the masses as low life sorts that would, could and only promulgate and perpetuate the low lifeness that is of itself. He did not think analysis would help the masses in this regard, but he did think it would reach some. Of course, a commentary as has been made over my entire professional lifetime has been of the failings of psychoanalysis, yet the problem has been the no one has shown the way to correct the problem. If you bear with me I hope to be able to do that.

The last story about Grotjahn was the first. I remember the first time I went to his office. The door was slightly open and he came out right on time. In that pixie way of his first words were, "This is my waiting room but no one ever uses it because I am always on time!" The entire time I knew him, was in consultation with him, or met him for lunch, I never used his waiting room because 'he was always on time!' This was the éntre to what I was later to learn from Bion's analysands regarding "the minimum conditions" of an analysis and this went both ways.

Bion used to say "There are two nasty facts. The first is that people need to depend on other people. The second is that you need to find someone who is dependworthy." Thus, if the psychoanalyst proves to be a person who is motivated by greed or other concerns than being 'on time' in a 'dependworthy way' we might very well have a situation develop where the patient would think, and perhaps rightfully so, that the psychoanalytic relationship was of no damn use to him or her.

As my colleagues of the past who tried and failed in doing the task I am imposing upon you, I feel it is incumbent upon me to give you not only the technical knowhow that I developed throughout the years as a result of having fine-tuned and technically harnessed paranormal sensitivities or extra-sensory perception, but also to give you a historical feeling so to speak of what went into the makeup of a psychoanalyst as I have done by presenting you Dr. Grotjahn, and will do with others. My work with Grotjahn was when I was just beginning to do psychoanalysis and really prior to any working knowledge of doing psychoanalysis. Nevertheless Grotjahn had a very good idea of me as a psychotherapist and wrote a pre-publication review of my book which was to be published by Allyn & Bacon, Inc., 1981, Boston. It was titled "Psychotherapy, Insight & Style: The Existential Moment" (Allyn & Bacon, 1981, Boston, 288 pp). Grotjahn was the first psychoanalyst who wrote about me which was helpful for an outsider, an unknown psychologist making his way in the world. I will quote his review verbatim in that it begins to give credibility to who I am; that is, making what may easily appear to be grandiose and omnipotent claims instead at providing a reality that transcends and transforms any that you have known.

Grotjahn wrote in a pre-publication review to Gene McCann, my editor at Allyn & Bacon the following: "Dr. Bergantino is obviously a gifted therapist who does not limit himself to academic study, but has the talent to experience many and differently oriented therapies as a patient. The proper subtitle of the manuscript would be: My Work as a Therapist, With Therapists, and in Therapy. Bergantino is a Lt. Colombo in psychotherapy: he goes into the (therapeutic) situation, finds out by himself, shows what he saw, and reports how he understood it.

His approach is consistently experiential. He is at his best when he describes his clinical observations, may it be as a student, patient, or as a therapist. He goes with open mind, courage, and youthful enthusiasm into the different aspects of existential therapy and it is this approach which makes the book valuable, even unique, and definitely and doubtlessly suitable for publication.

All therapists, young and old, beginners and well experienced veterans, feel the isolation of their profession and are (and should be) immensely curious to learn and read about the work of their colleagues.

Most cases as reported in the literature describe the patient's associations and productions while the therapist remains hidden in the mystery of darkness unrevealed. Dr. B. is an exception: the great advantage of his work is the openness and frankness with which the author reveals his experiences when treating patients or when accepting himself as a patient of another therapist."

Of further importance in my writing these reviews are the qualities in me that were to be developed as a psychoanalyst that are not necessarily in the training of a psychoanalyst via traditional training, yet are critical in being able to function in the ways I will describe.

For example, Carl Whitaker, M.D., prior to having trained me in family therapy, read my book and wrote both a pre-publication review and the foreword.

In the pre-publication review of 1/12/81 he wrote "The author as a therapist is a student of creativity and he offers a metaphorical elaboration that is both impressionistic, artistic and a stimulus for thinking. He is a professional reporter of interpersonal change models in the family therapy set and even intrapsychic change process in its twentieth century face. The book rouses powerful feelings and stimulates growth in its readers.

Reading this book is an active experience in the use of self in the field of psychotherapy, and as such, it both expands and enriches the community standards of practice of professional psychotherapists. That self is really our only tool. It's use is critical and evolving through each practitioner's professional lifetime."

Carl Whitaker, M.D., in the foreword to my book wrote, "The plethora of how-to-books is increasing. Barbara Betz stated that the dynamics of psychotherapy is in the person of the therapist. Abraham Maslow stated that the peak experience lasts two weeks. Winicott insisted that if you haven't been hated by your psychotherapist you have been cheated. Erenwald has stated that psychotherapy is the effort to evolve an existential shift.

Len Bergantino is trying to expand this operational territory by stretching the psychotherapeutic geology. He succeeds. Describing the therapist as a person of liberated wisdom, he dares to the chaos and anxiety of not knowing; he opens a gate to see and make the impact of psychotherapy more clearly. His description of beingness as a process is reminiscent of Paul Tillich. His grasp of responsible involvement with the patient as a discipline of self shows his own search for creative options. He makes no pretense of camouflaging the psychotherapist as a wounded healer. Furthermore, Len makes crucial the pattern of the therapist's search for his own healing and successfully validates the authentic trickery of the psychotherapist as a liberated spirit. The approach to his own craziness, the freedom from the culture bind, and the discipline of self each emerged as obtainable goals of that professional parent we call the psychotherapist.

Further evidence of his own search is illustrated by his impersonalized impressionistic response to the other searchers he uses as models. Simply reading his book leaves me feeling it would be meaningful to join in his search for his beingness. Though he would be enjoying himself and enjoying me as a patient, he would not be doing things to keep from being himself and thus I could be more fully myself."

The psychoanalyst who understood aspects of me that ranged into the paranormal in a way that gave full appreciation to my unique gifts was Donald Rinsley, M.D., F.R.S.H., Fellow, American College of Psychoanalysts and Fellow, American Psychiatric Association. The feeling I had when I read what Dr. Rinsley wrote was deep appreciation and gratitude as it was clear that here was a man who had no need out of hatred or envy to write a review that would be limited by his own limitations. He felt secure enough in himself to write about me as full as I was. His review was published in Bulletin of the Menninger Clinic, Vol. 47, No. 5, September, 1983. He wrote "There is no doubt that some people possess a healing capacity and that others do not; nor is there any doubt that a Zulu witch doctor, a Puerto Rican curandero, a Navaho medicine man or a voodoo spiritist may remit symptoms more effectively than the best trained psychotherapist or psychoanalyst. The differences between healing and therapy are not inconspicuous even as both may readily dissolve into quackery in the hands of the exploitive and the unscrupulous. A wise Freud once commented that the function of psychoanalysis is to convert neurotic misery into ordinary human suffering, a point of view to be dismissed only at one's peril even though it doubtless reflected the essence of Freud's depressive personality. From such few considerations as these emerge questions concerning the differences separating healing and therapy, the features that unite them and the goals and objectives they may be noted to share. And whatever answers to these questions may satisfy those who propound them will reflect whether one's Weltanschauung considers the world to be a vale of tears or, after the fashion of the Gallic optimist, Coué, a place where everything keeps getting better and better.

Dr. Bergantino's book in scholarly and even entertaining fashion sets out to address issues such as these. The blurb on its book jacket states that it "integrates 17 prominent therapists' styles and problem solving techniques..."Its more accurate subtitle, The Existential Moment reflects the author's searching awareness that effective psychological healing, or psychotherapy, or whatever one chooses to call such interpersonal transactional processes ultimately expands one's awareness, hence one's knowledge of one's self, one's surround and the relationship between them; and further, that such awareness and knowledge develops in saltatory fashion, deriving from unheralded and even momentary experiences of insight, illumination ("aha!") or unconscious internal change. So far so good, but there is after all nothing new in that, so why read yet another book devoted to arresting human experiences that many believe to be inexplicable and unteachable?

There are at least two answers to that question. To begin with, the book reflects the personal odyssey of a trained, disciplined yet open-minded professional psychologist who has drunk deeply at the wells of an number of acknowledged healer-therapists whose work he has carefully studied and evaluated, among them, Viktor Frankl, Wilfred Bion, Bob and Mary Gouldings, Frederick Perls, Milton Erickson and Carl Whitaker. A unique feature of Dr. Bergantino's presentation is his detailed accounts of these therapists' hour-to-hour work, drawn from his own personal experience and from verbatim descriptions provided by their students and analysands, offering fascinating and instructive insights into the therapeutic labors of admittedly gifted treaters. The book is thus replete with clinical material, excerpts from therapeutic encounters and direct reports of those precious "aha"-type moments, conveyed within a disciplined epistemic context that presents each example in terms of ethical professionalism rather than exemplary amateurishness.

Again, the book reflects its author's ongoing growth and development as both thinker and therapist. Dr. Bergantino has gone to great length to converse and consult with both primary and secondary sources, delving into the what and the how, ferreting out illustrative clinical situations and indicating how he has proceeded to synthesize and integrate what he has learned from them and from his own therapeutic work. His book is indeed a literate statement of how one clinician has made of himself a therapist and his statement is both informative and poignant.

As I read this book my thoughts returned to a little-known 1962 Psychiatric Quarterly paper by Ernst Federn, the son of the psychoanalyst_Paul Federn, entitled "The Therapeutic Personality, As Illustrated by Paul Federn and August Aichorn." It described in some detail the uniquely intuitive therapeutic work of these two outstanding clinicians, drawn from the author's own experience of knowing them both; Federn and Aichorn brought disciplined artistry to their respective therapeutic tasks in working psychoanalytically with "difficult" cases, Federn with psychotics, Aichorn with disturbed adolescents; both readily sensed suffering and never flinched from addressing it; both could occupy honored places in Dr. Bergantino's book. I learned much from that paper and I have learned much from Dr. Bergantino's book as well.

Psychotherapy, Insight and Style is an absorbing work, to be returned to time and again after one has read it through, to be thought about, mulled over and placed on one's bedside table if not under one's pillow. It is a book that the experienced clinician will read with knowledgeable satisfaction and that the nascent therapist will read with excitement. And both will profit from what it has to tell."

The reviews I am including and the comments from other reviews are important either because they were written by psychoanalysts and can put what I do and have to teach into a psychoanalytic perspective closer to what has been thought to be psychoanalysis from the past; or those who have contributed important understandings of my work that are better descriptions than I can do of illuminating what must be incorporated into the expansion of psychoanalysis for it to be curative in the future.

Jim Simkin, Ph.D., analyzed by Fritz Perls when Perls was still a psychoanalyst, and later premiere gestalt trainer, better in speed and skill to Perls himself, wrote the following review: "I know of no comparable books in the field and believe that the subject is an area of growing and continuing interest. I believe that the author's ideas are useful and important. The existential moment (which psychoanalysts might say is the same as 'insight') is an important concept and an addition to the psychotherapeutic literature. Professionals could benefit directly from this book in that Bergantino describes how it is possible to integrate a variety of psychotherapeutic approaches." Further, in a way Jim Simkin was an important person in my pursuing the objective of writing this book with the mission with which I set out. I spent a week working with him as a patient-model in Big Sur, California in 1979. He found out of both my talent and my ambition long before I knew about it or had that kind of confidence. He said in a way that has stayed with me all these years, "Go for it!" I am! A few years later when I was having a bit of difficulty cracking the workshop circuit as an "outsider" he told someone that he knew would be in touch with me the following, knowing that I would get the message: "When thinking about all the therapists I have trained or seen (including Fritz Perls)-Bergantino, Him I think about! Him I consider! He is a man of depth. He is a man of substance." This was an unusual statement for Jim because by his own standards he did not train me. I was a patient model for one week. To be in training one had to train for one month, two months or three months and would receive a gestalt certification if he thought you were someone he would or could certify after three years. Jim was very picky about who he certified and very stringent about giving out compliments. So knowing that came from him and was intended to get to me has provided the lifetime boost I am certain he intended to give me. I knew him well enough to know that's how he was and that's perhaps the only way he could give such a compliment.

Dr. David Barstow, Editor of Pilgrimage: Psychotherapy and Personal Exploration, Vol. 11, No. 2, 1983 wrote one crucial paragraph in his review that is critical in terms of what has evolved into what I hope will be the "liberation of the psychoanalyst" as being the kind of person who is well disciplined yet able to work as a free and liberated person. Barstow wrote: "Why not say it right off; I think this is a marvelous book!...The action in therapy is at non-rational levels; the therapist needs to risk sounding 'crazy' in order to direct attention to what is happening at the personal primal level. The therapist who is willing to move beyond the professional role of always being careful and 'correct' thereby opens up the possibility of having a more powerful and personal therapeutic impact. I loved this book; I hope you will, too." This comment is critical as an attitude in being able to do the kind of psychoanalysis written about and practiced by Wilfred Bion!

Bion's work involves the "transformations" of the quality of being of patients (Becoming 'O'). Ernest Rossi, Ph.D. wrote of this quality in me when he wrote a review of my book in The American J. of Clinical Hypnosis, Vol. 24, No. 3, January, 1982. He wrote "....a new understanding of what it means to be a creative therapist continually living in the present's potential for change and transformation...focuses on the precise and often provocative and shocking techniques that are useful in helping patients break out of their learned limitations to realize their potentials for creative change." It was this quality in me that helped me develop the courage to integrate some of Wilhelm Reich's work as well as John Rosen's methodology of "Direct Analysis" into the "minimum conditions" of and for an analysis that is curative at the level of the psychotic core written about by Bion, Rosenfelt, and certainly inspired by the work of Melanie Klein. The work of John Rosen and Reich should not have been thrown out when the individuals themselves were discredited, as they are a necessary ancillary to being able to do the work that Bion wrote about.

Moreover, an attitude of being open to the chaos and anxiety of "not knowing" on the part of the psychoanalyst is a sine qua non of everything Wilfred Bion was and everything he wrote about. In my own personal growth and work as a psychoanalyst it was not only important to be able to work in this manner, but also to have attained a state of being whereby I actually have the ability to live in this manner. While "technical neutrality" is a must on one level, the patient can always tell if the analyst is phony baloney at the deepest levels and core of being. In other words this book will help you move toward being able to work in the ways of which I write if you are the sort of person that is willing to pursue your own Being to finer and finer discriminations of infinity, or Becoming 'O', as Bion wrote. If you are not, you might as well put this book down right now and attempt to develop as many ingenuous ways to destroy my work, and Bion's too, (the destruction of the links to relationship through 'K'-Knowledge usually works), so no one will find you out that you are living a life and developing some sort of psychoanalytic method, the purpose of which is to be able to remain in "bad faith" with your own Being and still earn large sums of money doing psychoanalysis.

David Keith, M.D., wrote of me in Journal of Marital and Family Therapy, Vol. 10, No. 1, January, 1984, "Psychotherapy books provide_an explanation of a particular point of view. Those that are most meaningful turn out to be an experience. Dr. Bergantino wrote this book with the intention that it be both experience and explanation. I am satisfied that his intention is realized." Of those who have written psychoanalysis-Freud, Kohut, Klein, Kernberg, Searles, Federn, and on and on, only Bion has written the experience itself. That is, when you read his work, if you develop the kind of attention required to experience the subtleties of what he has done, it is being supervised or you are being supervised en vivo when you read it. I am proud that Dr. Keith wrote I have done this with a book I have written in psychotherapy. It is my every intention that be the sole purpose for the way in which I write this book in psychoanalysis, to give the reader the experience that will shift the analyst to a higher level of capacity to function as well as an openness to the kind of experience required to do a bigger job as a psychoanalyst, a job more in line with what Freud had in mind when he created psychoanalysis.

Most books write about the benefits of psychoanalytic method in a way that does not transmute the experience to you. Others write with a keen eye about the pitfalls of psychoanalysis without showing the methods required to fill and fulfill the functional steps required to make a psychoanalyst capable of functioning in a way whereby he or she is capable of doing the job he or she purports can be done. IT IS MY EVERY INTENTION, MAKE IT ABSOLUTELY CLEAR, THAT IT IS WITH THE DEEPEST RESPECT I WRITE THIS BOOK FOR PSYCHOANALYSTS IN THAT I THINK THEY ARE THE ONLY ONES WHO ARE DISCIPLINED ENOUGH TO BE ABLE TO GRASP THE POSSIBILITY OF BECOMING THE KIND OF PERSON REQUIRED TO DEVELOP THE CAPACITIES TO FUNCTION REQUIRED TO SUCCESSFULLY TREAT THE

PSYCHOTIC CORE OF THE PERSONALITY THAT GOES BOTH UNDETECTED AND UNTREATED EVEN IN THE SO CALLED NORMAL NEUROTIC. IT IS ONLY IN THIS WAY THAT PSYCHOANALYSIS CAN LIVE UP TO ITS PROMISE TO MAKE A DIFFERENCE IN THE UPGRADING OF MANKIND IN A WAY THAT CAN TURN AROUND WHAT WE KNOW AND SEE AND HAVE AS A DOWNWARD SPIRALING SOCIETY!

While neither Freud nor Dr. Bruno Bettelheim were particularly known to be religious fellows, and in fact, because of Freud's viewpoint analysis has taken on a non-sectarian perspective or one not particularly concerned with the supernatural or God, per se, Dr. Bettelheim told me in personal communications two different things. The first time he said Freud told him, "The Americans will never understand analysis because they do not understand it is the fight for man's soul!" The second time he said Freud told him, "The Americans will never understand analysis because they do not understand the relationship between sex and death." (Personal communications with Dr. Bruno Bettelheim were at his home in Santa Monica, California during 1988 in sessions in which he supervised me). Much of what Dr. Bettelheim transmitted to me made me view him as the link between the past and the future in that he would help me write the kind of book that would fulfill Freud's comments of what the Americans lack in terms of being able to do a psychoanalysis that matters at those levels-those of life and death itself! So when you read this book, understand always, those are the stakes for which I played the game and that is the commitment those who hired me had to pay in order for me to be willing to play. While I feel proud of having become the kind of person and psychoanalyst who could do this, perhaps it even says more about both the kind of person I worked with, and the desperation they had felt to be willing to approach the work at that level. 110% was required of myself and the patient. Nothing less had a chance in the fight for one's life!

So it is not my intention to write a book about psychoanalysis that may if it does well for an "outsider" take its place among other written works of psychoanalysis. It is my intention to write a book, the subtleties and discriminations in capacity to function as a psychoanalyst are such, that it forever changes the addition of the kinds of training of psychoanalysts which will give them the opportunity to develop the kinds of capacities I am writing about in this book. These capacities are both teachable and can be developed. I know because I did not have them prior to certain kinds of training. I developed them and learned to utilize them as part and parcel of doing and expanding upon much of Wilfred Bion's what were thought to be psychoanalytic conceptions into what I view as an extension of psychoanalytic technique that I am hopeful will give those that have the wherewithal to begin to develop not only what I have written about but also capacities that transcend my own personal limitations. It is a book that I intend to be able to provide the kernel for advancement of psychoanalysis to infinity over the next hundred years or so in terms of the unification of psychoanalytic technique with finer and finer discriminations of Becoming 'O', that is, movement toward 'pure Being' on the part of the psychoanalyst who can enhance that on a sustained level in the patient. It might be viewed if never conceived before as one of my patient's put it, "like trying to catch mercury."

DR. BRUNO BETTELHEIM

I first met Dr. Bettelheim when I was on a program with him and Erik Erickson among others at UCLA in 1983. Dr. Heinz Kohut was also there, whom I shall get to later.

Dr. Bettelheim, with my extra-sensory channels in full working order was perceived by me to resemble Yul Brenner in "The King And I". As Yul Brenner was quoted as saying, in regard to the part, "I am the King!" Dr. Bettelheim had this kind of air about him. He responded to a large group of know it all psychiatric and psychological types from West Los Angeles, a group of about 900, with no mercy whatsoever. The primitive process was one of him kicking their all-knowing psychological asses from one side of this huge coliseum to the other, until they were more humble about their meager clinical knowledge. If you were half alive and half astute you most probably would have the experience of having had the living shit beat out of you until you became open to learning in the first twenty minutes.

However, Dr. Bettelheim then had the capacity to rouse you from the dead, to psychophysiologically wake you up to yourself, your mind and your own thoughts. He challenged all comers! He feared none! If you took him on you had better know what the hell you were doing!? He roused clinicians to become more noble than they were with who he was and how he worked.

This is what pisses me off about the son of a bitches who waited until he died before they took their shots at him. Most of these weasels would have pissed their pants rather than take the old boy on when he was alive! He was the King! (in the sense that Yul Brenner was the King).

I sent him a copy of my book so inscribed, although I do not remember the exact quotation. It was about a paragraph long. It was as challenging as he was, poking fun at his bald head and resemblance to

Yul Brenner in "The King and I," nevertheless, not shortchanging who he was and what he did in the least. I just let him know I was around!

The next time I saw him was at UCLA giving a course on "FREUD AND MAN'S SOUL" right after his book came out by the same name (Alfred Knopf, NY, 1983). Here quite a few in the audience went after him and that is when Bettelheim was at his best, when he was challenged in public! When they asked him why he wrote 'Freud and Man's Soul', he contemptuously retorted, "Because I am the only one left Who Could!" He was great! I assume this was prior to his first stroke. I wrote him the following letter at his home at that time which was in Portola Valley, California. It was dated May 14, 1983 and read as follows:

> "Dear Dr. Bettelheim:
>
> Every once in awhile, as it happens for me, on occasion, several years apart, I am fortunate enough to attend the kind of experience that makes a major change in the nature of one's life, one's work, and basically, how one views the nature of man. From a psychoanalyst's point of view, even the entire question of the task of the analysis itself.
>
> The nature of your presentation-the nature of your book 'Freud & Man's Soul'-the depth of your responses at both a thinking and emotional level-and a 'personal' level gives one a very different perspective about how the task of analysis might be viewed. The comment of Freud, in a letter to Jung-'Psychoanalysis is a cure through love'. The experiential understanding that man's soul is what the analysis is all about, and must be the top priority. This perspective made an indelible impact on me and my work is different. Thank you for being all that you are.
>
> Respectfully yours,

Len Bergantino, Ed.D., Ph.D."
On May 19, 1983 Dr. Bettelheim wrote back to me as follows:

> "Dear Dr. Bergantino,
> Just a note to thank you for your letter. It is very encouraging to be told that one's efforts occasionally are appreciated. It gives one courage to go on, and we all need that. Because as one gets as old as I am, one has one's anxieties that one may get out of touch with what younger people are interested in, fears that one has a tendency to worry that one might be too much involved in one's own concerns which no longer are of interest to anybody else. This is why a response such as yours is so welcome.
> With my best personal regards,
> Cordially yours,
> (signature only) "Bruno Bettelheim"

In the latter part of 1986 and early part of 1987 I was an integral political part of a new group in Southern California which was a local chapter of Division 39, American Psychological Association, Division of Psychoanalysis. In our meeting there was a debate as to whom should be invited to speak for the March 6, 1987 meeting. A good number of the group were all for another fairly well known analyst. I was pushing for Bettelheim. They asked me, "Why don't you want so and so?" I vehemently stated, "Because he doesn't exist!" They kept asking me what I meant as if they either didn't or could not possibly understand anyone relating to them on that level. When they then turned the question around and asked me why I wanted Bettelheim, as the King himself might have phrased it, I vehemently stated, "Because he exists!" Needless to say it was my only victory with this group and they invited Bettelheim to present on "FREUD'S VIENNA".

I was asked to both write the promotional material and to pick up Dr. Bettelheim at his home, now in Santa Monica, and to escort him to the presentation. I wrote the following:

"BRUNO BETTELHEIM, PH.D.-FREUD'S VIENNA Powerful, impactful, brilliant, engaging! Dr. Bettelheim provides an experience and an understanding of Freud that creates both a factual and an impressionistic response in the total being of his audience that has the possibility of forever changing the way one views and practices psychoanalysis. He brings a deepened humanity to what one might have considered a psychoanalysis to be, both clinically and technically, that you feel in every inch of your bones, and it changes who you are-and that changes what you do both clinically and technically.

This is my experience of Dr. Bruno Bettelheim.

Written by
Len Bergantino, Ed.D., Ph.D.
Treasurer-SCC-Div. of Psychoanalysis"

When I picked Bettelheim up he was awkward in social conversation. He didn't have that much to say. However, one of the things he told me was what a nice car I had. I was driving a 1977 Dodge Diplomat that my parents left me after they passed on and it was very special to me. I still have it in 1995. What that told me about Dr. Bettelheim was that he was not a man who was impressed by glitz and material things. He was a man who had depth and substance.

When I presented him I referred to him as a "great man". He corrected me saying, "Not so great." In retrospect he was correct, however, he was at the next level. Of those who have trained and heavily influenced me only Milton H. Erickson, M.D. and Wilfred R. Bion, M.R.C.S. were great. However, Bettelheim certainly was on the next rung.

I had been a psychologist caught in the war between the American Psychoanalytic and the psychologists who were frozen out if they were clinicians and it was too late for me. However, the first clinical psychologist accepted straight up into the Southern California Psychoanalytic Institute for training (Southern California Psychoanalytic Institute was exclusively for medical doctors until this first clinical psychologist) as a result of psychologists winning the case of Welch vs. The American Psychoanalytic was there that evening. He told

Dr. Bettelheim he had just been accepted. He asked two very pointed questions to Dr. Bettelheim which Dr. Bettelheim answered candidly.

First, he said, "What kind of clinicians do Institutes customarily accept?"; "and second, What happens to them as a result of the training?" Dr. Bettelheim replied as follows: "Well, I can't speak for Southern California but I can speak for the Chicago Psychoanalytic Institute (I believe he also said, 'of which I am a member). They pick mediocre clinicians who will not make any waves and by the time they get out the training institute crushes every bit of creativity and clinical acumen beyond mediocrity that they have or might have had. And of the few creative or gifted clinicians that were able to sneak in past the entrance committee, they are crushed by the time they graduate from the Institute." The man was gaping with his mouth open as were all the rest of us; both at so candid a response, so accurate a response, and so devastating a result for all parties concerned. Dr. Bettelheim came right out with it that the American Psychoanalytic and its training institutes were in "bad faith", although he did not use that exact phrase, everyone knew what he meant. (I have a video tape of this presentation somewhere among my collection).

Another analyst who was a training analyst of the Los Angeles Psychoanalytic Institute, the other medical training facility in those days in Los Angeles, Dr. Richard Edelman, told me in a personal conversation, "I never read the psychoanalytic journals any more because they always say the same thing."

In other words psychoanalytic training crushes everything that is alive and lively in that way it has turned a fresh and refreshing Freud and many of his gifted followers into the kind of in stone dogma that the mediocre can practice and earn a living by doing.

And those mediocre, out of fear, have kept out the gifted clinicians who might have made a difference over the past ninety years or so in developing and advancing the clinical acumen to do the kind of jobs that I refer to in this book, thereby having saved years of suffering for many many patients over many many years. That in fact was Bettelheim's message!

My work was directly related to and expanded upon the work of Bion with the integration of other kinds of training I felt were invaluable to the treatment of the psychotic core. I knew that if this could not be done analysis would continue to put on band aids and never reach the depths of what ails people. Most of those whom I had seen, clinicians included, my patient paid $625 per week (30,000 per year) after they already had one or two three to seven year analysis plus combinations of psychotherapy that put them in the 20 years dues paid category before they got to me. They were desperate and they were dedicated. They were the kind of people psychoanalysis should have been able to cure the first time around.

Yet my fascination with Bettelheim was that he knew Freud and was in Freud's original training group. In other words if there was ever a classical Freudian, it was Bettelheim. It was in his blood. He exuded it in every part of his Being. So I felt it would be important to be supervised by Bettelheim in that I knew I one day had to write this book, and I wanted a grass roots perspective with depth and breadth to contain what might later be viewed as the outrageous and the bizarre.

I had five supervision sessions with Dr. Bettelheim, although many various and sundry kinds of communications after those sessions. He charged me $100 per supervision session. I told him I was surprised that he did not charge me more, that my fee was $125 per hour. He asked me how much money I made a year doing analysis. I told him $240,000 per year. He said, "That is a very great deal of money. I never made more than sixty thousand per year tops, when I was at The University of Chicago." I said, "Yes, but you were Bruno Bettelheim and you were at the University of Chicago." There was a mutual respect between us.

Bettelheim, when he supervised me, was a bit quick, in a hurry. He did not have a great deal of patience and could initially be caustic. For example, when I told him of some of the Reichian interventions or direct analysis physical interventions I used in the psychoanalytic frame, Bettelheim responded,

"Dr. Bergantino, I cannot supervise you. I am not familiar with your methods!" "Your methods are violent!"

I said, "Bettelheim, just shut the fuck up and do your job. You're the only genius left. Everyone else is dead!" This seemed to have a calming effect upon him for a little while before he went into, "Dr. Bergantino (screaming out with that Viennese accent), the Nazi's methods were effective too!"

At this point I looked him right in the eye and said, "Bettelheim, what the fuck makes you think I won't get up off this chair and snap your neck like a twig!" The old man, stroke and all, in his late eighties, had a lot of balls. He looked me right in the eye, sitting up as straight as he could and said, "Dr. Bergantino (screaming out with that Viennese accent), I am not afraid of you!" At which point I said, "Well let's get on with things then!"

All I can say is that if you had the range of personal responsiveness that I had Bettelheim was an absolute pussy cat.

Another time he was complaining about my methods, telling me that even though I was correct, and Reich was Freud's most gifted training analyst, the American Psychiatric Association discredited him and would therefore not pay attention to anything I had to say.

I looked him right in the eye challenging him full out and said, "Dr. Bettelheim, can psychoanalysis as you know it offer anything to the kind of problems I am treating in that I should reconsider what I think and what I do?" Again, he sat up straight in his chair, looked me right in the eye, and said, "No, psychoanalysis will make no difference at all in treating the difficulties in the patients you describe." At this Bettelheim became more tolerant of me and what I was doing, always with respect, but dubious that I could sell it to what he viewed as a constricted bad faith group of colleagues who couldn't get out of the way of their own constipation. The first page I had written was page five of this manuscript. He read it and said, "They will never read it. You have to do it as Marie Cardinal has done it in a book called "The Words To Say It" Van Vactor & Goodheart, Inc. 1983. You have to write your clinical cases showing them exactly what you do."

So Bettelheim helped shape my thinking for this book, the overall perspective from which I view analysis, the way I am writing the book, the task of an analysis as being to save man's soul, and many more things.

More personally, he was a genius and he could supervise me and provide value to me as a clinician whether he thought he knew what the hell he was doing or not. I knew he was the link between the past and the future, at least the last one I would ever meet.

On 6/3/89 I wrote him this letter:

> "Dear Dr. Bettelheim,
>
> In terms of whether or not there is a God, I have direct evidence there is ONE. Without 'knowing' this at the most primitive level I would never have the courage to embark on my plan, which is karmic mission, karmic destiny. I am sent down here to open up the training of institutes so the institutes and the outlaws can do the job that needs to be done-which is why psychoanalysis was created in the first place. It is the only method of treatment that has the minimum conditions to do the job, only no one knows how to do an analysis.
>
> What I am saying to you is that your personal responsibility is bigger than your fear. That is why you wrote "Freud And Man's Soul." You were inspirational that day at UCLA! The problem as you said, is that there was no comment from the American Psychoanalytic about your book. I told one analyst that I would write the book that demonstrated all that was in my ad and my letter. He said, 'No one would have to read it'.
>
> Have courage my friend. I 'know' you are a sick old man who has many irrational fears that dominate the life of a sick old man who has many fears; that I 'know' that you have gone out of your way to be collegial with me and kind to me in my situation. In anybody's situation but yours that would be quite enough. (Bettelheim wrote 'A Good Enough Parent', and was apparently confronted with the issue far more

than he found comfortable, in this situation by me). In your situation, this is not the case. You are Bruno Bettelheim and you have a special responsibility to psychoanalysis and to mankind. You cannot say that you 'do not know'. You 'do know' and I 'know' that you know. You are the link between the past and the future! I am the missile! Just go for it! Things will turn out well all the way around! I promise!

Of course you will do what your conscience guides. I must do the same. I see Dr. Barron as the loophole, whether a small group of psychologists want to persecute a psychologist who will make it a public issue that they are no better than their persecutors, or if they give me the forum I will break the American and the International through economics unless they learn what is required to do an analysis.

To do that of course, they would have to take a look at the entire curriculum of what goes into the making of a psychoanalyst and what is required to do what I write about, which is where they are tragically stuck.

Common, help me do it! Once you get the hang of it and see that you can take the next step and there you are, still alive and kicking in the midst of it all, it actually gets to be fun!

I am clear that I have hit the weak link in the chain in Barron's group. It certainly wouldn't hurt if they received whatever you wanted to say in support of the mission as the (APA-American Psychological Association) Scientific Award Winner of the Year in Psychoanalysis. We could blow them away in the first round on this one!

What could they say? Bettelheim's gone off his rocker. Or, Maybe the time is here for revolution. Even someone such as Bettelheim, the grand old man of the old guard, the heir of Freud himself, is backing this change. The worst thing they could do is revoke your award, and you don't need it anyway. (He has the Goethe Medal of Honor, of which he was most proud).

I assume that you understand I am writing this letter to you with my understanding that you are a genius who will understand this karmic tiger in a jungle with the primitive certainty I present you, and that I am the most gifted clinician of my time. I just think at this stage of the game the clock is moving, there is much to be done, and there is no use waiting for politically crazed bastards full of envy, hatred, greed and jealousy to come around peacefully to such a recognition in the psychoanalytic political arena. And there is no sense in doing it as an outsider because, then when I die, things will be as if I was never here. You don't want that to be the summation of your life, do you! Heart to Heart,

Len Bergantino, Ed.D., Ph.D.

P.S. What I claim about myself I always offer to back up in public demonstrations and/or video. My role models were Garibaldi, Bismarck, Talleyrand and Muhammed Ali-who would never have gotten a title fight if he hadn't driven a bus onto Sonny Liston's lawn, had all fifteen of his crew come out and yelled, 'I'm the greatest! I'll take that big ugly ole bear in seven!" He got the title fight. Sure enough, he took Liston in the seventh round! (Actually my own clinical assessment of my capacity to utilize the therapeutic use of self in a teaching and training capacity is that of all who trained or influenced me that I have seen, only Wilfred Bion and Milton Erickson could work at that level.) (Francesca Bion, in a personal conversation with me when I was sharing what I did and the intensity with which I did it and told her I can do that for six hours a day in workshop format, stated, "Bion used to do eight!" I can only say, I developed myself so I can do it, but Bion was a tank to be able to sustain eight! That I never tried.)

I then sent a second letter to Dr. Bettelheim also dated 6/3/89. It went as follows:

> "Dear Dr. Bettelheim,
>
> A thought came to mind that would be of value to psychoanalysis, to psychologists throughout the country, and to you. What if you were to take an add out-send in a simultaneous submission with mine. I'll pay for the add. Say whatever you want and set up whatever kind of training you feel is imperative to the advancement of psychoanalysis-perhaps in the realm of supervision given your age-groups, conference call groups, supervision via telephone. Too Madison Avenue? Common, the world needs what Bruno Bettelheim has to offer on a much larger scale than they are currently able to gain access to it as a result of the kind of institute situation that has so to speak, put even you, too far out to pasture for the good of mankind.
>
> These are ideas, just ideas. Dismiss them. Refine them. Enjoy them.
>
> Warm Personal regards,
> (just my signature) Len Bergantino

Bettelheim's response to me was fear. I said, "How the hell can you be afraid of what I am talking about. You were in Buchenwald! You looked the tiger right in the mouth and in the eye and here you are to tell about it."

(Bettelheim on several occasions stated to me that when he was in Buchenwald, the German Concentration Camp as a prisoner, the Germans would have two lines. For those that hung their heads down and their eyes did not meet the German guards and their shoulders slumped over, to the gas chamber they went. For those that showed strength, walked straight up, looked the Germans in the eyes, they went in the other line which was a work group. This was a very important point to Bettelheim as he mentioned it over and over).

In retrospect I can see that I miscalculated Bettelheim's mental state at the time as a result of his first stroke. He said that while I was right I made him nervous. He was not the Bruno Bettelheim that he used to be and he could not function as he used to function. He said, that if he could, he would have been up to the challenge. But, now, all he wanted to do was avoid anxiety that might cause him another stroke because he did not think he could tolerate another stroke.

I don't know how many hours Dr. Bettelheim and I were to gather after the hours I paid him for supervision, but as I was in a vicious custody battle and lawyers were eating up my income in sucks of ten thousand, eight thousand, five thousand, thirteen thousand, etc., Dr. Bettelheim felt a great deal of compassion for me. For a man who was old and no longer making money he did not charge me one dime. I am certain it was at least twenty hours for which he did not charge me.

AFTERMATH

Bruno Bettelheim committed suicide. The tragic question is whether or not he was able to save his own soul. He was not a great man and he had a "closed heart", or closed heart chakra, that if one had extrasensory perception you could both sense and feel. So did Kohut who tried to overcome it by putting a focus on empathy in psychoanalysis. In other words my view of these people with extra sensory perception is a little like an ex-ray machine in front of which they stood naked.

So Bettelheim wrote about, and taught me about doing the kind of analysis that would save one's soul. Yet, in the Judeo-Christian, at least if you are raised a Catholic, which I was, to commit suicide is to cheat God, and as I later developed, may even put you in a Kharmic situation that one would hope to grow beyond.

Yet, for a man whose heart chakra was closed, he did all that! He was generous. He was a genius and his unconscious mind was a clear as a bell, which is why he could supervise me no matter what I did and no matter what he thought he did. He was good to me. One just didn't or couldn't feel deeply personally touched at the heart level in his presence because he did not have that personal capacity. But what the hell, he could help you become a King! He wasn't envious or hateful. And his judgment was so quick and so skillful in terms of knowing to do the right thing, it is highly unlikely that he would make a harmful mistake, when I knew him, or before.

Another thing Bettelheim told me was that Dr. Spock was the worst thing that ever happened to American parenting. After his death there are those that say Bettelheim hit some children and some patients at the University of Chicago, Sonja Shenkman Orthogenic School for children, of which he was the director. My clinical assessment of Bettelheim is that he was quick and intolerant, although never intentionally hurtful. I do not doubt that he hit some children at the University of Chicago Orthogenic School. I do doubt those that immediately condemn Bettelheim for doing so. His brilliance and clinical judgement were so acute and his unconscious so clear, I am certain that if and when he did so, it most probably had a beneficial affect for the children at a time when there was another philosophy of raising children-"Spare the rod and spoil the child". I am certain Bettelheim would not take any shit from those children, and I am also certain that to the last one of them, they would all have become more of themselves for having known him.

I suppose my personal regret is in not having seen or been able to assess the degree to which Bettelheim's intolerance was applied to himself after his first stroke. He stated many times that he could no longer type; that he was dependent upon a maid; that he could no longer do the things he did; and that if he had another stroke he didn't think he could live through it, or that life would be worth living. So he just about out and out told me, but why would I have heard him? Why would I think, that stroke or no stroke, Bruno Bettelheim, the survivor of Buchenwald, would ever kill himself or be so intolerant of his limitations that he could no longer stand to be alive so far less than he was? For that I am deeply and truly sorry, Dr. Bettelheim. Alas, you were right and I was wrong. On one occasion he was frantic with fear that what I was proposing would kill him, that it would cause him so much anxiety, it would kill him. Despite all that, we liked each other and were what I have written. I suppose he said this in a lot of ways to others, that the down side of being Bruno Bettelheim was that no one would listen and no one could hear him.

He stated he had not seen his grandchildren or his daughter in nearly a year one of the last times I saw him. As to how much this may have bothered an old man who really had no one, even if he was Bruno Bettelheim, I do not know. The feeling is one of being unfortunate. It is hard to believe that perhaps no one gave a shit about him, because I did. Then again, what a foolish fantasy that so little caring of a deaf person may want to make Bruno Bettelheim not commit suicide? At first I was judgmental and even pissed off. Then I wondered, "What would I really do if I were in his place with his equipment?" and "Everytime I have been a judgmental asshole there has always come a circumstance where I have done the same thing." My hope was that down the road I would not have to eat my initial judgement or lack of compassion and find myself facing a choice such as made by Dr. Bettelheim...

It is most difficult when a man is not around to defend himself and judgements are made posthumously. There was the quality in him of being impatient, perhaps with my shortcomings as well as his own. Yet, when he would say, "Dr. Bergantino, Get On With It!" I would retort, "Shut the fuck up! You're the doctor and I am the patient and you're supposed to listen!" When I told him what he was doing in this way he always became more patient and things went well. I knew that was the price, certainly, of working with this genius. (My comment was not accurate in that he was the supervisor and I was the supervisee, but the point was to make the point, and that I did.)

Moreover, what I am saying is that it is not for ordinary men to judge Bruno Bettelheim because he was not ordinary. One cannot judge the nuances of a great one unless you have the same or similar capacities to know how it was to be in his shoes and then have called the shots that he called. One of the problems with history is that is written by the ordinary and the mediocre, not by the Paganini's, the Caruso's, and the Toscanini's.

THE FEAR OF THE ORDINARY AND THE MEDIOCRE

By 1985 I was training therapists internationally and had a psychoanalytic practice earning about $240,000 per year. The better I got, the more gifted I became, the more I was frozen out.

I received the following letter from Donald Rinsley, M.D., Fellow-American College of Psychoanalysts and Senior Faculty Member in Adult and Child Psychiatry, Karl Menninger School of Psychiatry on July 1, 1985. (I met Dr. Rinsley when he presented at a major workshop of master clinicians in Los Angeles at UCLA along with Dr. Otto Kernberg, Dr. Harold Searles and Dr. James Masterson. It was after that meeting that he reviewed my book and wrote a review published in 1983.)

He wrote:

> "Dear Len:
>
> How nice to receive yours of June 24th, and to learn of your upward spiral! I'm very pleased indeed to believe that my little review of your book has contributed to your success!
>
> Frankly, Len, I have long been eructatively fed up with the sort of territorial cupidities and other evidences of narcissistic nonsensicality so many of the colleagues display. Such antics reveal the essentially limbic nature of people as it comes to be expressed in envies and jealousies to which you allude in your letter. When I read your book I knew at once of your outsider-ism (cf. Colin Wilson's seminal book of the same name--The Outsider) as well as your talent; since I know I am good also, I do not need to do the Big-Daddy-in-Cat-On-A-Hot-Tin-Roof bit, viz., to shit on one's sons out of envy and fear that they will appropriate my penis-cum-wife-cum-everything-else!

> I trust your family are in good health. Keep in touch.
> Most sincerely,
> (signed Don)
> Donald B. Rinsley, M.D., F.R.S.H.
> (Lond.) Associate Chief for Education
> Psychiatry Service
> Clinical Professor of Psychiatry
> University of Kansas School of
> Medicine Kansas City

About this time I had already been paid to train psychotherapists in Australia and my work had been described as "a kind of mental precision that electrified the Australian therapeutic community." And had lasting therapeutic impact."

I did a mini-workshop at the Humanistic Psychology Association Yearly Convention at Wentworth Castle in Sheffield, England in 1985 entitled "The Therapeutic Wizardry of Dr. Len Bergantino". The Brits were rather put off by the title, a rather conservative group. Only 12 showed up. Then they found out I could really do it and the entire conference of 300 wanted me to do another one the following day, however, I had prior arrangements so I left. I said, "You should have got it the first time! Anyone who would make such a statement about his work at an international level had to be able to back it up!"

Then I was invited back to Australia in 1986 and did workshops for psychiatrist, Barry Blicharski in Sydney and Yaro Starak, Clinical Social Worker and head of a gestalt training institute in Brisbane.

Dr. Blicharski wrote in a letter of September 5, 1986 "We will be inviting Len Bergantino to return to Australia and I recommend his work, both clinical and teaching, in any situation." Yaro Starak wrote in a letter of September 8, 1986 "Dr. Bergantino has a unique ability to transfer his teaching methods in a live and expressive manner that has proven to have lasting impact on his audience. He has our highest recommendation as a workshop leader."

In 1986 I trained psychotherapists in Seattle and on December 30, 1986 received a letter from Kathleen Murphy, Ph.D., executive Director, Northwest Family Training Institute commending my work.

In March, 1987 I reached the pinnacle of my capacity to work as a psychoanalyst and to train others as one, even to the degree of working with extra sensory perception and psychic phenomena. I did a workshop at the American Psychological Association Mid-Winter Convention entitled "Psychoanalysis and the Problem of Thinking". This work was a direct expansion upon the conceptual subtleties of psychoanalytic technique as written about by Wilfred R. Bion. Two comments of note were made. First, Sam Kirschner, Ph.D. a well-known clinical psychologist and workshop leader on the East Coast of the United States said of me, "A healer who uses psychoanalytic principles. As was Ferenczi to Freud's group, the most gifted clinician of his time." A second psychologist whose name I did not get said, "One of the greats! You should have been invited to present at the Ericksonian Conference in Phoenix." (The one he made reference to was the one with all the greats such as Bettelheim, R.D. Laing, etc. Needless to say I was not invited and have remained one of the best kept secrets in the field.)

On November 19, 1987 I gave the best psychoanalytic mini-workshop I was given the opportunity to do. In fact, a psychiatrist who was a political enemy of mine but put the video tape together called it "BETA ELEMENTS: THE PSYCHOANALYTIC GENIUS OF DR. LEN BERGANTINO". Unfortunately the workshop had to be marketed to psychoanalysts through the Southern California Society of Clinical Hypnosis, a group then composed of physicians, psychiatrists, dentists and psychologists. It was given at the Los Angeles County Medical Association. It was announced as such:

"BETA ELEMENTS AND THE PRACTICE
OF PSYCHOANALYSIS"

Guest Speaker-Len Bergantino, Ed.D., Ph.D.

Wilfred Bion, M.R.C.S., the great British psychoanalyst, wrote of beta elements. He further wrote about his experience with Melanie Klein in that "he came to make choices between contradictories based on what his senses told him." He wrote about the theory of the container, which most analysts seem to agree with, that it is the task of a psychoanalyst to contain the split-off emotional experience and projective identifications of the patient in order to put them back into the patient and make it safe for the patient, as the good mother would do. The problem is this, that these beta elements that analysts thought Bion wrote about from a conceptual frame of reference, actually Exist! The question then becomes how can one do an analysis if they do not perceive with their senses these beta elements because they would not know what needed to be contained and the underlying psychotic thinking disorder aspects of patients' personalities, even those thought to be neurotic, could not be dealt with authentically beyond the point with which a psychoanalyst could pick up the beta elements. Through new_developments in psychoanalytic technique which I will demonstrate with audience participants, I will show how these beta elements can be put back in the patient so that whatever thoughts emerge when the patient in more whole in terms of his or her natural being are in fact authentic, and the expansion of thought can occur while the patient is moving toward finer and finer discriminations of the enhanced quality of his or her being (Becoming 'O', Bion). Strangely enough, I developed the capacity to sense these beta elements as a result of my work with Milton H. Erickson, M.D. *Without this method patient experience cannot be detoxified. The further problem is that to do this work one has to be able to successfully treat the archaic primitive liquid symbiotic transference described by Harold Searles, M.D., who is ahead of his_time in sensing the subtleties of the archaic primitive work that needs to be done if cure is to take place in the practice of psychoanalysis. Without the technical tools to deal with this phenomena, one must either avoid it by not working at such depth, or be taken under as a crocodile might whip one to the bottom of a swamp!

The video of this presentation was viewed by James Grotstein, M.D., author of Splitting and Projective Identification; (Jason Aronson Publishers), and training analyst of The Los Angeles Psychoanalytic Institute. Further, Dr. Grotstein was analyzed by Wilfred Bion for a second training analysis. He wrote me the following letter of December 30, 1989:

> "Dear Len,
>
> I finally had the pleasure of viewing your tape. I found it very impressive. It helped me to understand better where you are coming from and to be able to observe first hand your intuitive way of approaching people. Your technique reminded me of an elegant sophistication of Gestalt along with Erickson and Bion.
>
> My intimate knowledge of the members of my study group (Interdisciplinary Group for Advanced Studies in Psychosis--'IGASP') suggests to me that this tape, unfortunately, is not for them. They are not like me nor like you. They are more conservative in their attitudes and tastes and are especially defensive about Bion. Many of them have been analyzed and/ or supervised by him, and I believe, to quote Bion, 'it would produce more heat than light!" I think there would be such debate over 'beta elements' that the beta elements encountering contrary beta elements would create a beta element cacophony.
>
> On the other hand, let me gently broach the subject to them at the next meeting and see what they say. I will let you know in either case.
>
> Thank you very much for letting me see the tape. It was really educational for me to watch the way you work. You are truly talented.
>
> I hope this year brings you more happiness than any preceding.
>
> Warmest regards,
> James S. Grotstein, M.D.

JSG/sf

P.S. (Dr. Grotstein's handwriting) While this letter was being typed, I learned that Don Rinsley had just passed away!"

It was after receiving this letter that I realized I would have no chance to train psychoanalysts or use the "gift" of talent I had developed to pass on to others unless I wrote a book that could turn the psychoanalytic universe and perhaps the clientele it serves in the metropolis areas right on their ear. This is what I am attempting to do in that I do not live my life having the capacity of a Toscanini, a Caruso, a Paganini, and never have a concert hall to play in. In music Paganini said, "There is only one Paganini!" The way he played they filled the halls and indeed, "There was only one Paganini!" In Psychoanalysis, everybody better claim to be one of the group or they will never play again, even if they are frozen out and their talents are not acknowledged on the widescale basis that merit of the work itself would bring.

I was light years ahead of how analysts were being trained and I had learned all that I could from doing analysis in the office seeing patients from 3 to 7 years five times per week. I realized there was a point of diminishing returns to continue doing something I no longer could learn from doing and could not share with my professional community in that I was not an insider of a medical psychoanalytic institute and therefore frozen out by design, and really too old to pursue it with the zeal of a more youthful analyst going into the profession once Welch vs. the American Psychoanalytic opened the gates for psychologists, clinical social workers and marriage, family and child therapists.

Yet I was invited back to Australia for a third time to train therapists. This time it would be Melbourne, Brisbane and Newcastle. This was perhaps the most important trip of my professional life in that I learned through the experience of doing it exactly what was required to train psychoanalysts to be able to do what Wilfred Bion wrote about. Further, I learned what was required to extend psychoanalytic technique beyond what Wilfred Bion wrote about.

I had titled the presentation in Brisbane where I was the key presenter at the conference as

"THE-THING-IN-ITSELF

The link between experiential approaches to psychotherapy is the movement toward finer and finer discriminations of pure being, to feel, to think and be able to move and live with the swiftness of universal life force itself, while sustaining a state of imperturbable composure. This workshop will show you how to do this through the experience itself in ways you will be able to begin to use in your own lives and work."

However, when the video of the working with an audience of 300 was made I realized it was a workshop to train psychoanalysts. What was shown in this video I announced as follows in the professional newsletters. Here is one from the Los Angeles County Psychological Association Newsletter December 1988/January 1989.

"PSYCHOANALYSIS: STATE OF THE ART"

- 1 hr. 43 min. video cassette (VHS)-$45
- An expansion of the conceptual work of Wilfred R. Bion, M.R.C.S. into psychoanalytic technique.
- Becoming 'O'-Demonstrated use of beta elements to <u>detoxify</u> (Kernberg's work stops here) psychotoxic states, contain projective identifications at microcosmic levels in a way that reconnects patients to vital life force through means of sense perception, sustained depth of feeling, access to unimpeded flow of the unconscious put into conscious formulations expanding upon the capacity to think. A movement toward finer and finer discriminations of 'pure' being and 'pure' thought, even 'thoughts without thinking' while being able to think and respond in the emotional line of fire.
- Demonstrated technique to work with underlying psychotic thinking disorders even in neurotics as well as narcissistic and borderline personality disorders.

  'Reference to techniques that are helpful in working with <u>liquid</u> archaic symbiotic transferences (such as those treated by Searles for 15 and 25 years in which he does not claim to have a successful method of treatment. Reference-<u>The Borderline</u>

Patient) to restore a solid 'nuclear self' to patients who never had one.

Kohut, in How Does Analysis Cure wrote 'the analytic dissolution of defensive structures that have formed around a persisting hollowness in the center of the patient's self cannot be achieved-even in cases where this central hollowness is experienced as painful by a would-be analysand.' Kohut was wrong. Depending upon how far the analyst has traveled in Becoming 'O' and how the analyst can point out the evidence through the experience it-self, patients will stand the prepsychological chaos that is required once they have a taste of self.

•\ Primitive Mental States: For psychoanalysts to be curative of primitive mental states at deep emotional levels-it is imperative that the quality of being of the analyst be curative-otherwise patients will respond to the primitive mental states of the analyst even though the analyst does not act out. This is why Bion saw the life work of the analyst in Becoming 'O'. A method will be demonstrated where dis-ease free states of being provide a deep inner tranquility that primitively lets the patient 'know' that the analyst humanly accepts even what patients view as the most repugnant parts of self."

It is interesting what the professional community did with these announcements, but I shall get to that later.

I did have some training analysts who became friends and respected my work. One was Fred Vaquer, M.D. who was chair of the continuing education committee of the Los Angeles Psychoanalytic Institute in 1988. He said that if I applied to present at the Institute with another training analyst who was a member of the Institute, it was likely to be accepted. Richard Edelman, M.D., training analyst who was analyzed for a second training analysis by Wilfred Bion offered to be the discussant. The presentation was submitted as such:

"BETA ELEMENTS: AN EXPANSION OF THE CONCEPTUAL WORK OF WILFRED R. BION, M.R.C.S. INTO PSYCHOANALYTIC TECHNIQUE

Presentor: Len Bergantino, Ed.D., Ph.D./Discussant-Richard Edelman, M.D.

LEARNING THROUGH THE EXPERIENCE ITSELF

Beta elements that Bion wrote about from a conceptual frame of reference actually exist! The question then becomes how can one do an analysis if they do not perceive with their senses these beta elements because they would not know what needed to be contained, therefore the underlying psychotic thinking disorder aspects of patients' personalities, even those thought to be neurotic, narcissistic or borderline, could not be dealt with authentically beyond the point with which a psychoanalyst could detect, detoxify and interpret these beta elements.

Becoming 'O'-Demonstrated use of beta elements to detoxify psychotoxic states of being, contain projective identifications at microcosmic levels in a way that reconnects patients to vital life force through means of sense perception, sustained depth of feeling, access to unimpeded flow of the unconscious put into conscious formulations expanding upon the capacity to think. A movement toward finer and finer discriminations of 'pure being' and 'pure thought', even 'thoughts without thinking' while being able to think and respond in the emotional line of fire.

This kind of work permits psychoanalyst to develop technique to do jobs that have either never or rarely been done: 1. Form a solid nuclear self in a patient who never had one-a job Kohut said couldn't be done; 2. Work successfully with the kind of ambivalent archaic liquid symbiotic transferences that Searles wrote about treating with limited success over 13 and 18 year cases; 3. Detect and work with underlying psychotic thinking disorders-even in narcissistic, borderline and neurotic patients; 4. Detoxify psychotoxic states of being (Kernberg's work stops here) and return patients to natural states of being where affect is connected, life force and the fight for that life force is sustained; 5. Help psychoanalysts' quality of being (Becoming 'O') become enhanced so they may be curative of primitive mental states at deep emotional levels, even in patients thought not to be in treatment for that problem. Otherwise, patients will respond to the primitive mental states of the analyst even though the analyst does not act out. The end result would be an analysis whereby the analyst blocked quality of being would leave patients in primitively stuck places with self and a significant other whereby that patient's life would remain tragic even after a long analysis.

Donald Rinsley, M.D., Fellow, American College of Psychoanalysts in a review of Dr. Bergantino's book, Psychotherapy, Insight and Style: The Existential Moment, Jason Aronson Publ, 1986, made reference to Dr. Bergantino and his work in the following way: "There is no doubt that some people possess a healing capacity and that others do not; nor is there any doubt that a Zulu witch doctor, a Puerto Rican curandero, a Navaho medicine man or a voodoo spiritist may remit symptoms more effectively than the best trained psychotherapist or psychoanalyst." 'Bulletin of the Menninger Clinic Vol. 47, No. 5.

Len Bergantino, Ed.D., Ph.D. is in the private practice of psychoanalysis in Beverly Hills, CA.

Richard Edelman, M.D.-check with Dr. Edelman directly to see what he wants you to write about him. 310 275-0205."

The response of the Los Angeles Psychoanalytic Institute continuing education committee, composed of training analysts, one of which was very apologetic to me but said he had to close ranks when it was a matter of professional psychoanalytic matters, was, "Rejection because I publicly stated that I was a psychoanalyst and that I stated that I practiced psychoanalysis." A more appropriate response would be "We don't dare expose what you have found out and legitimize it and you for fear we will be shown to be inadequate and you will cost us a bloody fortune of approximately $150,000 per analysand." (1980's fees)

I received $625 per week each Monday equaling $30,000 per year per patient.

As I was the only one who could treat the underlying psychotic care of the personality I was paid $625 to hold the time open (once for 6 months) for those on vacation

CHAPTER TWO-I WAS TRAINED BY MILTON H. ERICKSON, M.D., WILFRED R. BION, M.R.C.S., AND GOD IN ORDER OF ASCENSION

I received a doctorate in Counselor Education at The University of Southern California in 1971, an Ed.D. The entire program at that time was humanistic existential and learning through experience. The bottom line was counseling is psychotherapy and in a sense the professor with the major impact in the department was a guru of sorts and therefore I was trained to both be one and think like one if there is such a thing. The bottom line of this kind of pursuit was that I was never trapped in the culture bind as Carl Whitaker put it in his foreword to Psychotherapy, Insight & Style: The Existential Moment, which was my_doctoral dissertation in clinical psychology under the tutelage of Peter Marin at International College. (Ph.D, 1977)

However, at the University of Southern California the emphasis was on Sartre. I wrote an 83 page paper on "Being and Nothingness" for my advanced techniques course and received a "B+" with a single comment, "Not quite enough!"

For all the books one reads in a lifetime if it is a good book perhaps you remember the major theme or one major point. Sartre wrote a great book and what it all boiled down to was this:

The thing missing in psychoanalysis is the thing-in-itself. My search through the years was to show this to be true, that what was missing was a quest to move toward 'pure being' and thus analysis was not curative because so to speak, the analyst or the qualitative being of the analyst was not considered to be of major importance during the analysis. This would be similar to having somebody puke in your soup while they are cooking it and yet trying to convince you it is both tasty and nutritious.

Okay, where do we go from here. Once I became sensitive enough or competent enough to realize what Sartre wrote was true and the major problem to an analysis that was curative, then the snag was to find someone who had a chance of showing me how to solve the problem. Otherwise, the entire venture was a hopeless one. One old doc Paul

Guggenheim, MD that I treated whose father was analyzed by Freud was trained and analyzed at Menninger's in the fifties. The son was bright enough to come to the conclusion that Psychiatry had little to offer and instead went into allergy and surgery.

Fritz Perls, formerly a psychoanalyst and then creator of gestalt therapy, said, "Lose your mind and come to your senses". There was a key, however, the gestalt therapists lost their minds and were never able to develop methods that went far enough to develop their senses in a way where they would have minds attached and functional with the total quality of being of the person, or therapeutic use of self. Thus, they went by the wayside. I was a three year graduate of Erv. Polster, Ph.D. & Miriam Polster, Ph.D.-The Gestalt Training Center-San Diego (1976-1979), which is why Dr. Grotstein commented that he thought what I did had elements of a sophisticated gestalt therapy having integrated the personhood of Wilfred Bion and Milton Erickson into my therapeutic use of self while I did it. He did not say on its face this looked like psychoanalysis to him as he knew it; yet, perhaps what he saw was a kind of analysis that solved the problem as Sartre posed it, Becoming The Thing-In-Itself Michael Paul, M.D., who supervised me in my first psychoanalytic case for two years (Dr. Paul was analyzed by Bion and is now a training analyst of the Los Angeles Psychoanalytic Institute) used to say that psychoanalysis was like "good gestalt therapy". He was trained in gestalt prior to his training in psychoanalysis. In retrospect I can say that the gestalt training and supervision I received from the Polsters gave me the development of the equipment from which I could pay the kind of attention to experience to make the transition to paying attention to the most subtle, most difficult primitive transferences.

Reich's work with character armor and character defenses; it dealt with life force and life energy and what he referred to as the blockage thereof.

Yet, these kinds of training while inadequate in themselves in that they do not contain the minimum conditions under which the subtleties of the primitive transference can be analyzed at a depth that would be healing; and further, because no method has yet been found to "lose your mind, come to your senses, and regain your mind", nevertheless would have been helpful if included in the analytic curriculum. In other words I am not saying throw out the baby with the bathwater. I am saying that analysis is the only method of therapy that has the minimum conditions of cure, it just doesn't have the ingredients necessary in its training process to actualize its potential. And to a large degree this is a result of its own corruption.

I had the unusual experience of having been trained by many world renowned therapists. Among them were Carl Whitaker, Erv & Miriam Polster, Walter Kempler, Stanley Keleman, George Bach, Jim Simkin, Bob & Mary Goulding, and Albert Ellis. Yet, if it were not for Milton Erickson and the grace of God I would never have stumbled upon the method, sensitivities or knowledge that I will get to once the foundation has been built for such reading.

B.C.-A.D., B.E.-A.E. BEFORE ERICKSON-AFTER ERICKSON

I read Uncommon Therapy: The Psychiatric Techniques of Milton H. Erickson, M.D., Norton, N.Y., 1973. I read it and finished it around_April, 1977. I was in awe in that some of the things done were totally out of my range of experience and even seemed quite unbelievable to me. I wondered if this fellow Erickson was still living and thought that if he was I would look him up and go for training. The book mentioned Phoenix, Arizona. I called Phoenix information and asked for a Milton H. Erickson M.D. I was given two addresses that were the same address. (Erickson was noted for the confusion technique but this may have just been serendipity.) I called and said, "I'm looking for Dr. Milton H. Erickson." The person answering the phone in the s l o w e s t, l o n g e s t, most drawn out way imaginable said, "Y e ssss". I am laughing as I write this but you can't imagine how unnerving that was for him to answer the phone in that manner.

I said, "I have just finished reading your book, Uncommon Therapy, and would like to come and see you." He said, in the same manner, "T h a t w i l l b e f i n e." I said, "However, I want to read your other book, Advanced Techniques of Hypnosis and Therapy (Grune & Stratton, 1967, NY) first". He said, "T h a t w i l l b e f i n e." Again, thinking about working with Erickson is fun now, however, it wasn't fun then. Practically everything he did threw me into chaos, something no therapist up to that time had been able to do (and frankly, no therapist since that time, however, I was not analyzed by Bion. I suspect he would have been the other one to do it.)

It was a ridiculous proposal to read an advanced techniques book of Erickson's work without any experience in hypnosis or the kind of therapy he did because I got so experientially lost I didn't know what end was up. After getting to know him it became apparent to me, as one of his talents was to have your next so many moves on the chess board figured out before you did or did them; that he was fully aware of the stupidity of my ways yet gave me enough rope to hang myself.

I called up around the beginning of August, 1977 and said, "Dr. Erickson, I have tried to read and integrate the advanced techniques book and I am totally lost. I want to come and see you the weekend of September 11th." He said, "Let me get my book. (long pause). There is a small group coming that day, but, 'C O M E! Y O U W I L L G E T WHATYOUWANT!"

Again, this was quite unnerving and I agreed without knowing the address, where I was going, how to get there, where I would be staying, and what time it started. Further, this triggered a series of questions in retrospect. "How does he know what I want? I don't even know what I want. How can he be so certain I will get it? But he was so sure of himself. That is why I agreed to go and forgot the details. (This was the first time I ever heard anyone demonstrate what I will later refer to as "primitive certainty", which is crucial in the development of the analytic use of self to be able to do the kind of work of which I write).

I called him back and asked all the questions that were unanswered. He said, "The sessions begin at 11 a.m. Call Mrs. Erickson from the airport for details." (Click-hung up the phone). I had all the information I needed yet was totally exasperated.

Then I talked to a colleague and former supervisor, Al Weinstein, Ph.D., clinical psychologist, who told me he had driven all the way to Phoenix and Erickson was too sick to work. I called Erickson a third time, about two weeks apart, and said, "How will I know if you are well enough to work. I don't want to come to Phoenix if you can't work." He said, "Call the day before." (Click). Again, I had all the information I needed but was even more frustrated than the previous time. In a way Erickson's behavior of "no wasted energy", like the movements of a Zen Master, created such a chaos before I got there that my receptivity to change was significantly increased just to reduce the tension and anxiety of his doing it again, and again while I had to withstand this chaos and anxiety of 'not knowing'.

I went with my wife as I was married then. We pulled up to a rather modest ranch style house. I thought, this is small and has no accoutrements of wealth or status, similar to the psychoanalyst's homes in Beverly Hills that I had visited. I wondered why such a world famous person lived so moderately.

Mrs. Betty Erickson answered the door and told my wife and me to go around to the side of the house where there was an office.

The office was rectangular and not too big. It had a desk on the left with a purple telephone on it. There was a bookcase beyond the desk and a few of Erickson's books were there with purple book jackets. There was an American Society of Clinical (1977) Hypnosis Journal that had just come out that month and had purple lettering in that this particular issue was dedicated to Dr. Erickson and his work, I believe in honor of his 77th birthday.

Three more people attended that day. I do not remember them except for an American Indian woman named Dawn White, who was soon to get her doctorate and go about doing what was needed with her people. There were five of us altogether.

Mrs. Erickson wheeled Dr. Erickson into the room. There were no social courtesies. He looked at each of us as if he had one huge eye in the middle of his head that could see you totally psychologically naked and the feeling was one of being "taken off balance" and feeling a good deal of discomfort.

Without saying anything Dr. Erickson handed us each a sheet of paper and said, in that hypnotic, slow pace, "Write your name, date, marital status, number of children, highest degree and your occupation." I wrote down gestalt therapist as that is what I did at that time.

Dr. Erickson collected all the papers, still without saying anything of a personal nature to any of us. Then, he looked right into my eyes in the way that created the anxiety when he came in and said the first words out of his mouth, "You forgot the date and your marital status." In retrospect that comment was the beginning of the end of my marriage (official separation in 1986 and official divorce in 1990). In other words his first shot was that if I was going to get divorced I was waiting much too long to do it. Although I did not know that I knew this at a conscious level and can only write in retrospect. The experience at the moment was great embarrassment in front of my wife that I forgot her on the short list. In any case that was Dr. Erickson's entire diagnostic history. He had developed such skill that he could pay attention to "minimal cues" and know where things were going very rapidly.

Of the five in the room, he looked right into my eyes and said, "So you come all the way from California and you are avoiding the hot seat!" (Gestalt Term) (Erickson spoke to people in their own language. For example using the "hot seat" is a gestalt therapy term. Use own language) I was a quick witted sort that could come back and depotentiate a therapist in seconds. I was thinking of saying, "All the seats in the room look the same." Before I had the time to mention it, which was a matter of seconds, he came right back more forceful than he did the first time and said, "Now that I mention it, you are still avoiding it!" This created so much chaos and anxiety in my stomach that I got up and moved over to the chair next to his wheelchair.

Erickson made it a point to speak to people in their own language. I wrote down "gestalt therapist". He used the words "hot seat". Further, he was all dressed in purple. He had a purple silk shirt, purple silk pants, purple knitted booties over his feet which were so swollen from gout they looked like cement blocks and a purple string tie, the kind worn by Westerners. He had polio, his lips were paralyzed and his tongue was dislocated. He could not move his arms very well, although I believe it was his left that moved more than his right. He had myastenia gravis. I took one look at him when Mrs. Erickson wheeled him in and I thought to myself, 'No matter how tough my job is it couldn't possibly be as tough as this old gent just to get along each day.'

There I was sitting in the chair next to his wheelchair. He said, in a very challenging way, "So you're a clinical psychologist, eh!" I said, "Yes." He said, "I'll bet you don't even know why I am wearing purple!" I, in the same way I would have commented about all the chairs looking the same said, "I guess it's just part of Dr. Erickson's style." He, in an even more challenging way with the intonation that I was a jackass said, "I'm colorblind! It's the only color I can see!" He proved his point in about three minutes. He was the teacher and I was the student. He was the therapist and I was the patient. He was the supervisor and I was the supervisee. I say all three because he did all three in a single process of telling stories, or using the 'teaching tales', a process which I will get to. The way he set the frame, that we were not pals and there were no social courtesies was extremely important in him setting the frame-a hierarchy, in which I was both able and willing to learn. There was also a fear that if my unconscious modus operandi were to mess with this fellow he was quick enough and ruthless enough to turn me every which way but loose.

This first day was a Saturday. The American Indian woman Dawn White was sitting on the floor next to me. I found out later that Erickson was letting her stay in the guest house and she had attended his sessions for about a month. He said something to me. The feeling I had was one of not understanding. I turned to Dawn White and said, "What did he say?" She said, "He said you know more than most." However, he said it in a way that I was still feeling stupid and the hierarchy was still intact. He then looked at me and said "You will be interested in me for awhile and then you will move on." I was so interested that I was certain he was mistaken, but he was not mistaken. It was uncanny the way he called his shots.

He looked me right in the eye and said, "Well, young man, what can I do for you?" What came out of my mouth surprised me in that at a conscious level I thought I went there to learn hypnosis. I said, "Dr. Erickson, I have heard about your unusual talents. I wonder if you could help me stop moving." He asked me if I wanted to experience trance and I said that I did. I was aware at first that every part of me wanted to challenge him and to prove what he did would not work. However, what he did provided me with such physical relief that I could not lift my arms when he challenged me to do so; or, he had helped me so greatly in a matter of twenty minutes that I just didn't want to move at the deepest levels. It was a level of deep deep peace that I tasted, that Erickson worked in, and that I had only experienced in the way of being of one other individual, the great British psychoanalyst, Bion, two years later. As you will see, this is no small point. He said, in a very challenging way, "Well, do you think that you are hypnotized!?" I said, "Yes."

As a gestalt therapist I had a good intuition and I could track experience pretty well, one step follows another (in the patient). The basis for my development as a psychoanalyst was "Good Gestalt Therapy" as taught to me by Dr. Erv Polster, Ph.D. However, as was I, I have never met a gestalt therapist who had access to his unconscious mind with any degree of freedom other than Jim Simkin. There was a conscious control and an inability to break free from such conscious control. Further, if it were not for this very unusual method I was about to experience, being in the right place at the right time in history, I am certain I was born that way, I would have lived that way, and I would have died that way. People who have that degree of conscious control over the years that I have seen as patients would not have changed by any ordinary means of therapy in terms of a loosening of controls that would gain them access to their unconscious were it not for what Erickson showed me and I learned how to do. These people are referred to as "cement heads". They can be lawyers, judges, doctors, very intelligent people, but their heads are like cement blocks. No access to the unconscious or to the primitive unconscious and not amenable to psychoanalysis or psychoanalytic interpretation of an unexpected sort, such as Bion would do.

That first day I awakened from what Dr. Erickson did as a trance induction after about 20 minutes, however, I never did leave the hypnotic feeling state for the entire four and one half hours that he told stories.

THE TEACHING TALES OF MILTON H. ERICKSON, M.D.-THE PROCESS

Most psychotherapists and psychoanalysts work with patients for fifty minute hours, or even worse, forty five minute hours (which I will explain later in terms of the multiple deficits caused by the five minute shortchange). Erickson commonly worked between 80 and 120 minutes with patients. He would tell stories at a very slow pace. His view of it was that after so much "concentrated attention" people would naturally get tired and wander off, and when their resistance was down or they were less guarded is when most of the work happened. It would be like saying "I will zap you when you are out on your coffee break".

My experience of the process was somewhat different and not known either in Ericksonian or psychoanalytic circles, either by accident or on purpose. There was the great man in front of me telling stories. As a young therapist I wanted to learn everything he knew so I could develop myself to that degree. Thus, and as most patients do for their own reasons, I focused every bit of attention upon him and what he did. I watched his every move. My focus was totally externally oriented. Only he didn't stop. He kept going and going and going, and finally, I was getting very tired putting in all that work concentrating upon him.

My mind began to <u>wander off aimlessly</u>. He continued to tell stories. The experience was one of drifting out, usually somewhere that seemed insignificant although somewhat pleasurable in that I was not listening to Erickson or concentrating upon what he was doing. It was a <u>relief to wander off aimlessly</u>. However, then all of a sudden, as if a "red_neon sign were flashing before the middle of my eyes or forehead, depending upon whether my eyes were open or closed", That red neon sign was somehow directly related to what appeared to be aimless stories without a point and provided "insight", "illumination", in a matter of moments that could change the course of one's life forever. (My first book focused on 'the existential moment'. This was one type of an existential moment.)

Time after time during the first four and one half hours the experience was one therapists have written about as "Aha!" Later that day, if one considers the following in the context of a psychoanalytic interpretation of projective identification, I said to Erickson, "Dr. Erickson, your stories have pinpoint accuracy!" (as it felt as if he was inside your head to be able to tell the kind of stories he was telling once the cement head qualities of focusing on what he was doing dropped off after the first 80 minutes or so). Dr. Erickson said in that slow pace,

"Oh, No. I am just an old man who tells stories. It's your unconscious mind that has the pinpoint accuracy." When he said this I thought he was being falsely modest, however, his comment had two effects. First, it gave me the confidence to believe it was true in that the more I did it, in fact it was true. Second, the more I did it, that is trust my own unconscious mind in 'knowing' with 'primitive certainty' that the story going through my mind does indeed have 'pinpoint accuracy' for that particular patient at that moment in time; the more the pinpoint accuracy developed to a point of trust, accuracy and therapeutic artistry at the 97th percentile. One can only say in retrospect as a student of a great master, Erickson was the first of two that did not suffer from envy, hatred and not want their offspring to surpass their own talents. He once said to me, "I can't understand why a two legged skater would want to imitate a one legged skater, anyway!" Of course, he didn't live long enough to find out where that was to develop, but he made it clear in two places already, that he thought I had more going than he did. Maybe it's true. We shall see. The amazing thing was that he bold-facedly told me without reservation in a way that I would never forget no matter how far the chips got down in my life. I never lost confidence in my ability or faith in myself. And for that alone, I shall always love Dr. Erickson. I suppose of all those that trained me the only two I saw that I was certain I could not outwork at the time were Bion and Erickson, in that they both worked with as fine-tuned discriminations as it was possible to develop in the most brilliant of minds, the most dedicated of beings, and with the kind of therapeutic selves that would and could work at the finest levels of discriminations until they became finer and would live their lives continuing to do so. By 1986 I could out work any therapist in the world. I backed up what I said giving a workshop at Wentworth Castle in England entitled "The Therapeutic Wizardry of Dr. Len Bergantino." There were no two I respected more than Erickson and Bion. Mrs. Erickson wrote to me several years after Dr. Erickson's death and said his comment to her about me was "I respect his dedication to the work." Erickson was dedicated to the work and Bion to Being. One helped me see the other.

The reason I am writing of this aspect of Dr. Erickson's work to be incorporated into the doing of a psychoanalysis at the levels at which I write it that of all those therapists I have ever seen or been exposed to, "only psychoanalysts as a whole even have a chance at developing what I will write about because the level of dedication required to do so means going all the way, no holds barred." Freud was this sort of fellow and so was Melanie Klein this sort of woman. Herbert Rosenfield demonstrated this kind of sensitivity in regard to osmotic transferences in his book, *Impasse and Interpretation*. Harold Searles, wrote of archaic liquid symbiotic transferences in his book entitled "The Borderline Patient".

At the end of the first day my ex-wife and myself had about one and one half hours with Dr. Erickson in a private session. He talked only to me, again starting off saying, "Well, what can I do for you, young man?" I looked him right in the eye and said, "Dr. Erickson, you are the foremost psychotherapist in the world! When I get out of here, I want to be as good as you are!"

This was the kind of question, except for Bion, that hooked most of the other great, world renown therapists that had trained me, into either falsely building me up with what I would refer to as 'therapeutic placation', or actually boldly and forthrightly attempting to murder their younger offspring through the most sophisticated and subtle maneuvers of hatred and envy imaginable. The better the therapeutic skill in someone who hadn't moved beyond this, the worse it could have been if I had not met Erickson and Bion. And for that I am deeply and forever grateful!

Erickson responded to me, with no axe to grind, "Where do you think you stand now?" I looked him both competitively and fiercely right in the eye and said, "Top of the average!" (I had been in private practice five years at that time and was 35 years old). He said, in a way that removed all pressure from me internally as well as externally, "Well, why don't you be the best top of the average you can be then, you'll never be Milton Erickson!" The feeling tone from him was one of "I don't care if you become better than me or not, however, for you to become whatever you can become, it is important that you not have to compare yourself with or to me on the way up, and just be free to develop yourself to the best of your ability." This comment took me out of the quagmire in which I had been stuck no matter who I had trained with or how good they were supposed to be. Erickson freed me in that moment! This is the job a father is supposed to do for a son, only father's do not know it is the job and they are not in the emotional place to do it. This was one turning point without which I would not have been able to advance either personally or professionally.

The job Erickson did for me is the job a father is supposed to be able to do for a son, without which, the son can never earn his full rights as a "warrior".

Another unusual facet was the fee Erickson charged. It was $40 per hour. At the time I was charging $75 in Los Angeles. However, on one occasion he trained ten students for about six hours and one of the students asked what the charge was. This included many licensed psychiatrists and psychologists. He said, "Well, I have to come out with $40 an hour. Why don't you all chip in and if some of you can't afford that, find some way to pay me back in the future!" He said this, not expecting to live too long, and not expecting any money back in the future. He was referring to "good works" of those he trained. There I was getting trained by Milton Erickson for $4 an hour. I wrote him a check for $40 an hour because that is what I wanted to do. He gave one the feeling that you were working with a "saint".

The last time I saw him there were fifteen psychologists and psychiatrists there. He looked around the room at us with that intimidating piercing eye that made you feel like he could look right through you and he said, "I can take no responsibility for blindness! I can take no responsibility for blindness!" We all had M.D.'s or Ph.D.'s and yet he thought we were blind. I came to find out he was right. The problem was what kind of details were required to be able to pay attention to the kind of "minimal cues" that Erickson paid attention to that allowed him to do what he did and call the shots that he did; for the most part without missing and without error at the stage of the game I met him.

Most of Erickson's students made the mistake of thinking one could learn to do what Erickson did by learning a form of brief therapy that was Ericksonian and learning to pay attention to external cues; such as Dr. Ernest Rossi has written about in many of his how to books about Erickson. This is not true. Erickson and Wilfred Bion were the two most dedicated human beings I ever met as well as the two most dedicated clinicians. I found that one had to develop his or her internal sensitivities to be able to develop the therapeutic use of self with the same resonance and precision as Paganini was able to play his Stradivarius violin. Erickson's work was referred to as "magical" and_Bion's as "mystical". On one occasion Erickson asked a young lady if she thought she was hypnotized. She said, "No!", very defiantly. He leaned over from his wheelchair, and with his left arm, which moved somewhat better than his right given the polio. He flipped her arm and up it stood. I had never seen anybody call his shots like that before, and I suppose I looked a little dumbfounded with my mouth open. Erickson said, "And look at ole Dr. Bergantino over there. He believes in magic. He doesn't know all I do is pay attention to details!" Again, the question was, what kind of details did he pay attention to? Well, it took me ten hours a day for a year to find out. There was an unusual combination of one of the two most dedicated clinicians I ever met working with one of the most dedicated students he ever had. (Mrs. Betty Erickson informed me after his death that his comment about me was "I respect his dedication to the work." Coming from Erickson I know of no higher compliment; particularly in that I never saw him give one to anybody).

I remember the day a man came all the way from Orange County in California and he said, "Dr. Erickson, your work is just marvelous." There was a bit of a patronizing kiss up style and sound to the compliment. Erickson said, in a disgruntled way, "Yeah, everybody tells me that." The man did not seem to get the message as he again made a patronizing comment about Erickson's work. Erickson looked at him and said, "I never want to see your face again as long as I live!" The power with which he said it and given who it had come from I experienced as awesome. To my even greater surprise the man got up, walked over to the wheelchair where Erickson was seated, kissed him on the forehead, and left. I kid you not, I saw it happen!

Erickson didn't waste any energy when he thought working with someone would go nowhere. He once kicked me out until I learned the principles of William of Occam, of whom I knew not. I went to the library and looked it up. Occam's Razor-"Multiplicity Ought Not Be Posited Without Necessity". Erickson would only spend time with you if you developed yourself to be able to work at the razor's edge in terms of the development of the therapeutic use of self.

On one occasion he began by looking at us (about fifteen psychiatrists and psychologists) and saying, "You wouldn't believe the psychiatrists and psychologists I train. They all have amnesia!" Then he repeated it. "You wouldn't believe the psychiatrists and psychologists I train. They all have amnesia!" It was his amusing way of making us look at our own stupidity and lack of self-discipline.

When I was president of the Southern California Society of Clinical Hypnosis in 1987 I gave a presentation of the Ericksonian Storytelling non-stop for about two hours. One of the brightest people there and one of the most disciplined, was an oriental woman who was a psychiatrist. She was smart enough to understand the task and she said "Dr. Bergantino. I marvel at what you do. However, when I do hypnosis I give the patients a few suggestions and it helps things along. To do what you do requires a lifetime dedication to self-development, to the quality of your being, and to the sustaining of access to your unconscious. I marvel at watching you do it but this is much too difficult for me. I just want to use hypnosis and give people a few suggestions and help them along. This is when I began to get the idea that what I was really talking about was a method of "reverse psychoanalysis" and only the most dedicated of the psychoanalysts, who already had done a great deal of work in the development of access and flow to the unconscious would have an opportunity to learn to do what is required to work in the ways I describe.

A rather ordinary clinician who was somewhat disenchanted with me once blurted out, "Bergantino, when are you going to teach something somebody can learn?!" She had a point. Those I want to train are those that already know everything and we can begin from there. In one of Bion's books he began the book by making that statement, not as a matter of arrogance, just as a matter that without knowing all of what there was to know about psychoanalysis the reader would be quite lost as to what experience was being conveyed by the book.

Before I get into a more detailed description of "reverse psychoanalysis" (a term coined by James Grotstein, M.D., Training Analyst, Los Angeles Psychoanalytic Institute & Society, when he was exposed to the storytelling or teaching tales part of my work), I am going to tell you a few more of the stories of my experience with Erickson in that the kind of human being you become is tantamount to your developing the kind of self-discipline to be able to do the work as will be described in this book.

The last time I saw Erickson he said, "My muscles are rotting away and there is nothing I can do to stop it. Young Steve Langton came down from Michigan to work with me and he saw that this was the case. He went back to Michigan very depressed. He sent one of his colleagues down to work with me about a month later. I looked him right in the eye (and Erickson had the spirit of a Viking) and I said, "I understand that Young Steve Langton is prematurely morning my death. Well, I want you to tell Young Steve Langton that dying is absolutely the last thing I plan to do!" Can you picture this, Erickson in the face of death itself challenges the grim reaper with fire and abandonment! Can you get a sense of the feeling it gave to those present to meet the challenges of their lives without being quitters, babies and whiners!

The title of one book written about him was "My Voice Will Go With You: The Teaching Tales of Milton H. Erickson", Rosen, S., Norton 1983. He spoke at this slow pace "Margaret Mead told him_she had only heard in a rare African tribe relatively free of disease." Between the disease free pace; the awesome sense of personal presence; the exquisite sense of self-discipline as applied to the development of therapeutic skill, and the sense of personal impact that his interventions had on his patients, his voice did indeed go with you. For years to this day I can hear Erickson's voice exactly as he spoke the words.

Erickson has said "Much has been said about the solid rock of truth, but little has been said about the shifting sands!" "Into every person's life should come a little confusion and a little enlightenment." These comments were also related to the work of Bion, who often made interpretations that even the San Diego Psychoanalytic Society and Institute found that they were left in a state of "not knowing, chaos and anxiety". When they said to Bion, "Dr. Bion, we do not understand a word that you have said over the past hour and one half", Bion replied, "Well, I am speaking ordinary conversational English!"

Erickson made a point of speaking to people in their own language. This sounds simple enough, but let me give you an example of what it was like. When my ex-wife and I were there in 1977 he carried on a conversation with me in front of her in English in which she did not understand a word he said. Then he carried on a conversation with her in front of me in English in which I did not understand a word that he said to her, and she understood everything he had said to her, just as I had when he spoke to me. Without ever making an interpretation one could certainly understand that we spoke two different languages and had nothing in common as a result of the experience of being shown that to be the case.

I never thought I had the capacities to tell stories, so don't get discouraged if you like doing this and find it difficult to begin. I began by telling stories for five minutes, then ten, then fifteen, and after several months my unconscious mind was developed the bases of reverse analyzing enough to make an assessment in the first five minutes writing down four or five things that came out of my unconscious on a piece of paper (called automatic writing); and then, with pinpoint accuracy telling stories from my unconscious mind to the unconscious mind of the patient get an existential shift. Erickson always worked with an end result in mind which involved manipulation and control. I never did. My work was true psychoanalytic in that it was based on, as Bion put it, the abandonment of memory and desire. I found only with such abandonment could existential shifts occur where "transformations in being" would occur. In this way my work transcends Erickson's work.

I did this storytelling twenty five hours per week for one year between 1977 and 1978 and that very slow pace, from my unconscious mind to the unconscious mind of the patient. Several things happened from there.

First, I became a master at "reverse psychoanalysis" and the use of storytelling as insight. Second, I developed extrasensory perception in that my senses were cued into my own body in the disease free state of being Margaret Mead stated she had only experienced in Erickson and that I had only experienced in Erickson and Bion. Third, I made some direct requests of a spiritual nature to the Almighty and got what I asked for; thus turning my entire existence upside down for many years. One must be careful about one what asks for?

The following section deals with the first development,

REVERSE PSYCHOANALYSIS: THE UTILIZATION STORYTELLING AS INSIGHT PSYCHOANALYSIS

Submitted by
LEN BERGANTINO, ED.D., PH.D.
Private practice of Clinical Psychology
Beverly Hills, CA 90210

■■ ■

Between September 11, 1977 and the time of his death in March, 1980, I had the good fortune to have been exposed to the wisdom of one of the foremost hypnopsychotherapeutic geniuses to ever practice the state of the art, Milton H. Erickson, M.D. One day after a seminar composed primarily of his teaching tales, I said to him, "Dr. Erickson, your stories have pinpoint accuracy", somewhat in awe of the effect his storytelling was having on me. He said, "Oh, No! I am just an old man who tells stories. It is your unconscious mind that has the pinpoint accuracy." So it is what the wisdom of Dr. Erickson has evoked in my unconscious mind that I have created and write about a method that expresses my views and in no way is intended to represent the views of Dr. Erickson. Erickson was known for his work utilizing uncommon methods of behavior modification and often stated his views about the inadequacies of psychoanalysis. Further, to my knowledge he never wrote about or told stories about 'insight' therapy. Thus, there may be instances where there are similarities, but this article is not intended in any way to represent Ericksonian hypnosis, but to represent Bergantino's view of a method evoked in him by Erickson, entitled "Reverse Psychoanalysis: The Utilization of Hypnotic Storytelling As Insight Psychoanalysis."

At the conclusion of a story while Erickson was engaging in his 'teaching tales', "one brave student questioned him. 'Were you directing the story to someone in the group for whom you sensed it was relevant?' 'No', he replied. 'Were there several of us what you felt needed to examine something illustrated in the story?' 'No.' 'Were you hoping to fixate our attention as an indirect hypnotic induction?' 'No.' 'Well, was it a metaphor meant to convey something at unconscious levels?' 'No.' 'Well, then, why did you tell the story' queried the baffled student. Erickson smiled. "I just thought it was an interesting story about good therapy!" (Hammond, 1984).

UTILIZATION OF SENSORY PERCEPTION, PACING, AND 'TIME' IN GAINING ACCESS TO THE UNCONSCIOUS AND IN DEVELOPING THE CAPACITY TO THINK

Before any pinpoint accuracy can be developed in storytelling from the unconscious mind of the analyst to the unconscious mind of the patient, the analyst has to have access to his or her own unconscious mind on the basis of an unimpeded flow from moment to moment over long periods of time. So things must begin with the training of psychoanalysts in this hypnotic method that will help them develop the capacity for pinpoint accuracy in storytelling. (Includes getting the crust off the unconscious between Friday and Monday)

Step one is having a storyteller-trainer who can tell stories at a particular and slow pace, with a particular rhythm, with a particular cadence, as if the constancy of that analyst were as steady as a metronome. This pacing helps the trainee or patient, over the course of perhaps eighty to one hundred and twenty minutes, although sometimes within the fifty minute hour, develop an unusual ability to perceive and focus on sensory awareness. This ability to attend to the sensations at a slowed_down pace, over a long period of time will happen, because it feels so good and so natural to be able to do. In a 'sense' it is regaining the kind of sensory awareness one might have had when they were babies.

The tremendous value of this process to psychoanalysis is that without it psychoanalysis cannot cure underlying psychotic thought disorders, because thoughts that are founded in the being of the person and are evoked by being able to pay attention to sensory awareness. To the degree this capacity is limited, what you have are thoughts being said as if they were disconnected to the thinker, or even worse, the evacuation of thought as manifested in psychotic thinking disorders. So, the storytelling method has the capacity to help patients tune into sensory awareness in a way that evokes thought. That includes the ability to pay attention to what Jung might have referred to as the collective unconscious, or might otherwise be referred to as primitive preconceptions.

In terms of gaining access to the unconscious the length of time of the session may be even more important. If patients are in what Melanie Klein may have referred to as the paranoid-schizoid position, they are usually quite frightened because they are not able to tune into sensory perception in a way that they know the thoughts they have as it relates to the reality of the moment. So you find patients whose eyes are bugging out, as if to say, "If I look at you long enough and hard enough, perhaps I will see reality." This is a false premise, and in fact, they are looking in the wrong direction. They need to look inward as opposed to focusing on the other person whom they think they mistrust. They really mistrust themselves, but do not know it.

The advantage of the storytelling, and the patient may have eyes open or closed, although closed is an advantage, is that after so long a period of time of continuous storytelling-80-120 minutes-patients get sick and tired of trying to figure out what the point of the analyst might be. So there is a loosening of control, providing the analyst is a trustworthy character, if nothing else, through sheer exhaustion of trying to maintain the tight tense control during what is being provided by the analyst-a very relaxing environment in which stories are being told.

When the patient begins letting go or giving up of control due to fear, what begins to happen is that where the patient's mind was being evacuated, the patient begins to notice, amidst the pleasant sensations, and the variety of sensations they notice, that there may be a variety of places to which their minds wander. Also, they may go in and out in terms of attention to your storytelling, and their unconscious minds may begin to give them pinpoint messages that are extracted from the stories. These are not necessarily the messages intended by the storyteller. In fact, the best way for this method to work is if the storyteller tells stories from his or her unconscious without any particular agenda, desire or manipulation. In other words there is a purity of being involved in the quality of being of the analyst-(Bion-Becoming 'O') that helps to enhance the trust of the patient, and that is most enhanced without manipulation and without desire on the part of the analyst.

Further, this slow process helps patients contain sensations and emotions they unconsciously can't stand and have been splitting off from. The soothing environment provided by the pacing and storytelling make it possible for patients to contain material and experience they previously felt were too painful. This is particularly useful in treating the borderline personality disorder who splits off to such a degree that there is almost a constant state of irritability. This is for the most part also true with obsessive compulsive personality disorders. Of course, narcissistic personality disorders like it just because it feels good.

This is the beginning of the access to the unconscious. The pinpoint accuracy continues to develop, both in terms of the patient's unconscious mind tuning in at the exact moment it needs to extract a particular message from the storyteller, thereby enhancing a trust of the unconscious in relationship to others; and also, gaining access and trust in terms of where their unconscious minds drift off to when they are not involved with the story. *So patients are learning to develop a balance between paying attention to self, others and environment at the unconscious level-and learning to trust their own capacity to do this. This work is a preface to psychoanalysis and makes a transition possible for patients who were not capable of being treated by insight.* On the average, two sessions per week for about ten weeks would prepare a non-insight oriented patient, the kind that Erickson would customarily treat through his uncommon strategies, for an insight therapy that would perhaps begin with a twice per week psychoanalytic psychotherapy, or possibly with a five time per week analysis.

After this point the constancy of the analyst as an object and perhaps the continued utilization of pacing as if to be offering the "good breast" on a constant basis, is of the utmost importance in terms of the success of the analysis.

THE GOOD BREAST

Patients are very sensitive to what they are being fed. Patients who cannot think and who have relatively no access to their unconscious minds cannot work with insight therapy because they would have relatively few productions, be too embarrassed, say very little, and not be able to tolerate psychoanalysis. The preparatory method I propose feeds the hungry patient, and as Erickson would say, permits them to "enjoy the benefits of passive learning". Until the patient is properly fed through the storytelling which gives the patient some access to sensory perception, to the unconscious, and to the capacity to think, and until they are permitted and even encouraged to 'enjoy the benefits of passive learning', seeing there isn't very much else they can do anyway, patients cannot be given the opportunity to develop themselves as whole and fully functioning human being. I think this is where Erickson's view of brief therapy was short sighted. It did not offer the methodology to help patients become whole, solid and mindful. It did, however, in this author's opinion, help those patients who were stuck in the ways of mindlessness turn the tragic corner in their lives and live a happier and more functional life than they otherwise would have done. The storytelling is the "good breast" that makes the opportunity to become whole in terms of the quality of being of the patient-as a person with access to mind, conscious and unconscious, a viable alternative to being just functional. It provides the opportunity to have access to personal abundance.

THE USE OF SENSORY PERCEPTION BY THE PSYCHOANALYST

The more the capability of the psychoanalyst to know on a sensory level what is going on in the here and now, the better chance that psychoanalyst has to provide a healing environment as well as an extraordinary degree of empathy. This takes a good deal of experience at paying attention to sensory perception cues and in being able to trust them.

In terms of providing a healing environment, when the psychoanalyst is with some patients it feels hard to breathe, a constant sense of irritation, and a difficulty in maintaining the force of energy necessary to keep the storytelling going-and in particular, to keep it going while providing a full breast-that is, without the psychoanalyst letting his or her energy become depleted by the patient who saps his or her own energy, thereby projecting this energy sapping experience upon the psychoanalyst.

By telling stories over the course of 80 to 120 minutes, and for the most part, even in the first 20 minutes, the steady pace and control of the quality of the feeding by the constant object of the analyst, will stop the energy sapping quality of the patient because the patient will be receiving the constant flow of nurturance necessary to relieve the irritation. This kind of environment provides the patient the best opportunity for learning to provide such environment through self-discipline. This gives the patient the best opportunity to turn around the kind of process that irritates and weakens the immune system, thereby giving the patient the best opportunity to create a strong resistance to illness in all the forms that such Eastern ways might be helpful. Alan Walts (East vs West) To turn this around, though, patients must understand the level of discipline involved. It is not a kind of hypnotic pace that one enters for ten or twenty minutes per day. It is a quasi-hypnotic pace that a patient maintains throughout all phases of daily functioning. So this becomes a sixteen hour per day job, and if the patient suffers from insomnia, it may be a twenty four hour a day job. With such dedication to keep control over this pace so the body is nearly always in a nurtured state, the patient has the possibility for optimum health and optimum functioning. Such a method can even help heart attack patients turn around such problematic states where they previously have had very low cure rates. Of course, either the storytelling and/or the analysis must also deal with the dynamic that motivates the heart attack type behavior. But without the pacing or feeding the dynamics and storytelling will be of little use in helping patients get control of themselves. The psychoanalyst has to take control first of the crazy out of control part of the patient. The use of sensory perception and storytelling as a non-stop flow of communication does just this. It prevents the manic, agitated, or hyper pace from intruding back into the pre-analytic experience. Analytic interpretations must in later phases of treatment also maintain the kind of quasi hypnotic pace, taking into consideration the space between analyst and patient, and the kind of sensory perception environment the patient is projecting. This creates a transformation of being that permits both patient and psychoanalyst to work at the level Bion wrote about in "Transformations."

The second primary use of sensory perception on the part of the analyst is to provide a kind of empathy that is so in tune with the patient's moment to moment quality of being, that the analyst knows by shifts in sensory perception, and areas in which the patient splits off from pain, exactly what stories to tell to reach the problem areas. For example, if the analyst feels a sharp pain in the heart, the stories would be stories that help people live along the path of heart, or moving stories, or heartwarming stories. If the therapist notices pain on the sides of the temples it may indicate anxiety and/or anger at confined thoughts on the male-(R) or female (L) sides of the personality and body. The analyst can assume the patient is trying hard to do something with the storytelling and needs to give permissions at this point. For example, interrupting the story with the permissions 'you don't have to be perfect', 'you don't have to please me', 'you don't have to be strong', 'you don't have to hurry up', and 'you don't have to try hard' will usually release the problem with thinking or the pain in the head (tortured thoughts). As you become more familiar with the patient you may find there are usually only one or two of the permissions required to release the pressure of having to perform, and you can go right back into the story or a different story, and as Erickson used to do, you may lead in by talking about "the value of interrupted learning."

If you are sensing pains in the lower back or the genitals that you would not have if your patient were not in the room you can assume strong sexual injunctions on the part of the patient and begin telling those kind of stories. This may all sound rather strange to someone who has not developed sensory awareness but with each day a psychoanalyst practices they can get a little closer to being able to do this kind of work. Of course, after analysts get basic training in this method, they may not feel confident in using it in the office. This would be a mistake. I remember the first patient I worked with in this way. I mentioned my unusual experience with Dr. Erickson and he said "Something is missing." I said, "What's that?" He said, "You're not doing it". I said, "I don't know how to do it." He said, "Go ahead. Take a chance. I trust you." And so it was that I told my first group of stories and lasted for five minutes. I was so excited and enthused. I practiced and practiced, session after session. I began to be able to tell stories from my unconscious to the unconscious of the patient that lasted ten minutes, then fifteen, then fifty, then two hours. Once, I did it for two three hour segments in a row (6 hrs.) in one day. It all started out with five minutes.

ACCESS TO THE UNCONSCIOUS

There are some problems in developing such a method. First, there is quite a resistance to sluggishness or feeling sluggish about maintaining the kind of energy and clarity required to do the work. This can be conquered by sheer effort at not giving in to the lazy sleepy feeling. (Similar to how analysts feel when ending off Friday and having to take the crust off the unconscious when beginning Monday's session.

Second, there is the problem of intuition, or paying attention to what you don't know that you know, as Erickson might say. Intuition, a sense about a patient, may cue the next story that you will tell. As a psychoanalyst continues to learn to trust intuition and unconscious occurings that become available almost in a stream of access to the unconscious, so the art form of reverse analysis via the method of storytelling at a very slow pace manifested by both Bion and Erickson will develop.

THE USE OF AUTOMATIC WRITING IN HELPING THE ANALYST

When I begin a session I usually have a purple pen and a pad. I tell some of the stories about Erickson, who always wore purple, so I use the mystical powers which can be used for patient benefit by having the purple pen. Further, it reminds me of the respect I had for my teacher who worked much in the way a Zen master might, and when I am sensing and juggling the story to invade the unconscious moment by moment in a way that I can "sense" is going to make the impact, I for some reason feel the spirit of a Viking in doing the work.

What I do is have the person begin to tell me about themselves, in whatever way they start talking, for about five minutes. During that five minutes I may jot down certain sentences, phrases, a pattern, or even verbatim paragraphs. But from the writing in the initial five minutes, automatic writing in that it is from my unconscious while I am in the state Margaret Mead told Erickson was relatively free of dis-ease and that she had only experienced in a rare African Tribe relatively free of disease and I only experienced Bion & in the presence of Bion and Erickson that a set of stories begins to weave together in my unconscious. That is the meat of what I will tell during the length of time that I work. One only knows so many stories, I suppose, and I use a lot of the same stories. Many of my stories are about Erickson's stories to me on what he thought 'good therapy' was all about, but I utilized whatever unconscious wisdom was transmitted to me and whatever unconscious wisdom of my own (at 75 years old they are mostly my own), enables me to juxtaposition the story in terms of helping that patient enhance the quality of his or her being at each moment I am telling the stories. Usually, there is at least one spot during a session_where it feels as if there is a little snap (existential shift) that occurs in the head of the therapist, which indicates a possible impact in a patient, the magnitude of which will create an existential shift in a patient's life.

Many other stories come out of my own life history, and ways I sense and intuit I can make impact at that moment of the work, and then punch it in there. (Carl Whitaker, MD trained me to invade the unconscious). Once it's in the unconscious, it can never be taken back or removed. The patient has it for good.

STORYTELLING ITSELF

Erickson once wrote to me, "Much has been said about the solid rock of truth, but little has been said about the shifting sands." The many volumes of Erickson's work are dealing with the shifting sands. The works of many analysts deal with the solid rock of truth, But I think, knowing how to shift the sands can help people who would never avail themselves to the solid rock of truth, be able to make transitions. I think to work short of being able to utilize both tools, does not give patients the best opportunity to live full lives. If one has the capacity to do so, and does not, it is clearly in "bad faith". I think the goal of an analyst's work must be to give that patient the best shot at a full life that they are able to provide. To work in "good faith" may mean you would choose not to do hypnosis with certain patients if you see they are committed to stagnation and living in bad faith. To work with these patients may only give them a tool to cop out on themselves and their lives.

Why I think psychoanalysts will be able to accept this method, is that the psychoanalyst can continue to be the thing-in-itself (Becoming 'O'), to the best of his or her ability. That is, this method of storytelling is not just a matter of hypnotic suggestion to create a hypnogogic experience that will alter or relieve some symptom instead of being the experience itself. This method of storytelling involves telling the kind of stories that make people think about 'what they want to do with their whole lives', (words Erickson used). This kind of storytelling goes for the_patient's bottom line. There are no holds barred. It is intended to move the patient's life in ways that free patients to live, grow and develop. These are the kind of stories intended to help people turn the tragic corner in their lives, and if they so choose, to avail themselves to living the kind of lives that go beyond functioning well, but approximating closer and closer levels in terms of approaching their own being, of_course, which they will never quite reach, but which is life's work.

THE PSYCHOANALYST AS A SOLID OBJECT

One of the primary issues with patients who have not turned the tragic corner in their lives, or who have not been able to maintain such a turn on any sort of consistent basis, is the issue of homicidal and suicidal primitive feelings and ways of behaving at work. These people destroy their life force in some of the most awesome ways. Further, the psychoanalyst can practically count on a good number of them trying to discredit or destroy the "good breast" that will be fed to them before that "good breast" ever touches their lips. Thus, the issue for the psychoanalyst is how to avoid being murdered so the storytelling and further therapeutic work can take place without the death instinct predominating.

To avoid being psychologically murdered the psychoanalyst must know two things. First, there must be a trust in the analysts unconscious and in the unconscious of the patient, that the patient does indeed want to get well; does indeed want to experience the benefits of what is going to be offered; and that even though the patient will do his or her best to discredit the psychoanalyst, they really want him or her to succeed. So the psychoanalyst must develop an <u>attitude of confidence, of assuredness, that the patient will get what he or she came for</u>. (Erickson said this to me!)

Second, the part of the patient that is psychologically attempting to murder off the "good breast" must be stopped. While you are attempting to help the patient on the one hand gain confidence in the wisdom of his or her unconscious mind to help provide for the well-being of self, you at the primitive level must with solidness, prove beyond the shadow of a doubt, much as would a Zen master, that the crazy part of the patient knows nothing. <u>You must prove by the evidence of who you are, what you say, the authority and respect that you command by the quality of your being, your wisdom, and your "intimidation" of the patient's crazy part, that you are the teacher and the patient is the student, and that it would be a foolish notion that the patient even venture to consider it otherwise</u>. Without doing this where required, the patient will not take you or himself seriously.

Next, the psychoanalyst must <u>be enough on top of the life force of self that the psychoanalyst is convincing</u>. That is, when life force stories are told, the analyst must be believable. There must be an authenticity that is conveyed in terms of the quality of being of who that psychoanalyst is.

<u>TENACITY</u>

I remember being a freshman or sophomore in college and being an excellent ping pong player. I had the capacity to hang tough in the clutch and if the score was 18 to 18 I knew I would win at least eight out of ten because I wouldn't fold under the pressure. At this time I remember playing a young fellow who played eight hours per day, and who was ranked third nationally in the boy's division. He did win but something he said has always stuck with me. I had a rather awkward style one would learn by playing backyard ping pong while he had a style that was very professional. But he said, "You are very tough to beat. You play every point as if it's the game."

When dealing with the homicidal and suicidal primitive phenomena of patient's it is critical to be able to maintain this attitude. It is critical that you not give into discouragement or defeatism, especially at times when patients feel it is hopeless. There is a difference between going with the hopelessness as a therapeutic strategy and actually giving in to feeling whipped. It is only this kind of spirit, constancy, and tenacity in terms of the psychoanalyst's maintenance of life force in the face of the patient's spiritlessness as well as homicidal and suicidal terror that can calm and cure the patient suffering such a plight.

THE STORIES THEMSELVES

When telling stories, particularly when beginning with a patient the story should encompass the kind of struggle from which the patient suffers. The story should have a beginning that metaphorically, and sometimes concretely as well, deals with the patient's difficulty in turning the tragic corner in his or her life. By concretely, I mean it may also deal with the particular problem that would focus the attention of the conscious mind. For example, the following story has two main themes. The first, and the basic reason it can be told to anyone as one of the first stories, is that it deals with the difficulty of becoming the kind of person who will build his or her life upon the solid rock of truth. If this does not make a significant enough impact, when patient's cheat, you never know when the devil is going to move the fence. This is the_kind of issue that all people face in their lives-how to become solid, honest upstanding people who live their lives with integrity.

The second issue is a specific one that would make the story particularly valuable for overeaters. The interesting phenomena when telling such a story is in hearing the patient's response sometime later regarding what part of the story got through to the unconscious mind and effected a change in their lives.

A BEGINNING STORY-THE NAZIS AND THE CONCENTRATION CAMP

I worked with a minister who was in Nazi Germany during World War II. The minister was working with a group of people, all of whom were overeaters. Every one of these people, right down to the last one said, 'they couldn't stop themselves from eating'. Subsequently the Nazis captured the minister and all the members of his group and put them in a concentration camp. The Nazis fed them only bread and water. Day after day, only bread and water. Further, the Nazis had lavish meals. They had the finest meats, steaks, fish, potatoes, green beans, and the most luxurious pastries. They had such an abundance of food they could not eat it all. So they put their leftovers, which were both quite significant in quantity and quality on the inside of the prisoners' side of the fence, only they used the area for target practice. The minister said, it was the most amazing thing he ever saw. In all the years they were in the concentration camp, with all the food that was there, steaks, fish, pastries, vegetable, potatoes, chicken, roast pork, roast beef,-all the finest delicacies included, not once did he ever see even one member of this group, all of whom said they couldn't stop themselves from eating, not once, did any member of the group ever touch one piece of food. He went on, in amazement, again saying, that each member of the group said "they couldn't stop themselves from eating." The minister said he made a decision when they were all released from concentration camp after the war, that from that time on, he was only going to work with honest people".

I told this story to one overweight patient, and months later when he was significantly thinner he said, "That story you told me about the concentration camp with all that food. Every time I went to eat more than I should I saw those bullets coming at me. I could hear the sound of them and feel them whistling by. Those bullets stopped me cold" The interesting thing is that I didn't mention the bullets. This was a creation of his unconscious mind which helped him to do a job he needed to do. It was what my story evoked in his unconscious that permitted his unconscious to come up with the thoughts, memories, feelings and actions it had, to help him live a happier and healthier life. Further, he said he could hear the bullets and feel them whistling by. So he was telling me that I reached him at the auditory and kinesthetic levels. I never tried to do this strategically, because I felt the strategy would get in the way of the thing-in-itself, that is, the quality of my own being. But I always trusted that if I was in tune with my unconscious and the unconscious of the patient, I would tune in on the appropriate wave lengths to reach him, and get a high hard fastball, or at least a curveball through to the unconscious of the patient so that the patient's own evoked resources would provide the necessary existential shift-in helping that patient live his or her life more healthily and more happily.

A CREATIVE STORY-BRER RABBIT

I made this one up as I was going along. I had a patient who came to me after a seven year analysis. He was president of a multi-million dollar corporation, wanted to think of himself as a nice man, and therefore had a difficult time acknowledging the homicidal feelings that were occurring during the high powered and very stressful executive meetings, over several hours duration. His complaint was that he stopped breathing because he was so tense. During the sessions he was a lot of fun to work with because his mind flowed so freely. When working with neophytes who have never had an experience that helps patients make connections quickly with their unconscious, the work would be more tedious than when working with this fellow. Further, the man was highly stressed and was projecting this stress onto me as if to say, "Dammit! Hurry up and do something! I need a cure and I need it fast!"

Well, of course, this isn't the way cure happens. It happens slowly, so the first thought I had was to slow the man down and just keep telling stories at a very slow and monotonous pace. I knew his feeling would be that he couldn't stand it, and that my work would perhaps increase both his toleration and patience-although I had to be ready to stand an assault. Further, while he was president of the corporation I didn't think he felt comfortable using power.

The images that came to my mind were of "Uncle Remus who was sitting on his rocking chair singing zip id dee do dah, zip pid ee aee, oh mister blue bird, just ah singing away. zip pid ee do dah, zip id ee aeh". This was from a movie entitled "Song of the South" put out by Walt Disney when I was a little boy. But for some reason, in the depths of my unconscious mind, there was this totally relaxed Uncle Remus without a care in the world-a lovable character indeed, just singing away, unaffected by any pressure. Next, I began to tell stories about Brer Bear, Brer Fox, and Brer Rabbit. Amidst these what I thought to be irrelevant and time wasting stories, I would make the comment, "It's good to be King!". The image of a Mel Brooks movie, "The Creation of the World, Part I", came to mind where Mel Brooks, in his own zany way, kept making this statement, "It's good to be King!"

Prior to this session, the week before, I made up the following story. "People are like flies. They just keep buzzing around. BZZZZ. BZZZZZ. And your problem is that you don't have a big enough fly swatter. Now can you imagine having a huge fly swatter and seeing these people buzzing around. Bzzzz. Bzzzz. Now can you imagine yourself just smashing these people off the walls and seeing them splatter!"

I felt this story would evoke and have him enjoy his homicidal fantasies about people, who he saw as gnats who were always pestering him, who would never leave him alone, who he perpetually wanted to get away from. When he awakened from trance, and during the trance I had put in the suggestion of amnesia as an option, so if he felt he couldn't tolerate the awareness at a conscious level, it could remain at the unconscious level, he said, "I didn't remember a thing that happened. I just had a sense that this session was a total waste of time and that you are a crazy man." However, he said "crazy man" with the implication that he enjoyed both my creativity and my willingness to give free expression to what frightened him so much in himself. Also, he seemed appreciative I gave him the opportunity to have an amnesia if he felt he could not tolerate the feelings during the session.

Now back to the Brer Rabbit session. About mid-way during the session, as the patient's impatience and hurriedness mounted to an explosive level, he woke up out of trance, and screamed at the top of his lungs, "Bergantino, you are a maniac!", to which my response was to continue on telling stories about Uncle Remus, Brer Rabbit, Brer Bear and Brer Fox, as if he had never come out of trance and as if the incident never occurred. In retrospect, I think my ability to contain this outburst without any discomfort whatsoever made him feel safe with these feelings in himself. Second, I did not fold, but remained constant in not buying into his hurry-up drivenness. The remainder of the session went on uneventfully.

When the patient returned the following week, as I was seeing him one time per week, he reported the following: "You are not going to believe what happened. I was at one of these stressful six hour board meetings. It was about forty five minutes into the meeting and I felt the pressure mounting and I was holding my breath. I screamed at the top of my lungs, while I looked fiercely into the eyes of the other six board members, "Brer Rabbit!", while pounding my fist on the table and keeping a straight face-a deadly serious look! The other board members were in total shock, and I just played right over it as if it hadn't happened. When they asked what was the matter I said, "Oh, nothing. Nothing. Let's just get on with the meeting." Three hours later I did it again. Again, I told them, "Oh, it's nothing" and proceeded on with the meeting. It felt good to feel powerful. "It's good to be King!" Then I told my wife about it. A few days later we all got together for an important business function and a couple of the executives came up to my wife and said, "Have you heard about", and before they could finish she with a straight face said, "Oh, you mean Brer Rabbit." And in a rather apologetic tone said, "I don't want to talk about it".

Now the thing about this unconscious storytelling is you never can figure out exactly what a patient's unconscious mind is going to give them as a solution to the problem, but it certainly can prove to be interesting!

A SEXY SUPERVISION STORY: A release of Psychosexual Inhibitions in one session via Reverse Analysis of both the patient and the supervisor.

I had a woman therapist call me to have me see a woman patient that she was seeing for one hypnosis session. The woman therapist was dressed in black in very matronly garb. Outside of saying hello and good bye I said nothing to her at the conscious level. Her patient was about 26 years old, looked very masculine, and said she wanted to get to deeper levels.

I began to tell a story about Freud. "You know Freud knew what it was all about. He said it all had to do with sex. He wrote about sex. He spoke about sex. You know, with that Oedipal thing, and that Electra Complex, and it was hard to tell who was who and what was what, and even then, it was intolerable. Why Freud went to a scientific meeting in 1903 among his colleagues and he started to speak of his ideas about sex in this very professional jargon, and they knew what he was talking about. One of his colleagues jumped up in fury yelling, 'This is not a matter for a scientific convention. This is a matter for the police!" Well, admittedly things were pretty hot in Freud's day when it came to sex, but it's just as hot an issue today.

I keep referring to "hot" to connect her up sexually while dealing with the countertransference issue that the therapist was functioning as the police. Then I went on to tell a story about a patient who had "very kissable lips", while I looked the patient right in the eye in a way that was both fatherly and appreciative of her femininity. I told her another story, the punchline being that every time she went into a restaurant and saw a bottle of 'red ketchup' this would unconsciously pair her with sexual thoughts and feelings.

I received a note from her therapist a week later saying that her patient showed up for the next therapy session with a new hairstyle, "a permanent", and was wearing a stylish new red outfit. The insight from the one session and the solidness with which I dealt with them; even the outrageous quality, was quite freeing to the patient in getting the courage to challenge her therapist where they both were suffering from sexual inhibition.

The therapist said that I had given her a great deal with which to think about and to continue her work.

Each of these sessions had the characteristic of my utilizing outrageous unconscious material that was freeing, or in the first story about the Nazis and the concentration camp, aiding with necessary self-control and self-discipline. Further, there is the characteristic of juxtapositioning to get the football through the defensive line so to speak, or get the unconscious material to reach the unconscious mind of the patient. In each case, only one such insight caused an existential shift in the person's way of living life. Whether it be "the bullets", "Brer_Rabbit!, or the "Red Catchup", all the psychoanalyst needs to do is tell the stories from the therapist's unconscious in a way that empathically tunes into the crisis of that patient's life at that moment in time, and sooner or later, one impactful insight will get through to move that_patient's life.

REFERENCE NOTE

Erickson, M.H. Personal communication wherever his name is mentioned between the dates of September 11, 1977 and the time of his death in March, 1980.

REFERENCE

Hammond, D.C. Myths About Erickson and Ericksonian Hypnosis. American Journal of Clinical Hypnosis, 1984, 26, 236-245.

ARTICLES EXEMPLIFYING THE STORYTELLING AS WELL AS VERBATIM COMMENTARY FROM TWO MINI-WORKSHOP DEMONSTRATIONS

(Analyzing fragments of thought & restoration of sense perception via transformations of being)

During the early phases of the work I thought of it as hypnosis and described it as such in these articles and workshops. However, the process is "reverse psychoanalysis" and it was never learned by anyone practicing hypnosis other than Erickson used to tell stories four and one half hours at a time at this slow pace and Bion used to make paragraph long psychoanalytic interpretations at the same pace. It gives one a control over the entire psychoanalytic environment in which the possibility of transformations in being are much more likely to occur, as well as a restoration of sense perception in those where it was destroyed as children. This restoration is the sina quo non of being able to do psychoanalysis in working with underlying psychotic thinking disorders because it is the sense perception that is the first step toward identifying & analyzing fragments of thought.

I will start by showing you the short articles to give a more easy to integrate frame of reference of how it is done; and then move onto the longer more difficult to follow workshop format that looks like a bunch of run on sentences but they are stated in perfect sensory timing to the participants in the room, and their unconscious psychophysiological processes.

First is "Hypnotic Storytelling As An Unconscious Supervisory Process", initially published in The American Society of Clinical Hypnosis Newsletter, October, 1984, Volume XXVI, No. 1. The second is Successful Hypnosis in the Treatment of Hyperemesis Gravidarum, The American Society of Clinical Hypnosis Newsletter, March, 1985, Vol. XXVI, No. 3.

The fourth is a non-published audio tape transcription of a one and one half hour demonstration of non-stop storytelling I gave to an abnormal psychology class at the University of Southern California on January 8, 1983.

It teaches Ericksonian storytelling as a basis for Reverse Psychoanalysis.

The fifth is a two hour demonstration of Ericksonian Storytelling in the Dept. of Sociology at the University of Southern California with social work students learning psychotherapy. There was one woman at this session who volunteered to work as patient in a demonstration who was appalled and nauseated at Erickson being a cripple and she reported she could not stand cripples. By the end of this work there was a transformation in that she had a great deal of internal strength for cripples, realizing that while Erickson was a cripple who suffered from polio, arthritis and a variety of other maladies, he was a powerhouse of strength in many other ways. Somehow this rubbed off on her insides as a result of the storytelling, as well as her unconscious mind. In other words the changes brought about were insightful and visceral at the same time. (A subject-object merger). Me being the subject—her the object.

The third is an article entitled Overcoming Test Performance Anxiety published in The Southern California Society of Clinical Hypnosis Newsletter, August, 1985.

All these articles exemplified "reverse psychoanalysis", a method of storytelling from the unconscious mind of the analyst to the unconscious mind of the patient or group of trainees-based on the pathological projective identifications those patients and trainees emitted to and effected the unconscious mind and psychophysiological processes of the analyst.

The "Sexy Supervision Story" is an example of a one session turnaround in a lifelong personality characteristic of a patient and her therapist.

Len Bergantino, Ed.D., Ph.D. 450 N. Bedford Drive, St. 300 Beverly Hills, CA 90210 (213) 273-8705	}	Primary office where I did psychoanalysis from 1981-1991.

OVERCOMING TEST PERFORMANCE ANXIETY

by Len Bergantino, Ed.D., Ph.D.

450 N. Bedford Drive, Suite 30
Beverly Hills, California 90210

Private Practice of Clinical Psychology

p. 130 b

A young female of twenty six came to me after an unsuccessful bout of three months with law school, a year layoff, and now, an acceptance and beginning of medical school. She was a bundle of anxiety covered by skin and her guts were like jelly. Each time there was an examination she was certain she was going to flunk it and would call me in a panic for an extra hypnotherapy session.

The problem was in providing a stable gut level environment for her. I told her hypnotic tales about my own fear of statistics as a graduate student. I told her about my very hard work to compensate for my fears; the extra tutoring I received from the student across the hall in the dormitory; and the ten hour examination with ninety two problems. Further I told her I was convinced this course would flunk me out of the doctoral program and felt tremendous pressure. When the final grade postcard came back in the mail I had ninety out of ninety-two problems correct and an A plus for the course. I thought the student across the hall was playing a joke on me, but when I asked him, he was as shocked as me, as he got a B plus for the course. I realized after this life long mathematics block and fear of being tested, that if I plugged away at it I could pass any examination.

In the storytelling the part of the story that created the existential shift in the woman's perspective and ability to perform is underlined.

I presented a personal story at a hypnotic pace that was very calming. It had the elements of fear, struggle, and overcoming the fear and struggle by hard work and determination upon which success and further self confidence would be built.

This set the reframing of the patient seeing herself performing with superior qualities in herself which she had refused to own due to her own anxiety about test taking as well as fear of abandonment.

Also, I put in the suggestion of creativity on the part of my instructor - who drew the mean, median and mode by comparing different ice creams of the month, and when I least realized it, statistics had gotten into my unconscious mind without my even knowing it. So I set up an unconscious fail safe in addition to conscious success. The certainty I had as a hypnotist was internalized and helped the student have the 'guts' for the task, particularly in

(Please turn page)....

THE AMERICAN SOCIETY OF CLINICAL HYPNOSIS NEWSLETTER

March, 1985 Vol. XXVI, No. 3

in a lifelong personality characteristic of a patient.

For hypnosis or training in hypnosis contact

Len Bergantino, Ed.D., Ph.D.
450 N. Roxbury Drive, St.30
Beverly Hills, CA 90210
(213) 273-8705

Len Bergantino, Ed.D., Ph.D., has presented Ericksonian Storytelling and Teaching Tale methods as part of a workshop in training marital and family therapists at the International Gestalt Institute of Australia in Brisbane, Australia. Further, he has recently been selected to the Board of Directors of the Southern California Society of Clinical Hypnosis.

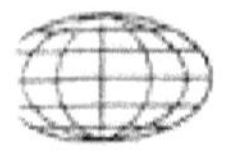

OCTOBER 1984
VOLUME XXVI, Number 1

The American Society of Clinical Hypnosis

Clinical Corner Interesting Case Reports

HYPNOTIC STORYTELLING AS AN UNCONSCIOUS SUPERVISORY PROCESS

Len Bergantino, Ed.D., Ph.D.

A therapist asked for a consultation for hypnosis for her therapy patient, and requested that she be present. While she did not state it clearly, this was a request at the unconscious level to help the therapist with sexual countertransference issues that were blocking the patient's growth. The patient stated that she wanted hypnosis to help her 'peel an onion', getting to deeper levels. It was agreed from the onset that it was going to be one session.

The patient complained of being stuck in the past, feeling like a four year old. She recalled an incident of wetting her pants, following her teacher around screaming. She complained of washing her hands all the time - "everything was dirty and the intensity gets worse during my period". She complained of washing her hands forty times per day, living in fear of being an adult, and feelings of chronic emptiness and of being "stuck". The patient's therapist sat quietly throughout the session.

The hypnotic method entailed my looking at the patient and the therapist, getting an impression of them, and then tuning into my unconscious and doing what might be referred to as a "reverse analysis", that is, an insight oriented hypnotic storytelling where the insights occur indirectly relating to both what was going on with the patient and the countertransference problem that existed between the patient and her therapist. However, this entire process was metaphorical, and dealt with at the unconscious level. The method is an indirect metaphorical method of hypnosis that is experienced solely as hypnosis by the patient, while at the unconscious level it serves the dual function of being both hypnosis to the patient and supervision regarding countertransference issues for the therapist. The supervisory aspects are not at all obvious, because stories were told only to the patient, the therapist was spoken to directly only upon entering and leaving.

The metaphors I tell revolve around my work with Milton H. Erickson, M.D. I tell stories about him much as Carlos Castenada wrote about The Tales of Don Juan, only using unconscious specificity depending on the patient or the group to determine which story, which inflection, which pace, the particular wording and reframing, etc. So the same story is never told the same way twice, and always has a purpose that is intended for the unique personality or personalities being treated.

Sensing this woman was quite fearful, I set up the metaphor of amnesia, telling two stories about two patients who had an amnesia, but were cured. One was about a next door neighbor of mine who was a doctor, using hypnosis in medical capacities. The woman was in the midst of making difficult choices in terms of her husband's employment being out of California, not knowing if she should give up a job she liked very much in California, having two children, and going to see Dr. Erickson to learn more about hypnosis for professional reasons. I said that I was curious about her work with Dr. Erickson, but when I asked her she said the strangest thing happened - "I can't remember anything that happened during the entire week I was there. The only thing that is different is that every time I go into a restaurant and see a bottle of red catchup, I have a visual image of Dr. Erickson and I taking a hot jacuzzi together". Then I said, can you believe that? She had an amnesia for everything else, and all her problems were resolved. She moved out of state, has a nice ranch, enjoys her work, is a good mother to her children, and enjoys her husband, and the only thing she remembered was a bottle of red catchup! I told one other Erickson story, the punchline being, "and he looked at this 26 year old woman, and said - take it from an authoritarian old man like me that you have very kissable lips". To deal with the resistance I said Dr. Erickson was always concerned about the conscious and the unconscious mind. This woman's conscious mind tended to discount her unconscious wisdom, and as she got up to leave she said, "But Dr. Erickson, how is that going to help me stop coughing and sleep tonight?" Dr. Erickson turned over his right shoulder and began to sing, with his paralyzed lips and dislocated tongue, "The lip bone is connected to the cheek bone, and the cheek bone is connected to the neck bone, and the neck bone is connected to the chest bone", and then he turned around to the group with an all-knowing chuckle and said that *he knew* that Barbara would sleep very well that night. (The patient's original complaint was an asthma attack and up all night coughing, but I generalized the certainty that the red catchup and kissable lip metaphore would get the sexual job done.

When the patient came to see me she looked sexless and masculine. When I asked her at the end of the session if there was anything she wanted to say, she said she had the realization that she could just change, and she didn't have to wait a long time or suffer a lot to do it. When I asked the therapist if there were any thoughts or feelings she had, she said, "Only that you have given me a great deal with which to think about and continue my work", indicating that there had been a shift in the therapist's countertransference relationship to the patient. Later, the woman's therapist reported to me that the patient showed up for her next session with a new hairstyle, "a permanent", and was wearing a stylish new red outfit.

When the patient was leaving my office, her conscious doubts took over and she asked, "Can one hypnosis session make a difference?" I firmly and with gusto and challenge replied, "You only had to be born once, didn't you?" The patient replied, "Yes"

THE AMERICAN SOCIETY OF CLINICAL HYPNOSIS NEWSLETTER
March, 1985 Vol. XXVI, No. 3

129

Clinical Corner Interesting Case Reports

Successful Hypnosis in the Treatment of Hyperemesis Gravidarum
by Len Bergantino, Ed.D., Ph.D.

The following report exemplifies successful utilization of storytelling as a method of hypnotherapy with a life threatening situation - in this case, the life of an unborn baby. The question presented by the patient, a pregnant woman, was whether she was going to have yet another abortion because she could not tolerate excessive vomiting. The treatment was brief, taking only three weeks. Of course, the method described here may not always work, but when there are no clear-cut alternatives, Ericksonian hypnotherapy via storytelling is something physicians may want to consider.

It is the job of the doctor to have the skills to build confidence on the first meeting, and to set up a failproof system which puts the appropriate degree of responsibility in the hands of the doctor and helps the patient come to trust both his or her own unconscious mind and the doctor. The doctor can set the proper frame by establishing rapport with the patient, enlisting the conscious mind as a cooperative companion, and setting up the conscious-unconscious way of thinking so the patient gets used to the idea that much of the work done by the doctor may not be understood by the conscious mind, but will be understood by the unconscious mind (even though the conscious mind doesn't know that it knows).

Further, for the first twenty minutes of the first session I did a diagnostic assessment of both the patient and her husband, who was forced to accompany her to the session due to her nausea, overall fatigue, and condition of severe vomiting. Rapport was established both with the patient and her husband. The husband only attended the first session, as the patient was able to get a ride from other members of the family who waited in the waiting room.

The Treatment of Hyperemesis Gravidarum

This condition involves excessive vomiting beyond the first three months of pregnancy. A physician referred this patient, who reported vomiting seventeen times per day. She said this condition existed with a prior pregnancy which she was forced to abort because of her inability to tolerate the vomiting. She feared that if the excessive vomiting and nausea was not helped by hypnosis, that she would need to have another abortion.

After the initial diagnostic work, I began to tell stories at a very slow soothing and relaxing pace for the remainder of the fifty minute hour during the first session, and for the full fifty minutes of each ensuing session. It is important to begin to use the hypnosis during the first session because the patient is suffering and the most human thing the therapist can do is to begin to provide the condition of relief as soon as possible. This patient was straightforward, cooperative and appreciative of the relief she felt both during the session and for the remainder of the day or days between sessions.

There are situations where patients are so overcontrolled that the therapist may have to postpone utilizing hypnosis during the first session until the part of the patient that wants to deny the therapist a success is put in checkmate. However, this was not the case with this patient. I saw her four times the first week, four times the second week and once the Monday of the third week, and her vomiting and nausea stopped.

The dynamics were clear during our work. She had a death instinct that prevailed over her life force, and she was quite mistrustful and at times hateful of her husband, despite her conscious report that things were fine between them.

So my stories were geared to the dynamics of life force: a variety of stories where people would do things they enjoyed that were pleasant, stories about babies and the sense of abandonment they had when they took their first step, and perhaps she could remember how she looked as a baby and how it felt to be held. A second set of stories were geared to the enjoyment of hatred of people, the problems people caused, how Sartre said "Hell is Others", and how she could think of the fun and enjoyment in hating her husband at times. This helped her accept her own degree of hatred and anger and to not punish herself for feeling that way. With the relief of her self hatred, plus the introjection of life force via the life force stories, the vomiting stopped and the nausea was significantly reduced so that she could tolerate the pregnancy.

The telling of the stories at a slow pace using as velvet a touch as I was capable, to create the physiological sensation of well being, and the psychodynamics of the stories geared to the patient's unconscious mind, seems to have created one "insight" or release after another in freeing that patient from the places in which her mind was locked. This combination was responsible for her call six months later, telling me with great joy and excitement that she had a beautiful baby girl and thanking me for helping her.

FOR TRAINING IN HYPNOSIS CONTACT: LEN BERGANTINO, ED.D., ABPP
DIPLOMATE IN FAMILY PSYCHOLOGY - AMERICAN BOARD OF PROFESSIONAL PSYCHOLOGY
CERTIFIED AND APPROVED CONSULTANT-AMERICAN SOCIETY OF CLINICAL HYPNOSIS
TRAINED BY MILTON H. ERICKSON, M.D. (1977-1980) + CARL WHITAKER, M.D.(1981-82)
12301 Wilshire Blvd., Ste. 300, Los Angeles, CA 90025 Tel. (310) 207-8818

Author: HOW MASTER CLINICIANS INTERVENE, Jason Aronson Publ. N.J.

Doctorate -University of Southern California - 1971.

FOR TRAINING IN HYPNOSIS CONTACT: LEN BERGANTINO, ED.D., ABPP

DIPLOMATE IN FAMILY PSYCHOLOGY-AMERICAN BOARD OF PROFESSIONAL PSYCHOLOGY

CERTIFIED AND APPROVED CONSULTANT-AMERICAN SOCIETY OF CLINICAL HYPNOSIS

TRAINED BY MILTON H. ERICKSON, M.D. (1977-1980) + CARL WHITAKER, M.D. (1981-82) Mentored by from 1982-1994)

12301 Wilshire Blvd., Ste. 300, Los Angeles, CA 90025 Tel. (310) 207-8818. Office and telephone from 1991-1996 - Post Analysis.

Author: HOW MASTER CLINICIANS INTERVENE, Jason Aronson Publ, N.J.

Doctorate-University of Southern California-1971.

Southern California Society of Clinical Hypnosis
COMPONENT OF THE AMERICAN SOCIETY OF CLINICAL HYPNOSIS
8151 W. CENTURY BOULEVARD • SUITE 1114 • LOS ANGELES, CALIFORNIA 90045

P. 130 a/ August 1, 1985
No. 1/85

"OFF TO SEE THE WIZARD"
by Len Bergantino, Ed.D., Ph.D.

A title meant with the utmost respect for my teacher, Milton H. Erickson, M.D. - and not dissimilar to the patient's first call and expectation for hypnosis. I called, telling Milton I wanted to see him individually the weekend of September 11, 1977. He said, "Let me look at my book" - (pause) - There's a small group coming that day, but come - you'll get what you want."

I had all the ambivalence of anyone making that call for hypnosis. His response was so confident. He was so sure of himself. But how does he know what I want? Well, he is the doctor. That comment was said so solidly in answer to a question every patient wants to know, "Doctor, can you help me?" that I decided to go off to see the wizard.

I learned - patients making the first call want reassurance and they want the message delivered with conviction.

BERGANTINO CASE REPORT - OVERCOMING TEST PERFORMANCE ANXIETY - ENCLOSED

Len Bergantino, Ed.D., Ph.D., became internationally renowned when he presented Ericksonian Storytelling and Teaching Tale methods as a part of a workshop in training marital and family therapists at the International Gestalt Institute of Australia in Brisbane, Australia last summer. (Members who were present at our first meeting last September will recall his fascinating presentation on this subject). Len is not only a practicing psychologist in Beverly Hills but a prolific and thought provoking writer. A case report on his methods was printed in the "Clinical Corner" of ASCH Journal of Hypnosis, October 1984, and we are privileged to enclose another of his case reports with this Update.

* * * *

OVERCOMING TEST PERFORMANCE ANXIETY

A young female of twenty six came to me after an unsuccessful bout of three months with law school, a year layoff, and now, an acceptance and beginning of medical school. She was a bundle of anxiety covered by skin and her guts were like jelly. Each time there was an examination she was certain she was going to flunk it and would call me in a panic for an extra hypnotherapy session.

The problem was in providing a stable gut level environment for her. I told her hypnotic tales about my own fear of statistics as a graduate student. I told her about my very hard work to compensate for my fears; the extra tutoring I received from the student across the hall in the dormitory; and the ten hour examination with ninety two problems. Further I told her I was convinced this course would flunk me out of the doctoral program and felt tremendous pressure. When the final grade postcard came back in the mail I had ninety out of ninety-two problems correct and an A plus for the course. I realized after this life long mathematics block and fear of being tested, that if I plugged away at it I could pass the examination.

13092

In the storytelling the part of the story that created the existential shift in the woman's perspective and ability to perform is underlined.

I presented a personal story at a hypnotic pace that was very calming. It had the elements of fear, struggle, and overcoming the fear and struggle by hard work and determination upon which success and further self confidence would be built.

This set the reframing of the patient seeing herself performing with superior qualities in herself which she had refused to own due to her own anxiety about test taking as well as fear of abandonment.

Also, I put in the suggestion of creativity on the part of my instructor - who drew the mean, median and mode by comparing different ice creams of the month, and when I least realized it, statistics had gotten into my unconscious mind without my even knowing it. So I set up an unconscious fail safe in addition to conscious success. The certainty I had as a hypnotist was internalized and helped the student have the 'guts' for the task, particularly in reducing her fear of abandonment and its effect on test taking behavior. That is, she had the fears of a little girl who would be abandoned by her parents if she did poorly on tests.

The result was that she passed her coursework during the first year of medical school to enable her to enter the second year. Last time I saw her she was entering her third year, still with success. Her anxiety was reduced and her recall, attention and concentration were able to occur in accord with her full access to her capabilities. Further, this increased her motivation to succeed.

A storytelling method of hypnosis based on the fears, struggles, and test taking success of the hypnotherapist as a constant and solid object, can relieve test taking anxiety, increases performance in terms of recall, attention and concentration, and develop the belief in self and attitude of success that builds upon itself as well as giving the patient the steadiness of 'guts' to handle what is thrown at her in the line of fire.

* * * * * * * *

by Len Bergantino, Ed.D., Ph.D.
450 N. Bedford Drive, Suite 300
Beverly Hills, CA 90210
Private Practice of Clinical Psychology

* TRAINING FOR PROFESSIONALS IN HYPNOTIC TEACHING TALES
2nd Sat. of each month, 10 a.m.-12 noon -$40

*WORKSHOPS ARE OFFERED throughout the United States and Internationally.

OVERCOMING TEST PERFORMANCE ANXIETY

by Len Bergantino, Ed.D., Ph.D. 450 N. Bedford Drive, Suite 300 Beverly Hills, California 90210 Private Practice of Clinical Psychology (1981-1991)

Primarily Psychoanalysis with some clinical hypnosis influenced by Milton H Erickson, MD. and some Family Therapy, influenced by Carl Whitaker, M.D. Both of whom trained me and had my utmost respect!

■■ ■

A young female of twenty six came to me after an unsuccessful bout of three months with law school, a year layoff, and now, an acceptance and beginning of medical school. She was a bundle of anxiety covered by skin and her guts were like jelly. Each time there was an examination she was certain she was going to flunk it and would call me in a panic for an extra hypnotherapy session.

The problem was in providing a stable gut level environment for her. I told her hypnotic tales about my own fear of statistics as a graduate student. I told her about my very hard work to compensate for my fears; the extra tutoring I received from the student across the hall in the dormitory; and the ten hour examination with ninety two problems. Further I told her I was convinced this course would flunk me out of the doctoral program and felt tremendous pressure. When the final grade postcard came back in the mail I had ninety out of ninety-two problems correct and an A plus for the course. I thought the student across the hall was playing a joke on me, but when I asked him, he was as shocked as me, as he got a B plus for the course. I realized after this lifelong mathematics block and fear of being tested, that if I plugged away at it I could pass any examination.

In the storytelling the part of the story that created the existential shift in the woman's perspective and ability to perform is underlined.

I presented a personal story at a hypnotic pace that was very calming. It had the elements of fear, struggle, and overcoming the fear and struggle by hard work and determination upon which success and further self-confidence would be built.

This set the reframing of the patient seeing herself performing with superior qualities in herself which she had refused to own due to her own anxiety about test taking as well as fear of abandonment.

Also, I put in the suggestion of creativity on the part of my instructor-who drew the mean, median and mode by comparing different ice creams of the month, and when I least realized it, statistics had gotten into my unconscious mind without my even knowing it. So I set up an unconscious fail safe in addition to conscious success. The certainty I had as a hypnotist was internalized and helped the student have the 'guts' for the task, particularly in reducing her fear of abandonment and its effect on test taking behavior. That is, she had the fears of a little girl who would be abandoned by her parents if she did poorly on tests.

The result was that she passed her coursework during the first year of medical school to enable her to enter the second year. Last time I saw her she was entering her third year, still with success. Her anxiety was reduced and her recall, attention and concentration were able to occur in accord with her full access to her capabilities. Further, this increased her motivation to succeed.

A storytelling method of hypnosis based on the fears, struggles, and test taking success of the hypnotherapist, along with the introjection on the part of the patient of the hypnotherapist as a constant and solid object, can relieve test taking anxiety, increase performance in terms of recall, attention and concentration, and develop the belief in self and attitude of success that builds upon itself as well as giving the patient the steadiness of 'guts' to handle what is thrown at her in the line of fire.

# # # #

Article 4 & 5 Transcribes could not understand the words. It was left as is rather than manufactured.

JANUARY 8, 1983

ONE AND ONE HALF HOUR DEMONSTRATION OF NON-STOP STORYTELLING

in abnormal psychology class at University of Southern California I remember working with Dr. Erickson and it's rare that Erickson would work with a patient in his old age. He was basically trained as a psychiatrist and psychologist but I did have the good fortune to see him work with a woman named Barbara. Barbara called up in a crisis. Erickson always found a way to meet the needs of a person in a crisis. He told her to come right over. And she did. He asked her if she wanted to be hypnotized and she said she did. While she was in trance for about 40 minutes. At the end of that time her eyes opened and she said "but Dr. Erickson how is this going to help me stop coughing and sleep tonight?" Erickson looked at her and he said "Take it from an authoritarian old man like me that you have very kissable lips!" Barbara just beamed. Erickson had touched her heart. Women need that to feel like women. Otherwise they can't give it back to men. I remember a woman physician who lived next door to me, she worked at Children's Hospital. It was leukemia patients-children. She was a very quick hypnotist. Used to be able to help them when they were vomiting and gagging. And her husband worked at UCLA in cancer research. But he was unhappy there. He didn't have the proper research laboratory. UCLA reneged on the minimum conditions necessary for him to live a happy and full life employment wise. So he went and he found two jobs at the University of Texas Medical School. But his wife liked her job at

Children's Hospital-Los Angeles. Of course Dr. Erickson was living at this time. And whenever there was a worthy cause he would take time out of his busy schedule to meet the demands. She got the entire staff at Children's Hospital of psychologists, psychiatrists and MD's who had to use hypnosis call Erickson up and Erickson took a full week out of his schedule. Erickson was certainly a fascinating, powerful therapist. And I was very curious about what had happened for the entire week. So I asked her and she said "I can't remember." She said "the only thing I know is that every time I see a bottle of red ketchup in a restaurant I have this image of Dr. Erickson and myself taking a hot jacuzzi together." Now who would have ever thought that a woman struggling at which job she should stay with Children's Hospital or Texas, or should she go with her husband, or should she stay here and live her life by herself? What about her professional identity? She had two children. The issue of parenting. Being a single parent, being married. Moving to a new place she didn't know if she would like it. She didn't know if she would make it. She liked what she had in some ways. Her husband didn't. With all these issues she would have thought she would ever say to me. Erickson often used amnesia state. So, the only thing her unconscious mind knew was that every time she saw a bottle of red ketchup she would see herself with Erickson in a jacuzzi. A hot jacuzzi. Another therapist I sent to see Erickson had a similar experience. He was there for 2 1/2 days and he said the only thing he could remember about it was as he was leaving Erickson had a bowl of strawberries. And he took a strawberry and he bit into it and he said "uummm strawberries. It's good to eat the kind of fruit that you enjoy eating." And he said "here have one." Of course Erickson had polio, arthritis, gout, his lips were paralyzed. And his tongue was dislocated. I remember the last time I saw him a young psychotherapist dashed in and asked how he was doing. He said his muscles were rottening away. And there was nothing he could do to stop it. He was in tremendous pain. But he enjoyed teaching of students. And he made it a point to do what he enjoyed doing.---Psychologist I referred to Erickson. I heard a tape of Erickson working with him. I always talked to him about problems with his child. With his children. Or his child. He had two but then there was the other one. Of course with his wife that made four. And this man was a perfectionist. Erickson talked about how many stupid mistakes children made. Over and over he must have spent 40 minutes of this tape talking about this stupid mistakes children would make. He----a very difficult problem for this man. He ended it in 40 minutes. He was so sick of hearing Erickson talking about stupid mistakes. He began to accept those stupid mistakes with his first child, his second child, then the third and fourth child. Who knows probably----child. An organization. The company's organization. Who knows how many children you have. The administrators, the sales people, financial officers, engineers, foremen, workers. They all have children. They all want to enjoy themselves. It's true that every bit of enjoyment has to be earned. It's a problem in how to keep the child in child's play should always be taken seriously. Child's play is something that ought to be comprehensive, rebuilt, reorganized and replanned. We develop just as children develop.------A happy hood.----with a friend, parent by yourself. A very happy event. I'm going to stop for a minute or so and let the details of that happy event go through your unconscious. That happy event is the key or the success to a business organization.----that child is protected, nurtured, and cared for. And every bit of enjoyment has to be earned that way. The pathways. The works of human achievement serve as if-----work of gods. Man has a different kind of achievement. Human achievements. Human achievements.-----is whether you made a mile stone decision. Or a no stone decision. Because you did spell it "milstone." Not that I'm interested in your spelling but in your unconscious message. By thinking it is a mile stone-----if it is a mill stone around your neck. See mile stone certain people are rewarded for. You may even think of it as a human achievement. But a mill stone is referred to as----. A mill stone around your neck. Of course $6500 a month is a lot of cabbage. But how much cabbage can you eat. Only rabbits live in a cabbage patch. Well obviously you've been able to take a sick company and make it work. You have clear thinking, you know what your goals are for a company. You know how to achieve. You're successful.-----is the joy of success. One problem. Are you the kind of person who needs a mill stone around your neck. Who would just move from one mill stone to the next. You live a terribly unhappy life. Can you stand success. Is this desire to use your extraordinary skills and clear thinking and meeting company goals. People continuing wanting to move on to new territory. Well that's interesting, challenging, exciting. But it takes its toll. Burdensome, it's a mill stone. I'm not saying this is necessarily the case. But there is a suspicion about it.-----your last stop or your next stop. Maybe that's not important to know. First you've met your obligations to-----and that's important. You've always been guilty if you hadn't done that. But now you've done it and you can move on. You can begin to make-------. Cause you'd be guilty if you didn't. But the question is can you-------. Because if you don't you'd be guilty there. And that might be the worse guilt. So then you dealt with the question if you've built up a sick company.-----is it risky or is it------? Which company is it that you're most worried about? Second time I saw Dr. Erickson I walked in. As soon as I sat down there was a group of us there, he began to tell stories about his work career. When he graduated from medical school he took a job at the Rhode Island State Hospital. It was a life time job with fringe benefits. Erickson always talked about whether someone was left thumb or right thumb. He liked the staff. He enjoyed the patients he was working with. It was a life time job. One day he was working with a patient who was an ex-prize fighter. He went into the patient's room. The patient acted as if the bell had just rung and the round started. He began to measure Erickson off for the kill. Erickson backed up right to the wall, straightened out his arm with his knuckle in a-----. He lunged forward, hit the patient in the throat and knocked him out; And escaped from the room. The authorities said he had to go. Under no circumstances was he to hit a patient. Erickson found a job at the Massachusetts State Hospital. It was a life time job. Good fringe benefits. And he like the staff; he liked the patients he was working with. He was beginning to become very very good at hypnosis. But the problem was he was beginning to publish widely in hypnosis. The problem was that this was before the American Medical Association which accepted hypnosis. And so they warned Erickson. Erickson didn't call it hypnosis. Everyone knew it was hypnosis. The American Medical Association began to bring pressure on Massachusetts State Hospital.

And they said he had to go. They were so anxious to get rid of him they got him a job, they fought on the job at Wayne State University----. It was a life time job. Good fringe benefits. They had teaching he loved doing. Teaching the medical students.----over a hundred publications. He loved that job. He just turned in his 50's. He was riding his bicycle and he fell. He reactivated his childhood polio. He had arthritis that was getting worse by the day. The doctor said if he wanted to live he would have to move to Phoenix, Arizona. Here he was at 52 years old. He had been in Civil Service his whole life. He'd never done private practice. Move to a new city, crippled. He put a back office in his home. He started seeing people out of his home. That's where it started. He said he never knew at the age of 76 that he would be working quite so hard and quite so well known. He made such an impact on the psychotherapeutic community. The whole thing was a surprise to Erickson. Erickson did come from some strong stock; that would take on that kind of a job if he had to. His parents were born in Wisconsin. Norwegian descent. They wanted to move from Wisconsin to Nevada. All they had was a covered wagon and a horse to pull the wagon. They put all their belongings in the wagon and they moved from Wisconsin to Nevada. It must be 1500 miles. They didn't like it in Nevada. So they walked back. Erickson's father had his first heart attack at the age of 73. Doctor said he was going to be laid up for several months. This infuriated him. He said several wasted days. In seven days he was up and around. He had his second heart attack at the age of 78. The doctors were certain that this would lay him up for several months. He said "umf, another seven wasted days." And he was up and about in seven days. Carrying about his normal activities. His third heart attack came when he was 83. He said I'm a bit older now. Not quite as strong it's gonna be ten wasted days. In ten days he was up and around again, functioning well. His fourth heart attack was at the age of 94. He says I only wasted ten days I don't think these heart attacks are gonna kill me after all. I'm losing faith in them. At the age of 97 he was walking out with his daughters. He forgot his hat and when he went in and they hadn't seen him for awhile. He didn't come out when he was supposed to get his hat. They knew what had happened. Dealing with the issues of death and depression and suicide and homicide. The problem with----demands and requests are realistic. When you say work hard and consistent you mean work other people into the grave for what you pay them. You mean working yourself into the grave. When you say take care of yourself and your health. I don't see how----sick companies at all. You go from one sick company to another sick company. You almost have to work for yourself so you can carry your health and yourself.----redevelop your mind. Seems like what you've learned how to do is to hang in and not give in to the-------.-----depression, lack of energy, woundedness. The continuous feeling of being knocked out of the ballgame. Knocked out and the energy needed to take in and put out and give of yourself. Do not give up. I've worked with someone four days a week in analysis over several years. The work in the consistency of developing the tools which to pay attention themselves and their own thoughts and their own fears.----murder off and murder others off. And murder themselves off and murder me off. It's a full time job. It's developing the discipline and consistency. Then you have feelings that are undisciplined and inconsistent. Just because you feel that way it doesn't mean your mind needs to be engulfed by your feelings. In fact it's quite the contrary. Bion, the great British psychoanalyst said that the difference between an officer and an enlisted man, was that an officer could think and respond in the line of fire. What do you mean the line of fire? Well these feelings you have. The question is whether they'll engulf your mind or not, whether you'll be able to work consistently. To think and to stay afloat. You can contain those feelings of depression while you still move forward, whichever direction you seem to go. Erickson said he would only read good books. Books by Thomas Mann, or Henry----. He would read the last chapter first. He would try and figure out what happened the chapter before. Then he would read that chapter and try and figure out what happened the chapter before. Then he would read that chapter and try and figure out what happened the chapter before. He would read the whole book that way. The last point he mentioned here is to do things that you really wanted to do with the family.??? Family life is important. I remember before I had family therapy family life really wasn't working out that well. The man who wrote the foreword in my book is Carl Whittaker. And after Erickson died Whitaker was the guest speaker at the International Ericksonian Conference: The Evolution of Psychotherapy. So I got to meet him, and we did a private therapy session together with a couple. I said "I would like you to teach me family therapy, but you live in Wisconsin and I live in California." He said "Do you have a speaker phone?" I said "No. Why can you supervise over the speaker phone?" "Yeah." "You does therapy over the speaker phone?" "Yeah." I said, "Alright, I'll get one. But I've been doing mostly individuals, couples and hypnosis and hadn't seen a family in so long I was beginning to wonder if there were any in Los Angeles. San Diego was different. When I practiced there it was more of a family town. Los Angeles everyone was divorced." God was good to me and he sent a couple of families. Whitaker supervised me over the telephone from Wisconsin to Los Angeles. And he said no family therapist is trustworthy enough by himself to not to get sucked into the games of the whole family. Get yourself a co-therapist." It was pretty hard in Los Angeles. Everybody sort of in their own thing. There is a driving problem. And the fees are twice as much. He said "Well, get your wife." I said well she's not a therapist. It didn't occur to me that I had taken her with me all the times to Erickson and to George Bach and to Walter Kempler. She had even worked with Whitaker a couple hours in May 1982. So we had a lot of couples work. So I asked my wife and she said alright. She said I'm not a therapist. When I told Whittaker that my wife wasn't a therapist he said "That's alright she'll know what your bullshit is." She agreed but then she didn't show up for the first supervision session. So Carl said "where is your wife?" I said "well she's been up all night with the kid." The baby was just born. "Well you're doing co-therapy how can I supervise you if you're doing co-therapy? He says, why don't you ask her? I said well alright I'll ask her. She said "get the hell out of here. I've been up all night with the kid. Don't bother me." But she did say I'll come the following week. Carl had asked me how he could take me seriously. He said, You want to learn family therapy and she wasn't there. Then I happened to mention that my folks were out visiting from Connecticut. And he said your folks are in the house and you didn't invite them up to be in the session. This was a supervision session. And I said well I had mentioned it to them. What did they say? They said they were not interested. Did you tell them it was important to you? No. How come? I guess I was----. "How can I take you seriously that you want to learn family therapy!" Well he got my goat. So I told my parents and they were going back to Connecticut the following Wednesday. So I made an appointment with Whitaker on a Monday. And I said I wanted them there. They said "No way, we're not going!" I said, "You're going!" "We're not going." So then I went over to my wife's parents. I told them I wanted them there. My mother in law was wishy washy. My father in law said he wouldn't go unless my wife's brother and his girlfriend (not his wife) were there. I hadn't spoken to them for a year and a half. So I told him if he wasn't there I'd never do him another favor as long as I lived. My folks saw what a pain in the ass they were being and decided they could be better parents by showing up. My wife's brother and his girlfriend, were more upset than we figured about the family alienation. So they came. I put the squeeze on my wife's parents so they showed up. So we had eight of us and a baby in my room with a speaker phone talking to Dr. Whitaker in Wisconsin. It went a 40 minute. At the end of the hour Whitaker said "Well looks like you guys are just warming up. Maybe you want to let it go for a while." We went another hour and fifteen minutes. And they said "Hey can you get that guy back? This was pretty good." Shocked me. Nobody wanted to be there when I started it. I said I think so except my folks are going back to Connecticut. Well we could set up a conference call, Connecticut to Wisconsin to Los Angeles. So we did. And we worked the first three sessions three weeks in a row. Things were getting warm. My father in law says to Whitaker, "Carl thank you but no thank you." He said, "I've had it with this. This is too upsetting. And I'm not coming back" so Carl says "You don't have to come back but I don't have to see the family." I got a call the Thursday night before the next meeting and my father in law was in doubt all this time. My mother in law says "Dad's not going to come. He's too upset. And he will return to family therapy when everything is better. When everything is worked out." So it seemed hopeless. It seemed like I was defeated right there. I hung up the phone. Depressed, discouraged. Then I thought what would Erickson do. So I called back and I said "I want you to tell Dad that I want no further contact with any member of the family until he returns to family therapy. I don't have to pay for a cancelled appointment you can-I have to call Whitaker. You can let me know by 7:30 tomorrow morning. I had a call at 7:30. Says well Dad is too upset this week but he will return the following week on a permanent basis." We met for twenty five weeks. During that time we learned how to use power in the family politics. We learned how to get through stuck spots that seemed hopeless. One member of the family did something that used to drive me right up the wall. That person did it to Whitaker. It had the effect of kicking him in the balls, choking him and twisting his stomach all at the same time. And I was amazed that it happened right there in the session. And I said "Hey Carl, how are you gonna handle that one?" And he said "I'm gonna enjoy it. What else can I do with it." That was the big key because here a person does that kind of behavior sort of dampens everything. But they want to be enjoyed. So the task for you is to contain the behavior and enjoy them. And to stop the behavior when you can. To say what's on your mind and to call each thing that goes through your mind. Don't let anything slide. When you let it slide all it does is build up resentments. You have a cool barb wire fence between you and your spouse or other family members. So go for it. You can say and do the most outrageous things. As long as they got the family spirit in mind. If you live and let live it'll work out.???I did that with final solution. The harder family. What's good for you is good for the family. Is good for all the family members. You keep those things in mind and it all works out. (Karmically) Not necessarily in the temporal world.

"Your request was that I make two full hours of tape. But I think I've pretty much covered everything I have to say here. In terms of the time it's taking me-it took me a half hour of reading and thinking about your request. And then making some unconscious notes with my purple pen from which to tell my stories from. And I have to have the tape made and get to the Post Office. I think our time is up-it feels to me like we're about even. Should this phone work ever be of interest to you my phone is 424 293-9511 let it ring 7 times, and leave a message.

It's okay with me to work with me if you need things in the future. Let me know what happens. What you decide to do. And how things are going for you. Until me meet again."

USC

TWO HOUR DEMONSTRATION OF ERICKSONIAN STORYTELLING IN THE USC DEPT. OF SOCIOLOGY WITH SOCIAL WORK STUDENTS LEARNING PSYCHOTHERAPY.

Bergantino-It all started with my reading therapy "Uncommon Therapy: The Psychiatric Techniques of Milton H. Erickson, M.D." Norton, 1973-Get original copies. Erickson was a creative genius who needed strategies to help people turn around the tragic corner in their lives. He knew how to juxta position what was happening in their psyches and in their environment in a way that their life began to work for them. Now, what Erickson evoked in me what was perhaps quite different than he ever thought about what he did or what he taught. When I met Erickson in 1977 he was quite old and confined to a wheelchair. He did some demonstrations in hypnosis, but most of what he did was tell stories, hour after hour, 3 or 4 hours straight hours he told stories. USC Teacher Dr. Carl Broderick-This class is used to that already.

Class laughs.

Bergantino-What I found with his stories was first of all, and I am going to try to teach it to you in a way that you may be able to start to implement them or to practice with them in the training. Again, there were things that he evoked in me. I don't know that he necessarily thought about them this way. But he talked in a pace like this (slow), hour after hour, after hour. Now what would begin to happen and my thoughts about it, people who live in the Western World are a little too much with the environment as opposed to with themselves. It's a little too speeded-a little too fast-a little too much pressure on earning a living. Or for whatever reasons. Keeping with the center of oneself seemed to be quite a difficult task. Now, Erickson again would talk at a pace like this hour after hour after hour. What would begin to happen is first of all, you would stop trying to figure what he was doing. After 80, 90 minutes you'd give up on that and your mind would start to drift out. Well, between where you drifted and where you would come back in you would either from the stories he told have unconscious flashes that would create existential shifts or movement in your life; at least this is what happened to me; or you would begin to develop access to your unconscious and a trust in wherever it went. As I later became interested in psychoanalysis I saw that people who were very controlled, or, perhaps in what Melanie Klein referred to as the paranoid schizoid position would have an opportunity to develop an unconscious mind where perhaps they were the sort of people, who previously would evacuate thought. That was one thing that happened. The other thing that happened was with the amount of time Erickson did that, storytelling at that slow pace, I began to develop an access to sensory perception that I never experienced before. For example, right now there is a kind of speeded quality in the room a little bit. When working with ESP and individuals I go into a trance state, then I see what these sensory perceptions are between myself and my patients; if I get pains on the side of the head it usually has to do with anxiety or anger or self-hatred, or self-torture. The patient is projecting Beta elements via severe pathological prospective identification. Bion referred to this as projective identification. So, what that patient is showing me, how it is to be him, is what I first pick up on a sensory level. That tells me what the reality is of where to go. It's like an automatic cue or to where to tell the story. If I get pain in the heart area, usually the person has a problem in living the path of heart. If I get stomach nausea the person usually suffers from lying to themselves. But there are all sorts of combinations, particularly in terms of where people project off. Pain might be in the middle of the stomach usually has to do with conflict. So becoming sensitive to one's sensory awareness; from that sensory awareness develops the capacity to contain emotions and to evoke thought. So this method of hypnosis or perhaps it's a reverse psycho-analysis; it could be thought of in those terms. It goes from the sensing perception to the emotions, to the evocation of thought, and that's the process that takes place. Now, another tool I learned in hypnosis is automatic writing. When a person starts to talk and they have come into my office for a hypnotic session, I usually have them talk for about 5 minutes. During that time I'll jot down-of course I'll use a purple pen-Erickson always dressed in purple. Whatever magic goes along with the pen when you are doing hypnosis, you don't take it seriously-you know how to use it. Patients say things about five minutes at which time I'll jot down certain things on my pad which also has purple on it, and as I do that certain words seem to leap out in an impressionistic way. When those words leap out from what I do in the automatic writing that's the basis for the story I'm going to tell you in the next 45 minutes. Those stories appear from my unconscious mind and the unconscious mind of the patient. The very pin point accuracy and the very specifics I think in the next context my work is different from Erickson. Dr. Erickson's said my stories had pinpoint accuracy. That kind of response really kind of helped me along. What I have on the pad is the basis for the story telling. From that point during the sessions any switches that takes place that has to do with sensory perceptions-what I know at the moment is taking place. Any comments or questions at this point before I do a demonstration?

Question-Just to make sure I understand or part of it anyway. You use more than most of us do your own reaction to the client. I can tell when I'm bored with a client or not comfortable. It sounds like you become very very tuned in to how your body reacts to register the input you get from a client.

Question-Do you feel that it is idiosyncratic that due to the particular location of the split of pathological projection identifications via Beta elements they are in specific places?

Actually I don't think you're idiosyncratic when people have those kind of problems they usually inflict dis ease those particular parts of the body. You have a person focus in on paying extra sensory perception then they know the anatomy of things.

Question-Based on any statistical--------?

Just my own knowledge and paranormal experience.

Question 4-What you're saying is their problem evokes on you the bodily reaction? And you use your bodily reaction to determine what their problem is?

Great statement of what I do.

Let me say this in a couple ways. One, for example Tom said that he might feel bored sometimes. Instead of making a direct confrontation of boredom or something like that.-----------

Let me show you how it works-demonstration

A woman begins while I do automatic writing.

There's something that I discovered about myself and---There's something that I do--add values to that I'm real curious about that I cry.-----especially when I was a little girl. Someone in a wheelchair or someone who look like they have difficulty walking, or have polio braces on, or------something like that. When I first met him when I was back in Seattle during the winter time in my back yard. I was about two. I was playing with this beach ball with this neighbor boy, his name was Jimmy and he was four. He had polio braces on his legs. And I knocked the ball I guess what you would call out of bounds, down an embankment into sort of an orchid bush. There were plants in the backyard. My father told me that I had asked him about that experience. He said he came out the back door because I was shrieking like somebody was doing something to me. He said when he came out I was just standing there crying. All that was happening was this little boy was retrieving the ball. I was just standing there. The information that I forgot to include-----was that perhaps what was happening was I was having my first experience having to------somebody who was disabled. And experiencing some kind of guilt. And I related that to having power as the only child in my family. Sort of in between my mother and my father. That's as far as I got with it.

Class/Audience laughs.
???

What I'd like you to do is put your arms on the side of the chair, feet flat on the floor. Focus your eyes on any particular spot----. There is no need to talk and no need to move. If you can remember when you were a little girl, learning many very difficult things. Things that you don't even know that you knew. You learned the letters of the alphabet, how to discriminate between an A and a D. Which way the stems went on a b and a p. How to dot your T's and cross your I's. And add and subtract 1 and 1 is 2, 2 and 2 is 4. And many other difficult things that you don't even know that you knew. Now all of these learnings are part of your unconscious mind. Your unconscious mind is all the thoughts, memories, feelings and actions in it that you need to live a happy healthy life. As I recall Erickson worked with a patient who spoke only in word salads. No one could communicate with that patient. Erickson went out to the park bench, the man spoke 3 hours of word salad. Erickson wrote down every word. At the end of the man's word salad. He said "name's Erickson!" He went home that night and spent 6 hours writing out a 3 hour word salad in counter point to that man's word salad. The next day he went back to that park bench; the man spoke a 3 hour word salad. Erickson replied with a 3 hour word salad. This went on for 2 straight weeks. At the end of each day Erickson would say "Name's Erickson!" At the end of that second week the patient said to Erickson, "Erickson you're the only damn guy here who can speak English!" Why don't we go down to your office and talk!" When Erickson was 17 he had his first bout with polio. That bout of polio was so bad that he overheard the doctors tell his mother that he would never see the next sunrise. When they left he called his mother and father in. And he told them that he was furious that the doctors had upset his mother so. Would they please move the mirror in his room facing the crack in the door; where he could see the through the window on the other side of the house, where the sun came up. "He said he would be damned if he didn't see the next sunrise." When I met him he was 77. Erickson had a cane most of his life after his polio. And there's a story with his cane and his crippled walk. He got a call from a woman who said she didn't know what to do, she was beside herself about her daughter. Her daughter said her feet were too big. She wouldn't leave the house, she cut off all her relationships with her friends, with school, with the church she went to. And Erickson said to the mother; "sounds like you have a cold; Why don't I come to the house under the pretense of giving you a physical examination and see what the situation is?" Of course Erickson limped. Looked like a cripple. The mother was on the bed. She had a fever and a cough. And Erickson asked the daughter if she would be so kind as to go into the kitchen and get a wet cloth that he could put on mother's forehead. Which she did. As she returned he positioned himself in a way where she was directly behind and Erickson fiercely stepped on her foot. As he did so he turned around telling her "If you would grow those damn things big enough a physician like me wouldn't be in such an awkward situation!" Erickson might have been crippled, but there was surely no question that he could use his authority. In fact in some ways he was one of the two least crippled people I ever met. I remember when I first went to see him. There were no social amenities. His wife wheeled him in and he sort of looked around at you, and you couldn't tell if he was looking at you or through you. And he said, "You came all the way from California, and you're avoiding the hot seat." Of course all the chairs in the room looked the same and I had a pretty quick answer for everything. Before I could come back and say anything he says "Now that I mentioned it I see you're still avoiding it." It was like boom, boom. So I got up and moved over to the chair next to his wheelchair and he says, "What can I do for you young man. Actually there is a preface to that." He said so you're a clinical psychologist huh? I bet you don't even know why I'm wearing purple!" This man might have looked crippled but he sure didn't think cripple. He sure didn't act cripple. So I said "Well I guess this is just part of Dr. Erickson's style!" He said "Huh, I'm color blind! This is the only color I can see!" But he made it clear within the first 3 minutes he was the doctor or the teacher and I was the student. Now that is the way he set that frame using his authority. He set the conditions in the first 3 minutes where the therapeutic change could happen. And I would take him and myself both seriously. He was the first person I ever met who could do that. I had a patient who came to me after a 7 year analysis. And he said he had trouble when he was a high powered executive. He had trouble and he stopped breathing at these executive meetings. He was so tense. While he was president of the corporation he didn't feel very powerful; in fact he sort of acted like he thought people were gnats or flies, that would just buzz around and bother him. And he wished they would go away. During one session with him I began telling stories that people are like flies; they just buzz around. BUZZ, BUZZ. They just keep bothering you buzzing around. I said, But your problem is you don't have a big enough fly swatter. Now can you imagine just seeing those big flies, and you with a big fly swatter smashing them off the wall!" Now I suggested an amnesia state for this man but I didn't know if his conscious mind could tolerate what his unconscious mind felt. So as to whether he remembered or not after the session was in particular up to his own unconscious mind. The only thing he said at the end of his session was "Bergantino you're very strange!" He came back the second week and he was driven; just in a hurry to get everything. Everything he could possibly get. He was bothered by people. Harassed by himself. And absolutely driven. The memory that was evoked in me was watching a movie called "Song of the South" when I was a little boy. There was a character named Uncle Remus. Who sat on a rocking chair on a porch somewhere down South. Singing zippidy-do-da-zippidy-di-ee-a-oh-Mr.-Blue-Bird just singing away. And Uncle Remus would tell these stories about Brer rabbit, Brer bear and Brer fox. And I thought this was the perfect method of treatment for this man. So I continued to tell these stories about Uncle Remus, Brer Rabbit, Brer Fox and Brer Bear. It was about 25 minutes through the session and the man awakens from a trance state and screams at the top of his lungs, "Bergantino you're a maniac!" These were all the projections that were going on in his own mind. He couldn't tolerate it. So it was okay if he said I was a maniac, because I could enjoy it. I could enjoy his homicidal and suicidal fantasies and thoughts. I totally ignored his response and just continued telling the stories about Uncle Remus, Brer Rabbit, Brer Fox. Of course Erickson often uses the confusion technique as to whether Brer Rabbit or Brer Fox or was it Brer Bear or Brer Rabbit, or Brer Rabbit or Brer Bear came first in the order. And what sequential outcome would that have on the vast knowledge of the resources of the unconscious mind because in every person's life should come a little confusion and a little enlightenment. Erickson often talked about the value of interrupted learning. There was a therapist he was working with who was actually quite well known. And when I looked at the man he looked very fearful initially. And Erickson looked at him and said "for you young man I've got a surprise! I've got a genie in a magic lamp!" The guy sort of backed up and he said "well do you believe me?" The man kind of backed up again. He thought it over for a long time and said "if it were anybody but you Dr. Erickson I'd have you locked up but with you I'm not sure." And with that you could see the beginning of a trust and a faith in someone he thought was dependable. Bion said, "There are 2 nasty facts; people need to depend on other people, and then you need to find someone who is depend-worthy." This fellow in my office who came back and Erickson always talked about the value of interrupted learning. This fellow in my office who came back the following week and said "you're not going to believe what happened." And also there was a movie out called "The History of the World Part I" by Mel Brooks. And there was a line in there "It's good to be king!" And I would keep interspersing that comment with the Brer Rabbit stories. It's good to be king. The guy came back the following week and said I don't know what you did. I don't know how this happened. But you're not going to believe this. So he goes on to tell me the following story. He said he was at one of these executive meetings 45 minutes into the meeting and he couldn't breathe. He felt tremendous pressure at the top of his lungs with a fierce look in his eyes. He looked at those people and he said "Brer Rabbit!" And they were all shocked. And he said "oh no it's nothing." And he went on for another 3 hours and he did it again. He had the greatest time playing this little joke, only which he knew what the joke was. Enjoying his own craziness. Enjoying the fact that it's good to be king. He was the vice president. He could do any damn thing he pleased. There was a business meeting a few nights after and he had told his wife about this, who he was very affectionate towards. And a couple of executives came up to them. He became part of something he could own something. He could enjoy something. He could play with and he could feel powerful about. How one ever gets from storytelling and clinical hypnosis to analysis is a very strange story in itself. But one of the things I remembered was reading a story about Freud. He wrote about the Oedipus complex, and the Electra complex. Everybody knew what he was really talking about. And in 1903 he was at a scientific meeting with one of his colleagues got up and screamed from the top of his lungs, "This is not a matter for a scientific meeting! This is a matter for the police!" I suppose we all don't quite live in the era that Freud grew up. I saw Erickson working with a woman who was the only patient I ever saw him work with. All the rest were trainees. But this person lived in Phoenix and was one of the last patients that he saw. She was suffering from asthma, And she couldn't sleep all night. She was in a panic. She came in and Erickson asked her if she wanted to be hypnotized. She said that she did. She was in trance for about 20 minutes. And Erickson has a way of saying that at the unconscious level in his own words that. These are also called Drivers in Transactional Analysis. I am a clinical member of the International Transactional Analysis Association (ITAA)-1500 hr & exam-1975 she didn't have to try hard. She didn't have to be perfect. She didn't have to be strong. She didn't have to please me. She didn't have to hurry up. And you could see a softening. When this session was over she said "But Dr. Erickson how is that going to help me stop coughing and sleep to night?" And Erickson said "Take it from an authoritarian old man like me that you have very kissable lips." This woman just beamed! It was if he reached in and touched her heart! Erickson always dealt with this problem of the conscious mind versus the unconscious mind. In the conscious mind's trying to negate with the unconscious mind had benefitted from. And then she got up to leave. Her conscious mind took over again. And she said "Dr. Erickson how is this going to help me stop coughing and sleep tonight?" And Erickson began to sing "the lip bone is connected to the cheek bone and the cheek bone is connected to the neck bone and the neck bone is connected to the chest bone. He was facing the door where the woman was leaving then he turned around to the group and in an all knowing way he said that he knew that Barbara would sleep very very well tonight!" And he said it in a way with such confidence there was no question in any ones' mind that that's exactly what would happen. I need to do a bit of automatic writing here for a moment. Is there anything you would like to tell me at this point. The second day I saw Erickson I said Dr. Erickson will you hypnotize me again and he said "By the very fact you've asked the question shows that you're already half in trance and you can stay for as long as you wish, And come out when-ever you wish feeling very very relaxed and refreshed. And I thought how will I do that at the conscious level. (That ratifies trance). My unconscious mind remembered the pace at which he spoke, the heaviness in my hands, the heaviness in my legs, change in your muscle tone, change in your respiration rate, change in your blood pressure, change in your heart rate. So it was Erickson's gift that I could use this for however long I wished. Even all day long if I wished. I'm going to begin to count to 10. And at the count of 10 you gradually and gently return to a wide awake relaxed and refreshed position. Your unconscious mind will continue to give you and extract what it needs for the stories I've told you today. In coming to a resolution of the particular problem you brought up today. 1, 2, 3, 4, 5, 6, 7, 8, 9, and wide awake at the count of 10. Thank you for volunteering. Any comments, questions or thoughts?

Comment----------feel just the opposite of how I felt when I felt so burdened from whatever I felt. It was kind of like I don't know why I was feeling so good and I could have just been giggling of the stories of Brer Rabbit. That's what I wanted to do. Except I didn't giggle but inside I giggled while you were telling the story.

Any other thoughts or comments?

Question-Were they all true stories?

***I have magic telling stories about Brer rabbit!"

Answer-They were all true stories. The only thing I do with the story even if I tell the same story many times is I??? juxtaposition the story to the patients' unconscious mind, using minimal cues. My unconscious versus that person's unconscious in the best way I think it would sink in and get through the conscious mind's defenses.

Question-I got the feeling that you had a certain number of things that you felt you had to cover-----prioritize------

Answer-Well I wrote down things from which he (Erickson) said and that was the meat of the session. There were a couple of things I didn't do because as the work started it shifted and it seemed inappropriate. There were a couple of things I didn't do because I didn't have the foggiest notion why in the hell I wrote it down. So I just trusted, well if it is gone it shouldn't be there. And I shouldn't do it and maybe I'll do something else.

Question-What did you write down? How do you decide--------

Answer-It just comes to me in the 1st 5 minutes and I write down with a purple pen. Here purple came into my mind. Actually it wasn't purple, but then she said people in a wheelchair. Then I had to go to a story where Erickson was standing. The closest I could come to him before polio was when he had a cane. So then I show a guy with a cane but he's powerful. With one shot (boom) I invade her unconscious mind and she is forever changed. The girl's back to school resumed the relationship with everyone. It turns the whole thing around. It's a different way to reframe looking at a cripple.

Question-I heard you talking about spirit. Seeing and not seeing the purple in the spirit of Erickson.

Answer-There was something with the breathing that made me think about the asthma. I have here I knocked the ball out of bounds. Referring to sports, but I have no recollection where I read that. Something about an orchard which didn't come up in the context. Something about pressure in the mind, which I used TA. TA talks about the 5 drivers. You don't have to be perfect, you don't have to be strong. And I sort of put them in an Ericksonian context to release pressure. There was a comment about a bad experience and manipulating somebody. What I got is that was said is a bit of nausea. So I thought I was off the point and the next thought I had was the Freud story. Then I figured if all that came together there would be no problem with power. Or whatever sequence that comes together you'll be equipped with full power. What happens again is it wasn't that slow as we were going through like that. Within the first 5 minutes.

Question-Your assumption is the parts that you forget must not be important.

Answer-Not relevant, not important for this time. And if it comes back I talk about the value of "interrupted learning."

Question-Why not assume the opposite?

Answer-It implies a mistrust in the unconscious. What I learned to do in my work with Erickson was have an implicit trust of what was going on with the unconscious, and kind of a stream of flow.

Question-Reaction---------

Question----------I guess I was curious about your sensitivity or response to your stomach.

Answer-Using pain projected from patient onto my body (Beta elements) as cure from which to tell stories or make psychoanalytic interpretations. Two, one was pressure here one visual was pressure here in the eyes and the third one was here but not for long. Just at that one point. Maybe a significant point. So I think any other questions or comments about it?

Question-I feel that I in turn my some different experience to the previous experience to get a feeling of some kind of release.

Figure out transition

Answer-At your conscious level you don't know why but at your unconscious level you experience some relief. I thank you again for sharing that. I think that's again in a sense of what the kind of work is about getting that kind of release. I had no strategies to do that. Difference (Between me & psychoanalysis) Erickson thought about his work more as manipulation and changing people's behavior. I thought about it as just going with your pure and authentic flow of unconscious stream as I could. You figure it there was going to be a release (release = existential shift) it was going to happen in that context. Without any desire for you to be any particular way. So I think the desire of the reverse psychoanalyst needs to be out of the way to be most effective. Which I think is quite different from Erickson would have thought about. And what I think might be termed as kind of a reverse psycho analysis.

Question-It seems there are all kinds of analyses. But I'm wondering why you never talked about the story about the executive and what your thought was on that?

Answer-I thought he had homicidal and suicidal feelings that were quite frightening to him. And were not permissible to commend to his mind or his-those kind of primitive preconceptions were not permissible for him to experience. By working in sort of a hypnotically crazy way he became permissible and he wheeled a certain power where he was psychologically doing the absurd for which he was not responsible. With that there was just a lot more gusto in everything he did.

Question-Why the story here?

Footnote:

*** Most times I could get an existential shift-release-every time out!

Answer-Why the story here. He was crippled. He was crippled in a primitive sense. And he overcame that somewhat during those 2 sessions. I was thinking of crippled, I was also thinking in terms of having access of primitive preconceptions.

Question-----------I'm just wondering how much knowledge you incur as you go along?

Answer-All of the time. I do it with the sensory perception. How do you mean how does that change now?

Question-I was wondering if you touch---------

Answer-You heard the report about it. And you heard there was a release. So that's from her point of view. From my point of view I noticed when your face got soft. When your eyes were softer. When you felt open to me. When you seemed to at one point or somewhere along there I thought I screwed up on one of the stories.

Question-That's what I was wondering how---------?

Answer-I had a nauseous feeling and I thought is it her? Is it me? Then the though came it is me.

Question-Was that at that point when she almost looked like she was trance?

Answer-Could have been.

Question---------

Answer-I forgot that I was in the office for a minute.

Comment-----------I had to let go of it. When I came back I heard how he stepped on her foot and I was really puzzled. It was like I missed it.

Answer-It sounds like what happened to you is your unconscious mind left you kind of in some chaos. Some confusion about it. And yet some excitement and some joy about it. It must have been a good one. And in its own time in its own way, it may be significant for you. It will be interesting to see which way that happens. I see where it's about that time.

Question-You'll be back next week?

Answer-I'll be back next week.

Several people talking in background.

REVERSE ANALYSIS AND ITS UTILIZATION BY THE PSYCHOANALYST TO DO THE WORK

The methods described are both methods of hypnosis and contain many of the tools necessary to make psychoanalysis an effective method of treatment-that is, tools the psychoanalyst must possess and integrate into the practice of psychoanalysis if that analyst is to be able to know the sensory experience of what the patient projects onto the analyst, and then be able to make the kind of interpretation that helps the patient contain both the sensory experience and the emotions from which there is violent splitting so that patient may be able to develop thought as thought is connected to sensory experience, emotion and the quality of being of the patient. Without these tools psychoanalysts would be hard pressed to work with primitive phenomena and entrenched characteristics in a way that would make any consistent impact. Further, the method makes possible the transition for patients who were not able to be treated by insight. It permits a passive learning that allows the development of access to the unconscious. Further, the method can provide an existential shift in the life of the patient in accord with the psychodynamic of the stories being told and the release that occurs. The method can be taught in workshop format.

I began doing many workshops with the Ericksonian Storytelling and I am going to include both announcements of these workshops and how I marketed them; in that each time I thought things through anew they focused on different variables. And secondly, as hypnotists, psychoanalysts and even Reichians have been attempting to learn how to teach and train the development of "sense perception" as it relates to the development of thinking and the access to the unconscious; and as the profession has failed to date; I think the repetition of what I am presenting is important to not only the cognitive understanding but the experiential integration. I will follow these workshop announcements and experimentation with new ways of thinking about and describing the experience with two more (the thing-in-itself, which Sartre felt was the best way to learn-through the experience itself) presentations of "reverse psychoanalysis" with non-stop Ericksonian Storytelling. Some of the same stories are used in different contexts, on different days, with different audiences and the art of it is to juxtaposition the nuances. Erickson often said people might have to hear the same story three times before it registered at the unconscious level; although neither Erickson, nor Bion, nor myself ever told the same story in exactly the same way twice. As Bion stated, “experience is not repeatable!”

Let me next present a book review written by me of Healing in Hypnosis, Vol. I, Irvington Publishing, NY, 1983. The book was written by Ernest Rossi, Ph.D. and Margaret Ryan and Florence Sharp. However what I extracted was the particular focus Erickson had on the development and utilization of sense memories. This was published in The American Psychological Association, Division 30, Psychological Hypnosis Newsletter in August, 1987.

BOOK REVIEW: HEALING IN HYPNOSIS: VOL. 1

edited by Rossi, E., Ryan, M. & Sharp, F.
Irvington Publishers, Inc., New York, 1983.

Review submitted by
Len Bergantino, Ed.D., Ph.D. 450 N. Bedford Drive, Ste. 300 Beverly Hills, CA 90210

■■ ■

Healing In Hypnosis is what this book is. It has gems of genius and wisdom from Erickson himself at differing stages throughout his career. The implications for experiment are enormous from the material included for what might otherwise be considered hopeless cases. Of particular significance are comments that can be utilized in forming a treatment strategy for those who are paralyzed. "Milton foraged through his sense memories to try to relearn how to move. He would stare for hours at his hand, for example, and try to recall how his fingers had felt when grasping a pitchfork. Bit by bit he found his fingers beginning to twitch and move in tiny, uncoordinated ways. He persisted until the movements became larger and until he could consciously control them. And how did his hand grasp a tree limb? How did his legs, feet, and toes move when he climbed a tree?'

'These were not merely exercises in imagination; they were exercises in the activation of real sense memories-memories that sufficiently restimulated his sensory-motor coordination to enable him to recover." This book is full of such passages which can evoke methods of treatment through hypnosis for those that are hopelessly up against it and in need of healing. The book stimulates the reader's creativity to continue in the tradition of Erickson himself, to persevere until that thought to be hopeless can either become hopeful, or, that which is also transmitted through the book that the reader might evoke in the patient the capacity to live as spirited and as full a life as possible-the life of a Viking, if you will!

Once again, clinicians can only appreciate the dedication of Ernest Rossi in tracking down throughout the entire career of Erickson, valuable material, the subtleties of which are presented in a way that can be transposed by clinicians to other situations to facilitate the kind of healing that Erickson knew about.

Erickson taught and developed methods which can be expanded upon from his own personal suffering. When teaching a group of students he said "In thinking all that through, you will first have to start with thinking: 'My hand is in my lap. To pick up an apple over there I'll have to lift my hand, and that means I'll have to bend my elbow-which means I'll have to lift my elbow-which means I'll have to lift my forearm-which means I'll have to lower my hand-which means I'll have to feel the apple with my fingertips.' You yourself can think through that process".

The first example showed Erickson's use of sense memory and the second shows how a plan may be developed for practice by the patient which can link sense memory development to thinking step by step in a slow and patient manner.

Another important concept that Erickson believed and utilized was "when one part of the brain is damaged you can call upon another part of the brain to develop the lost learning."

The ramifications of this concept, in addition to the prior two, for those in need of rehabilitation, children with developmental delays and their frightened parents, points in some very meaningful directions in which clinical hypnosis, as it continues to develop, can help people turn the tragic corner in their lives. So it was that Erickson dedicated his life's work, and so it is that Ernest Rossi continues this heartfelt quest. And this book provides the means by which the subtleties of the psychological and the physiological potentialities at their most subtle discriminations in patients can begin to be utilized. On a scale of one to ten, give this book a ten! * END OF BOOK REVIEW

Next we will take a look at the teaching tales in terms of naturally occurring rhythms in the creation of a healing environment. The focus here is the beginning of a link between a finer vibration when doing a psychoanalysis as it relates to a transformation of being in the patient. Wyckoff ties this right back to the work of Mesmer and Reich (again, we haven't been able to implement to much of the work of our therapeutic forefathers due to the destruction of experience through hatred and envy and through the way knowledge itself is presented to satisfy the mediocre.

HYPNOTIC TEACHING TALES OF MILTON H. ERICKSON, M.D. AND NATURALLY OCCURRING RHYTHMS IN THE CREATION OF A HEALING ENVIRONMENT

Unpublished as???
Requests for reprints should be sent to
450 N. Bedford Drive Ste. 300
Beverly Hills, CA 90210

Couch Canyon office from 1981-1991.

■■ ■

Milton H. Erickson, M.D., told stories to me hour after hour, after hour, at a very particular pace. This unique, and slow pace, in accord with the natural rhythm of people, provided a healing environment. After a time, usually ninety to one hundred and twenty minutes, there occurred a letting go of control in people. This letting go of conscious control made access to their unconscious minds and sensory perceptions increasingly more available.

Ernest Rossi, Ph.D., a serious student of Dr. Erickson noted that Dr. Erickson often wondered why his own sessions were lengthy and leisurely and ranged between 90 to 120 minutes (Rossi, 1982). Dr. Rossi describes the time span of 90 to 120 minutes as an ultradian cycle. He defines ultradian cycles as "A multioscillatory system of 90 to 120 minute variations in psychophysiological process" (Rossi, 1982). Thus, what Dr. Erickson was doing was utilizing ultradian cycles as a way of accessing the unconscious minds of patients. Teaching Tales paced over such a period of time provides a kind of hypnosis that corrects the patient's disruption of the ultradian cycle, thereby establishing a healing environment to treat the basic physiological mechanisms of psychosomatic illness, by restoring what is the natural energy or life force of the patient. "A Healer who is in contact with perhaps a finer vibration can heal many people and will be refreshed by the effort" (Wyckoff, 1975). Although it may not have been his purpose, Dr. Erickson had such a fine vibration in his work, and to the degree the vibration and the pace become more fine-tuned, is the degree to which the healing environment is provided; contingent upon the appropriate amount of time necessary for the natural processes to unfold via the utilization of ultradian cycles. An interesting comparison, "And so we see that perhaps for such a man healing is not a question of doing, but-as LaoTzu indicated-of being. Perhaps then to understand something of Mesmer's animal magnetism, the Life Force, it is not required of us to 'think' or to 'do', but to allow something to be done" (Wyckoff, 1975). I told teaching tales hour after hour at this fine-tuned pace with a fine tuned vibration, and often talked about "the benefits of passive learning".

While Dr. Erickson utilized a patient's own real sense memories from somewhere in that patient's life and felt that the utilization of these sense memories would create the basis for filling developmental gaps in a unique way, it is also possible to utilize a real sensory perception and experience, the thing-in-itself, the vibration, and utilize that centering to take control over psychophysiological processes-such as psychosomatic illness or heart attack type behavior.

The left hemispheric processes that override the ideal balance with right hemispheric processes in the brain and, are associated with parasympathetic functions, thus have the opportunity to regulate themselves naturally. Thus, Dr. Erickson referred to his method of hypnosis as "naturalistic". The pace of the experience (fine-tuned vibration) itself over 90 to 120 minutes can become imbedded so the patient can learn on many levels to maintain the more natural pace, thereby learning to create an optimum state of health in which the patient can then function without, or at least with reduced, psychosomatic problems. This kind of self control over the course of the full day, and not just as an occasional post hypnotic suggestion or for ten or twenty minutes per day, can create the kind of self-discipline over ten hour periods of time that permit optimum states of being to occur, and for increased fine-tuned sensory perception as a guide to both health and as an organismic point of moment to moment self direction. I suppose when you hear tales such as a Buddhist monk who meditates all day long every day being able to heal people by projecting some kind of healing energy upon them, you might think that the limits of hypnosis as it is conceived and extended upon with the utilization of ultradian cycles has infinite limitations. The limitations are in the hypnotist and the self-discipline of that hypnotist as opposed to the limits of what hypnosis can achieve. The degree to which the clinician develops such discipline is the degree to which a healing environment can be provided. The degree to which the patient develops such discipline as a result of working with the hypnotist is the degree to which cure can take place. In a presentation Dr. Rossi said that Dr. Erickson was in a trance state many many hours per day and suggested that was the best way to get a sense of how to do hypnosis and utilize the natural rhythms of the ultradian cycles (Rossi, 1984). Of course, what we do not know is what level of achievement Dr. Erickson may have reached on this scale were his body not continually racked with pain in his later years.?

HYPNOSIS AND ULTRADIAN CYCLES: A NEW STATE(S) THEORY OF HYPNOSIS?

By
ERNEST L. ROSSI

This article is printed in its entirety with permission of Francis and Taylor Analytic Publishers in London, England.

■■ ■

The similarities between the behavioral characteristics of ultradian cycles (a multioscillatory system of psychophysiological processes involving many parasympathetic and right-hemispheric functions which have a 90-minute periodicity throughout the 24-hour day) and those of the "common everyday trance" lead the author to propose a new state(s) theory of hypnosis. The background for this proposal developed over eight years of observing the clinical, hypnotherapeutic techniques of Milton H. Erickson, whose work appeared to utilize a similar 90-minute periodicity. The ultradian theory of hypnotherapeutic healing proposes that (1) the source of psychosomatic reactions is in stress-induced distortions of the normal periodicity of ultradian cycles, and (2) the naturalistic approach to hypnotherapy facilitates healing by permitting a normalization of these ultradian processes. Research problems involved in the validation of these proposals are discussed, and the author's initial clinical approaches to utilizing ultradian cycles to facilitate hypnotherapy and posthypnotic suggestion are outlined.

Hypnosis and Ultradian Cycles: A New State(s) Theory of Hypnosis?

A salient characteristic of Milton H. Erickson's (MHE) work with patients, as well as with hypnotherapeutic training groups, was that the sessions were lengthy and leisurely; they usually ranged between 90 to 120 minutes, or more. Even in his advanced years when his available energy was precarious, MHE's hypnotherapeutic sessions were still longer than the standard 50-minute hour. For many years the author wondered about this, and also wondered why MHE would choose a particular moment in the session to introduce trance. Sometime or other during those leisurely interviews with their traded memories and anecdotes, it would suddenly become apparent that the patient was quietly nodding his head in a slow and rhythmical fashion — with lids closing over faraway-looking eyes. A hypnotherapeutic trance was being induced in an indirect manner that once again had escaped the author's attention.

It soon became apparent that the author was missing the initial moments of hypnotic induction because he was focusing his attention on MHE rather than the patient. MHE was continuously observing the patient with a careful and highly focused attention: he would monitor the patient's heart rate (by observing pulsations in the face, throat, legs, or hands), the speed of reflexes (eye blink, swallowing, respiration), and the degree of overall body movement. In his later years MHE would usually wait for the patient's physical and mental processes to "quiet down" before he induced trance, explaining that he was waiting to utilize those "natural" periods of quietness and receptivity. We soon began to call these quiet periods the "common everyday trance" (Erickson & Rossi, 1976), because it seemed they were a part of natural everyday life. The housewife staring vacantly over a cup of coffee, the student with a faraway look in his eyes during the middle of a lecture, and the driver who automatically reaches his destination with no memory of the details of his route, are all varieties of the common everyday trance.

This author now conceptualizes the common everyday trance as a generalized movement toward parasympathetic and right-hemispheric dominance in all the psychophysiological and behavioral processes listed in Table 1. In Erickson's work, as soon as a patient began to manifest an individual pattern of these behaviors in clinical interview. MHE would deepen it into a hypnotherapeutic trance through direct or indirect suggestions. MHE usually gave important suggestions only when he sensed that the patient had achieved "a state of *response attentiveness:* that state of extreme attentiveness in responding to the nuances of communication presented by the therapist" (Erickson & Rossi, 1979, p. 2). In Table 1. response attentiveness is categorized as a form of social behavior in which the subject (patient, listener, client) is manifesting very close attention to the speaker (therapist, lecturer, friend) via (1) focused eye contact; (2) open and receptive body language; (3) an attitude of interest and expectation; (4) quietness of body (spontaneous catalepsy) except for occasional stereotypic agreement responses (head nodding yea, leaning closer to speaker, etc.); and (5) an acquiescence in accepting suggestions.

TABLE 1

Behavioral processes changing during the common everyday trance, as summarized from Erickson and Rossi (1976-1980).

Hypnotherapeutic Intervention Periodicity (90-120 minutes)

Psychophysiological Processes

Heart rate
Peripheral blood flow
(blushing, blanching, coldness of extremities, etc.)
Eyeblink & motility
Pupillary responses
Swallowing
Respiration
Lack of exaggeration of startle response

Motor Behavior

Response latency
Economy of movement
Decreased muscle tonicity (face "ironed out")
Spontaneous catalepsy
Altered vocal qualities

Sensory-Perceptual Behavior

Relaxation and comfort
Feeling "distant"
Spontaneous illusions and hallucinatory phenomena

HYPNOSIS AND ULTRADIAN CYCLES

Cognitive Behavior

Amnesias
Literalism
Autonomous ideation and fantasy
Time distortion and time lag in conceptual usage

Social Behavior

"Take a break" periodicity (90 minutes)
Response attentiveness
eye contact
open and receptive body language
interest and expectation
body quietness
suggestibility

Most observers presumed that MHE evoked or induced the behaviors characteristic of the common everyday trance listed in Table 1 with his direct and indirect suggestions. Recently, however, the author had suggested that these behaviors might be a natural biological expression of the rest phase of the ultradian cycle that takes place physiologically every 90 to 150 minutes throughout the 24-hour day (Erickson & Rossi,

1981; Rossi, 1981). The author had proposed that the rest phase of the ultradian cycle and the common everyday trance were identical. Thus the essence of MHE's "naturalistic" approach was that he utilized the ultradian cycle (the common everyday trance) by nudging it into a state of response attentiveness through his interesting stories, momentary surprises, fascinating facts, and so forth (Erickson, Rossi & Rossi, 1976), until a hypnotherapeutic trance was obviously manifest.

More recent research on the ultradian cycle, however, indicates that this proposal may have been too simple — research into ultradian cycles has become vastly more complex as it has proceeded. With this increasing complexity, though, the skeins of its possible relatedness to what we call "hypnosis" are becoming ever more intriguing. In the following section 1 shall outline some of the history of and current developments in ultradian cycle research, as well as demonstrate its relevance for hypnosis.

Ultradian Cycles: A Multioscillatory System of 90-to-120-Minute Variations in Psychophysiological Processes

Ultradian cycles are so named because they are of such short duration that many complete oscillations take place within the 24-hour circadian cycle. Research on ultradian cycles dates back at least a generation, when it was reported that stage REM occurred cyclically throughout the day, as well as at night in infants and during the day when adults slept. Dement and Kleitman (1957) concluded that the 90-to-100-minute cycle was a "Basic Rest-Activity Cycle" (the BRAC hypothesis), which ran continuously throughout the 24-hour day. Kleitman (1963) concluded that this basic rest-activity cycle (the BRAC model) was an endogenous oscillation of the central nervous system that had profound implications for physiology and behavior.

Tables 2 and 3 list the major behavioral processes identified as characteristic of the ultradian cycle, along with the researchers who have investigated them. Table 2 was arranged so that the correspondence between the behaviors of the ultradian cycle and those of the common everyday trance listed in Table 1 would be obvious. A general slowing of the reflexive processes of heart rate, pupillary response, eye blink and motility, respiration and swallowing, are characteristic of both the common everyday trance and of the rest phase in the ultradian cycle. However, Kleitman's original conception of the basic rest cycle has undergone significant modification: with more recent research, many of the diversified, cyclic, psychophysiological processes loosely conceptualized as ultradian in Tables 2 and 3 have been found to be out of phase with one another, and different neurophysiological sources have been found to account for them (Kripke, 1982a; Kripke et al., 1978). For example, there is no consistent phase relationship between the dominant REM-NONREM cycle and the very well documented gastric motility cycle (Lavie & Kripke, 1981). In general, however, the movement toward parasympathetic and right-hemispheric dominance that are characteristic of the common everyday trance can be found as psychophysiological polarities of the ultradian cycles presented in Tables 2 and 3.

Ultradian cycles are thus an incredibly complex, multioscillatory system of 90-to-100-minute variations in psychophysiological and behavioral processes (Kripke, 1982a). They are no less complex, in fact, than the widely varied hypnotic phenomena which the author proposes to be associated with them. It is precisely this correspondence in complexity that lends credence to the view that ultradian cycles could be one of the important psycho-neuro-physiological foundations for hypnotic phenomena.

TABLE 2*

Behavioral processes that have been studied experimentally in ultradian cycle research and have been found in the common everyday trance and hypnosis.

Dream (REM) Sleep Periodicity (90-100 minutes)	Dement & Kleitman, 1957
	Kleitman, 1963, 1969
	Kripke, 1974, 1982a
Hemispheric Laterality	Klein & Armitage, 1979
	Kripke, 1982a
Psychophysiological Processes	
Heart rate	Lovett, 1980
	Orr et al.. 1974, 1976
Peripheral blood flow	Lovett, 1980
	Romano & Gizdulich, 1980
Eyeblink & motility	Krynicki, 1975
	Ullner, 1974
Pupillary response	Lavie & Schulz, 1978
Swallowing	(See "Appetitive Behavior" in Table 3)
Respiration	Horne & Whitehead, 1976
Motor Behavior	
Response latency	Globus et al., 1970
	Kripke, 1972
	Kripke et al., 1978
	Lovett & Podnieks, 1975
	Meier-Koll et al., 1978
	Orr et al., 1974
	Podnieks & Lovett, 1975

Muscle tonicity...	Katz, 1980 Lovett et al., 1978 Rasmussen & Malven, 1981 Teirney et all., 1978

In a recent summary statement of ultradian cycle research. Kripke (1982a) indicated how many of these behavioral and psychological processes are associated with REM and endocrine metabolism:

> The wealth of phenomenology which has been uncovered in pursuit of the BRAC hypothesis should console any investigator troubled that the hypothesis remains controversial. Dramatic behavioral cycles have been discovered, both in man and lower primates, and perhaps these cycles have important ethologic functions. Cycles in fantasy, hemispheric dominance, and perceptual processing have been described. The significance of these cycles in both normal and pathologic psychologic functioning deserves our attention. Episodic hormone secretion seems to be a fundamental property of endocrine metabolism, and it is somehow related to the REM cycle. The suggestion that the pituitary is only responsive to intermittent releasing hormone stimulation is particularly exciting, for it suggests one way in which ultradian cycles may be a functional necessity. The early stage of search for cycles must now give way to more analytic studies which explore the mechanisms and functional implications of each ultradian cyclic process. (pp. 30–31 in unpublished paper; 1982a in the forthcoming publication)

If our proposed identification and/or association of ultradian cycles with hypnosis is correct, the above quotation suggests incredible new vistas for the future development of therapeutic hypnosis.

The Ultradian Cycle, Stress, and Psychosomatic Reactions

Orr, Hoffman, and Hegge (1974) reported that almost all their human subjects showed a stable ultradian cycle when under quiet, bedrest conditions. When subjects were stressed with extended performance tasks (observing responses monitoring three panel meters hidden behind front-surfaced mirrors), however, they experienced major disruptions in the amplitude and patterning of their ultradian cycles. In association with Stroebel's earlier work with rhesus monkeys, the investigators concluded that "psychosomatic-like" responses (heart rate alterations, ulcers, gastritis, asthma, and skin rashes) resulted from stressors' continual disruption of the ultradian cycle. The highly individualized dynamics of this disruption process, which is also characteristic of psychosomatic (and hypnotic) responsivity, was emphasized in their conclusions:

> .... (a) The same stressor can produce quite different physiological and behavioral response patterns in different subjects; (b) behavioral stress can produce disruptions which are clearly manifest in terms of altered biological rhythms; and (c) there appears to be no simple relationship between a physiological response and specific behavioral responses. (p. 1,000)

The implications of this association between disruptions of the ultradian cycle by stress and psychosomatic illness are profound. If the major proposal of this section is correct — that therapeutic hypnosis involving physiological processes is actually a utilization of ultradian cycles — then we can finally understand in psychophysiological terms why hypnosis traditionally has been found to be an effective therapeutic approach to psychosomatic problems: *Individuals who override and disrupt their own ultradian cycles (by ignoring their natural periodic needs for rest in any extended performance situation, for example) are thereby setting in motion the basic physiological mechanisms of psychosomatic illness.* Most of this self-induced stress could be conceptualized as left-hemispheric processes overriding their ideal balance with right-hemispheric processes and associated parasympathetic functions. *Naturalistic therapeutic hypnosis provides a comfortable state wherein these ultradian cycles can simply normalize themselves and thus undercut the processes of psychosomatic illnesses at their psychophysiological source.*

Sensory-Perceptual......................................Lavie, 1976
Lovett, 1976
Lovett & Podnieks, 1975
Rorschach alterations.............................Globus, 1966, 1968
Visual illusions......................................Gopher & Lavie, 1980
Klein & Armitage, 1979
Lavie et al., 1974, 1975, 1977

Cognitive Behavior
Observing response...............................Kripke, 1972
Meier-Koll et al., 1978
Orr et al., 1974
Fantasy...Kripke & Sonnenschein, 1978

Social Behavior...Delgado et al., 1976
Lavie & Kripke, 1981
Maxim et al., 1976

"Take a break" periodicity
(90 minutes)
napping time...Lavie & Scherson, 1981

---

*Because of space limitations, the notation *et al.* will be used when there are more than 2 (rather than 3) authors.

TABLE 3

Behavioral and psychophysiological processes that have been studied experimentally in ultradian cycle research that have not yet been associated with the common everyday trance and hypnosis.

Appetitive Behavior	Friedman & Fisher, 1967
	Hiatt & Kripke, 1975
	Kripke, 1972
	Lewis et al., 1977
	Oswald et al., 1970
	Reinberg et al., 1979
	Weda, 1922
Hormonal Behavior	Bykov & Katinas, 1979
	Eriksson et al., 1980
	Filicori et al., 1979
	Friedman & Piopho, 1978
	Levin et al., 1978
	Millard et al., 1981
	Quabbee et al., 1981
	Shiotsuka et al., 1974
	Simon & George, 1975
	Stiner et al., 1980
	Tannenbaum & Martin, 1976
	Tannenbaum et al., 1976
	Ullner, 1974
	Weitzman, 1974
	Yen et al., 1974
Temperature Alterations	Hunsaker et al., 1977
Urine Flow	Lavie & Kripke, 1977
	Luboshitzky et al., 1978
Psychoactive Drug Sensitivity	Naber et al., 1980
Smoking	Friedman & Fisher, 1967
Neuroendocrinal Functions	Kripke, 1982a
Penile Erections (in sleep)	Ohlmeyer et al., 1944

A more exact understanding of how an individual's ultradian cycles manifest themselves could lead to the development of more deeply involving hypnotic states wherein the ultradian characteristics of therapeutic trance are utilized for psychosomatic healing. In the following section, I shall examine how clinical research in this area could proceed.

Clinical Research on the Ultradian Theory of Hypnosis

It would be tempting to immediately propose the obvious research approach of determining if there is a correlation between scores on hypnotic suggestibility scales and indices of the ultradian cycles. There are two sets of problems with such an approach, however: problems from the side of ultradian research, and problems from the side of the "kinds of hypnosis" involved in the usual laboratory or clinical use of hypnotic suggestibility scales.

From the ultradian side, Kripke — who is perhaps the most prominent researcher in this area — recently commented to the author, "The more we study the ultradian cycles, the more elusive they seem" (1982b). As was noted in the previous section, it is the very irregularity and variability of these cycles that recommends a possible commonality with the similar variability of hypnosis and hypnotic phenomena. Because of this wide variability together with the many sources of large but indeterminate errors of measurement, however, we would not expect to find many statistically significant correlations. With so many imponderables of experimental design involved in investigating these elusive phenomena, any lack of statistical correlation would simply not be convincing evidence against the proposed relationship between ultradian cycles and hypnotic phenomena. As in high energy particle physics, the elusiveness of the phenomena under investigation, compounded by the limitations of our methods of measurement, leads to an uncertainty principle. Perhaps because of this factor, Kripke demurred when the author proposed the familiar type of correlational investigation — and, to date, no such work has been done.

From the side of the “kinds of hypnosis” used with standardized hypnotic suggestibility scales, there are difficulties related to the above problems of measurement (Bowers, 1982; Hilgard, 1982a & b). Further, a standardized administration of scales like the Stanford and Spiegel’s Hypnotic Induction Profile does not take into account that quality of *response attentiveness* that Erickson felt was of essence in his form of therapeutic hypnosis. A high degree of clinical skill is required to recognize, facilitate, and utilize response attentiveness in each unique clinical situation, so it remains an open question as to how it could be standardized and scored in an objective manner.

Until these experimental design problems are solved in a convincing manner, we must make do with more traditional clinical approaches to explore the proposed relationship among hypnotic phenomena, ultradian cycles, and psychosomatic illness and healing. In an effort to develop a systematic clinical approach to this problem, the author has begun to ask himself a basic question: *How could hypnotic suggestions be associated with ultradian cyclic phenomena to produce specific therapeutic effects or new hypnotic phenomena that could not be produced in any other way?* For example, there are a myriad of possible associations between hypnotic suggestion and the neuroendocrinal and hormonal factors in ultradian cycles listed in Table 3 that could be explored to produce fascinating and entirely new effects. A renaissance of exploration in therapeutic hypnosis will be initiated by those workers with the requisite clinical skills and psychophysiological knowledge to investigate these new vistas. To date, however, the author has been limited in his private practice to investigating the use of posthypnotic suggestion with ultradian cycles, as outlined in the following section.

Utilizing Ultradian Cycles in Posthypnotic Suggestion

The basic principle utilized in this section is Erickson’s view that the most effective means of facilitating posthypnotic suggestions is to associate them with behavioral inevitabilities. We know that it is inevitable that a patient will walk out of the office, go home, eat, sleep, dream, go to the bathroom, work, play, etc. Erickson usually associated posthypnotic suggestions with these kinds of inevitable daily behaviors (Erickson & Rossi, 1979).

The experienced clinician could immediately think of many ways of utilizing the ultradian cycles as psychophysiological and behavioral inevitabilities that would give posthypnotic suggestions associated with them continual reinforcement throughout the 24-hour day. This report can only outline a few approaches the author has been exploring with some success in clinical practice during the past three years. Obviously the needs of the individual patient determine which approach will be used. (These approaches are not mutually exclusive, and it is often more effective to blend two or more together.)

1.\ *Associating a Heightened Sensitivity to Ultradian Behavior with Hypnotic Responsiveness and Posthypnotic Suggestion*

In clinical interview, when the patient's behavior indicates that a quiet period of the ultradian cycle is being experienced (each patient has his own pattern of manifesting the behaviors of Tables 1 and 2, which the observant therapist must come to recognize), the author will utilize it to initiate a hypnotherapeutic trance. He uses a variable pattern of double binding questions and statements that comment upon whatever ultradian (common everyday trance) behavior the patient is actually manifesting at the time. For one patient, it might run somewhat as follows:

> "I notice your body seems to be getting quieter in these last few moments, and you're not saying much as you look out the window that way. I wonder if that means your unconscious is ready to enter a comfortable period of therapeutic healing: And will it continue to develop as I continue talking to you? And how will you know? Can you feel your body getting even quieter? Are some parts of your body now more comfortable than others? That's right, you can adjust your arm just like that, so it can be easy and comfortable.

> "And are you letting yourself enjoy that comfort even more as it continues? Do you notice how your breathing and heart rate are quietly changing? Do your eyelids feel like they may become heavy and want to close, sort of by themselves? Will you be aware of the exact moment they close, or will you already be daydreaming by then — just wondering how healing happens. And will it happen mostly by itself, so you can just quietly enjoy it, or will you know there is something you must do to help it?"

This associative network focuses attention inward on the many behaviors that are compatible with the parasympathetic and right-hemispheric dominant portions of the ultradian cycle. The behaviors more characteristic of traditional clinical hypnosis — such as catalepsy, arm levitation, ideomotor head and finger signaling — can then be explored to assess the patient's readiness for hypnotherapeutic work. If it appears that deepening is required, the patient may be awakened so that the therapist can receive a report on just which of the ultradian cycle behaviors the patient was most aware of during this initial phase of the trance induction. Trance is then reinduced by the therapist, who now focuses his attention and pattern of suggestions and statements on those ultradian behaviors which the patient is most aware of.

After the body of hypnotherapeutic work is accomplished, posthypnotic suggestion can be greatly facilitated by associating it with the inevitable behaviors of the ultradian cycle throughout the 24-hour day. The patient is given suggestions that the hypnotherapeutic work can reinforce itself automatically during dreaming at night, and during those periods throughout the day when the patient just feels like "taking a break" — during which time he can rest while his unconscious continues the healing process.

2.\ *An Intellectual Presentation of the Ultradian Cycle with Posthypnotic Suggestion: Hypnosis without Awareness of It*

In this approach the therapist also begins by noting when the patient is experiencing some quiet portions of the ultradian cycle, but he does not tell this to the patient. Instead the therapist simply introduces an intellectual discussion of the "fascinating research that's being done on the ultradian cycle." The therapist indirectly induces trance by firmly focusing the patient's attention and facilitating *response attentiveness* with a series of questions and statements that utilize the patient's own special areas of interest — particularly the patient's interest in effective therapeutic work being accomplished that day. It could run somewhat as follows:

"You know, Mary since you are an engineer, I'm *wondering* if you are *aware* of the *fascinating* research that's *being done* on the ultradian cycle?"

The author never had a patient who was not interested, so he goes on to explain in impressive terms (adjusted to the patient's own vocabulary level and frames of reference) just what the ultradian cycle is. When the author comes to the part about the characteristic behaviors of the quiet (parasympathetic or right-hemispheric) portions of the ultradian cycle, he tends to slow down and emphasize with a subtle tone of inquiry those behaviors that the patient is currently manifesting. He then tells the patient that while it is only a "clinical hunch," there may be a relation between the ultradian behaviors and the patient's psychosomatic symptom (habit problem, or whatever). The patient is then enjoined to begin to tune into her ultradian behaviors throughout the day and notice if there is any relationship. Does the symptom tend to flare up when the patient does not allow herself to take a break during those portions of the ultradian cycle when the symptoms are manifest? Posthypnotic suggestions are then introduced by having the patient remind herself of the therapeutic work that needs to proceed "all by itself" during those "take-a-break" periods.

In this approach, then, a period of therapeutic trance is introduced by fixing and focusing the patient's attention and response attentiveness with an appropriately fascinating discussion that associates therapeutic suggestions with ultradian behaviors actually being manifested by the patient during this moment of the therapeutic encounter. The patient is not aware that associative connections are being formed between these ultradian behaviors currently being experienced and the apparent "intellectual discussion" that is actually loaded with therapeutic suggestions. When the patient later experiences these inevitable ultradian behaviors throughout the 24-hour day, the therapeutic associations will be evoked "covertly," and reinforced automatically within themselves, usually on an unconscious level. When the ultradian behaviors are particularly evident to the patient, she may become consciously aware of them and then reinforce some of the "suggestions" consciously, as directed by the therapist. The patient is consciously aware of the suggestions the therapist told her to associate with the ultradian behaviors, but she tends to be unconscious of other suggestions the therapist was associating with her ultradian behaviors under the guise of an intellectual discussion, interesting story, metaphor, etc. Thus both conscious and unconscious posthypnotic suggestions can be associated with ultradian behaviors so that they will be continuously reinforced on conscious and unconscious levels. The patient has no conscious awareness that a "hypnotic process" was used. Indeed, it is perhaps a matter of semantics. Is the process of associating conscious and unconscious processes with behavioral moods or ultradian cyclic behaviors a form of hypnosis? It is if one identifies ultradian behaviors with the Erickson-Rossi concept of the common everyday trance. Otherwise, the approach could be conceptualized as a new form of state dependent learning (Fischer, 1971).

Summary

The ultradian theory of hypnotic experience would view MHE as a brilliant innovator of many therapeutic approaches to facilitating naturally occurring oscillations of psychophysiological behavior characteristic of the ultradian cycle. Ultradian cycle research indicates that normal mental and physical health depend upon numerous naturally occurring rhythms, wherein parasympathetic and right-hemispheric processes have varying degrees of dominance every 90 to 100 minutes throughout the 24-hour period. Many, perhaps most, mental and psychosomatic problems could be understood as distortions of these naturally occurring "rest-activity cycles" induced by stress. Mental and physical stress distorts the normal periodicity of ultradian cycles and disrupts a variety of psychophysiological balances necessary for optimal functioning. Trance readiness, or the common everyday trance, may be understood as highly individual and variable but behaviorally recognizable portions of the ultradian cycle. Hypnotherapists can learn to recognize the behavioral characteristics of this naturally occurring cycle and facilitate hypnotherapeutic trance at this time by utilizing Erickson's naturalistic approaches. Hypnotherapy may be conceptualized as a facilitation of these naturally occurring ultradian cycles, during which parasympathetic and right-hemispheric processes can be maximized to facilitate healing.

REFERENCES

BOWERS, K. Has the sun set on the Stanford Scales? *American Journal of Clinical Hypnosis*, 1982, *2,* 79-88.

BYKOV, V. L., & KATINAS, G. S. Temporal organization of the thyroid in A/He mice (morphometric investigation). *Biol. Bull. Acad. Sci. USSR*, 1979, *6*, 247-249.

DELGADO-GARCIA, J. M., GRAU. C., DEFEUDIS, P., DEL POZO, F., JIMENEZ, J. M., & DELGADO, J. M. Ultradian rhythms in the mobility and behavior of rhesus monkeys. *Experimental Brain Research*, 1976, *25*, 79-91.

DEMENT, W., & KLEITMAN, N. Cyclic variations in EEG during sleep and their relation to eye movements, body motility, and dreaming. *Electroencephalography & Clinical Neurophysiology*, 1957, *9*, 673-690.

ERICKSON, M. H., & Rossi, E. L. *Hypnotherapy: An Exploratory Casebook.* New York: Irvington, 1979.

ERICKSON, M. H., ROSSI, E. L., & Rossi, S. I. *Hypnotic Realities.* New York: Irvington, 1976.

ERICKSON, E., ED'EN. MODIGH, K., & H." AGGENDAL., J. Ultradian rhythm in rat hypothalamic dopamine levels. *Journal of Neural Transmission*, 1980, *48*, 305-310.

FILICORI, M., BOLELLI, G., FRANCESCHETTI, F., & LAFISCA, S. The ultradian pulsatile release of gonadotropins in normal female subject. *Acta Europnea Fertilitatis*, 1979, *10*, 29-33.

FISCHER, R. A cartography of ecstatic and meditative states. *Science*, 1971, *174*, 897-904.

FRIEDMAN, A. H., & PIEPHO, R. W. Effect of photo period reversal on patterns for GABA levels in rat brain. *International Journal of Chronobiology*, 1978, *5*, 445-458.

FRIEDMAN, S., & FISCHER, C. On the presence of a rhythmic, diurnal, oral instinctual drive cycle in man: a preliminary report. *Journal of the American Psychoanalytic Association*, 1967, *15*, 317-343.

GLOBUS, G. G. Rapid eye movement cycle in real time. *Archives of General Psychophysiology*, 1966, *15*, 654-69.

GLOBUS, G. G. Observations on sub-circadian rhythms. *Psychophysiology*, 1968, *4*, 366.

GLOBUS, G. G., PHOEBUS, E., & MOORE, C. REM "sleep" manifestations during waking. *Psychophysiology*, 1970, *7*, 308.

GOPHER, D., & LAVIE P. Short-term rhythms in the performance of a simple motor task. *Journal of Motor Behavior*, 1980, *12*, 207-221.

HIATT. J. F., & KRIPKE, D. F. Ultradian rhythms in waking gastric activity. *Psychosomatic Medicine*, 1975, *37*, 320-325.

HILGARD, E. The eyeroll sign and other scores of the Hypnotic Induction Profile (HIP) as related to the Stanford Hypnotic Susceptibility Scales. Form C (SHSS:C). *American Journal of Clinical Hypnosis*, 1982a. *2*, 89-97.

HILGARD, E. Further discussion of the HIP and the Stanford Form C: A reply to reply by Frischolz. Spiegel. Tryon & Fischer. *American Journal of Clinical Hypnosis*, 1982b, *2*, 106-107.

HORNE, J., & WHITEHEAD, M. Ultradian and other rhythms in human respiration rate. *Experientia*, 1976, *32*, 1165-1167.

HUNSAKER, W. G., REISER, B., & WOLYNETZ, M. Vaginal temperature rhythms in sheep. *International Journal of Chronobiology*, 1977, *4*, 151-162.

KATZ, R. J. The temporal structure of motivation. III. Identification and ecological significance of ultradian rhythms of intracranial reinforcement. *Behavioral & Neural Biology*, 1980, *30*, 148-159.

KLEIN, R., & ARMITAGE, R. Rhythms in human performance: 1-½-hour oscillations in cognitive style. *Science*, 1979, *204*, 1326-1328.

KLEITMAN, N. *Sleep and Wakefulness* (2nd Ed.). Chicago: University of Chicago Press, 1963.

KLEITMAN, N. Basic rest-activity cycle in relation to sleep and wakefulness. In A. Kales (Ed.). *Sleep: Physiology & Pathology.* Philadelphia: Lippincott, 1969, 33-38.

KRIPKE, D. F. An ultradian biological rhythm associated with perceptual deprivation and REM sleep. *Psychosomatic Medicine*, 1972, *34*, 221-234.

KRIPKE, D. F. Ultradian rhythms in sleep and wakefulness. In E. D. Weitzman (Ed.), *Advances in Sleep Research*, Vol. 1, New York: Spectrum, 1974, 305-325.

KRIPKE, D. F. Ultradian rhythms in behavior and physiology. In F. M. Brown and R. C. Graeber (Eds.), *Rhythmic Aspects of Behavior*, Hillsdale, New Jersey: Erlbaum Associates, 1982a.[1*]

KRIPKE, D. F. Telephone conversation with Ernest Rossi, March, 1982b.

KRIPKE, D. F,. MULLANEY, D. G., WYBORNEY, V. G., & MESSIN, S. There's no basic rest-activity cycle. In F. D. Stott et al., (Eds.) ISAM 1977: *Proceedings of the Second International Symposium on Ambulatory Monitoring.* London: Academic Press, 1978, 105-113.

KRIPKE, D. F., & SONNENSCHEIN, D. A biologic rhythm in waking fantasy. In K. Pope & J. Stringer (Eds.). *The Stream of Consciousness.* New York: Plenum, 1978, 321-332.

KRYNICKI, V. Time trends and periodic cycles in REM sleep eye movements. *Electroencephalography & Clinical Neurophysiology*, 1975, 39, 507-513.

LAVIE, P. Ultradian rhythms in the perception of two apparent motions. *Chronobiologia*, 1976, *3*, 214-218.

LAVIE, P. Nonstationarity in human perceptual ultradian rhythms. *Chronobiologia*, 1977, *4*, 38-48.

LAVIE, P., & KRIPKE, D. F. Ultradian rhythms in urine flow in waking humans. *Nature*, 1977, *269*, 142-144.

1\ [*] Projected publication date of April, 1982, according to *Forthcoming Books Index.*

LAVIE, P., & KRIPKE, D. F. Ultradian circa 1½ hour rhythms: A multioscillatory system. *Life Sciences*, *29*, New York: Pergamon, 1981, 2445-2450.

LAVIE, P., LORD, J. W., & FRANK, R. A. Basic rest-activity cycle in the perception of the spiral aftereffect: a sensitive detector of a basic biological rhythm. *Behavioral Biology*, 1974, *11*, 373-379.

LAVIE, P., & SCHERSON, A. Ultrashort sleep-walking schedule. 1. Evidence of ultradian rhythmicity in "sleepability." *Electroencephalography & Clinical Neurophysiology*, 1981, *52*, 163-174.

LAVIE, P., & SCHULZ, H. Ultradian rhythms in the pupil. *Sleep Research*, 1978, *7*, 307.

LEVIN, B. E., GOLDSTEIN, A., & NATELSON, B. H. Ultradian rhythm of plasma noradrenaline in rhesus monkeys. *Nature*, 1978, *272*, 164-166.

LEWIS, B. D., KRIPKE, D. F., & BOWDEN, D. M. Ultradian rhythms in hand-mouth behavior of the rhesus monkey. *Physiology & Behavior*, 1977, *18*, 283-286.

LOVETT, J. W. Two biological rhythms of perception distinguishing between intact and relatively damaged brain function in man. *International Journal of Chronobiology*, 1976, *4*, 39-49.

LOVETT, J. W. Sinus tachycardia and abnormal cardiac rate variation in schizophrenia. *Neuropsychobiology*, 1990, *6*, 305-312.

LOVETT, J. W., PAYNE, W. D., & PODNIEKS, I. An ultradian rhythm of reaction time measurements in man. *Neuropsychobiology*, 1978, *4*, 93-98.

LOVETT, J. W., & PODNIEKS, I. Comparison between some biological clocks regulating sensory and psychomotor aspects of perception in man. *Neuropsychobiology*, 1975, *1*, 261-266.

LUBOSHITZKY, R., LAVIE, P., SOIK, Y., GLICK, S. M., LEROITH, D., SHENN-ORR, Z., & BARZILAI, D. Anti-diuretic hormone secretion and urine flow in aged catheterized patients, *T.I.T. Journal of Life Sciences*, 1978, *8*, 99-103.

MAXIM, P. E., BOWDEN, D. M., & SACKETT, G. P. Ultradian rhythms of solitary and social behavior in rhesus monkeys. *Physiology & Behavior*, 1976, *17*, 337-344.

MEIER-KOLL, A., POHL, P., SCHAFF, C., & STANKIEWITZ, C. Ein chronobiologischer aspekt stereotypen vehaltens. *Archiv fuer Psychiatrie und Nervenkrankheiten [Archives of Psychiatry & Neurological Sciences]*, 1978, *225*, 179-191.

MILLARD, W. J., REPPERT, S. M., SAGAR, S. M., & MARTIN, J. B. Light-dark entrainment of the growth hormone ultradian rhythm in the rat is mediated by the arcuate nucleus. *Endocrinology*, 1981, *108*, 2394-2396.

NABER, D., WIRZ-JUSTICE, A., KAFKA, M. S., & WEHR, T. A. Dopamine receptor binding in rat striatum: ultradian rhythm and its modification by chronic imipramine. *Psychopharmacology* (Berlin). 1980, *68*, 1-5.

OHLMEYER, P., BRILMAYER, H., & HUELLSTRUNG, H. *Pflu. Arch. Ges. Physiol.*, 1994, *248*, 599-660.

ORR. W. D., HOFFMAN, H. J., & HEGGE, F. W. Ultradian rhythms in extended performance. *Aerospace Medicine*, 1974, *45*, 995-1000.

ORR. W. C., HOFFMAN, H. J., & HEGGE, F. W. The assessment of time-dependent changes in human performance. *Chronobiologia*, 1976, *3*, 293-305.

OSWALD, I., MERRINGTON, J., & LEWIS, H. Cyclical "on demand" oral intake by adults. *Nature*, 1970, *225*, 959-960.

PODNIEKS, I., & LOVETT, J. W. Spontaneous rhythms of perceptual motor performance in intact and damaged brain of man. *Biological Psychology*, 1975, *3*, 201-212.

QUABEE, H. J., GREGOR, M., BUMKE-VOGT, C., ECKHOF, A., WITT, I. Twenty-four-hour pattern of growth hormone secretion in the rhesus monkey: studies including alterations of the sleep/wake and sleep stage cycles. *Endocrinology*, 1981, *109*, 513-522.

RASMUSSEN, D. D., & MALVEN, P. V. Relationship between rhythmic motor activity and plasma luteinizing hormone in ovariectomized sheep. *Neuroendocrinology*, 1981, *32*, 364-369.

REINBERG, A., MIGRAINE, C., AFFELBAUM, M., BRIGANT, L., GHATA, J., VIEUX, N., LAPORTE, A., & NICOLAI. Circadian and ultradian rhythms in the feeding behavior and nutrient intakes of oil refinery operators with shift-work every 3-4 days. *Diabete and Metabolisme*, 1979, *5*, 33-41.

ROMANO, S., & GIZDULICH, P. Suggestion of ultradian rhythm in peripheral blood flow. *Chronobiologia*, 1980, *7*, 259-261.

Rossi, E. L. Hypnotist describes natural rhythm of trance readiness. *Brain/Mind Bulletin*, 1981, *6*, No. 7.

SHIOTSUKA, R., JOVONOVICH, J., & JOVONOVICH, J. A. In vitro data on drug sensitivity: circadian and ultradian corticosterone rhythms in adrenal organ cultures. In J. Aschoff et al. (Eds.). *Chronobiological Aspects of Endocrinology.* Stuttgart: Schattauer, 1974, 255-267.

SIMON, M. L., & GEORGE, R. Diurnal variations in plasma corticosterone and growth hormone as correlated with regional variations in norepinephrine, dopamine and serotonin content of rat brain. *Neuroendocrinology*, 1975, *17*, 125-138.

STEINER, R. A., PETERSON, A. P., Yu, J. Y., CONNER, H., GILBERT, M., TERPENNING, B., & BREMNER, W. J. Ultradian luteinizing hormone and testosterone rhythms in the adult male monkey, macaca fascicularis. *Endocrinology*, 1980, *107*, 1489-1493.

TANNENBAUM, G. S., A MARTIN, J. B. Evidence for an endogenous ultradian rhythm governing growth hormone secretion in the rat. *Endocrinology*, 1976, *98*, 562-570.

TANNENBAUM, G. S., MARTIN, J. B., & COLLE, E. Ultradian growth hormone rhythm in the rat: effects of feeding, hyperglycemia, and insulin-induced hypoglycemia. *Endocrinology*, 1976, *99*, 720-727.

TIERNEY, I. R., MCGUIRE, R. J., & WALTON, H. J. Distributions of body-rocking manifested by severely mentally deficient adults in ward environments. *Journal of Mental Deficiency Research*, 1978, *22*, 243-254.

ULLNER, R. E. On the development of ultradian rhythms: the rapid eye movement activity in premature children. In L. E. Scheving et al. (Eds.). *Chronobiology.* Tokyo: Igaku Shoin, 1974, 478-481.

WEDA, T. *Archives of Psychological Monographs*, 1922, *8*.

WEITZMAN, E. D. Temporal organization of neuroendocrinal function in relation to the sleep-waking cycle in man. In *Recent Studies of Hypothalamic Function*, International Symposium, Calgary, 1973. Basel: Karger, 1974, 26-38.

YEN, S. S. C., VANDENBERG, G., TSAI, C. C., & PARKER, D. C. Ultradian fluctuations of gonadotropins. In M. Ferin et al. (Eds.). *Biorhythms and Human Reproduction.* New York: Wiley & Sons, 1974, 203-218.

PSYCHOANALYSIS AND ITS RELATIONSHIP TO THE WORK OF MILTON H. ERICKSON, M.D.

Dr. Bruno Bettelheim wrote of the value of stories and storytelling in The Uses of Enchantment. Dr. Milton Erickson told stories in an unimpeded flow. Dr. Erickson's work evoked in Dr. Bergantino a method of telling stories from the unconscious of the analyst to the unconscious of the patient in an unimpeded flow. These stories are told_in accord with the analyst's conscious as well as unconscious moment to moment experience of the patient, in that even the same story is never told the same way twice.

The method can be utilized to 1. Bypass the resistance. 2. Create relatively dis-ease free states of being that are most valuable in treating psychosomatic disorders and in utilizing Bion's conceptual framework in working with underlying psychotic thinking disorders.

The work of psychoanalysts and the work of Milton H. Erickson, M.D. have been too far apart for too long. There is much to be gained by a unification of the theory and the experience.

Len Bergantino, Ed.D., Ph.D. was trained by Milton H. Erickson, M.D. from 1977-1980. Psychotherapy, Insight And Style: The Existential Moment, authored by Dr. Bergantino and published by Jason Aronson, Inc., Pub., 1986, has a chapter done in cooperation with Dr. Erickson of Dr. Bergantino's personal and technical work with him. Dr. Bergantino has presented this work in Australia, England, Canada and throughout the United States.

"This work is valuable in that the analyst may begin to access the primitive unconscious of patients who would otherwise be inaccessible to analysis, and who after these methods, can work with analysis as a method of treatment. It is a method of "reverse psychoanalysis" to help the very needy so they may begin the work." (Len Bergantino)

Restoring The Sense Organs is the key to being able to do Bion's work with underlying psychotic thinking disorders. The storytelling precedes the analysis.

Title of Workshop Proposal: Ericksonian Storytelling: A Hypnotic Method To Restore The Sense Organs, Create Dis-Ease Free States of Being, Gain Unimpeded Access To An Unconscious Mind, And Bypass Conscious Resistance

Workshop Leader:	Len Bergantino, Ed.D., Ph.D. Private Practice of Clinical Psychology 450 N. Bedford Drive, Ste. 300 Beverly Hills, CA 90210 (1981-1991)
Position:	Past President-Southern California Society of Clinical Hypnosis (1987), which is a component society of The American Society of Clinical Hypnosis, of which I was also a member.
Mailing Address:	450 N. Bedford Drive, Ste. 300 Beverly Hills, CA 90210 USA (1981-1991)

This workshop, however many hours in length, will be a transmission of the culture of who Milton Erickson actually was as a person and what he actually did in terms of therapeutic use of self in the way Erickson actually did it. To my knowledge I am the only one of his students who is actually able to utilize this method in a non-stop manner from my unconscious to the unconscious of the patient and/or group of hypnotherapy doctors in training. Erickson used this method to teach, supervise and therapize simultaneously working nearly exclusively from the unconscious. Margaret Mead told Erickson the only time she heard the pace at which he spoke was in a rare African tribe relatively free of dis-ease. I have found this particular pace to be the key in working successfully with psychosomatic illness, when the unconscious is worked with via the storytelling simultaneously. While Erickson used this method non-stop for four and one half hours at a time when he trained me, I have found a way to be successful within fifty minute hypnotherapy sessions, and many times gain an existential life shift in one session. That is, the tragic corner of where a patient is stuck in their lives gets turned around as if one were using a ju-jitsu lever. I will work in a way that brings conscious understanding without disrupting the primary unconscious pacing experience necessary to do the work.

Dr. Wilfred Bion's psychoanalytic interpretations were a paragraph long at exactly the same pace or vibration that Margaret Mead told Dr. Erickson she had only heard in a rare African Tribe relatively free of disease. Bion had more in common with Erickson than he did with other psychoanalysts and vice versa.

AS TOLD BY LEN BERGANTINO, ED.D., PH.D.

THE HYPNOTIC TEACHING TALES OF MILTON H. ERICKSON, M.D.

AND THE CREATION OF A HEALING ENVIRONMENT

MARGARET MEAD told Milton H. Erickson, M.D., that THE PACE AT WHICH HE TOLD STORIES, WHICH IS THE PACE AT WHICH THESE STORIES WILL BE TOLD, WAS THE PACE OF A RARE AFRICAN TRIBE THAT WAS RELATIVELY FREE OF DISEASE.

A method of storytelling utilizing insight, that accesses the unconscious mind of the patient via the clinical application of a series of stories. This creates a series of releases that result in existential life shifts in addition to the benefit of the healing pace which helps to_create a new psychophysiological reality for the patient that can become both steady and internalized in the face of external difficulties. This method of hypnosis is particularly beneficial as adjunctive treatment with the difficult and sometimes even life threatening medical referral. Its advantage is that it has both a way of dealing with psychosomatic processes and psychophysiological processes simultaneously, and bypasses resistance because the storytelling is an indirect method of accessing the unconscious in which the patient is not told to do anything directly. Further, it has the advantage in that most people like to listen_to stories, particularly stories that contain the wisdom of the ages, such as those of Dr. Erickson.

The method will demonstrate how to combine the use of storytelling, automatic writing in the initial assessment of the patient, the utilization of sensory perception as a moment to moment diagnostic tool, and the pacing of which Margaret Mead was referring, to create a healing environment in working from the unconscious mind of the hypnotherapist while accessing the unconscious mind of the patient.

This method will be taught experientially, as Dr. Erickson himself conducted his teaching seminars, for the most part with a stream of unconscious uninterrupted storytelling. This will expose the psychotherapist to a working knowledge of the experiential effects over a period of fifty to one hundred or one hundred and eighty uninterrupted minutes and give the participants the kind of experience they will then be able to begin to transmit to their patients.

FOR MEDICAL DOCTORS AND DENTISTS who may have to endure some unenjoyable and stressful situations with patients regarding patient treatment and follow through, gaining the ability to bypass resistance by telling one or two appropriate and well timed stories may create the kind of release in the patient that will help the treatment be effective as well as reduce the stress for both doctor and patient.

This method of teaching and demonstration through the experience of the stories themselves, in addition to learning the method, is intended to give the workshop participant the experiential flavor and sense of how it was to have been there with Dr. Erickson. Bion's use of the_long winded Psychoanalytic interpretation enabled the patient to attain disease free status of being relatively free of character armor (Reich) in pursuing Power and finer discriminations of pure being. Bergantino is the only one who could do all of the above as a way of life.

UPLIFTING THE HUMAN SPIRIT- GAINING ACCESS TO THE

UNCONSCIOUS IN PROVIDING THE HEALING THERAPEUTIC

ENVIRONMENT OF MILTON H. ERICKSON, M.D.

When referring to Milton H. Erickson, M.D., DeStefano (J. of Marital And Family Therapy, Vol. 8, No. 4, Oct., 1982) wrote "What is often lost in the plethora of technical detail described is the remarkable presence of the man and the way those with whom he worked felt personally touched by him. Techniques that often get rigidified by the students of the master lose vitality, creativity, and the central theme that what is most often effective comes out of the personal experience of the therapist."

This will not be the case when I teach you the Ericksonian therapeutic environment which contain the "minimum conditions" involved in doing effective hypnotherapy, effective psychotherapy and effective psychoanalysis-as one psychoanalyst described the method_as "reverse analysis", as I will teach through the experience itself. Dr. Erickson, over the three years in which I was involved in training experiences with him, never did anything that wasn't psychotherapy. He was a master clinician, and within that context utilized his hypnotic techniques and hypnotherapeutic genius. While the course is the thing in itself for those practicing hypnotherapy, it provides the essential ingredients to be developed by psychotherapists and psychoanalysts in their own particular disciplines if they are to provide a healing environment.

The problem in practicing Ericksonian hypnotherapy and psychotherapy, if one is to gain knowledge in being able to work with whatever is thrown at you, and Dr. Erickson was often a last resort in working with cases that were otherwise regarded as hopeless-is that techniques themselves won't do it. Dr. Erickson provided an experience from the moment you walked into his office. It was a rare occasion when he ever taught in the usual fashion of discussing anything cognitively. From the moment he set eyes on you, you were immersed in the kind of experience that would help you become the kind of person and the kind of therapist who could utilize his or her own personal attributes in creating a kind of hypnosis or psychotherapy that would work for you and the patients with whom you work. It may or may not resemble Erickson's work as he practiced it, but he provided all the elements from which your unconscious mind could extract what it needed to begin to practice the lifetime art of doing hypnosis and psychotherapy with the facilitation of a healing therapeutic environment. It is to these ends, and in this way, and with the utmost respect for my teacher, Dr. Erickson, that I will teach this course.

Saturday and Sunday 11 a.m. to 3 p.m. text required is Bergantino, L. Psychotherapy, Insight And Style: The Existential Moment. Allyn & Bacon, Inc., Boston, 1981.

ERICKSONIAN STORYTELLING

by LEN BERGANTINO, ED.D., PH.D.

■■ ■

Milton Erickson told stories four and one half hours at a time at a pace Margaret Mead told him was relatively free of dis-ease. This was the method by which he taught, supervised and therapized simultaneously. Through this method one can restore the sense organs, create dis-ease free states of Being, gain unimpeded access to an unconscious mind, and bypass conscious resistance. Bergantino did this in his workshops which were the thing in itself or as close to pure being as humanly possible.

VIDEO TAPE-3 hours in length-Ericksonian
Storytelling Send $50 in United States currency to:

Len Bergantino, Ed.D., Ph.D.
450 N. Bedford Drive, Ste. 300
Beverly Hills, CA 90210
United States of America
1981-1991

Those interested in hiring Dr. Bergantino for workshops may call him at

(424)293-9511

The Hypnotic Teaching Tales

of Milton H. Erickson, M.D.

• A method of regressive psychoanalysis utilizing insight, that accesses the unconscious mind of the patient via the clinical application of story telling. This creates releases that result in existential life shifts. This method of hypnosis is particularly beneficial as adjunctive treatment with the difficult and sometimes even life threatening medical referral.

LEN BERGANTINO, ED.D., PH.D.

- Trained by Milton H. Erickson, M.D.
- Southern California Society of Clinical Hypnosis Member, Board of Directors
- Author: Psychotherapy, Insight and Style The Existential Moment

3rd Saturday of each month, 10 a.m. – 1 p.m.
$40.00 per month

Contact: LEN BERGANTINO, ED.D., PH.D.
450 No. Bedford Drive, Suite 303
Beverly Hills, CA 90210
Telephone (213) 273-8705

Margaret Mead told Milton H. Erickson, M.D., that the pace at which he told stories, which is the pace at which these stories will be told, was the pace of a rare African tribe that was relatively free of disease.

Ernest L. Rossi, Ph.D., in <u>The American J. of Clinical Hypnosis</u>, Vol. 24, No. 3, January, 1982 wrote a <u>review</u> of

<u>PSYCHOTHERAPY, INSIGHT AND STYLE: THE EXISTENTIAL MOMENT</u>

"While Bergantino thus emphasizes how the personal and human element transcends all technique, his book does focus on the precise and often provocative and shocking techniques that are useful in helping patients break out of their learned limitations to realize their potentials for creative change."

The chapter regarding Dr. Bergantino's training with Milton H. Erickson, M.D. is beneficial for those interested in learning the basic premises from which one can begin to utilize the 'hypnotic teaching tales' both in terms of the clinical application of storytelling and the therapeutic tenets necessary to set the frame in which the work can take place. The book can be purchased by sending $27.50 to Dr. Bergantino at the above address.

Margaret Mead told Milton H. Erickson, M.D., that the pace at which he told stories, which is the pace at which these stories will be told, was the pace of a rare African tribe that was relatively free of disease. This is the key to the work of Dr. Len Bergantino and Erickson.

Ernest L. Rossi, Ph.D., in <u>The American J. of Clinical Hypnosis</u>, Vol. 24, No. 3, January, 1982 wrote a <u>review</u> of

PSYCHOTHERAPY, INSIGHT AND STYLE: THE EXISTENTIAL MOMENT

"While Bergantino thus emphasizes how the personal and human element transcends all technique, his book does focus on the precise and often provocative and shocking techniques that are useful in helping patients break out of their learned limitations to realize their potentials for creative change."

The chapter regarding Dr. Bergantino's training with Milton H. Erickson, M.D. is beneficial for those interested in learning the basic premises from which one can begin to utilize the 'hypnotic teaching tales' both in terms of the clinical application of storytelling and the therapeutic tenets necessary to set the frame in which the work can take place. The book can be purchased by sending $27.50 to Dr. Bergantino at the above address.

Telephone (213) 273-0705

LEN BERGANTINO, Ed.D., Ph.D.
Clinical Psychology (PL3837)

465 North Roxbury Dr., Suite 810
Beverly Hills, California 90210

192

September 1, 1981

Dear Marion,

Please write the following statement about my presentation

STORYTELLING AS A THERAPEUTIC TECHNIQUE:

Wilfred R. Bion, M.R.C.S., in his novel (Memoir of the Future-The Dre[illegible] Imago Editora Ltd., Rio de Janeiro, Brazil, 1975, p. 204) about psychoanalysis, has the character 'MYSELF', when confronted by the character 'Bion' about obscurity, state indirectly, what might be viewed as the aim of the clinical practice of psychoanalysis "...I am suggesting an aim, an ambition, which, if I could achieve, would enable me to be deliberately and precisely obscure; in which I could use certain words which could activate precisely and instantaneously, in the mind of the listener, a thought or train of thought that come between him and the thoughts and ideas already accessible and available to him."

"Into each life some confusion should come ...also some enlightenment" Milton H. Erickson, M.D. As Dr. Erickson evoked this storytelling method in me, I write "While every human being has limitations, Dr. Erickson presupposed a view of consciousness that has unlimited possibilities and did his best to provide the kind of open-ended environment so his patients could [illegible] possibilities. He did [illegible] to [illegible] in which patients were able to [illegible] go of conscious control and begin to trust in their unconsciou[illegible] processes and their inner wisdom. (Bergantino, L. Psychotherapy, Insight And Style : The Existential Moment, Allyn & Bacon, Inc., Boston, 1981, p. 228) Storytelling is a way to provide such an experience.

It is to these ends that I intend to get an experiential assessment of the group, make contact in the ways that occur to me at the time, and preferably, if I have a volunteer, and I assume I will, to do an assessment and demonstration of an actual 50 minute session. At that point I will open up discussion of what I do, but perhaps answer and respond to questions at the unconscious level. I would hope to present [illegible] which will give interested participants [illegible] to begin using storytelling in their own practices. If [illegible], I will [illegible] of paper, asking each participant to request one issue on which they wish to work, and begin telling stories to the group at the unconscious level. Depending upon how much time the first experience takes, I may do this as a second part of the experience.

Sincerely,

Len

cc: interested colleagues

ACCESS TO THE UNCONSCIOUS THROUGH STORYTELLING

This is an experiential course for those whose lives are intertwined with the story; those who produce stories, executives who earn their living by making decisions about which stories to choose, those who act the parts of stories, those who direct people in stories and last but not least, those who write stories. Each of these disciplines and art forms require an access to the unconscious unimpeded by conscious constraints. The attainment of a stream of access to the unconscious can be quite difficult to attain given the everyday pressures of life. The instructor has a unique method of storytelling and pacing, that over the course of consecutive hours provides that kind of freeing and access to unconscious processes by also helping to create an altered physiological state so that the unconscious subtleties of experience will be accessible. The course can be valuable for those who are having trouble blocking in terms of what they have to do with stories. This is a course for those who do have the ability to flow with the story, and is not a course for the concrete person who would have a difficult time making the unconscious connections and transitions in such a short course.

9:30 a.m. to noon and 1:30 p.m. to 4 p.m. on a Saturday

Instructor-Len Bergantino, Ed.D., Ph.D.-private practice of clinical psychology, Beverly Hills, CA

Monday, September 24, 1984 Los Angeles County Medical Association Southern California Society of Clinical Hypnosis

Hypnotic Teaching Tales In The Creation of the Healing Environment

I will demonstrate how to combine the use of storytelling or teaching tales with sensory perception in automatic writing. And working from the unconscious of the hypnotherapist to the unconscious of the patient.

What I'd like to do tonight is talk a little bit about the kind of-Carol-I need this microphone. Carol. I studied with Milton Erickson between 1977 and the time of his death. When I studied with Erickson he primarily told stories. He would do a few inductions. But primarily told stories. What Erickson talked about was what's involved in that person's unconscious mind. So all I can say about what I'm going to present tonight is an experience with Erickson evoke this kind of method of clinical hypnosis. I'm not sure he would speak about it this way. I'm not sure he would think about it this way. I was fortunate that he evoked such a method in myself. Because it had a lot of personal benefits. In the work with him-he used to tell stories hour after hour. 3-4 hours straight. During that time there was an access that took place to sensory perception that I had never experienced before. It was like a fine tuning of a sensory field, or an energy field or what a person projects. Almost as a psycho-analyst would think about projective identification. What is it that presides in that patient in terms of that person showing you how it is to be done. Those sensory vibrations which I never had access to before as result of the work with Erickson I started to-I would sense pain in the heart area. And when I would tell stories they would be stories of the heart. Like pointed the direction in which my stories would go. Furthermore, it pointed the direction almost immediately. So I could alter my story or the juxtaposition of a story. For example there may be 50 stories I know about Erickson. And I might tell one 4 or 5 times. But each time I tell it there is a different juxtaposition in terms of what's going on moment to moment. In the existential moment one might say. Now what happens this is a form of insight there. So what happens in that time if the work is done correctly. Usually an existential shift. Some sort of release in that person's unconscious mind with whatever dynamic they were bound up with. And they feel freer to get on with whatever stuck. Now the additional benefit of the sensory perception was that for example when working with certain patients who split off from emotion, split off from sensation projected out into the environment. Because the pain is intolerable for them to stand. With this use of sensory perception two things happen: one if you're doing this kind of story telling you can create an environment of wellness comes to mind. Ernie Rossi wrote about it in terms of-----ultradian cycles. Erickson used to work long periods of time. Ernie wrote it saying 90-120 minutes. In that time there is a certain break point. And I think Erickson met a lot of his impacts within that period of time. So, at a sensory level I think people in the western culture tend to live a bit out of tune with their internal clock. Erickson told his stories at a pace like this a f t e r h o u r. Pretty soon if everything's going at a pace like this hour a f t e r h o u r a f t e r h o u r. Your own internal clock gets to be like a metronome. You get external phenomena that might influence your behavior or throw you off center. You become much steadier. Much more stable at maintaining that center. What I found since 1977 in my self is that whatever hypnosis-whatever way it can be useful in adjunct to medical kinds of problems. If this kind of environment is created. The-----environment, the introduction.

People have their best chance at utilizing the hypnosis to take care of their particular psycho-sematic difficulty. Now what I further found out that this sensory experience gets you an almost immediate access to primitive experience. An analyst might speak about it in terms of primitive preconceptions. So then what you have is certain patients with thinking disorders. You have an immediate tune in, a way to help them contain the experience. And a way that gives to evoke thought with their minds customarily----thought. So, when I begin to work I use automatic writing. I use a purple pen. Erickson always dressed in purple. A lot of his stories although I've done my best in maintaining my own identity in this and I'm clearly the person doing the work. A lot of stories that I tell were either stories that Erickson told or were stories about Erickson. Erickson's view of it-there were stories about good therapy. My view of it I'm trying to juxtaposition moment to moment to get an existential shift on an insight level. When a person comes in I have a pad, a purple pen and whatever magic I can use I use it as long as I don't take it seriously. The stories build around purple okay so they build around purple. It helps sometime. The first 5 minutes of an interview a person tells me what brings them to the office. At that time I write down whatever goes through my unconscious mind. It may be concrete sentences. It may be a paragraph. It may be a thought evoked. It might be recognition of a story from which that person said. But within that 5 five minutes I've got the basis on a page or a page and a half of 50 minutes worth of stories. The rest is going to be a 2 hour session and it might be a little longer than 2 full pages. The stories of my unconscious reaction to what I sense that person's unconscious mind. What's going on about that. If there is sometime in the session that I get stuck I don't quite know where to go. I go back to the automatic writing. Whatever the unconscious mind says I go with that. My best bet is to stay centered, trust my own unconscious. And not get distracted. That's the introduction-I think it pretty much explains what I do. I think what I'd like to do at this time is-my intention is to try and give you something you can take from here and you can start to try out in your own office. Start to work with. What I'd like to do is-and I promise to keep it light. Is have a volunteer I can demonstrate this style with. And then after talk about the kind of thinking as it was happening that went into the stories and the kind of responses I would make. Also you might notice on a sensory level once that pace get started what kind of things you begin to notice in your own system that cue you in to what kind of experience you might work with. In terms of someone who volunteers. If you have a knack of liking stories or feeling the sense that you flow well with metaphors all the better. Come right up here. What do you like to be called?

Nikki.

Bergantino-Nikki, can you tell me in a short period of time in this demonstration here what-something you might be interested in that might be of value to you in terms of perhaps what your conscious or unconscious mind-----experience from what I've said so far? Something that might be a problem that you feel okay about bringing up here.
That's not too big or not to small, something you might benefit from.

Nikki-How about something perfectly vivid lying over me?

Bergantino-Anything you might want to add to that?

Nikki-It's kind of confusing-------

Bergantino-Can you say a little bit more about what you mean?

Nikki-I'm kind of------it's a problem outside and inside. Visible and invisible. It has a lot to do with the inside picture of myself. A way of looking, viewing things------. It sort of an amount of confusion.------ kinds of things that I want to do.

Bergantino-Can you say a little bit more about-------?

Nikki-Okay. I think it boils down to the advantages and disadvantages. Things-there are advantages to be-----. They're not really terribly obvious. But they're very definitely there. There's also advantages to being at my ideal ways and some of those are internal and some of those are

Bergantino-You said something about pictures?

Nikki-It's hard for me to picture the way I look. I can see what I look like in a mirror. But my internal picture of how I look shifts. Goes in and out and changes. And colors the way I perceive myself when I look at myself projectively in a mirror.

Bergantino-What exactly is that in and out shift? What does that look like?

Nikki-It looks like seeing almost a photo album of different pictures of myself and of the way I look. My mental picture of myself changes depending on how I feel about myself at the moment. And depending on where I'm feeling in my head. So that I see myself heavier than I really am. Sometimes slimmer than I really am. And sometimes as just a little confused where I can't get a clear picture at all.

Bergantino-What I'd like you to do is keep your feet flat on the floor, hands at your sides. You can pick any spot in the room you wish. If you can remember when you were a little girl learning many very difficult things. You learned the letters of the alphabet. How to discriminate between an A, and a D. Which way the stems went on a b, and a p. How to dot your T's and cross your I's. Add and subtract 1 and 1 is 2, 2 and 2 is 4. And many other difficult things you don't even know that you knew. All of these learnings are a part of your unconscious mind. Your unconscious mind had all the thoughts, words, memories, feelings and actions that you need to live a happy, healthy life. During this session those unconscious experiences I'm going to begin to evoke. I can remember the first time I saw Erickson. His wife wheeled him in. He was crippled, he had polio, arthritis. His lips were paralyzed, his tongue was dislocated. He had gout. His feet were swollen like cement blocks. I took one long look at Erickson and I thought how tough??? tough my life is, I can't compare how tough the old guys life is! When Erickson was 17 he had his first bout of polio. According to the doctors they told his mother he would never see the next sunrise. The doctors left. He called his mother and father in and told them he was furious at the doctors. He told them to please move the mirror facing the crack in the door where he could see in the other room where the sun came up. He said he would be damned if he wouldn't see the next sunrise. He forced himself to stay awake all night. When I met him he was 77. Erickson told me about a story a boy named Joey. Joey was quite a problem to his mother. His mother was beside herself. She called Erickson. He told her to come right down and bring the boy down. The boy went into the office saying---- You can't make me do anything! Erickson looked at

him "You're absolutely right young man! I can't make you do anything! I want you to leave to go out into my waiting room I'm going to talk to your mother. Because she needs counseling. He talked to Joey's mother. It took tremendous effort on Erickson's part to make her realize that it was going to take every bit of strength she had to hold Joey down while she sat on him. She was afraid of hurting him. She was afraid of being too tough on him. It took every bit of strength she had. The story went like this. The next day mother sent her older daughter off to school. Joey got up. She cooked him a dish of oatmeal. He threw it in her face. She got him on the floor. She sat on him. He kicked, screamed, tried to bite her. He spit at her, swore at her. She kept saying Joey I'd like to let you up. You've got me stumped. I don't know how to solve your problem.

I can't let you up until the problem is solved. This went into the third and fourth hour. Finally Joey had to go to the bathroom. His mother said alright you can go to the bathroom. If you come back and resume this position. During the fifth hour Joey said he knew exactly what to do to solve his problem. She said I have one more chapter to read in this book. When I finish that chapter I'll let you up. This was the beginning of the sixth hour. Joey got up and said he was hungry. His mother said you can't have dinner until you've had lunch. You can't have lunch until you've had breakfast. Seeming you missed breakfast I suggest you go to bed and get a good night's sleep. Get up bright and early and we'll start all over. He got up in the morning. The mother made Joey oatmeal. Joey thanked her. He ate every bit of it. He came back and told his mother he apologized to the neighbors, to his peers at school, to his teacher. He promised he'd never behave that way again. Things went along alright for a while. Joey got into a fight with his sister. The sister made fun of him. She asked that he explain in details. He was shaking in his boots. Mother told Joey those were normal kind of problems. Things went along pretty well for about 6 months. He said bring Joey down. Joey walked into the office stamped his foot down and said you can't make me do anything. Dr. Erickson asked Joey's mother to come into the back room. It made a distinct difference to have a clear separation of generations; adult-child. A clear separation. One language was for adults and one was for children. When the mother left Erickson said, Joey, I'll bet you can't stomp your foot as hard as you can a hundred times. Joey said oh yes I can. Erickson said I bet you can't even stomp your foot as hard as you can even twenty times. Joey said oh yes I can. One woman called she had a severe attack of asthma. And she was up all night coughing. Erickson asked her if she wanted to be hypnotized. After about 20 minutes you could see the muscle tone had changed. Erickson always talked about the struggle between the conscious mind and the unconscious mind. Difficulty in terms of the conscious mind.-

-----of the unconscious mind. She said but Dr. Erickson how is that going to help me stop coughing and sleep better. Erickson looked at her and said take it from an authoritarian old man like me you have very kissable lips. The woman just beamed. She had never been told that.

She never knew that about herself. When she got up to leave she said, ("Dr. Erickson, how's one session going to help me stop coughing and sleep better tonight?") Dr. Erickson turned over his right shoulder to the door and said, you only had to be born once, didn't you! And then with his paralyzed lips and dislocated tongue and began to sing the lip bone is connected to the cheek bone, the cheek bone is connected to the neck bone, the neck bone is connected to the chest bone. In an all knowing way he said he knew that Barbara would sleep very very well that night. Erickson often used the confusion technique. It was hard to tell which image matched which image. And what internal viewpoint-

----to what external viewpoint.-----one might have.----inside yourself what that might look like. The external verses the internal. When I went to Erickson I was a type A personality. I could hardly sit by the pool for an hour. I was about 30 pounds heavier than I am now. I started-the second day I was there. I said "Hypnotize me again". And it felt so good the second day I was there. Dr. Erickson hypnotized me again. He said by the very fact you've asked the question----you can go as

deeply as you wish for however long and come out wherever you wish. Of course I hadn't the foggiest notion of how to do this. My conscious mind panicked. Erickson bobbed and weaved his head a little bit. And all these-----they were true to my own nature. They needed to become

clear. I was able to remember a light trance. When I got back to my office I was telling one of my patients about this extraordinary person I had the good fortune to train with. I don't know how to do it. He said go ahead and take a chance! I trust you! So I began telling my first set of stories. It lasted 5 minutes. I was quite pleased. The next hour I tried it again. It was like anything else. You keep pitching baseballs you learn how to pitch better. When I went to a restaurant. I went to the movies with my wife and two friends. I had this image in my mind of a cheese cake. All night it was all I could think of this cheese cake. I looked at the menu and there was cheese cake. I noticed at the sensory perception level a small green salad. I lost 15 pounds without ever going on a diet. Seeing what my instincts, sensory perceptions. But then I started to try to lose weight. Once I did that the critical part of my mind took over. That happened for about a month. Then I gave up trying. I lost 30 pounds without going on a diet. I didn't go to Erickson to lose weight. Anything you would like to say about what you experienced?

Nikki – I was trying to catch what you were doing while listening to stories.

Bergantino-Thank you for sharing-----. Thank you for volunteering. Any thoughts, feelings, comments, questions?

Question--------

Bergantino-The only way I can pay attention to my own sensory perception is------for me to go into trance state. That helps to create the trance state.

Question---------automatic writing.

Bergantino-Some things I just took down verbatim. Advantages to being overweight. Advantages equals ideal weight. Then I wrote tries to picture the way I look. Shifts in and out. Changes. A photo of different pictures---heavier, skinnier. At this point my sensory awareness was lousy. Then she said confused. Can't get a clear picture at all. The nausea which was some kind of I thought primitive way to cut off the experience. It was the primary cue on a consistent basis.---on the right track. And of course with the word confusion then I could say this image or that image. In or out. This way or that way. But all the time focusing----confusion. Focusing on the sensory of where the nausea

was. The nausea and the confusion were the cues primarily from which I built the stories. It just happened to be those stories. It could have been any story. But these things just happened to fit this particular experience. I was surprised at the-at what came out in terms of my own weight loss of 30 pounds. I haven't thought about that in a long time. As I told it I started experiencing where I would imagine the cheese cake I was nauseous. And when I imagined the or when the-----. I could feel the difference each time I said the difference. I had made the assumption at some deep level that would be transmitted to me. Much as the analyst would say if you work with a solid object that solid object becomes an introjected into the patient. The patient becomes the thing in itself.

Question-----------?

Bergantino-I thought that-I had to trust my unconscious mind that that was the right story. That's what came out so I trusted-I thought about it was she wouldn't necessarily pick up on that part of the story or her unconscious mind would extract a different message from it. Or it would turn it around in a way where that part of the story might be useful to her in a way that I don't know about. But I trusted that was the right story to tell at that time. I had to go with it.

Question--------?

Bergantino-That particular one I read in the advanced techniques. I read all the works and I had over 3 years experiences and then all the letters he wrote. Within that frame work and then whatever experience I built up sense my own life personally in my own work. But I suppose as I go along I hope to have more of my own stories.

Nikki-That one was right on target in a in a very peculiar way. No in the surface part of the story but in the------.

Bergantino-Can you share a little more about what you mean by that.

Nikki-It was almost like trying to analyze a poem. It resonated the way a poem does. When the surface meaning of a poem is the not the important thing. It's the echoes the poem evokes. And that evoked an awful lot of echoes with the right on the target of the problem. I would probably have to go into very deep trance to do automatic writing.

Bergantino-If I'm doing training and analyses or family work I'll wear red. But I tie this in with Erickson and whatever mystique or curiosity about purple or. Sometime people will say I was going to mess up again but I just saw this purple and it put me on the right track. Essentially it gives me age. I'm 41 and he was 79 and I picked up 50 years without consciously knowing how to use that. Where I can identify that when it works with a patient I'll do it. Erickson also made a point of knowing the difference magic and just paying attention to detail. It wouldn't be-----that if I didn't know the difference.-----is kind of an awesome show of showmanship. So then I had to find out what kind of details fit for me. Quite different-----for him. And more of a sensory experience insight and he evoked the kind of experiences that had a lot to do with development of thinking. When I first went there I------. I don't know what he would think if he ever found out he turned me into a psycho-analyst.

Question--------------?

Bergantino-Those are your thoughts about it. My thoughts about what's evoked in my particular style. Which was evoked in me from the experience I had.--------he thought about it. I guess it was in the particular books he wrote. I'm not speaking of that I'm speaking about what I think and what I do can make the difference------. I don't pretend to be a spokesman for Erickson although I use stories about him to do what I want to do in sessions.

Question-----------?

Bergantino-It depends. What I trust is what comes through the unconscious. Sometime sometime not. One person I saw in the workshop in Australia. She said I'm sick of Erickson. I'd rather see more of Bergantino. And I had to do a different kind of work.

Question--------------?

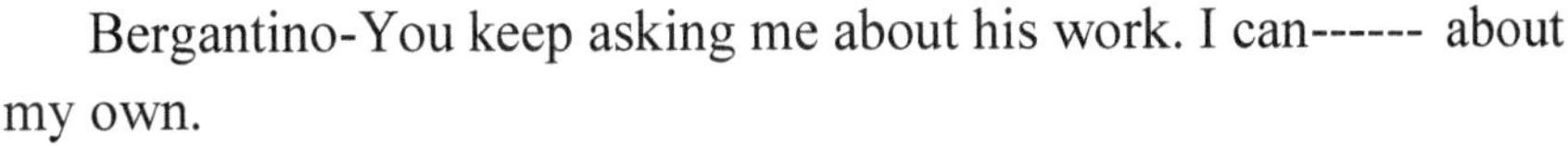

Bergantino-You keep asking me about his work. I can------ about my own.

Question----------- ?

Bergantino-No no no. Most of my talk was about how I use stories about him as an insight----- therapy to create an existential shift.

Question------------ ?

Bergantino-I've only used the stories about him to do the work here. Then what went through my unconscious to do the work here in a different kind of pace I use. I was tuning into my own center to get that pace.

Question------------?

Bergantino-I think that's true. I think he could be quite an authoritarian.

Comment----------

Bergantino-Yea. I saw him working directly but someone had mentioned directly he had this tremendous problem.

Comment------------

Bergantino-One of the things Erickson knew how to do was intimidate the hell out of someone in the first 3 minutes. When he set a frame like he was the doctor and you were the patient. He was the teacher and you were the student. He set that so clear that maybe you could learn something. He set the environment on how to do it. So people had to take him seriously. Anymore comments or?

Comment-----------

Bergantino-I think the issue here is what language was effective including unconscious following the hypnotist and the unconscious mind from the subject. And according to the subject's report there were 3 levels of experience. One was which------. And that's all I'm going to demonstrate was the method I used with whatever language----- effective in that situation.

Nikki----------I was aware of what you were saying at a very conscious------verbalizing level------without any difficulty.

Comment-----------

Bergantino-I think there's a difference in what you described and in how I intended for this work to be. And the mean would come from the sense experience connected up with the thought. There's a different concept in you describe what you think about Erickson.

Comment-The funny thing is-----------

Bergantino-You may have a variety of conceptions about what you think thought is. You may in fact-----to the experience that thought is connected to experience.

Comment----------

Bergantino-That's not thought that's-------.

Comment---------------

Bergantino-I'm about ready to call it quits. I've got to say one more thing. People who-therapist who----say that they feel liberated, freer, vitalizing and gets firmer. I enjoyed being here and I appreciate everyone of you for coming. Thank you.

THE FOLLOWING DEMONSTRATION OF ERICKSONIAN REVERSE PSYCHOANALYSIS TOOK PLACE AT THE UNIVERSITY OF SOUTHERN CALIFORNIA IN THE DEPARTMENT OF PSYCHOLOGY SOMETIME BETWEEN 1983 AND 1986.

■■ ■

Bergantino-Could the fellow right here move back a little bit. So I can see everybody. Milton talked to me about doing a presentation in clinical hypnosis and particularly how it related to over weight-the issues of overweight and alcohol. I thought perhaps in the spirit of my mentor Milton Erickson, I would show you how he might work in hypnosis. And I guess at the unconscious level what may come out in terms of working with alcohol, over weight issues and or any personal issues that you might want to bring up here. Erickson was a master of indirect suggestion and storytelling. And when you worked with him he would often times go into his office and he would tell stories and 4 1/2 hours later he would stop and his wife would wheel him out. The process was somewhat frustrating at first. It was a pace like this that he began to tell the stories. A very slow pace. In retrospect I think the western world moves at a certain pace. And you hear about people in the eastern cultures moving at an entirely different pace. Now Margaret Mead told Erickson that the only time she ever heard pace like the one that I'm demonstrating for you today was a rare African tribe. She said the thing that she noticed about that tribe is that there was very little disease in the tribe. Ernie Rossi who wrote, co-authored many books with Erickson has written papers about ultradian cycles. He said Erickson often worked with people between 80 and 120 minutes. And during that time I can recall a variety of things happening. I had wondered why no one else in the group spoke. Seeing there was a group of us there. Erickson just kept on talking at a pace like this. Then I began to try to figure out what he was doing. That was another hopeless situation. After about hour and a half after that I got sick of trying to figure out what he was doing. Then I began to drift off. Erickson always talked about the different between the conscious mind and the unconscious mind. If you're going to do hypnosis there's a very important double----to know.

Because it's a fail proof system. Your conscious mind may not understand everything that I say. But your unconscious mind has all the thoughts, memories, feelings and actions that you need to live a happy and a healthy life. Through the hypnosis those thoughts, memories, feelings and actions are evoked. And you may wonder whether they'll gonna begin between the time of 4 and 6 or whether they'll begin between the time of 6 and 8 tonight. Or between 8 and 11. Perhaps during your dream state. Or in the morning. Or will it be in the afternoon. Or the evening. The past, is the present, is the future, and they're all now! Erickson often worked with confusion states. He said in every person's life should come a little confusion and a little enlightenment. Erickson often told stories about patients----. He told a story about a patient

named Pete. Pete was an ex-convict. He lived most of his life in jail. But he'd been out for the last 7 months. He had a job working as a bartender. He was living with a girl. And he was drunk every night for the last 7 months. His girlfriend got sick and tired of him and she threw him out. Pete feeling very desperate walked 18 miles in the blazing hot desert sun in Phoenix Arizona. Parched throat, cotton mouth, blistered feet, aching body, dispirited. He got to Dr. Erickson's office. He knocked on the door and he asked him for his help. And Dr. Erickson gave it to him. Pete became furious. He slammed the door. Walked another 18 miles back to town. Talked his girlfriend into taking him back in. Resumed his job as a bartender. He was drunk every night for another 2 weeks. His girlfriend was sick and tired of him. She was fed up. She threw him out again. Pete feeling more desperate than he had the first time walked another 18 miles. Blazing hot sun in Phoenix Arizona. Blistered feet, cotton mouth, parched throat, dispirited. Erickson often talked about the value of interrupted learning. I remember he used to answer the telephone right in the middle of his hypnosis session. People wanted to come and see him from all over the world. He would say, "What's your highest degree? Call me back when you get it!" He would just go on with no wasted energy. When Pete got to Dr. Erickson's office he knocked on the door. He asked him for his help. Dr. Erickson said "Pete you asked me for my help and I gave it to you! You told me to shove it! So I shoved it! And now if you want my help now you're gonna have to beg me to take your boots!" Dr. Erickson went on to explain what he meant by that. That was his convicts code of honor that he really meant business. Without that sort of commitment one couldn't really expect very much of anything. Pete understanding the full nature of the request became furious. He slammed the door. He walked another 18 miles in the blazing hot sun of Phoenix Arizona. He got back to town. He talked his girlfriend into taking him back in. He resumed his job as a bartender. He was drunk every night for another week and a half. His girlfriend said she was sick and tired of him. She said she was fed up with him. And she was throwing him out for the last time. Pete feeling the most desperate he felt yet. Walked another 18 miles exhausted. The alcohol wearing away at his body. Dissipated. Got to Dr. Erickson's office suffering, depressed. He took off his boots, knocked on the door. And he begged Dr. Erickson to take his boots. Dr. Erickson said "Pete come on in. All I want you to do is go out in to my backyard. You can stay as long as you need. There's an old mattress out there you can sleep on. If you get cold at night Mrs. Erickson will give you a blanket. But I don't think you will be because it's summer time. If you get hungry ask Mrs. Erickson and she will give you some pork and beans. And think about what you want to do with your whole life." Of course Erickson always managed to get those suggestions in when you least expected it. Now sometime they were direct. People were kind of off balance and waiting expectedly. Sometime they were indirect. He always tried to speak to a person in their own language. Figuring out the way they needed to hear it to get the job done. When Pete had been out there for a time. It was Sunday afternoon. It was Dr. Erickson's birthday. His daughter and his granddaughter came to visit. And they looked out the back window and they saw Pete. They'd asked Dr. Erickson if they could go out and spend some time with him. He agreed. They spent the better part of Sunday and Monday with Pete. It was a short time later. Pete asked for his boots back. And he told Dr. Erickson that he never knew that girls and women like that really existed. Dr. Erickson said he heard from Pete about a year later. That he had a job the he enjoyed very much. He was living in a relationship that he found quite meaningful. That he was dry. Erickson often said he couldn't work with alcoholics through hypnosis. I suppose this is the degree to which one considers an alcoholic. I understand that there are some programs being started to work with business executives who might not be considered the kind of alcoholic that's hospitalized. The kind of alcoholic who drinks too much. Has something on the ball that could be motivated. Or has the motivation. I remember seeing the times I was with Erickson he trained people. He was old. He was crippled. He had polio, crippling this arthritis. His lips were paralyzed. His tongue was dislocated. You would take one look at Erickson and you would think no matter how tough my job is it couldn't possibly be that tough just to survive everyday. The last time I saw him a psycho-therapist asked him how he was doing. His feet were swollen like cement blocks. He had gout. He said his muscles were rottening away. And there was nothing he could do to stop it. Practically had to use trance states all day long to deal with the tremendous pain. Which is perhaps how he happened to perfect so many techniques. The therapist asked him about this and Erickson said but I enjoy teaching the people. And I work 6 days a week. Bion said that "And I make it a point to do what I enjoy doing. When Erickson was a youngster with his first bout of polio he was 17 years old. He overheard the doctors tell his mother that he would never see the next sunrise. When the 3 doctors left he called his mother and father in. And said that he was very angry at the doctors for upsetting his mother so much. And all he could move were his eyes. And he asked them to prop him up in the bed and to move the mirror facing the crack in the door; which would then face the window where the sun came through. And he said he would be damned if he wouldn't see the next sun rise. He forced himself to stay awake the entire night until the sun came up. That Viking spirit is something Erickson transmitted to me through his hypnosis. And I suppose when you tell your stories you can transmit it to your patients through your stories. He never gave up. He never quit. There is a story of a schizophrenic patient in a hospital. He spoke only in word salads. No therapist could communicate with this person. He stayed out on a park bench. And spoke only in word salads. Erickson went out there with his note pad. The man spoke 3 hours in word salad not making any sense at all. Erickson took down every word. At the end of the 3 hours he said "Name's Erickson!" He went home; spent 6 hours writing out a word salad in counter point to the one he took down. He went back the next day and the patient spoke a word salad for 3 hours. Erickson spoke the word salad he had written out for the next 3 hours. At the end of this he said "Name's Erickson!" He did this for 2 straight weeks. At the end of this time the patient said to him "Hey Erickson!" You're the only damn guy in this place who speaks English! Why don't we go down to your office and talk!" He said now you know how to build your practice. I had the good fortune to see Erickson work with one of his patients. He had very few left when I saw him. He was really trying to pin point where he spent his energy. Where it would make the most difference. This woman called who was in a panic. She hadn't slept all night. She had an asthma attack. She was coughing all night. Erickson asked her to come over immediately. She did. He asked her if she wanted to be hypnotized. She said she did. She must have been in trance for 20 minutes. Now if you looked at her you can see that her muscle tone" had changed. Her respiration rate had changed. Her blood pressure changed. Her heart rate had changed. Erickson always asked people to keep their feet flat on the floor. Their arms at the side of the chair. He thought that was the best way to go into a trance. Or he would utilize whatever the patient presented him. One man came in and he kept walking around the office. He said he couldn't possibly sit down. Erickson asked him if he would continue to walk in a square until he would either chose the chair on the left or the chair on the right as he began to go into a trance. As the woman had visible signs of hypnotic-

----trance. She came out of hypnosis. Uses where the conscious, unconscious way of dealing things was quite useful. Because the conscious side was very negative. And she said "But Dr. Erickson but I don't see how this hypnosis stuff is going to help me stop coughing or sleep tonight!" And he said "Take it from an authoritarian old man like me that you have very kissable lips." Well Barbara just beamed. As if her father never got that message across to her. She had no sense of confidence about that. As she got up to leave. Her conscious mind took over and she said "but Dr. Erickson how is that going to help me stop coughing and sleep tonight." The woman was sitting about here. His wheelchair was about here. She was looking, standing at the door and he turned over his right shoulder. Erickson was a stickler for details. I remember one time him asking a woman, do you think you're hypnotized. She said no. He reached over and flipped her arm upward and it just stood there! He used to be able to call his shots like that. I never saw him miss. This rather astounded me at the time. He looked over at me. And said "Look at old Dr. Bergantino over there. He believes in magic! He doesn't know all I do is pay attention to details!" So Barbara was standing at the door and Erickson began to sing. The lip bone is connected to the cheek bone. The cheek bone is connected to neck bone. The neck bone is connected to the chest bone." And in an all knowing way he turned around to the group and he said in a way that her conscious mind couldn't deny that he knew that "Barbara was going sleep very very well that night." I remember the first time I called Erickson. I said I wanted to see him individually. September 11, 1977, Saturday. He said "Well let me look at my book, I have a small group coming that day. But come you'll get what you want!" I thought how the hell does he know. Well he is Dr. Erickson------. How can he be that

sure of himself. Is true I expressed somebody with primitive certainty. Only Milton Erickson, Bion had primitive certainty! But there was something about the way he said it. And I said "Alright I'll be there!" Erickson had a patient, a woman called-. I'm going to do some automatic writing for a second, which I will explain to you in a minute. There is a confusion in my mind at that time. One hypnotic technique is to do automatic writing and see what comes out of your unconscious mind onto the pad. As you get a sense of doing that where you center-whatever it says is what you do. It's just always right. Erickson was all dressed in purple. He wore a purple silk shirt, purple pants. He had purple knitted booties. In fact he even had a purple telephone. When his wife wheeled him in. He looked around and there were 5 of us. This was the first time I met him. There were no social courtesies. He handed out a piece of paper. He said put your name, age, the date, marital status, the number of children, occupation, highest degree. Well at the time I'd put down Gestalt therapist. Erickson looked over all the papers. I suppose he sized all of us up. He looked over at me and he said "You forgot the date and your marital status!" No one had never said hello to me quite that way. I put the date and marital status down, handed him the paper. He paused for a moment and said "So you come all the way from the California and you're avoiding the hot seat!" All the chairs in the room looked the same. And he said before I could think of anything, "Now that I mention it I see that you're still avoiding it!" He had a way to look at you. You never quite knew if he was looking at you or through you. His look sort of almost geared to the middle of your forehead. Rather intimidating. I got up and I moved over to the chair next to his wheelchair. He said, "So you're a clinical psychologist huh? I'll bet you don't even know why I'm wearing purple!" So I said "Well I guess its just part of Dr. Erickson's style!" He said, "Huh, I'm color blind. It's the only color I can see!" The way Erickson set the tone in the first 3 minutes. He made it clear that he was the teacher and I was the student. Or he was the therapist and I was the patient. Until that time all the other people I had worked with never did that. Or didn't know how to do it. And I never took them seriously. Erickson knew how to handle those conditions from the second someone walked in the office. And it's the way he dealt with the conditions for each individual that set the frame for the success of the treatment. If a patient was over weight-he might say, "I'd like you to over eat enough to lose 2 pounds a week. Or perhaps over eat enough to lose 2 1/2 pounds a week." A strange way to make the request. Over eat enough to lose 2 1/2 pounds a week. One woman called up, she said she called him because she wanted to lose weight. He said "Well, I want you to gain-I forget the exact amount. I think it was 20 pounds. I want you to gain 20 pounds and call me back when you gain it.-----If she's heard of Erickson of

course there was a certain amount of power that went with that. Being famous, known for unusual cases. Helping people turn tragic corners. The usual successes. Interesting book "Uncommon Therapy: The

Psychiatric Techniques of Milton H. Erickson, M.D." written by Jay Haley, about Erickson's work. Norton Press 1973. So the woman calls back ask for an appointment again. He said I you to gain another 10 pounds. She finally agrees. She calls back again and asked for an appointment. Erickson says well you've proven the point that you're in absolute control of your weight. I don't know what you need me for. That's kind of an extreme example. I think one of the points is very well made. How fast he was going to get rid of you. He did brief therapy. And he'd go off and say "I like to see people for a while. And I like to get rid of them. And I like them to refer me new patients." I remember the last time I went back and he said "You wouldn't believe the psychoanalysts, and the psychiatrists I train! They all have amnesia! I've got to tell them a first time—I've got to tell them a second time—and I've got to tell them a third time!" I figured that was my last trip he was talking about. A strange thing happened to me through weight loss. I didn't go there to lose weight. But the second day Erickson was working and I'd been hypnotized the first day. It was the first time I felt I could stop moving. And I felt so good. I said "Dr. Erickson will you hypnotize me again?" And he said "By the very fact you've asked a question shows that you'll already half in trance. And you can go as deeply as you wish. For however long you wish. And come out whenever you wish. Feeling very very relaxed and refreshed." Of course my conscious mind hadn't the foggiest idea of how to do this. And I felt anxiety for about 30 seconds to 2 minutes. And then I remembered the heaviness in my hands from the previous day. Perhaps the heaviness in your fingertips. The heaviness in your legs. Perhaps a numbing sensation in the sides of your temples. Of course Erickson always bobbed and weaved his head. About a quarter of an inch of pace in which he spoke. All those recollections came back. And I went into a very light trance. About 20 minutes. When I got back to Los Angeles. I was seeing a patient on a Monday. And I was telling him about this unusual experience I had. And he says why yea, but something is missing. You're not doing it. I said well I don't know how to do it. He said "go ahead take a chance! I trust you!" So I told my first series of stories. I lasted for about 5 minutes. I was pretty tickled. So the next hour I tried it again. I made it 10 minutes. I did it every day and every hour. No matter who came I told him stories. I finally got up to doing 2 1/2 to 3 hour workshops. It all started off with that patient saying take a chance, I trust you. Now the story of course was my unconscious reaction to this group or to an individual patient. How will we know that anyway. See Erickson said "You can hypnotize yourself for as long as you wish. You can come out whenever you wish. Feeling relaxed and refreshed." Hell that was the best deal I'd heard in years. I used to be so driven I could barely sit by the pool for a half hour. Now I feel like I had to go work on a book, typewriter. Write something. So I didn't know at the time. But what he evoked in me was I suppose a cure for type A personality. I began to use that pace all day long. If I couldn't sleep. I'd use it all night long. And in a sense, I'm in that state now. Quasi trance state. If I do analysis I'm in that state. So what began to happen was I began to notice sensory perception the kind of things that I never noticed before. So I began to notice different sensations the patient would project off. If they had tension in the forehead. It split off that way. If they had conflict I would start to sense a pain in the center of my stomach. If they lied to themselves I would start to get nausea. If they had problems in lieu of the path of heart I would get stabbing pains here. But essentially I could also depend on the physiological phenomena to gear my stories to working with people. So I had the unconscious, the intuition and the sensory perception. The sensory perception-it was interesting I had a sense about it. You??? stalled there and had to break away from psycho-analysis. And he said lose your mind and come to your senses. But I think Gestalt therapists lost their minds but never quite had the methodology to come to their senses. The work with Erickson and the discipline of using that slowed down pace all day long helps you to come back to your senses. Then the issue once your senses comes back it's your first cue into reality. You know what's happening in terms of an existential moment. Almost immediately, if not immediately. Once you know what's happening you know where to make your comments. This later helped me develop a psychoanalytical technique, I think expands beyond where {psycho-analytic technique is today. In terms of knowing the immediate sense response, which then helps the person focus where they split off from feeling and put it back into them. Which then helps them be in touch with the emotion. Which you then as the therapist contain. Which has never been contained by no other. Which then detoxifies the experience. Which then helps the therapist and the patient stay on top of the life force for a full 50 minute hour. Which then provides the corrective emotional experience. As you over the years learn to master that paragraph that's about all you need to know.} At any case back to----. During these I always drive my car slower. I go into the restaurants. I remember going to the movies with my wife at the time and a couple of friends. And I was thinking about ordering cheese cake. We went to a place that specialized in cheese cake. I got into the restaurant. The image was up here. Right about here. (Right side of head) I could see the cheese cake up here. But at this different pace right out the pit of my stomach of here the senses-or instinct says "small green salad." With conflict. The image came back cheese cake. The instinct came back small green salad. Now there was a fight going on. But it struck me as so unusual. Because usually there was no fight; it was just cheese cake, pasta, etc. Whatever I grew up on. That's what people like to stuff their faces with. But I could now feel the instinct or desire based on my senses need because the pace was slower. So I ordered a small green salad. Then there was a matter of how I ate it. I took a bite. I chewed it very slowly making sure I tasted each bite until I felt satisfied. Then at the end of that bite I asked myself the question. Am I satisfied? Or do I want another bite? Well I'm still hungry. So I wanted another bite. As it was I finished the entire salad. Sometimes putting my fork down between each mouth full. Picking it up again. Putting it down again. Picking it up again. Over the course of 15 months I lost 30 pounds without ever going on a diet. I never had any intention to stay with any particular diet or give up any particular food. I just followed my instincts. And I lost 30 pounds without ever going on a diet. At that particular pace where I could sense what was organismic disgust and what I really needed to eat. I never had a sense of that before. I worked with a woman at the Southern California Society of Clinical Hypnosis who was very fat and very courageous. She came right up and said I want to work on the fact that I'm fat. So she handed her shoes over right there. I worked with her in this way. Telling her a story; not the Pete story, but another story, which had similar dynamics. The dynamics of the story were the-it was going to take every bit of control, this person had in her to sit on herself. To take charge of this problem. (Joey story) Then whatever stories went through my mind in relation to her-and while I'm doing an initial interview I take about the first 5 minutes if I'm doing hypnotic work. And whatever that person tells me in that first 5 minutes I use the automatic writing and the purple pen. From that first 5 minutes of information impressions pop out to me off the page. It's sort of like boom there's one story, boom ah there's another story. From these little notes here the first 5 minutes, 50 to 90 minutes of stories emerge. My unconscious mind in relation to that patient's unconscious mind and the information that was given to me in the first 5 minutes. What she described was a kind of extreme depths of experience. What I refer to as an existential shift; which is a shift in a lifelong characteristic of a patient. If you do this thing right you can get it in one session. She also told me in her work-I saw her again after that in another meeting. She said "Gees that work you did last time also helped me with this patient I was working with in my office using hypnosis. It helps the women who worked with the physician to get through her counter transference problem. So she could work hypnotically with a patient successfully. At this point I think what I'd like to do if anyone is interested is show you a demonstration of how I work if you came into the office with this particular method geared to an individual. Here I've done a group experience. But I'd like for you to have a sense of how you might do it. Later on as you develop your practice if someone comes into your office. Does someone have something you want to work with who-preferably if you find that you work well with metaphor. It would be easier for demonstration. For some people metaphor is not the best way to do it. Or storytelling. But if someone felt some kind of connection doing this work has any kind of desire to do that, I would be happy to work you for a period of time. Maybe 20 minutes.

What kind of thing do you want to work on? Anything special?

Bergantino-Anything at all. It doesn't make any difference. Are you volunteering?

Okay. General coping with stress.

Bergantino-What I'm writing down is not very out of the ordinary. I wrote down general - coping with stress. Can you say a little bit more about that.

When I feel a lot of pressure from school and work. And from my social obligations I get very cranky. And I have trouble sleeping and I get headaches.

Bergantino-Okay. I wrote down pressure from school and work and social obligations, cranky, trouble sleeping, headaches. Can you tell me the thought that creates the pressure.

I have too many things I have to do.

Bergantino-Okay. That's all the information I need. In fact there is enough there for a 50 minute hour. It would perhaps be better if I-I don't mind giving you my chair. If you keep your feet flat on the floor. Your arms on the side of the chair. There is no need to talk. There is no need to move. There is no need to move. If you prefer to keep your eyes open that's perfectly fine with me. I told her to do what she was already doing-utilize the resistance. There may be a time during the trance where you feel it's more comfortable to keep your eyes closed. If that time comes your unconscious mind feels that's the way to do it. That's perfectly alright. Just focus your eyes on the corner of this black tape here. Keep your eyes fixated on the corner of the tape. I need you to remember when you were a little girl you learned very very difficult things. Things you don't even know that you knew. You learned the letters of the alphabet. How to discriminate between an A and a D.

Which way the stems went on a B, and a P. How to dot your T's, cross your I's and add one and one is two. Two and two is four. Subtract, multiply, divide; and in many other difficult things. All these things----are part of your unconscious mind. It's all slow pace. In whatever slow way it chooses will help those thoughts, feelings, memories and actions. Begin to come into your life perhaps tonight----. If you feel comfortable close your eyes now. One of the great generals at least in my era was Mao Tse Tung. Mao Tse Tung took over all of China taking two steps forward and one step back; and two steps forward and one step back. And two steps forward and one step back. And two steps forward and one step back and China is a very big place. Thinking about Bismarck in history. Bismarck is The Iron Chancellor, old blood guts. Never let up-----workshop. The workshop leader said "Bergantino (Germany) you're always thinking about what you can do. You looked so tired when you got here maybe you should just go to bed and sleep for a while. That's all you need to do. Of course it was easier said than done. I didn't sleep that well. I would get so strung out. So stressed out during the day. My body would be jumping. When it was jumping I couldn't sleep. It's like drinking 14 cups of coffee. One right after the other. After Erickson taught me hypnosis I figured, what the hell. I'll try it at night. So I laid in bed stretched out almost as if one were in a coffin. Stretched out arms by your side straight out. I tried to go into the trance stage. The first 30 seconds and 2 minutes. It was very difficult. Semi trance state. So agitated I still kept jumping. These big hands coming down and grabbed my leg. My left leg. Then my right leg. And held it still. Every bit of agitation wanted to move. My unconscious mind creation held my legs perfectly still. Peacefulness. At the end of that 20 minutes. 4 or 5 hours. I was so tired I just drifted off to sleep. I was so tired I was just lying there. 5 minutes of trance equals 1/2 hour of sleep. 10 minutes of trance equals an hour and a half of sleep. An hour in trance equals 3 nights sleep. 5 hours in trance equals a week's sleep. So the rest my body got-------. One thing there is a conflict in the group. I don't know what that conflict is. Perhaps this story-----. When I worked with Erickson my head never stopped thinking. During that first trance state my eyes were closed. All I could see was the color purple. Your unconscious mind would give you amnesia states wherever you need some protection state. You don't have to try harder. You don't have to hurry up. You don't have to be strong. You don't have to please me. You learned how to drive a car. You didn't know how to put your foot on the gas. You didn't know how much to put your foot on the brake. You practiced and you practiced. When you were going 70 miles an hour, you came to a slow stop. You came to a slow slow stop. 53 miles an hour you came to a slow stop. While you were going 47 miles an hour you came to a slow stop. When you were going 34 miles an hour you came to a slow slow stop. When you were going 10 miles an hour you came to a slow stop. Now the interesting thing about------. Most people who are driven in stress---they work to that pace. The evidence was exactly the opposite. The person----is to take one step at a time. I have a busy law practice. I have telephones ringing off the wall. I've secretaries buzzing me. I've got files here to prepare for the next day. And then this pressure. The strangest thing happened. I was very worried about closing a million dollar deal. The man hated my guts and I hated his guts. It was a firm representative and I now have the case. I was in limbo. I was agitated. I don't know how long it took by the time my arm reached the phone, I had visualized the entire back pack trip-------. I picked up the phone----. The only surprise was my voice was friendly. A few jokes popped out. The next surprise was he was friendly and a few jokes popped out.---10 or 15 minutes I closed the deal and I was more successful---than I ever was. I use to feel that way in my office. My desk----overwhelming. If something urgent pops in I'll do it. It's interesting to see the way this happens. There's one more story I need to tell you first. I went to see Erickson work with a very well-known psycho-therapist. Who was quite controlled. Erickson said "for you young man I've got a surprise." You could tell the last thing this fellow wanted was a surprise. Erickson leaned over and said "I've got a genie in a magic lamp." And the man backed up a little. What a strange thing to say. Erickson leaned forward even more challenging and said "Well do you believe me!" and the man said, and then he said "if it were anybody but you Dr. Erickson I would have you locked up. But with you I'm not sure." You could see the beginning of the man's belief system change from negative to positive.

Right before your eyes. Erickson always delivered what he promised.----after the session. Erickson took out a toy genie and plugged it into the wall. A scream came off from-----and a genie appeared. The genie blew the man a kiss. Erickson said "surprises can be pleasant too." I'm going to count to 10 until you're wide awake and relaxed. 1, 2, 3, 4, 5, 6, 7, 8, 9, 10.

I don't feel anything that's particularly personal, That I can share with you. I don't know what to share. It's kind of interesting-that was the most relaxed I've been in a really long time. I actually took a moment to speculate on the fact that I couldn't feel the chair or my feet on the floor anymore. Underneath me. I was so relaxed. I actually noticed that I couldn't feel the chair. At first I noticed I couldn't feel the chair arms anymore. I felt wow. And then I realized I couldn't feel the chair beneath me or the floor. "Which was really interesting, I don't think this has happened before. I found myself drifting-you'd say things and my analytic mind wanted to tear them apart and say. Okays what's he picking up-----tell me this floor.------I'll just listen and don't be defensive. Like you'd say things and I'd start "yes, butting." Yes, but, yes but. I didn't state the problem and-----and evaluate. Right now. And I really focused on your voice. I really wasn't aware that I was sitting in this room with all these people. And it was sort of interesting when you said when I'd wake up I was so comfortable. When you said 10. And then you started counting back fast. I thought no. So actually I started pacing with you. And I actually shouldn't have woken up before you got to 1. Somebody have any questions?

Did you follow what he was telling you?

Huh hmm.

Did it make sense?

You mean in terms of the problems you presented?

Sometimes when you were talking about the backpacking. At first when you saw the color purple. I started seeing the color aqua. I said "Is that alright? Then I said of course.

Laughs

And then when you were talking about the backpacking I again had the sort of experience where I evaluated. I wanted-the last time I went backpacking I was cold. I was very uncomfortable because I was cold. So initially I saw the-----Meadows in Yosemite. And then I kind of looked at myself and said burrr. So I switched to lying on my sail boat. Which was something I felt was particularly----and the sun beam. Even though you were talking about a backpacking scene, I sort of picked up my own relaxing scene.

You're the perfect client Jill.

Laughs.

Jill-I was kind of skeptical. This is why I decided to do this. I decided you can't be skeptical unless you want to give it your all. Then if it doesn't work you have a right to complain.

Jill, aside from relaxation which would be----for the kind of stressful problem you actually-what do you think you gained from the story?

Jill-To be perfectly honest I'm not sure yet. That's sort of something that I'll see. I know that he mentioned some things like-you mentioned a couple of things. Unlovable, the little part of me that will always run no matter how relaxed I am that I've come to accept something that's going to happen. That's probably because one of the reasons I'm so driven is that I feel like I won't be loved unless I succeed. And he said I don't have to be perfect. And you know it pays to slow down. And if you slow down-I think I got a couple of I may have some new beliefs or try to give me new beliefs. Almost like Albert Ellis you don't have to belief these irrational things. And also sort of technique in that you know if you calm down and approach a situation you will be just as successful. So you know if you're expecting a lousy phone call take them in and relax and things will work themselves out. Because you're more relaxed. I don't know if it will work.

Bergantino-They already have.

Jill-They already have.

A comment to that is Jill looks to me very much like she looked in a lounge-----in the day. The way she usually does look when I went into her on Tuesday or Wednesday.

I think she look more relaxed. More----

Yea. She'll really relaxed.

Jill-And I actually feel very unpressured right now.

Bergantino-Thank you for volunteering. I appreciate you doing something. My pleasure.

Jill-You can have your chair back.

We've got about 10 minutes or something like that. Do you want to entertain fresh problems.

I thought I had some entertaining questions.

Whatever.

I have a question. Sort of going back to relaxation again, I'm wondering what you think the benefits of the therapy or aside from the benefits from relaxation are going into hypnotic type of state. What are its benefits-aside from that kind of feeling of calmness or slowing down.

Bergantino-I wonder if you might speculate and expand upon your sources of feelings about how you might answer that question?

I think what my questions probably is coming from is on one dream if there are any benefits in addition to relaxation possibly that the primary benefit of that kind of therapy is the relaxation and the calming down which we-it's very conducive type of----problem Joe was in----.

Bergantino-What I'm asking you is that you could expand on your thinking and see what other speculations you have about the possible value

PART II: SLIGHTLY OUT OF ORDER, I WAS TRAINED BY MILTON H. ERICKSON, M.D.: WILFRED BION, M.R.C.S., AND GOD IN ORDER OF ASCENSION

What I write now is still a preface to what I learned to do in terms of working with Bion's conceptualizations and extending psychoanalytic technique several light years beyond its current state of affairs. It is basically the part at which Martin Grotjahn removed from my entry book into the field, Psychotherapy, Insight & Style: The Existential Moment, Allyn & Bacon, Inc., 1981. First I will describe the experiences as I remember them; and then I will include a reprint that appeared in VOICES: J. OF THE AMERICAN ACADEMY OF PSYCHOTHERAPISTS: THE ART AND SCIENCE OF PSYCHOTHERAPY Vol. 17, No. 1, Spring, 1981.

STRANGE THINGS BEGAN TO HAPPEN

I was telling stories twenty five hours a week from 1977-1978, from my unconscious mind to the unconscious mind of the patient. I was doing this in the dis-ease free state of being Erickson exposed me to that Margaret Mead told Erickson she had only heard in a rare African Tribe relatively free of disease. I began to notice during sessions that pain would hit different parts of my body when I was working with a patient. I did not know what pathological projective identification was at this time, nor did I know of Bion or his work. As pain was discomfort I began to experiment blocking the pain with my hands; and sure enough, when I found the exact area from which the pain was being projected from the patient, my hand functioned as a shield to the pain. This struck me as strange, but then again, since having begun to be trained by Erickson, everything was strange. So I naively took things in stride, not really knowing what I was stumbling onto.

While this being able to block projected pain with my hands was rather novel, it was still a passive method of learning through thousands of repetitions where the pain came from. I had not learned to do anything about it, other than block it.

At the time I had a practice in San Diego and was doing 24 hours a week in two days while I was building my practice in Los Angeles and living in Los Angeles. I would fly down to San Diego early Wednesday morning and fly back late Thursday night.

However, in addition to staying in that mode of being described by Margaret Mead while working five hours a day on the average, I was also in that state most of my waking hours and during the night because at that time I suffered from insomnia. Later I will get to a most interesting facet of the insomnia in terms of Bion's work, but for now I will stay with my novelty with Erickson and his work. So I was averaging TEN HOURS A DAY OVER A YEAR IN WHAT MIGHT BE CALLED THIS DISEASE FREE STATE OF BEING.

One day I was treating a patient who had broken toes. I was very still, went deep into my unconscious, and felt a swirl of energy, almost like a tornado come down from above the back of my right side, and through my right hand (The Hand of God). It shot a laser beam of energy to her broken toes. She screamed. "The pressure! I can't stand the pressure!" As to why I knew what to do or how I knew, I have no explanation, other than IT WENT THROUGH ME AT THE DEEPEST LEVELS OF MY BEING WITHOUT ANY AGENDA. I said, the laser beam continuing to shoot, "STAY WITH IT FOR ANOTHER 30 SECONDS!" It was about two minutes in all. At the end of that time the energy beam stopped of its own accord and the woman said I have no more pain in my toes. She started to move her toes with her hands and they moved easily and readily. She had walked in with a severe limp and she walked out naturally without any limp and without any pain.

A different woman patient came in for her weekly session looking like death warmed over. She stated, "I have been to my physicians two times in the past week. They have given me different medications but nothing stops this earache. It hurts so bad I can't stand it." Again, I was in that deep state of being in which I later found transformations occurred via psychoanalysis using Bion's methods; but here I don't know why I just asked the woman to lie flat on the floor. I placed my right hand next to her left ear. There was no energy there whatsoever. I could feel nothing, only death. Her ear was dead or numb from a psychic energy point of view. With my right hand I began to move it around her body looking for anywhere I could feel energy. I found some right over her heart. I kept my right hand cupped over her left ear while my left hand remained over her heart. Energy began to run from my left hand over her heart to my right hand cupped over her left ear for twenty minutes. At the end of that time there was a slight pop and the energy stopped. She said, "I have no more pain", and upon her return the following week, she stated she remained pain free and her ear was "healed".

I left my old 1963 Plymouth given to me by my father down at Lindbergh Field, San Diego Airport, so when I flew down every week I would have a car to get around with. On this particular Wednesday I stopped at the gas station and checked the radiator, only it was so hot it boiled over scalding my arm leaving very serious burns that hurt very badly. I immediately drove to a drug store, as I had patients scheduled all day, and did not want to miss appointments for which I had flown to San Diego to see. I showed the burns to the druggist and asked if he had any ointments that would help. He said the burns were very bad and I should go to a hospital; that he had no ointments that would make any difference. I refused and went to the office with the pain. I had five hours of patients lined up with ten minute breaks between fifty minute hours. I greeted them at the waiting room door and then proceeded to my office where I did five hours of storytelling in the disease free state of being. I kept my right arm up on two pillows while I was doing this, as that was my damaged arm. If someone asked me if I knew how to hypnotize myself to do what happened I would have emphatically said "NO". It just happened, perhaps as when you hear a story of a woman who picks up the back end of a car to save her baby's life. It is not something she could ordinarily do. MY RIGHT ARM BEGAN TO FEEL AS IF IT WAS IN THE FREEZER, WHERE ICE CREAM IS KEPT, COLD BEYOND BELIEF. IT STAYED THAT WAY FOR FIVE HOURS. AT THE END OF THAT TIME WHAT

THE DRUGGIST DESCRIBED AS SECOND DEGREE BURNS WERE GONE AND THERE WAS NO PAIN WHATSOEVER. THE DRUGGIST TOLD ME I WOULD HAVE THE BURNS AND THE PAIN FOR AT LEAST TWO WEEKS, AND THAT I SHOULD GO TO A HOSPITAL! The burns were as bad as when I stayed at the pool in the sun at my high school graduation picnic and got sun blisters on inch high and 3 inches long over my body.

When I came home from the office to my home, my "wife at the time", would be in the courtyard seventy five feet away. I would put both hands up and shoot energy rays that would "burn her teats" and she would jump in amazement and with a kind of surprised delight.

Another Wednesday night in San Diego, a psychiatrist friend and his girlfriend and I went to see Charlie Byrd, the great Brazilian style jazz guitarist, at the Catamaran jazz club. The problem was there were only ten people there and Charlie Byrd looked catatonic, as if he just couldn't get into playing with only ten people there. I said to my psychiatrist friend, "Do you want to see Charlie Byrd play the wildest set of his life?" My non-believing friend knew I was having strange experiences, but really didn't fully believe what I was telling him. I said, "Watch, I'm going to shoot energy from my hands into Charlie Byrd", and I did. Charlie Byrd came on fire! My psychiatrist friend was laughing like a little kid in a sandbox who had just seen something he didn't believe, yet there it was. The three of us couldn't stop laughing for most of the set, and although Charlie occasionally looked up at what he must have considered rudeness on the part of his audience, he continued undaunted providing the kind of musical experience only Charlie Byrd could do! Sheer magnificence!

I was seeing a couple in Los Angeles. The husband was an attorney, a very rational fellow. The woman was very primitive and quite in touch on that level. As Erickson had spoken two different languages to my "wife at the time" and myself, I was in a playful mood toward these two. I nonchalantly moved my right hand up from my lap and the energy laser beam shot right to the woman's vagina. I did not move at all in my chair and if you did not feel the energy beam hitting you, there was no way to detect that it was happening. The lawyer and I were carrying on a rather involved intellectual conversation at the time and he noticed nothing. It was the kind of intellectual conversation she was always left out of as a result of marrying someone with totally different personal equipment. She immediately feeling the laser beam jumped up from her seat and said, "What are you doing!", kind of in a surprised, enraged and exhilarated state all at the same time. I nonchalantly looked over almost as if I didn't know what she was talking about so her husband would have no idea at all what was and had happened (and he didn't), and I casually said, "I just wanted to see if you were paying attention". I thought his intellectualism was compounded in that she cut off her own sexual heat in that neither had worked through the oedipal and electra complexes, nor could they sustain their psychosexual energy as a couple. She broke out laughing. He didn't know why. He and I just carried on the intellectual conversation.

I had lunch with Dr. Thelma Moss who did the research with Kurlian Photography at UCLA. She was convinced I was a healer and referred me a few cancer patients. Only now I had an agenda. I was being paid and wanted to help them. You know what happened. Nothing. It was like having a limp penis during a sexual encounter. In other words, if I desired to do something, or wanted to do something, I would almost always fail at it. If it just happened, and as Bion wrote, "there was no memory and desire", then I would have a healing or curative effect. However, this really began to mess with my head. Was I a psychologist? Was I a healer? How would I know if my ego wasn't strong enough to have no desire and just let it happen? How would I know of those who were supposed to die with the diseases they presented or those whom I was supposed to help? I was tormented! All of a sudden the honeymoon of my new play toy wasn't fun anymore! And I didn't know what to do about it?

ME-RELIGION-AND THE FIGHT FOR MAN'S SOUL

I was born a Roman Catholic. I studied the Baltimore Catechism at religious instructions and made my First Holy Communion. I had my Confirmation at twelve and went to Sacred Heart High School.

Basically, I didn't go to Church after high school, although I studied Neo-Thomastic Philosophy as part of my Masters Degree at a Jesuit School named Fairfield University in Fairfield, Connecticut. However, I did not go to Church nor had I prayed to God in about twenty years.

PRAYING

When you are a little boy or girl and you learn to pray to God you customarily say a few of the prayers you know and then ask God for what you want; or depending on the degree of narcissism you might ask for what you want first, then say a few prayers, while you are kneeling at the side of your bed, and then you go to sleep. What customarily happens is "nothing identifiable". However, it was from about 1987, after I met Erickson and was fully trained by Bion in one evening (which I will get to later), that I prayed every night and asked for the same thing. In fact, it was after both Bion and Erickson died. I was convinced they were the only two who could help me on the levels with which I was dealing and they were both dead. I had looked for help in the psychic area, but after Bion and Erickson, being as solid as they were and clinical just, one could tell a paranoid schizophrenic when you met one among the psychics. Most of these so called psychic healers were for the birds. In other words Erickson and Bion were so solid I could tell a phony anywhere after them. I did believe this could happen at the hand of God!

So I prayed and prayed to God that God would send Erickson and Bion back as my children, so they could help me in terms of what else I needed to learn to use the gift I had been given in the service of God. I did not do this because I was a religious person or because I thought of myself as a religious person. I did it because I was a serious dedicated professional and I was desperately and hopelessly stuck. Each night I would say my prayers, "nothing would happen that I knew about", and I would go to bed.

Further, if there ever was a "Doubting Thomas", I was one. I did not believe in anything that I did not experience first-hand. Perhaps given the training I have had is why God has granted me experiences others have not had. It forever affected what I am able to do in a psychoanalysis in terms of Freud's statement that "The Americans will never understand analysis because they do not understand that the purpose of it is to save man's soul!" When I speak at a level Bion wrote about as "knowing", the way I did analysis did that job for people.

Then there was this one night, I made the same request as always, that Erickson and Bion be sent back down as my children to help me finish the job I am supposed to do in the world given my gift. ONLY THIS PARTICULAR NIGHT THERE WAS A FLASH OF GREEN LIGHT THAT SHOT OUT OF MY HEART IN A SPLIT SECOND IN A SMALL WIDENING CONE AND SHOT THROUGH THE ROOF OF MY HOUSE INTO "INFINITY". That is, it only lasted a few seconds, moved and traveled with the speed of light, went through the roof and at that moment I could see through the roof; and the green cone in that split second continued to go into the sky forever into the distance near the moon. As Erickson used to ratify a trance, that_is, prove you were hypnotized, so God proved I had a "supernatural experience", the true nature of, I was not to find out until 1983. Even while this happened, so many strange things had happened to me with energy and psychic energy, I did not think much about it until several years later when it had a context that made sense.

I had terrible seborrhea, a skin problem that often left a raw red circle of about an inch in the middle of my forehead. I was an insomniac, so my mind used to visualize a large hand holding my left leg motionless for twenty minutes, at which point my entire body would go into the disease free state Margaret Mead described to Erickson. I would stay that way for at least five hours every night. I suppose I had suffered from neurasthenic exhaustion from someone who was "unable to stop moving". On the first occasion Dr. Erickson trained me he said to me, "So young man, what can I do for you?" I said, "Dr. Erickson, I heard about your unusual talents and I wonder if you could help me STOP MOVING." In other words, I was so driven that my leg used to jump all night while I thought about what I had to do the next day; and I could hardly sit by the pool for an hour without feeling that I had to be writing or working on something. I was not entitled to leisure enjoyment. Nevertheless, the disease free state brought the sensations of physical pleasure. However, on this one night, the "healing green light or cone appeared" and it stayed present right over my forehead for about five hours. When I woke up in the morning all the severe red raw circle on my forehead from the seborrhea was gone.

As far as curing the insomnia, when I was in this state I never used to move from one spot in the bed. Both arms were at my sides so "heavy they could not move". I never rolled from side to side or moved to the side of the bed my wife was on during the night. This is an important fact in another story that I am about to tell you.

As far as the insomnia it got better because if I were in the disease free state of non-movement I got more rest than I did the way I used to sleep; so it was alright if I drifted off to sleep; or if I just lay there for five hours in the disease free state of being. Either way I was rested and after a time I began to sleep again.

OLGA WORRALL-THE ONLY LEGITIMATE PSYCHIC I EVER MET

Olga Worrall was the psychic that Dr. Thelma Moss did the Kurlian photography with at UCLA where there are pictures of flames (psychic energy) coming out of her hands. She was going to a Mandala Conference in San Diego. I asked my "wife at the time" to accompany me. Ordinary people were asking Olga Worrall mundane questions like whether she could energize water. She had showed pictures of spirit photography and described out of body experiences and astral travel where she left her body and went great distances the outcome of which was that certain persons were healed.

Olga Worrall was different than all other psychics I ever met. She looked like a little old lady from the mid-west. She wore an old fashioned hat with a black veil over her face to begin with and then removed the veil but wore the hat. She had no ego investment at all in what she was doing. Further, she didn't charge anybody any money for any of her healings. They were done as part of her ministry at a Church in Baltimore, Maryland.

Olga would do her best for people, but she had a sense of when they were supposed to die-when it was their time, as opposed to when a "healing" would and could actually occur. This is something I found quite confusing in that I tried to do it for everyone no matter what God's agenda might be, which is the bottom line of why I got kicked down a notch out of the psychic realm of functioning in terms of a healer.

There were about 100 people in the room. Olga Worrall said that each person in the room could ask her a question. My "wife at the time" and I were sitting in the middle. Everyone got a question except when she got to me she skipped me and went to the other side of the room. Unlike the others I was going to ask her, "How do you know when you are a healer and when you are not? How do you know when to heal someone and when not to? How do you know if you are a fraud in that you cannot produce all the time? How can you stand being impotent as a healer as many or more times that you are able to offer anybody anything of value?"

She let everyone ask a question until she got to my "wife at the time". Then she skipped her. It was time to leave and I was totally frustrated and exasperated. I met someone who might have been able to help me and she purposely did not.

My "wife at the time" and me drove back from San Diego to our home in Los Angeles. I was tired. I went to take a 20 minute cat nap while I was in the disease free state of being Margaret Mead told Erickson she had only experienced in a rare African tribe relatively free of disease. Again, I never moved from one spot in the bed and I kept both arms down at my sides.

I had planned to take this cat nap, get up, and write Olga Worrall a letter telling her what I wanted and asking her to do an out of body experience to help me solve the problem. I was in bed only about ten minutes in a before sleep daze and a face came up with lightning speed almost like it was shot out of a pea shooter and grew in size in that instant until it was the size of my face and right 'in my face'. It was Olga Worrall's face-and there was just a head, no body. In the split second her face was right on top of my face she said, "I don't trust you! What are you up to anyway?" This shocked the hell out of me. However, what was equally shocking was the experience of my face coming from a distance in pea shooter style and meeting her face with full size and in that same split instant (very difficult to describe psychic time that deals with 'infinity'-in that it happens so quick-lasts so long-and yet is over in a split second; that is the experience of it) I said to her "I am the trickiest son of a bitch you will ever meet in your life, but I can trick people into getting better!"

At that very instant Olga Worrall's face drew away with the same speed at which it had arrived, going back into a little pea like ball of infinitesimal size as it disappeared into nothingness, into infinity. At that same instant my head and face drew back away from full size into the pea like shape into infinity. I realize I am describing two simultaneous experiences at the same time; and I am not doing this because I am crazy, only to give you an accurate account of what this psychic experience with Olga Worral in fact was.

Now for the "proof". Erickson ratified the trance so people would know they were hypnotized. How would I know whether I just had a dozing off for a moment and went into a dreamlike state and just imagined the entire thing. This could very well happen to a psychic experience that was so unusual every part of you would want to ignore it as never having happened so you would not begin to doubt your own sanity.

In the instant that Olga Worrall's face zoomed away and the next instant that my face zoomed away; there were two electric streams of energy that were buzzing on each side of my temple. This was different than any energy that I ever experienced and had the effect of a mini-electroshock on both temples. While this went on for about one and one half minutes to two minutes; the further "proof" was that I was rolling from one side of a king size bed to the other (a bed in which I had not moved off the same spot for over one and one half years while remaining in the "disease free state of being Margaret Mead told Erickson she had only experienced in a rare African tribe relatively free of disease") until the electroshock kind of experience ceased as quickly as it began. (I have never had any electro shock therapy and only use this as a description for others who have never had it in that they may know what I am describing-the feeling of two electrodes on the sides of your temples that go out about a foot and one half in length and stop as suddenly as they started.

When the experience ended I KNEW THAT I WAS AND WOULD BE THE BEST CLINICIAN IN THE WORLD AND THAT I WOULD NEVER USE MY PSYCHIC POWER AGAIN IN THE REALM OF A HEALER, BUT THAT I WOULD USE IT TO "DISTURB THE UNIVERSE IN THE REALM OF PSYCHOANALYSIS" IN THAT "PSYCHOANALYSIS WOULD BECOME THE KIND OF TOOL IT WAS INTENDED TO BE AND BE ABLE TO DO THE JOB IT PURPORTS TO DO!"

I only had contact with Olga Worrall on one other occasion. That is when my father was dying of lung cancer in 1983. She was very ill and I believe she died not to long after my father died on November 14, 1983. I asked her to reach back one more time and do an out of body healing. I was pulling out all the stops to save my father's life. I had not learned the lesson which got me kicked down from the healer level to the level of clinical psychology, that when it is someone's time, it is someone's time. Olga Worrall tried but nothing happened. My father died and then it was her time. Impotence in the face of God's plan was still a huge pain in the ass to my worldly mentality!

AGAIN, MAKE NO MISTAKE ABOUT IT, THIS WAS NOT A DREAMLIKE STATE, IN THAT I WAS NOT ASLEEP, THAT I SUFFERED FROM INSOMNIA, AND THAT I HAD NEVER ROLLED FROM ONE SIDE OF THE BED TO THE OTHER! THIS WAS AN OUT OF BODY EXPERIENCE THAT PROVIDED AN ANSWER TO AN ISSUE THAT TORMENTED ME!

The difficulty for the reader is the inclination to deny both the existence of God and what is considered to be the Supernatural as well as psychic experience-despite its repetitive proof throughout the history of mankind. I can only assume the reason I was chosen for these experiences to happen to me, given I was a very ordinary fellow in every other way, was that I have always lived my life on the higher end of personal integrity. Thus, with the training I have had with many world renown therapists, knowing much of what there is to be known, I perhaps was a likely candidate to resolve this issue for many generations to come, that the purpose of a psychoanalysis is to "save man's soul!"

Further, knowing myself, I am not one that at that time had dreams to which I could account for. Second, this entire experience with Olga Worrall happened in about twenty minutes. Third, rolling from one side of a King size bed to the other was about five feet across-in the face of my never having moved off one section of the bed in one and one half years of resting in a certain way.

Last but not least, when I called Olga Worrall in 1983, a good two years after this happened and reminded her of who I was, she knew exactly who I was and related to me in detail "knowing" the experience I had described happened between us. In other words we were both in sync. Furthermore, she was not accepting calls from people at that time because of her illness and she made an exception because it was me under the circumstances in which I called; which in retrospect had more to do with confirmation of the experience rather than saving my father's life when it had appropriately been used up.

Okay, so now I knew I was as some who have seen me work put it, "the most gifted clinician of my time". But what of it. What was I supposed to do with it, and would anybody acknowledge or receive anything I had to say or do anyways? As a matter of fact, the zeitgeist was moving in the other direction-that of education to be a clinician through academic presentation as opposed to the experience itself-a total bastardization of the process to gain even a modicum of competency; albeit it covers the proposition of no one having to expose themselves for the lack of dedication, the lack of skill and the lack of ability to make a difference that they have rightfully earned on their way to getting lost as clinicians, and even more important, as human beings. I came to know of those who I was either exposed to or trained by, only Bion and Erickson could work at the level of attention and detail that I write about, However, they were both dead and I was not. As I knew of the history of psychoanalysis and hypnotism, I felt that in terms of actual capacity to do the work, only Mesmer, Melanie Klein and Herbert Rosenfeld and Wilhelm Reich had developed the therapeutic use of self to the degree of which I am attempting to expand upon. I know that Melanie Klein had such ability because she turned out both Bion and Rosenfeld, who were her analysands; and the way Bion described her work as continually focusing him on his senses. I know that Rosefeld had gone beyond all others except Bion because of his writings on "osmotic transferences" in his classic work, "Impasse and Interpretation", Karnac Books, Lts., in London. Yet, perhaps the greatest difficulty I am going to have is best described by Dr. Donald Rinsley, Fellow, American College of Psychoanalysts in his letter to me of July 1, 1985:

Colmery-O'Neil
Veterans Administration
Medical Center

2200 Gage Boulevard
Topeka KS 66622

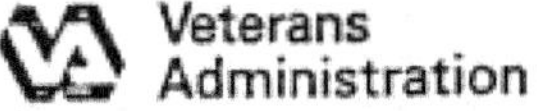

Page 252

1 July 1985

In Reply Refer To:

Len Bergantino, Ed.D., Ph.D.
10266 Kilrenney Avenue
Los Angeles, California 90064

Dear Len:

How nice to receive yours of June 24th, and to learn of your upward spiral! I'm very pleased indeed to believe that my little review of your book has contributed to your success!

Frankly, Len, I have long been eructatively fed up with the sort of territorial cupidities and other evidences of narcissistic nonsensicality so many of the colleagues display. Such antics reveal the essentially limbic nature of people as it comes to be expressed in envies and jealousies to which you allude in your letter. When I read your book I knew at once of your outsider-ism (cf. Colin Wilson's seminal book of the same name—The Outsider) as well as your talent; since I know I am good also, I do not need to do the Big-Daddy-in-Cat-On-A-Hot-Tin-Roof bit, viz., to shit on one's sons out of envy and fear that they will appropriate my penis-cum-wife-cum-everything-else!

I trust your family are in good health. Keep in touch.

Most sincerely,

Donald B. Rinsley, M.D., F.R.S.H. (Lond.)
Associate Chief for Education
Psychiatry Service

Clinical Professor of Psychiatry
University of Kansas School of Medicine
Kansas City

DBR:mtf

"America is #1—Thanks to our Veterans"

The following article is included to give the reader the information of what Martin Grotjahn, M.D. cut out of Psychotherapy, Insight & Style: The Existential Moment Allyn & Bacon, Inc., Boston, 1981, 288 pp. Grotjahn thought for a beginning book this would throw me beyond the bounds of which psychotherapy and psychoanalysis could accept. So I had it published as an article in VOICES: JOURNAL OF THE AMERICAN ACADEMY OF PSYCHOTHERAPY, Vol. 17, No. 1, pp. 45-55. Spring 1981. Of particular note is Dr. Ed Smith's comment at the end of the article. This was a first for VOICES. Also, I began doing workshops entitled:

THE THERAPEUTIC WIZARDRY OF LEN BERGANTINO, ED.D., PH.D.

I am utilizing the article in VOICES to establish a link between Mesmer, Reich, Erickson, hypnosis, psychoanalysis and the gestaltists search for sensory awareness and to lay the groundwork for much of what is to come in this book as a preface to the focusing of therapeutic use of self exclusively in the area of psychoanalysis.

THERAPEUTIC WIZARDRY of Len Bergantino, ED.D., Ph.D.

These seminars will teach you how to do what is often referred to as magical and unteachable in facilitating a therapeutic environment that is curative with individuals, families or hypnosis, regardless of therapeutic orientation.

There will be a focus on moment to moment detoxification and transformation of experience, the creation of a curative environment through pacing and accessing the unconscious, and development of the self in terms of working at the contact boundary with speed, precision and solidarity. There will be a focus on the therapists developing an enjoyment and toleration of their madness and that of their patients so that a countertransferential purity will develop.

Heavily influenced by Wilfred R. Bion, M.R.C.S. (psychoanalysis). Trained by Milton H. Erickson, M.D., (clinical hypnosis); Jim Simkin, Ph.D., (gestalt therapy); and Carl Whitaker, M.D., (family therapy).

1st. Sat. of each month 10 a.m. – 12 noon $40

Contact: LEN BERGANTINO, ED.D., Ph.D.
450 North Bedford Drive, Suite 300
Beverly Hills, CA 90210 (USA) – Tel.: (213) 273-8705

WORKSHOPS ARE OFFERED throughout the United States and Internationally upon request.

Therapeutic Wizardry

258

of LEN BERGANTINO, Ed.D., Ph.D.

This seminar will teach you how to do what is often referred to as magical and unteachable in facilitating a therapeutic environment that is curative with individuals, families or hypnosis, regardless of therapeutic orientation. There will be a focus on moment to moment detoxification and transformation of experience, the creation of a curative environment through pacing and accessing the unconscious, and development of the self in terms of working at the contact boundary with speed, precision and solidarity. There will be a focus on the therapists developing an enjoyment and toleration of their madness and that of their patients so that a countertransferential purity can develop.

DATE:	Saturday, November 9, 1985	TIME:	9:00am - 4:30pm	
PLACE:	Sierra South, Room #245	FEE:	Students	$35.00
			Non-students	$50.00

Dr Bergantino is the author of Psychotherapy, Insight and Style. He was trained by Carl Whitaker, M.D., Jim Simkin, Ph.D., and Milton Erickson, M.D. He has trained family and gestalt therapists as well as Ericksonian hypnotists in the United States, Europe and Australia. Dr. Bergantino is a diplomate of both the American Board of Psychotherapy and the American Board of Family Psychology and Director of the Southern California Society of Clinical Hypnosis. He is in private practice in Beverly Hills and is currently teaching at UCLA.

MFCC hours are available for this workshop.

. . . .

Please complete this form for advance registration: (Therapeutic Wizardry)

Name: ______________________________

Address: ______________________________

Phone: day ( ) ______________ evening ( ) ______________

Please make checks payable to CSUN Foundation and mail to: Center In Educational Psychology, M.H. 237, CSUN, 18111 Nordhoff St., Northridge, CA 91330. For more information call Natanya at (818)885-2544.

256
Voices:
the art and science of psychotherapy
HYPNOSIS AND
THERAPEUTIC PERSUASION:
REVISITED AND RETOOLED

Len Bergantino

HYPNOTIC TEACHING TALES
of Milton H. Erickson, M.D. as told by LEN BERGANTINO, ED.D., PH.D.

The utilization of storytelling to gain *access to the unconscious mind* and *restore sensory integration* where developmental gaps exist in those whose focus is on external objects – *concrete thinking.* The stories often have the additional effect of a series of psychodynamic releases that result in existential life shifts and symptom resolution. There will be a focus on *here and now nuances* on *sensory, conscious and unconscious* levels from which to make the *critical shifts in the stories* to meet the *individual needs* of the patient.

Trained by Milton H. Erickson, M.D., (clinical hypnosis); Jim Simkin, Ph.D., (gestalt therapy); and Carl Whitaker, M.D., (family therapy). Heavily influenced by Wilfred R. Bion, M.R.C.S., (psychoanalysis).

2nd Sat. of each month, 10 a.m.-12 noon – $40
Contact: LEN BERGANTINO, ED.D., Ph.D.
450 North Bedford Drive, Suite 300
Beverly Hills, California (USA)
Telephone: (213) 273-8705

WORKSHOPS ARE OFFERED throughout the United States and Internationally upon request.

465 North Roxbury-Suite 810
Beverly Hills, California
90210 (1970-1981)

Gestalt Hypnotherapy:
An Exploration in the use of Hypnotic Energy Passes and Kinesthetic Sensory Perception

Len Bergantino is engaged in the private practice of clinical psychology in Beverly Hills. He enjoys doing a balance among individual, marital couples, and family therapies in addition to clinical hypnosis. He teaches courses for professionals at UCLA Extension and is on the faculty of the International College in Los Angeles, where he offers tutorial study for doctoral candidates. He is eclectic, but consistently experiential in his approach to learning, teaching, and practicing. His new book, *Psychotherapy Insight and Style: The Existential Moment,* presents his work as a therapist, patient, and student with several well-known therapists who have influenced his view of how impact is made in psychotherapy.

I had always been able to diagnose the quality of a patient's being, that is, in terms of *to be or not to be,* by noticing the quality of the patient's vitality, or energy. Some patients looked as if they could barely maintain. Others looked quite robust. Most people were somewhere in between. In most cases of those in between, some days were better than others.

My existential and gestalt orientations primarily lend themselves to working historically. Thus, my diagnosis is often a moment-to-moment diagnosis and responsiveness. Part of what helped me to work in this way was my ability to see a haze that surrounds people. The haze appears dense and surrounds the patient's head and body down to the shoulders, an inch or two from the body. As most patients are sitting down when I work with them these are the only areas in which I pay attention to the haze for diagnostic purposes. This area usually is either dull or sparkling, and usually matches either the dullness or sparkle in the patient's eyes and skin. This tells me much of what I need to know in terms of *being or non-being,* or what level of aliveness and contact are present.

A few years ago I began to notice a sensitivity developing in my hands. That is, I could feel vibrations when I put my hands close to each other, or when I put them about two inches away from another person's hands or body. But I could only feel this energy near certain parts of their bodies, depending upon their particular levels of vitality or places where they have blocked energy.

For over a year I spent several hours a day either doing hypnosis with patients or using self-hypnosis. I was increasing my ability to know persons at the unconscious level and to begin to tell stories that fit their situation in life without them telling me very much in terms of a formal diagnostic interview. I came to trust my unconscious processes more and more as a method of doing hypnosis, whether it was imagery, storytelling, or sensing energy with my hands. My responses were what freely flowed through my unconscious mind in relationship to my *instantaneous and continued moment-by-moment experiential diagnosis of the patient.*

My greatest obstacle to developing a flowing unconscious trance state was a lazy or regressive feeling. For example, while I can now tell stories for the entire session as they flow through me, when I began I only had one-liners. In my experience, most people suffer from this kind of passivity to one degree or another. It took effort to continue to do it. At times I felt that it would be much easier to coast along at the conscious level. However, as I continued to make the effort, I found that my experiences continued to become more interesting. A childlike curiosity was becoming aroused in me.

Karagulla (1967) made an interesting comment when she said the following:

> Sensitives observe that certain activities, ideas or experiences seem to increase the inflow of energy into the field of a given individual. When an individual comes into the presence of a well-beloved person all three of his energy fields are intensely brightened. He appears to have more energy of a bright and scintillating quality in these fields. This is very apparent in comparison with his usual energy field. (p. 159)

Other patterns commented upon were that people with a tendency to enjoy intellectual discourse picked up energy; people with a tendency to get emotional first picked up energy and then lost it; other people were seen as sappers of energy, and when others were around them they would feel drained.

I had always thought about transactions between patient and therapist as either increasing the energy of both, decreasing the energy of both, or increasing the energy of one party while the other decreases. When therapy or hypnosis is going well, both therapist and patient feel refreshed.

For example, when a hypertensive patient walks in the door I immediately pick up pain on the sides of my head which is correlated to the degree of physical abuse the patient has perpetrated upon the body. Thus, I immediately do hypnosis to alter the pace until my head and the patient's body are both free of pain.

A basic premise to all my work with energy is that *the results achieved in psychotherapy and hypnosis depend upon the patient's own redistribution of his or her energy as a consequence of his or her interpretation into his or her own individual language of what he or she thinks (???or the energy comes directly from the Holy Spirit) was suggested. The hypnotherapist, who may use hypnotic energy passes, is not doing any magic at all. Patients take charge of their lives by whatever means their unconscious minds make available to them.* This understanding is important so the hypnotherapist does not suffer any delusions of grandiosity that there is magic in the hands, but realizes that no matter what the appearance, the magic is in the Hands of The Holy Spirit.

Hypnotic energy passes refers to a process whereby the hypnotherapist is in a trance state, and what flows from his or her unconscious is a particular attention to kinesthetic energy awareness. Then the hypnotherapist acts upon what comes from that tuned-in unconscious state in relationship to the unconscious needs of the patient. There is usually some movement of the hands and some focus on the feeling of energy vibrations. While there are many ways to establish authority to help the patient utilize his or her unconscious, this method was most useful for me in establishing authority and in ratifying trance. There is an empathic "I-Thou" contact between the energies of patient and therapist, just as two people make contact.

The following set of occurrences took place. They helped me to develop the use of hypnotic energy passes in a way that can be utilized with chronic pain, psychosomatic illnesses, hypertensive states, and addictive personalities. Many other areas are unexplored and could profit from further research and validation.

I was at a party one evening. I was sitting next to a woman. She would drift off into space while talking to me. I noticed heat in the center of my right hand (what felt like a tingly hot energy vibration). I passed the hand over her eyes in a downward manner. She became more centered within herself. It happened two other times with her that evening. Nothing was said at these times.

One evening my wife had a very bad headache. As a result of having had chiropractors work on a bad back of mine I knew how to press along the spinal column all the way up my wife's back, which usually resulted in relieving her of a tension headache. However, she said that her headache was not affected, and that she felt a pain in the middle of her eye. I remember feeling lazy, but making a decision to go into a tuned-in trance state. I felt that I knew exactly where I should press and how much pressure I should apply. I went to a particular spot and pressed very hard for about one and a half minutes. I felt that I knew exactly when her headache left. At that moment I removed my hand and said, "It's gone now, isn't it?" She said, "Yes." I was a bit surprised because my conscious mind did not know that I knew what to do or where to press. I found out that *when* I was that in tune with others they were much more receptive to suggestion than when I was in my ordinary conscious states.

On another occasion I was seeing a patient who lost 60 pounds while in hypnotherapy, but who was still the victim of her strong *sexual injunctions.* This particular day she came in with a *headache.* She said "I have been to the doctor and I have tried everything to get rid of this headache. But I have it for two days. I can't think of anything that will help and I can't stand it." I went into the same kind of trance state I was in when working with my wife. In this state I knew that talking therapy wouldn't make a bit of difference here. In fact, I sensed that my voice would only irritate her headache. I noticed a hot vibratory feeling in my left hand. (This feeling or sensation is probably there all the time but I would only pay attention to it intensely at certain times when I was in a trance state and when it felt appropriate to the situation between the patient and myself.) I walked up to her and placed my hand over a spot on her head where I sensed the pain existed. I noticed an extremely intense vibration between that particular spot and my hand, which is how I sensed where to place my hand. When that intense vibration subsided I intuitively knew that the pain was gone. I asked her, and she said her headache was gone. It took five minutes.

I was very curious about what had happened, so I decided to go a bit further. I began to hold my left hand over her right hand as she was sitting down in a chair. At first I felt nothing. Then the energy vibration began to build and became very intense. I began to move my hand up her arm, never touching her, but doing it from two inches away. I noticed a hot vibratory connectedness all the way up her arm. I moved over her face, and her chest, but the free flow of energy stopped when I moved the pass over her breasts, while keeping a distance of two or two and a half inches. I intuited that I should retrace my steps, so she would take the suggestion and begin to move her energy through all those areas again in the hope that she would move energy through the block this time. What was racing through my mind was this: "I'll bet she can break her sexual injunctions and ways of cutting off feeling in her genital area if she concentrates on moving her energy through the blocked area by taking the suggestion of following the hypnotic energy pass." After she moved her energy into and past her breasts, she was again blocked at a still overweight, dead, and listless stomach. I traced the energy all the way back, and this time was able to move over the stomach, over the genitals, and over the legs. After the experience I sat in my chair for about five minutes and neither of us talked. I asked her what her experience was like. She said, "My *entire body is pulsating.* I can't ever remember feeling this good!" It was becoming clearer to me that *energy follows thought.*

Giving came from the outside = Me my 16 hrs a day made the difference

A woman came in for her weekly psychotherapy visit looking deathly pale. She said she had been to her physician twice that week, and that she was taking medication for an ear infection, but that she couldn't stop the pain. She asked me if I would hypnotize her for pain, although I had never used hypnosis with her prior to this request. I had an intuitive sense to ask her to lie down on the floor. When I did the energy passes over her ear, and then over her body, I did not feel much energy vibration in either. There was virtually no energy over her ear. I felt stuck. I couldn't find a point of person-to-person energy contact between us that was strong enough for her to feel the energy sensation and then to begin to redistribute her own energy in a way that would focus on and remove the pain. I kept on for a bit and found only one small source of energy over her heart. I kept one and a half inches above her heart, never touching her, for about ten minutes until the energetic heat built up between her heart and my left hand. At that time I put my right hand over her ear and began to feel the energy build up there. I kept my right hand over her ear and my left hand over her heart for 20 minutes more. During this time there were both verbal and non-verbal suggestions that she could redistribute her energy and that her pain would cease. When the session was over she said the pain was gone and the color had come back to her face. *I began to realize that patient focus of attention on energy could take the place of visual imagery for those patients whose natural abilities were more in this line.* For those who are poor at imagery this could have implications in the work with cancer patients that Carl Simonton is doing, by kinesthetically feeling the energy instead of visualizing.

It was her envy this time

Another woman was a manic-depressive patient who was in a severe manic state. She walked into my office each time with fast little footsteps at a pace that appeared as if she hoped no one would ever catch up with her. There was a tremendous overbalance of energy about her head. I placed my hands around her head, two inches away, for about 20 minutes. The manic state ceased to exist as I felt many shifts in the energy patterns about her head, and a drop of the energy throughout her body. In other words, she became more connected or less disconnected with herself. At the end of the session she had the fresh look of a child. When she came back the following week she said that whatever happened helped her to feel so good that she wanted to experience it again. I told her that what happened was that she dropped the energy from her head throughout the rest of her body by using my hands as a suggestive tool, and that as her unconscious mind remembered how the energy felt when it dropped, she could begin to reexperience such energy shifts herself by practicing during the week. Since she felt a bit insecure of her ability to do this, my intuition and unconscious processes sensed that I should ask her to lie down on the floor. I passed my hand, two inches over her body, from the top of her head to the tip of her toes. The hand-pass suggestion was one of equal redistribution of energy. She did her part, and when I stopped, an equal distribution of energy could be felt by both of us, as opposed to all (Treat my??? depressing of cycle thinking in that meds) the energy being focused in her head. At the end of the session she again had that childlike quality instead of the severe manic state. She later reported that after a week she was able to keep her energy focused the way it was after the session I just described, and that she also felt sexual desire for the first time in over a year. Her sexual injunction was one of the reasons she had separated from her husband.

I was beginning to see that I had limited my psychotherapy and hypnosis in the past to exclude *kinesthetic ways* of working because they had never been exposed to me. I began to find that if I moved my hands around in different positions I could pick up what felt like vibration waves that would go all through my fingers on both hands. I could do this while sitting in my chair, a good seven to ten feet away from patients. I could sense when they had internal turmoil, when their system wasn't functioning well, when they were turning anger inwards, and when they were suffering from almost any degree of hypertension. As I moved my hands in different positions I would get different levels of vibration, and I would leave my hands in the position which had the greatest degree of vibration. As soon as the vibration stopped, I knew the unnatural physical state (such as hypertension) had ceased to exist. Patients' self-reports checked out 100% of the time in at least 60 different situations. Patients were able to utilize the suggestive qualities of the hand passes even at a distance of seven to ten feet.

I worked with one couple who were enjoying vibrant health, and they were able to experience the sensations in their hands. In a few minutes they were having the greatest time. They looked as if they were playing patty-cake, patty-cake with each other, only they were feeling each other's energy flow. They sat with their hands facing each other's hands. They would feel the energy rays connecting to each hand—and just laugh and laugh and laugh. It was such a fun and curious experience that I could certainly appreciate and partake in their laughter.

A woman was seeing me for weekly psychotherapy and hypnosis for hypertension. I held my hands out while sitting in my chair, about ten feet away from her. She gave herself suggestions to calm down and did so within two minutes. However, she also complained of pain from broken toes on one foot. She was walking with a noticeable limp and wore no shoe on that foot. I hadn't thought about working with her foot. When the vibrations in my hand began to disappear I knew her hypertension was reduced. Then I intuitively went into a deeper trance state and I focused a mental picture of an energy ray between my hands and her broken toes on one foot. I focused that picture with every bit of concentration power available to me. After a minute or two she screamed, saying that pressure was building up in her toes and that she couldn't stand it. Still about ten feet away from her, I intuitively told her to stay with it for another couple of minutes. She did, and at the end of that time she said that the pain was gone. She walked out with no broken toes.

A physician telephoned me asking me to see a patient in the hospital who was having his jaw wired. The patient couldn't stand the pain and didn't want to have to take medication when leaving the hospital. This was the first time I worked with a patient just recovering from surgery. He had cut off his energy to his face in his attempt to cut off the pain. Apparently this only caused more pain. By using the hypnotic energy passes the patient was able to reverse the process of cutting off his face from his body to reduce the pain. However, it took a full 50 minutes, given the severity of the situation. At that time he said he wanted to go to sleep. However, the wires broke so I never found out if there was a lasting effect in his ability to control the pain.

A man told me his insides were racing. At first I couldn't pick up any vibrations. This usually happens when I, too, am racing and in need of trance to slow myself down. When I slow down I become more present in the here and now, more sensitive, and more able to do impactful work. This is why it becomes imperative for me to keep a constant check on my own pace because I could easily get into the hypertensive pace if I did not keep constant self-control.

As I continued to move my hands around in a variety of directions I began to feel intense vibrations. He reported that his heart was beating more slowly, that it felt that his blood wasn't pumping as fast, and that his insides stopped eating away. The results were the same as if I had used a more traditional form of hypnosis.

After this experience he said that he wanted to learn to hypnotize himself. I insisted that he already had, but I sensed he wanted a method he could feel more conscious control over, so I began to use a hypnotic visual-imagery scene which he could then practice at home. When discussing the differences between the two experiences, he said that he felt the first helped him to focus his energy where it was needed at that particular time, and the second helped him create a feeling of over-all relaxation. I had a sense that this patient was much too traditional for continued energy pass work and would profit more from hypnotic visual imagery work which was more in line with his belief systems, which were being stretched even with the hypnotic visual imagery work.

The following is a verbatim commentary from a woman who had been seen by her physician for pain in her hip, but still had the pain when she came to her psychotherapy session. She said that her physician said she was suffering from bursitis. I focused my hand two inches over her hip. After about 20 minutes I asked her to report her experience. She said that the pain was gone and then went on to add, "It's like this energy. It's all forcing through the blood vessels, and I can feel the blood flowing through the blood vessels all over my leg. Now this leg [speaking of the other leg] doesn't feel that way." I commented, "That wasn't the leg that hurt, so perhaps there was no focus of attention given to that leg." She said, "But it tingled a little. But it's nothing like this leg (pointing to the one which was focused upon). This leg has a life of its own! There's all this energy in it! It's the strangest thing. You know how it feels when your leg falls asleep, and all the blood goes rushing down—the tingling—that's what it feels like. Only my leg hasn't been asleep. It feels like it's a positive energy." Whether her self-report was medically accurate or not is irrelevant. What is relevant is that she was able to use suggestion and metaphor to redirect her attention and *psychologically* focus her energy in a balanced way. I further suggested that she should continue treatment with her physician because I had no idea medically if the relief of pain had anything at all to do with the bursitis getting better. In fact there was always a possibility it would conceal a pain that should be there, which might not be helpful to her condition.

While I happen to be sensitive in kinesthetic areas—such as my hands, or the sides of my temples, or a twist in my stomach, or a pain in the back of my neck—in response to the physical states of being in which patients enter my office, I firmly believe that patients and therapists alike have far more sensitivities than they have permitted themselves to focus upon. For example, it is only within the past two years that I learned that I could feel energy. In some who are quite sensitive in particular areas, all that needs to happen is for the suggestion to be made. The couple I described earlier in this section were able to play more sensitively with energy in their hands in one session than I was able to do after practicing for six months. They were vital healthy people who were quite sensitive and open minded to the possibility of increased sensory perception. This just added another dimension of communication to their lives. These sensory-perception dimensions are usually peak experiences because of the lack of ordinarily paying attention to such phenomena. They are but a fine-tuned version of the here and now. That is why I feel they can be of value in hooking addictive personalities (smokers, drugs, alcohol, overeaters) on a natural high instead of artificial highs in learning to experience satisfaction.

There are many implications for the utilization of hypnotic energy passes in conjunction with visual imagery, a storytelling approach to hypnosis, or more standard forms of psychotherapy. My practice has been basically composed of normal neurotics who seek therapy more for personal growth than for extreme mental crisis (mental illness). So I have in the majority of cases used the hypnotic energy passes as a way to check out whether patients are a bit too hypertensive, and to help them regulate their own paces through the use of energy passes. In these cases patients have responded extremely well in nearly all cases. So in terms of using psychotherapy and hypnosis as a way of taking responsibility for positive health in a preventive sense of the word, the use of hypnotic energy passes is within the repertoire of the personal-growth-oriented psychotherapist and hypnotist.

It can be useful in helping obese patients feel satisfaction in their stomachs without eating. There may be reason to test out the effects of energy passes with manic-depressive patients as an adjunct to medication. With the manic-depressive and obsessive-compulsive patients, energy-pass work has had a balancing affect upon their physical states.

It can be used just for play, as a way of making positive contact between couples or patients in a group.

Patients must have a full understanding that hypnosis via energy-pass work is a *psychological* technique, and in no way is it a substitute for proper medical consultation regarding all situations that are physical in nature and/or may be a combination of the physical and the psychological. Further, it is also important that the energy pass be used as would any other hypnotic tool, and that no false representation be made in trying to take claim for medical cures.

In this way the false compartmentalization of the lack of the psychological as it relates to the physical and the lack of the physical as it relates to the psychological will be reduced. The focus of treatment will be *psychophysiological,* with the non-medical hypnotherapist helping to deal with the psychological as it relates to the physical, and the medical doctor handling the physical; while the medical hypnotherapist may be in a position to handle both sides of the coin.

Danger of Charlatanism and Mystification

If patients need an illusion of magic for the hypnotherapist to *get their attention,* or to ratify the trance state, all well and good. The important issue is that the work be completed in a way in which the patient realizes that the power to change rests within himself or herself. The hypnotist's use of magic in these terms can be very important when dealing with the cynical, skeptical type of patient who is able to pick holes in everything, thereby guaranteeing a rebellious stuckness in terms of both mental and physical illness. Change in the patient's belief system becomes critically important, and if energy-pass work can help do the job, all well and good, as long as the hypnotherapist doesn't believe that he or she can really do the magic. In such cases, the danger lies in the delusions of the professional.

Can Energy Passes Be Combined With Talk Therapy?

Yes, while my hands are moving about, making whatever suggestions they are making, while the patient's unconscious mind is interpreting suggestions in whatever way it needs to do so to focus the patient's energy in the places that are most needed, I do talk to patients. The talking or carrying on of a traditional therapy session while this process with energy is taking place is sometimes very useful since it can disarm patients who are reluctant to try something new. On the other hand, there are some occasions when it may be better to say nothing. Once the hypnotherapist gets an intuitive feel for doing the work, he or she will be able to act according to the flow of the unconscious.

Pain and Psychosomatic Illness

This has been a difficult area for hypnotists. Many authors report an 80 to 85 per cent ratio of symptoms being psychosomatic, but few speak of any psychophysiological psychotherapy or hypnotherapy. This leaves patients in a position of having surgery that might have otherwise been avoided by more harmless measures, such as the kind of hypnotherapy I am describing. It is best to try the harmless first.

Further, with the difficult chronic-pain population that tends to shirk responsibility and put blame on someone else because of their own feelings of helplessness and need to influence other people, kinesthetic energy-pass work can create an illusion of magic to establish authority by the hypnotist. Without this authority, the work might be sabotaged by chronic-pain patients. Of course, it might be sabotaged anyway, but the kinesthetic work increases the likelihood of success.

The vibratory sensations of the energy-pass work may even be thought of as a very mild form of stimulation that is along the lines of *electrical stimulation* used in treatment for pain control. Such energy-pass hypnotherapy might be acceptable to patients who refuse electrical stimulation because they do not like the more extreme sensations.

Further, while there have been a variety of studies indicating that hypnosis is not opiate mediated and that hypnosis does not release the endogenous opiate system in facilitating analgesia, it can be suggested that hypnotic energy-pass work needs further research to determine whether it would release the endogenous opiate system in the body.

Acupuncture is also a noted method of pain control. Its success is often explained by saying that the system of energy flow in the body is stimulated by the acupuncture points. Pain is thought of as an accumulation of excess energy. Energy flows through the *acupuncture* meridians. When there is an *energy block, there is pain.* Perhaps the hypnotic energy hand passes in some way break up the blocked energy, and that is what relieves the pain. Correlation studies using acupuncture and hypnotic energy passes would be useful for future patient populations whose belief systems preclude them from experiencing either one or the other of these methods.

Perhaps what is being described is a heightened empathy that helps a therapist use his or her body, mind, and feelings as a biofeedback machine that can also use suggestion and metaphor and do psychotherapy at the same time. The hypnotic energy-pass work is often done within the context of a storytelling approach where attention is paid to the moment-to-moment mental and sensory-perception cues going on in the hypnotist in relationship to the patient. The relationship between the hypnotherapist and the patient is always thought about in the context of making contact between "I" and "Thou." The primary difference between gestalt hypnotherapy and gestalt therapy is the unusual ways in which such interpersonal contact is made.

REFERENCE

Karagulla, S. *Breakthrough to creativity: Your higher sense perception.* Los Angeles: DeVorss and Co., 1967.

COMMENT

by EDWARD W. L. SMITH, Ph.D.
1145 Sheridan Road N.E.
Atlanta, Georgia 30324

This is a controversial article. In it Len describes a phenomenon which he has experienced. Most readers have not experienced that phenomenon, and I include myself among them. These days, my stance is skeptical respect for claims beyond my experience. I am very uninterested in the cults of pop-psychology and pop-metaphysics, or in their claims of knowledge and powers. At the same time I respect the reports of serious and conscientious people, and am stirred to interest or even excitement by these reports. Len is a man whom I like and respect. I have witnessed myself time and again evolve from skepticism (or even "solid disbelief") to familiarity with a phenomenon. I also have witnessed the clarification of illusions and the uncovering of untruths. So, I stand as respectful skeptic, usually open to being shown. And once shown compelling evidence I am quick to incorporate. I would like to investigate the phenomenon Len describes with him. My vote was to publish this article to stir us to consider and investigate.

Our labor is to bring all men to the healer in themselves. GEORGE Fox

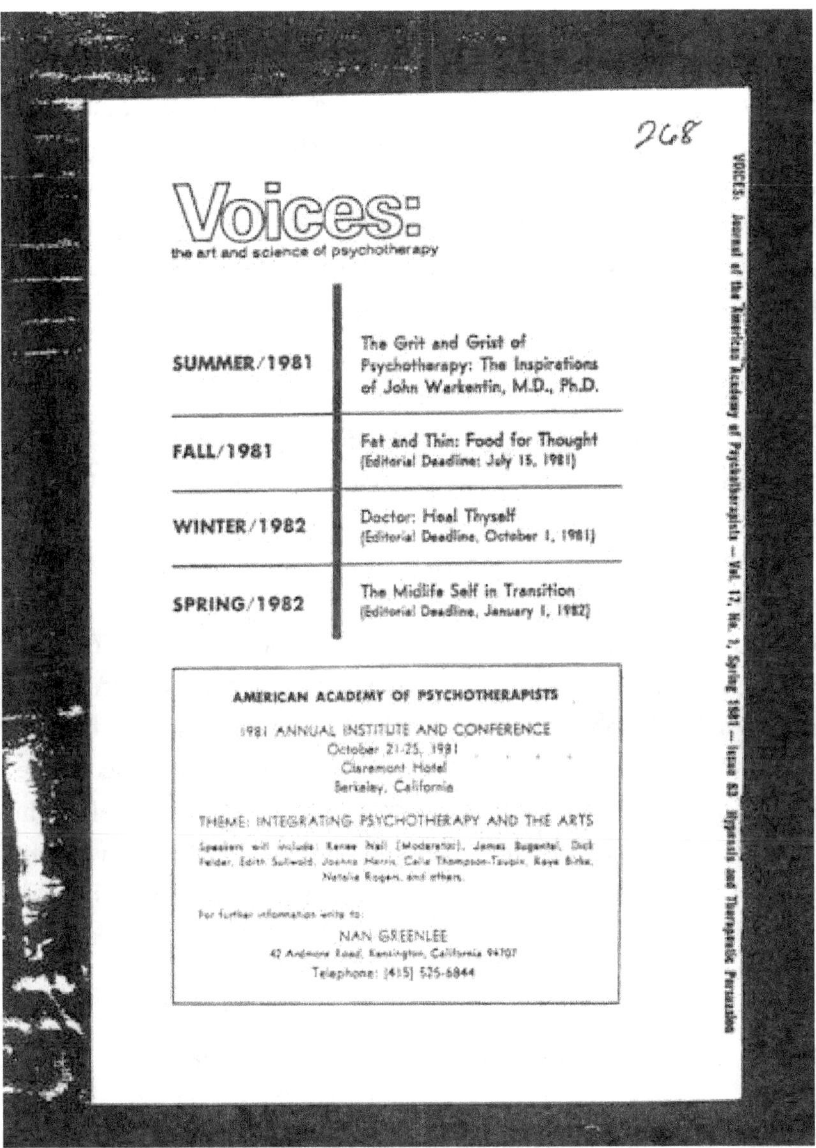

268

VOICES: Journal of the American Academy of Psychotherapists — Vol. 17, No. 1, Spring 1981 — Issue 63 Hypnosis and Therapeutic Persuasion

Voices:
the art and science of psychotherapy

SUMMER/1981	The Grit and Grist of Psychotherapy: The Inspirations of John Warkentin, M.D., Ph.D.
FALL/1981	Fat and Thin: Food for Thought (Editorial Deadline: July 15, 1981)
WINTER/1982	Doctor: Heal Thyself (Editorial Deadline, October 1, 1981)
SPRING/1982	The Midlife Self in Transition (Editorial Deadline, January 1, 1982)

AMERICAN ACADEMY OF PSYCHOTHERAPISTS

1981 ANNUAL INSTITUTE AND CONFERENCE
October 21-25, 1981
Claremont Hotel
Berkeley, California

THEME: INTEGRATING PSYCHOTHERAPY AND THE ARTS

Speakers will include: Renee Nell (Moderator), James Bugental, Dick Felder, Edith Sullwold, Joanna Harris, Celia Thompson-Taupin, Kaye Birke, Natalie Rogers, and others.

For further information write to:

NAN GREENLEE
42 Ardmore Road, Kensington, California 94707
Telephone: (415) 525-6844

WILFRED BION, M.R.C.S. (MEDICAL ROYAL COLLEGE OF SURGEONS): MY SEARCH FOR THE 'HOLY GRAIL' IN PSYCHOANALYSIS

I was divinely connected to Bion. No matter what I write there will be those who will never be satisfied with what I have written, but there it is. Not only was I divinely connected to Bion or I could have never learned what I did and I could never have done what I have done, and I could not know what I know, but I learned everything from him experientially only having met him one time. Of course, it was to take the next eleven years of my life to learn and master technically what I knew experientially in that night of May, 1979 when Bion was the invited speaker at the Franz Alexander Memorial Award at Rodeo Junior High School Auditorium in Beverly Hills, California.

On the day, in fact the exact moment that Bion died, I was about to put a letter in the mailbox at the corner of Camden Drive and Brighton Way and send it to him in London. However, the moment of his death was at the precise instant before I put the letter in the mailbox at which point "the wind was knocked out of me." Ten thousand or so miles away Bion's son Julian was climbing the Himalayas and at the precise moment of Bion's death the wind was knocked out of him. The second fact about Bion's son was how I was able to determine what had happened to me at the corner of Camden Drive and Brighton Way. That is the level at which I knew him, ceased to know him, and I got to know him again in different form (a story all in its own right). My daughter Lisa Francesca Bergantino is the reincarnated soul of Wilfred R. Bion!!! A direct request fulfilled by God.

What I am about doing is the writing of my life's work from 1979 through 1991. There was the "original paper I sent to Bion" which he wrote back to me was "evocative and stimulating" That is titled The "BEING OF" AND "BEING WITH" WILFRED BION, M.R.C.S. (Medical Royal College of Surgeons): A Clear Mind And A State of Discovery. However, I wrote that paper without any formal psychoanalytic context. Being in the presence of Bion from 8 p.m. to about 11:25 p.m. I stayed up all night and write a 37 page paper, evoked a clarity of thinking and feeling of passionately enthused excitement whereby I wrote the paper the very next morning and sent it to Bion that very day. It is said that his ability to "evoke thoughts without a thinker" had the effect of evoking such clarity and writing ability in his analysands. As for me, I went to him with extra-sensory perception, so I got the whole treatment in one dose; however my life has turned out for only having one shot at him in person.

Thus, what I am going to do is present what I have written about Bion in three sections. The first will be entitled "1995" and I will comment with the psychoanalytic knowledge and technical skills as influenced by "higher sense perception" that I have attained.

The second will present the forward to and the actual 22 (37) pages I had sent to Bion in that you may see what he found to be "evocative and stimulating."

The third was written in 1986 and is entitled "BION AND BEYOND: THE LANGUAGE OF EXPERIENCE", which is when I began writing a book that has taken me the longest time to overcome the resistance of doing. This is directly related to the facts of my life, which are also directly related to Bion and Erickson and what was to come later.

One might ask why all the fuss about Bion? So he was a gifted writer, and perhaps the leading psychoanalytic original conceptualizer since Freud and Melanie Klein; or perhaps his work even exceeds that of Klein. This is how the psychoanalytic community views Bion at the international level. If this was all there was about him, I would have not had the interest or passion to pursue what I am doing. Meeting him once changed the course of my life forever! A patient once asked_Erickson, "Can one hypnosis session make a difference?" Erickson stated, "You only had to be born once, didn't you!" I guess that's what happened.

I was after something but not quite sure what because I had never seen it. I only read about the possibility of it. My doctoral training at The University of Southern California was based on the existential psychoanalytic work of John Paul Sartre and the utilization of his master work, BEING AND NOTHINGNESS as a basis from which to do and view a humanistic existential psychotherapy or even a humanistic existential kind of psychoanalysis. Sartre wrote of and did existential psychoanalysis. Sartre described a quality of being and stated that the thing that was missing in psychoanalysis was "the thing-in-itself", in other words, the full being of the analyst. It is one thing to read and argue this point on a collegial basis. It is another to be looking for it without knowing you are doing so by seeking out and training with seventeen world renowned therapists and writing a book about it (Psychotherapy, Insight & Style: The Existential Moment, Allyn & Bacon, Boston, 1981). It is still another to get to a therapeutic use of self, like a Caruso, a Toscanini, a Paganini, where you actually have the sensitivity to experience in all the dimensions of splendor that are customarily associated with being in "the image and likeness of God", and having that hit you smack in the face when you knew it existed, but also knew that you would never attain it, and only a chosen few might ever come face to face with the likeness of God or any kind of experience that might be a momentary replica in its smallest dimensions to remind the human race of the greatness, grandness and glory of God-albeit only in the form of a human being who has lived a life worthy of the attainment of such magnificence. That was Bion! And me! And Erickson!

Of course my psychoanalytic brethren will say that I have idealized Bion-and that I have not worked through the paranoid schizoid part of my own personality thereby leaving my grandiosity in a place where I would and could idealize Bion. In 97% of the cases this could, would and might be true. In this case I am the real thing and I am presenting you the real thing. The question is whether or not you will get it even with the force with which I present it; or whether you will waste another hundred years seeing that the profession of psychoanalysis remains stagnant.

The problem among psychoanalysts today without a realization and focus on Becoming 'O', is that what they put into the interpretation on a primitive level is sputum, puke and puss. The fact one is well trained, or bright, or even brilliant has little if no effect whatsoever on the "severe pathological projective identifications of the psychoanalyst put into the patient", and in fact may make it more difficult for the patient to know that the psychoanalyst, on the scale of Becoming 'O', or moving toward finer and finer discriminations of pure being, in the image and likeness of God, for the purpose of the analysis-which is to save man's soul, is little more than a "purveyor of shit." This is not what Freud intended.

Much can be covered up by psychoanalysts under the benign word of countertransference. We all suffer counter-transferential problems to some degree or other. With the repetition compulsion we will play it out millions of times in our lives, many of which we will be on top of, and many of which we will not. Yet, what I am saying is that at the deepest primitive sensory levels psychoanalysts have not even begun to learn to deal with their countertransference's as they are related to the primitive nature of their own being and the splitting and pathological projective identifications in the psychoanalysts. In fact, as psychoanalysts, the state of the art today is that psychoanalysts can barely pick these phenomena up in that patient, let alone themselves. And if they do pick up the phenomena, they do so primarily with the "words" of the patient about four and one half years into the analysis as opposed to the immediacy of when the splitting and pathological projective identification are occurring (the existential moment or consecutive moments as detailed in Psychotherapy, Insight & Style: The Existential Moment and later titled Making An Impact In Therapy: How Master Clinicians Intervene, Jason Aronson, Inc., focuses on the range of interventions to_turn around the quality of being of the patient), which is required in moving toward finer and finer discriminations of Becoming 'O' in the image and likeness of God to save man's soul (Bettelheim, Freud and Man's Soul, 1983, Random House). Four and one half years for the brilliant and gifted analyst as opposed to an analyst who can pick up the most subtle and fine-tuned discriminations of splitting and pathological projective identifications as they are occurring, make interventions that "put them back into the patient's body in ways that the patient is mentally and physiologically whole at as many moments during the hour as are possible with the object in mind to have an unimpeded and uninterrupted flow of being or becoming 'O', something never fully attainable, but which we can only work toward.

Nevertheless, it is on this level that I am writing about Bion. For a human I had never met anyone nor ever experienced anyone who had traveled that far with themselves prior to meeting Bion. Let me tell you of my reflections of Bion in 1979 which you can later compare with what I wrote in 1979 and in 1986. It is all the more remarkable in that after Bion's death I searched among the top 26 analysts in Los Angeles, all M.D.'s, and sat face to face with each of them for the purpose of selecting a training analyst. All but one were purveyors of shit in the ways I shall describe the experience of Bion and those who were not. The other was clear minded but might as well have been sensorily dead and when dealt with on that level there was no one a person would want to spend any degree of time or money in the presence of, despite his many talents.

I have written these experiences seven and nine years apart and there is some overlap. Read all of it. For what I am trying to convey to you I assure you the overlap is necessary. Erickson stated he often had to tell a story three times before it registered in the patient's unconscious mind. For the purposes of this book, "YOU ARE THE PATIENT!" Further, while what I have written of Bion are seven and nine years apart, the "context" of each of these writings are different in terms of what I mean to convey and how I want to do it; so as Bion might have said, "The experience is not repeatable!"

THE STORY

I got a call from a psychiatrist friend who asked me if I wanted to go hear Wilfred Bion at The Franz Alexander Memorial Lecture at Rodeo Junior High School. It was May, 1979. I said, "No, I don't think so. I have heard some of this fellow Bion. His methods are formed in mathematical calculations and I had trouble in grammar school math." Yet at the very moments I was making these statements I felt a surge of excitement, of???ce that was unexplainable and certainly not congruent???oughts. I further stated, "I have no knowledge of psychoanalysis and no interest in it or anyone who does it."??? that I had met throughout the years didn't have??? despite my two statements, I enthusiastically??? agreed to meet him there. He brought his??? baby there among five hundred people).??? several years later that the politics??? Community Mental Health Center, and at the two major psychoanalytic institutes in Los Angeles (The Los Angeles Psychoanalytic Institute and The Southern California Psychoanalytic Institute, both exclusively M.D. institutes prior to Welch vs. The American Psychoanalytic) where heavy fighting between Freudians and Kleiniens, and a great deal of envy and hatred toward Bion existed. In fact, in many of these psychoanalytic circles they had excluded him to one degree or another throughout the years.

As one of my mentors, Carl Whitaker, M.D., may have put it, "They were trying to boil him in oil!" Over the years my very good friend has become Mrs. Francesca Bion, and in her recent visit to Los Angeles in July, 1995 I mentioned this point to her and what Bion said to me about it, and she said, "Oh, he just loved to work in that environment! He loved the challenge!" I had mentioned that one might expect a person to be annoyed with the lack of gratitude and appreciation for such an effort. She emphatically stated, "Not Bion!"

There were three M.D. psychoanalysts on the stage in addition to Bion. They were each going to present on different aspects of Bion's work as they understood and perhaps utilized Bion's legacy.

The first, I do not remember his name, although I would not tell you if I did. For the purposes of this story in this context I will call him Michael.

Michael began speaking of working with thinking disorders in children. As he began to speak I began to feel tremendous pain on each side of my temples, right and left. I knew it was coming from him. Although I knew it would look weird in such a large audience, I didn't care. I was both committed to do what-ever I had to do to maintain the quality of my own being at its highest levels, and I was a true experiential scientific researcher not bound by the culture bind of what was expected and common knowledge. In my own areas of psychotherapy I had transcended that, and in psychoanalysis I knew nothing on a formal academic level as would be taught in an institute.

In other words I was pre-institute material. Thus, I put both hands up in a direction toward him that would "block the painful rays of energy that were being pathologically projected from the M.D. psychoanalyst who treated children". I was able to "block the pain." When I put my hands down, the pain was there again. As he went on it became more severe. In addition there was a burdensome dis-spirited feeling, a sinking feeling and constant feeling of oppression in the chest area. I thought "the child would have to cure himself in spite of the analyst!" This thought came after the analyst stated that the child had only two sessions, the last two, in which he could think clearly. I did not realize the importance of this "thought without a thinker" at the time, that "the child would have to cure himself in spite of the analyst"; that is, in spite of the severe splitting and pathological projective identification of the psychoanalyst in a way that put the analyst's depressive and feelings of being overwhelmed onto the child. The pain on the left temple were tortured thoughts on the part of the analyst on what might be in an analyst who had become 'O' in a more nurturing fashion on the "female nurturant part of the analyst's thinking equipment". The pain projected and that would have incapacitated my own or at least hindered it, or the right temple, was a disturbance on the "masculine assertive" part of the personality of the presenting psychoanalyst. The chest area indicated the projections of depression and feelings of being overwhelmed. Now I am commenting from hundreds of thousands of repetitions of knowing exactly what part of the body is related to what thought or part of a thought (Bion-Second Thoughts) the instant I perceive the split off material with my own therapeutic use of self fine tuned sensory apparatus. So we have the repetition compulsion in the analyst; in other words if you were in session with him day after day, you would get the same primitive experience of where he was stuck on the scale of Becoming 'O'. That is "tortured thoughts on the left-or what is supposed to be female nurturant side of his personality"; tortured thoughts on the right, or masculine assertive side of his personality; and depression that knocks the wind out of you while you are being analyzed. So you are in the room with the analyst five days a week and you submit to severe pain on the left temple, severe pain on the right temple and overwhelming depression of feelings of the wind knocked out of you in your chest, and are supposed to carry on the analysis as if the analyst's interpretations will help you Become 'O'. In fact, the only way you could possibly succeed was in spite of the analyst, but the progress would be so slow because the analyst was such an impediment to the working through of the transference at the most primitive levels of being, that there would be a slowing down of the sensory integration required to restore thinking capacity.

The next fellow I shall refer to as Kenneth. He was brilliant in a sense, and people were taken with the eloquence of his verbiage. I knew this first fact because on a sensory level, where it hurt the sides of my head on both temples, with this fellow it was a matter of almost the sensation of bright lights flashing. Again, these are physical descriptions of sensations that have never been described before in writing, so I am doing the best I can do to come as close as I can to the description. Another way to put it was "good feeling and positive pulsations that had the feeling of brightness to them that pulsated every $1/16^{th}$ or so of a second."

However, at the same time there was a nausea in the pit of the stomach (equal to physiological disgust) and I thought the man is "lying to himself". This is a more common sensation than the others because man by definition engages in three types of lies-to oneself, to significant others and to all people in the world. The one to oneself is the most dangerous because it leaves the psychoanalyst in a position of "turning truth around on the patient" and believing what the analyst is saying and doing is the truth. This is a good way for everyone to wind up with their heads up their asses, and like cuckoo birds, going "CooKoo, CooKoo!".

Now to complete the trilogy of what I meant by "brilliant in a sense" in my initial description of the fellow, there was a pain being projected that was "heavy and dulling about a quarter of an inch to one half inch below the part that is referred to as "the crown" part of the top of my head. This is the part psychic energy people usually refer to as where the energy comes in or goes out. When I felt that heavy and painful dullness I thought, "Even though this man is brilliant it is of no use to him. The pain in the middle of the head nullifies the brilliance in that it is heavy and dull, and the nausea in the stomach distorts the energy that comes in or goes out from the crown. Again, all these phenomena were being projected from the speakers into and onto the audience without any conscious notice on the part of the audience, except for me who had been souped up for one year using the "disease free pace as a way of life that Margaret Mead told Dr. Erickson she had only heard in a rare African tribe that was relatively free of disease." Thus, it was as if I had an X-RAY machine and I was looking at the psychophysiological makeup of the analysts totally nude. When I say looking, it was also feeling, sensing in my body what was being projected onto me (and I always checked it out with my hands because if my hands could block out the pain then it wasn't coming from me. If you can develop this sensitivity in your hands it is a start toward the development of "countertransferential purity on the most primitive levels" because you will always know when it is you and when it is them; and this will help you to stop puking puss into the bellies of your analysands.). It clearly was them on all occasions of which I am writing. It is no wonder Bion found what I wrote in 1979 "evocative and stimulating." It was the direct and exact experience of his life's work by someone who didn't just conceptualize-it as most psychoanalysts treat his work today because they haven't a clue of what discipline of self is required to develop the kind of therapeutic use of self necessary to actually do the work. It is kind of like making a Stradivarius! Only instead of a violin you have an analytic use of self that plays that well!

You can well see the problem of having my work become widespread. The reader would have to acknowledge that many of their best shots are little more than the promulgation of puke, nausea, and organismic disgust that has the end result creation of another pussbag like self. Having no trust in the character disordered nature of psychoanalysts, albeit in some way less so than others and in many ways more so than others, it is my hope that this book will be widely read by those willing to pay for the analysis in that they will have an idea of what they are getting and what they are not getting.

The third presentor I shall refer to as Waldo. He began by describing himself as "exoteric", that is paying attention to that which is external to himself upon which to focus his attention and base his interpretations (similar to most gestalt therapists (see chapter following Bion entitled "Gestalt Therapy And The Problem of Thinking")-who have lost their minds, not regained their senses, and not regained their minds. I refer to the general characteristics of such persons as "cement heads". No matter what you say to them they can't transcend their own limitations and they are pissed off at you about it.

Waldo referred to Kenneth as "esoteric", meaning that the sum and substance of his interpretations came from the internal core of his being. I can only assume this was a high paid compliment in that Waldo had no way to assess the difficulties that were brought with the internal workings of Kenneth that tainted the esoteric with mud and sputum. One had a sense that Waldo was pretty good at tracking the experience of a patient one step behind the reported experience, but had a difficult time of it manifesting the depth of his own substance, which left him saddened to death, perhaps. I say this because what he projected was the feeling of "a huge dagger going through the heart that caused so much pain in me that I could barely stand it." What went through my head was "this man is such a liar he is going to kill himself with a heart attack." The cause of such sadness is life long and it is chronic. In other words despite the best that psychoanalysis has to offer, when the core of a person's being has been destroyed to such a degree, it is currently known to be irreparable. This is stated by Kohut in his last book entitled How Does Analysis Cure?, The University of Chicago Press, 1984, where on page 9 he wrote "My clinical Kohut experience suggests that the analytic dissolution of defensive structures that have formed around a persisting hollowness in the center of the patient's self cannot be achieved-even in cases where this central hollowness is experienced as painful by a would-be-analysand." (I will go back to pages 8 and 9 of Kohut's book at a later time, but for now this statement is enough to make my point in this context).

We can assume according to the literature, the works of Bion and others who have written about splitting and projective identification, that the payoff for the patient, or in this case, Waldo, is that the pain that is chronically there is not experienced Thus, in its full force I got the brunt of what was going on in Waldo at the heart level lying to himself about being permanently destroyed at the very core of his being which has left him with a central hollowness and superficiality despite the status he has achieved the status of training analyst, who received an M.D., and was of such stature among a city as large as Los Angeles to be invited to present on a stage with Wilfred Bion, no small feat in itself. The pain he projected was devastating and he had to lie to himself about it for he could not have stood the pain of what he might have seen in the mirror. Kohut, et al, on page 9 went on to say "Perhaps the basis of my conviction, as I implied before, is the feeling that I would not be able to maintain a reliable empathic bond with the patient when, at the end of his journey toward the basic transference, he would have to tolerate the protracted experience of prepsychological chaos and, not just temporarily but for long periods, borrow the analyst's personality organization in order to survive." Subject-object Merger)-I did it twice-Erickson & Bion-Dr. Mike Paul, MD., did it with Bion.

Bion was the only one I met prior to me that had the strength and clearness of personality in terms of Becoming 'O' whereby the patient would and could stand it. The problem was that the psychoanalytic frame even with the liberties that Bion took did not provide for the ruthlessness of method that would have to be brought into the frame to achieve the results of restoring the central hollowness of the patient's core to a solid, depthful and substantial being who might in fact be able to save his or her own soul as Freud had in mind.

However, Kohut does go on to illuminate about what might realistically be expected of an analysis with the advances that have been achieved up to and throughout the writing of this book when he wrote on page nine, "Of course, the fact that a therapist cannot accompany his patient into the lands of prepsychological chaos does not mean that he cannot be of help to him. While a nuclear self cannot be created by the therapy, the patient can still use the therapist as a self-object to build up new defensive structures. As a self-object transference establishes itself, in other words, in which the threatened defensive structures are offered not to the self-object therapist for his mirroring approval, or in which the self-object therapist's personality is used, via a township merger or goal-setting idealizations, to strengthen the patient's defensive structures." (see igniting and sustaining a nuclear self that has the capacity to think through storytelling, after the section on gestalt therapy and the problem of thinking.) Kohut wrote "As the result of straightforward educational activities from the side of the therapist, moreover, the patient can learn how to manage his defensive structures to his best advantage."

I was in the presence of Kohut in 1983 when he presented at UCLA and had the ability to check him out on my X-Ray machine so to speak. He was relatively clear in his thoughts and words, and there was a slight flickering green light being projected from the heart area. It made me think, "This man's battle was one of heart, and so from his own personal struggle he developed a kind of psychoanalytic interpretation that focused on "empathy" to the exclusion of aggression. There was a nausea in the stomach as there is in every "Kohutian" I ever met. If you kick him in the stomach, he will crumble! Yet, the slight "flickering green light" is what stood out. On a more personal level I had the thought he was having trouble keeping his own heart going, or he was not a man who naturally lived the path of heart. I think he died shortly thereafter, a year or so later, of a heart attack. (ANY CONNECTION BETWEEN MY SENSORY PERCEPTION AND HIS CONDITION? YOU TELL ME!)

AND THEN THERE WAS BION!

While Drs. Michael, Kenneth and Waldo presented, Bion sat there looking like a solid block of granite. That was the appearance he gave. No social courtesies, just Pure Being.??? Discrimination of Becoming "O". The only other time I had ever seen this kind of behavior was in Milton H. Erickson, M.D.

Then it was Bion's turn. Up to this point I was convinced I had not missed anything by being trained in other therapies than psychoanalysis, as the best in Los Angeles, I was certain, had relatively little to offer me in terms of who I was and how I wanted to be in the world.

Bion stood and began to speak. I will give you the feelings he "projected into the audience" as I describe the experience. He began by saying, "With all that's been said about me I can hardly wait to hear what I am going to say". The audience immediately began to feel warmed and included in mass. The longer he spoke the feeling was, and I have only had this one time in my life, like my entire body was being pumped up with a bicycle pump-filled with air, and then I achieved a feeling of fullness of being everything and all I was ever born to be Bion connected to God. That happened from just being in the presence of Bion while he spoke in terms of the level of Becoming 'O' he had attained in himself. When some referred to him as a "mystic" I suppose it was these and similar kind of experiences that happened in his presence for which there really was no way to explain it other than to describe him as a mystic. He spoke approximately one hour and forty seven minutes. During that time there was one slight twinge of pain projected from the right side of his temple, or the masculine assertive side of his personality. (Anser) There was no nausea in the stomach, no pain in the heart, and when he spoke very complex sentences and paragraphs the clarity and non-convoluted nature of himself and the congruence of his words gave one the experience, "if you were in a place to receive it", that "A WARM BATH WAS MASSAGING YOUR MIND AND YOU WERE IN THE PRESENCE OF THE CLEAREST FIRST GRADE TEACHER YOU WERE EVER LIKELY TO MEET", the result being that you were likely to develop a capacity to think that you never heard before and most probably did not know existed. Well, there it was, I had an experience the likes of which affected my entire life so that the pursuit of Becoming 'O' was put above all else. While all the cards are not in yet, it cost me everything I had known and treasured, or thought that I had treasured. In other words if you are the kind of person who is willing to play at this level, you have to play for all the marbles and be willing to lose them all, too. Saving your soul and the pursuit of the finer and finer discriminations of your own being are the sine qua non of your existence, and to those ends that you become, that you are countertransferentially pure, that you live the life of a Holy man or Holy woman, then you will be that psychoanalyst-perhaps not exactly like-but as Bion showed himself to be.

It was a long time ago and I did not focus particularly on the content of what Bion said, nor could I remember it. What was amazing to me was the clearness of mind to a degree I had never experienced in my life. Bion's statement of hardly being able to wait to hear what he was going to say was the showing of a man who could stand the angst of the unknown along with its accompanying accoutrements of chaos and anxiety, or as Kohut wrote about, pre-psychological chaos and their oscillations required toleration that could not be had to develop a solid nuclear self. Bion could not only stand this, he was that solid nuclear self personified, which is why I described him as a "solid block of granite". Again, you had to be there and experience Bion to understand the degree of Becoming 'O' by which he had surpassed all other humans I ever met. I did not realize until about 1987 in a presentation I gave entitled "The Search For The Holy Grail" that Bion was that embodiment of everything that Sartre wrote about and the lack in all other psychoanalysts was the embodiment of Sartre's comment, that the thing missing in psychoanalysis was the thing-in-itself; in other words, the pure being of the psychoanalyst himself; or as close to that pure being as might make a difference in the way the entire ball game is played. That is, the development of a solid nuclear self whose soul will be saved through the means by which the Churches and Synagogues failed, and that tool is psychoanalysis. This is in no means intended to demean or devalue our ministers, priests and rabbis. It is meant to show that the people are left to belief and good works to save their souls, even without the development of personal equipment that such an analysis as I am attempting to describe might help one attain.

There was an M.D. psychoanalyst in the audience who had been previously supervised by Bion. He wanted to present a case to Bion and came up to the stage. There was a table with a white table cloth. From the audience one could look up at the stage and see the legs of the participants below the white table cloth. They were all males so you could see their trousers. Bion sat straight up as "solid as a block of granite". He looked straight ahead, having little interest in making eye contact with the psychoanalyst being supervised, an M.D. Through the years I became experientially clear that Bion, Erickson and Whitaker (the later two having trained me) had the primary interest of being able to tap into their own unconscious mind and having constant and continuous access to it, and that the "eye contact" was often used by patients to seduce the psychoanalyst to become mindless, or lose their unconscious minds and become "cement heads", so the patients could remain in such a deluded state of false safety. Bion has written extensively on this throughout his works and he certainly was "not one on this evening to be seduced by contact".

OF PARTICULAR NOTE WAS THAT BION SPOKE THROUGH HIS OWN PRESENTATION AS WELL AS HIS LONG WINDED ALMOST STORYTELLING LIKE INTERPRETATIONS WHEN HE WAS SUPERVISING, AT THE PACE MARGARET MEAD TOLD ERICKSON SHE HAD ONLY HEARD IN A RARE AFRICAN TRIBE THAT WAS RELATIVELY FREE OF DIS-EASE! THIS PACE WAS S L O W. I had wondered, given Bion was English but was born in India, whether the Eastern Way of Being, during those early years of childhood, influenced the way he developed? Bion never varied from "his center", or the center core of his being. You could feel it when you were in his presence. He was not a man to be distracted by other peoples' bullshit.

Back to the supervision session, and there he sat. The supervisee was leaning over a bit and the audience could see, but Bion could not, that the man's right leg was bouncing back and forth and could not be still while he presented his case. He presented the case of a man laying on the couch whose right leg could not stop bouncing or moving, no matter what was said, or no matter how it was analyzed. The supervisee went into a fair amount of detail regarding his efforts that were to no avail. Again, without seeing the man's leg, and looking straightforward sitting there like a solid block of granite looking only into his own unconscious mind, Bion said, that "In such a case the receptor may not be receptive to the patient's movement." I thought, "Holy Shit! Bullseye in One Shot!"

I am not the shy type and I have pretty much met everyone I ever wanted to. Then again, to have the experience I have just described left me in awe where I did not do something I wanted to do and have forever regretted it. When the presentation was over Bion went into the hall before the entrance to the auditorium and he spoke with a few as the participants left. To my surprise not too many were after him and those he spoke with was only in passing. I wanted to ask him to go out for a few cognacs, but chickened out. Years later, after his death, his wife, Francesca Bion, told me he did not have a ride home that night. It was my one shot to hang out with Bion and I blew it!

However, I did go up to him and say, "Dr. Bion, it was a pleasure just being in the audience when you presented. It was like a warm bath massaging my mind." Bion was that night, and I am assuming he lived that way, always "BE-ON", that is in terms of responding at deep levels from his unconscious to the unconscious of the person he was with. Erickson and Whitaker were the only other two I ever met who were like this, but each had a different compilation of personal qualities that did not equal BE-ON or BION. Bion said to me, "I enjoyed myself very much and I always make it a point to do what I enjoy doing." However, at the moment in time he said this, as one would consider the timing of an interpretation of a psychoanalyst, "my entire body filled with feeling-that is, welled up with feeling", as I felt "so understood by Bion that he had somehow communicated to me that he "understood the central struggle in my life". I was standing there speechless, in awe, thinking that perhaps I should write him a check for a session. I did not, or could not speak another word to him at that time, We both looked at each other knowing we had more to say, but that was not the time it would be said.

My life was never the same after that evening and meeting with Bion.

My dear friend, Francesca Bion, who is the only adult in the world who knows what I know, stated to me two years before my writing this section in 1995 that "Perhaps when you write your new book you will include the "original paper you sent to Bion". While I wrote much about Bion it was filtered through his analysands in <u>Psychotherapy, Insight</u>

And Style: The Existential Moment in that I had no context in which to write what I knew in that I did not know that I knew it. To the extent I appreciated what they offered me at the time, it diluted what I am now able to give you some sixteen years later.

However, I do recommend the book as a preface to reading this book in that it shows the range or what I have brought into psychoanalysis; it shows how Bion effected some of his best analysands and what they had to say about him; and it is the only place in existence where I have dissected 12 hours of audio tape supervision of Dr. Bion supervising a then young psychoanalyst, Stephen Salenger, M.D., who was most gracious to let me quote verbatim even though much of what was said about him was personal and not flattering. Dr. Salenger made a conscious decision to do this because he felt it was important for the profession of psychoanalysis to "know" what Bion actually did and how he actually worked.

During my writing Francesca is still looking in the attic of her home in Oxford for the original sent to Bion, as she calls him. I refer to him as Dr. Bion, in that the respect that is due should never be lost. And again, I did not know him as well as she did. She earned the right to call him Bion, writing four books after his death that completed his work!!!!! So here is the short preface I wrote which I had intended to go into my other book, Psychotherapy, Insight and Style: The Existential Moment, but which was changed in its entirety by consultation with Bion's analysands.

The Original was entitled

MY REACTION TO THE "BEING OF" AND "BEING WITH" WILFRED BION, M.D.: A CLEAR MIND AND A STATE OF DISCOVERY.

* When I wrote it I did not know Dr. Bion had an M.R.C.S. and not an M.D. That is the British equivalent from the Medical Royal College of Surgeons.

Chapter 4 Part II

PREFACE TO WILFRED BION, M.R.C.S.

No matter how many times I read this section, I still feel a bit awkward putting out this reaction to a group of colleagues, some of which may find my methods of evaluation of Dr. Bion very strange indeed. Basically I evaluated Bion and his process using methods of higher sensory perception, and it was in those terms that I was able to quickly experience, perceive, and sensitively tune into just how extraordinary a man Dr. Bion really was.

Further, as his writings are quite complex, I believe it is doubtful that many people will be able to capture the essence of who he was and what he did that was extraordinary. Thus, I am writing this section in the hope that those who pursue the work of Bion may get an experiential feel or sensory impression from how I wrote about him, in addition to a sense of his process-of what he actually did in terms of responding and the effect that had upon people, namely me.

After experiencing Bion on this one occasion I wrote him two letters in great depth. The first asked him to work with me intensively for five to seven years. After he rejected, saying "the pressure of time". "I therefore am not free choose what I would like to do from amongst the many options". I wrote a second letter requesting that he reconsider. He graciously responded in a clear and potent way saying "I am glad that you appreciate the difficulty that I have in having to say "No" to requests which are made to me. I cannot even say that I would like to embark on a piece of work when I know that it can arouse false hopes."

Being gravely disappointed, but feeling a genuine warmth toward Bion, I sent him a letter wishing him well on his return from Los Angeles to London. He sent me a very friendly note and included "As I am not coming back I had better make this a farewell note. With every good wish for your continued work".

In the meantime I began to apply the principles I learned by experiencing Bion on the evening of which I wrote about. I had a??? schizoid-depressive paranoid patient who said she wished she could think clearly and creatively. I began to tell her a story, capturing the same feeling in my body and the same sensations and pace I describe when writing about Bion. I was using an Erickson form of hypnotic storytelling. My sense of presence began to expand and my thinking became clearer. I began to say thoughts without thinking. I have no memory of the content of what we were saying to each other, but both the patient and I felt it was the most creative clear thinking session we ever had together. I began to do this with several other patients.

The loss of not working with Bion was looming ever larger in my mind. I wrote him another note, hoping he would get it before he left Los Angeles. Basically I said that while I read some of his work and doubted if I would ever fully understand the subtleties of his system of psychoanalysis, "I could do what he does." I told him that were it not for what I felt to be an extremely moving primal connection between us and how he worked, plus my having an ability to do the kind of work that he exemplified through his being, I would have been much too embarrassed to write yet a fourth letter after he had been so generous in responding to the first three. I told him I was willing to go to London for three weeks the following summer so that I would have a chance to have enough continued impact where the kind of sensory impressions that I used in working would not fade. Bion wrote back,

"Dear Dr. Bergantino,

Many thanks for your letter of August 24. I am not yet sure what work I shall be doing here, but I do not think it would be practical to attempt an analysis in the way that you suggest. Perhaps I could get in touch with you at a later date; I shall let you know my permanent address at the earliest opportunity.

Best wishes,

Sincerely yours,
W R Bion"

I was both tickled that he was considering working with me if he planned to do any work, and afraid of giving up everything I had worked so hard to build in Los Angeles. I was in tremendous conflict about moving to England for five years, and then coming back to Los Angeles to start over again. However, I had decided to do so and had written Bion a letter to the effect that I was beginning to explore possibilities of getting a work permit in England and would wait until my book was published because it would perhaps help me build a practice faster in London. However, on the day I was going to mail the letter, I had a very strange feeling. I decided to hold off mailing the letter for a few weeks. I thought Bion was a man of his word and surely had time to permanently relocate and would write to me soon. About two weeks after I had written the letter and decided to hold it back for awhile, I got a telephone call from a colleague saying that she had been informed that Wilfred Bion had died about two weeks ago in London, and that she had confirmed it with one of the psychoanalysts in Los Angeles who was supervised by Bion. Bion was 82 years old. I felt sad and brokenhearted, with a very great sense of loss, perhaps as great as any I had known.

Perhaps now it will be clear why I should be willing to write such a strange chapter in what is an otherwise very legitimate book about the psychotherapies. But I was so sure that I was willing to move to London and give up all of what I have worked for in Los Angeles based on this one experience. Further Bion read the work and commented "Thank you for what you say; this work is certainly most evocative and stimulating."

Chapter 4 Part II: MY REACTION TO THE "BEING OF" AND "BEING WITH" WILFRED BION, M.D.: A Clear Mind And A State Of Discovery

I have heard about Wilfred Bion from time to time. However, the rumors did not particularly attract me to following up to see what he had to offer. I heard he was a genius who put psychoanalysis and psychotherapy into formulations that were as difficult to understand as calculus and that had too much of a resemblance to higher forms of mathematics-that is, too much for someone who vowed to stay away from numbers after a final statistics course in the doctoral program. I heard very few could understand him, but that all knew he was a genius. As my experience was diametrically opposite what I have heard, and as my experience of Dr. Bion was so significant just as a result of my being part of an audience of about 500 people hearing him and other panelists speak, I feel moved to write about what I consider to be <u>one of the most highly developed humans I have ever encountered.</u> That is, when Sartre_wrote about "Being and Nothingness" he must have somehow known about Wilfred Bion because he is living proof that humans can achieve the level of Being that Sartre talked about, although neither Sartre nor Bion would probably think about themselves in terms of achievement. The Language of Achievement nevertheless, it was Bion's Being that was healing. One moment flowed upon another as if one were to watch a ballerina dancing to perfection, or a Toscanini conducting a symphony. I experienced a <u>consecutive accumulation of existential moments</u>, and <u>my mind reached a state of clarity, and my body, a state of being, that I had never known before</u>.

Grinberg, Sor and Tabak de Bianchedi wrote, "One of Bion's greatest merits is that he had placed psychoanalytic theory and practice in a new dimension, preserving the most valuable classical contributions of Freud and Melanie Klein while approaching them from different perspectives (or 'vertices.'). He adds freshness and originality to them and stimulates a new attitude in the analyst by encouraging him to abandon rigid schemes and old clichés, thus opening up new ways of psychoanalytic thinking. The richness of his hypotheses, the scope of his theories, and the flexibility of his models, together with his advice of approaching the task of observation and investigation "without memory or desire," exercise an enormous attraction while at the same time provoking some uncertainty. All this tends to increase creative capacity, common sense, and the development of intuition, helping the investigator to get himself into what we would call 'the state of discovery.'" 13

"Bion speaks of the difficulties of expressing new ideas in familiar words; and this sometimes leads him to introduce terms that are intentionally devoid of meaning or to use familiar words in his own particular way." 14

"In reading Bion one often feels that the depth and strength of his ideas is equivalent to agitating the surface of the lake and altering the reflection. Bion's language contains what appears as doubts, half-truths, mysteries, uncertainties; conveying these aspects of his ideas is in practice an impossible task." 15

I have used Grinberg, Sor and Tabak de Bianchedi to give a description of Bion and his work for a few reasons. First, their description fits my experience in that. Just being in Bion's presence helped to increase my creative capacity; second, my responses to him were primarily in the areas of common sense and a highly developed intuition; and third, I entered into a state of discovery utilizing extra sensory perception abilities of a kinesthetic nature (pure sensation). Fourth, I have expressed my reaction in a primary process way that may make it difficult for some readers to feel a tie into their own experience. At times my reactions are a combination of pure sensation, a keen sense of observation and intuition as a means of evaluation. Fifth, is that while I am describing a process that I was able to experience due to particular sensitivities within myself, I was quite shocked at the nature of the experience in that it was so different from anything I had ever before experienced. While I am able to <u>experience people in kind</u>, <u>in terms of who they are and how they relate</u>, Bion's way of relating was so unusual that it was altogether out of my frame of reference. For example, for the first time I was able to have the experience of <u>thoughts without thinking</u>. The result was that for the <u>first time in my</u>

life I experienced my thinking capacity to be as full as my abilities to experience pure sensation and to know through intuition. I was an open channel receiving the experience of Bion and the other presentors. I was present in the here and now. However, to evaluate and experience Bion, I, in a sense, was functioning in a way that was 180 degrees from the sense of presence or being manifested by Bion. That is, while Bion was being all that he could, I was receiving and reacting to all that I could.

I maintain certain assumptions; "To feel clear headed, inspired and creative is an important state of being. 2) When I am responding in kind, what I see and experience people doing is what they do. That is, it is what they do when they do psychoanalysis in terms of the quality of their responses; and it is what they do when they relate to their wives and children. It is what they do because it is where they are in terms of the development of their own state of being along the continuum of "to be or not to be". While my description of the presentors sometimes gives the impression that the analyst does it to me, or that I am in a victim position, this is one of those half truths. That is, the analyst does what he or she does. When I am an open channel, or responding in kind, I am fully receiving all that the analyst does. In those terms it may appear that the analyst is doing it to me, while in fact the analyst is just doing what he or she is doing. When I do therapy in this manner I make the assumption that patients will do with me exactly the kind of things that make their relationships difficult or pleasurable with others-and therefore, only replace the characters in the cast. So, in a sense my reaction to Bion is the same as me being one of the characters in his cast.

While the process of evaluation I am going to describe may sound strange in the beginning, it is intended to help the reader get a feel for how my insights may be harmonized with outsights. And while I am a bit uneasy pouring out such a very personal reaction that may certainly be out of the mainstream of human experience, I nevertheless feel I must share this process for the reader to understand how I come about my idiosyncratic viewpoint.

I make a further assumption that strength, power and health are correlated to the quality of being that is manifested by a person. And in terms of the unusual physical and mental reaction I had to Bion, I further equate strength, power and health with the balanced quality of being exemplified by Bion in terms of clarity of mind plus intuitive knowing. But most important, all of these qualities were pure with Bion. That is, he was humble. He was in a state of being that transcended the needs of the ego to think well of oneself or to be an important person. In this way he was very different than the other presentors on the panel.

Friedman, when writing about primary process, said "there are no contradictions, and totally contradictory forces exist simultaneously without being in conflict with each other, such as love and hate, masculine and feminine desires." 16 Bion's presentation and my reaction are both primary process in nature.

And now for the remainder of my story!

A good friend kept talking about Kleinien psychoanalysis. While I had been well trained in many of the more popular therapies such as gestalt therapy, transactional analysis, humanistic existential therapy, and clinical hypnosis, etc. I never had any formal exposure to psychoanalysis. While I had an interest, I found it strange that when he asked me to go I felt very excited.

My sense of the large audience was that it was a very bright, mentally expansive, yet physically reserved group. I thought, this must be the kind of patient analyst's work with. When the evening began I realized I was going to get more than I bargained for, as there was a panel of training analysts who would also present their view of Dr. Bion's work interposed with how that work was most significant in their lives and practice of psychoanalysis. This was beginning to feel like a rare_opportunity because I wasn't aware that the analytic community was as vigorous as I found it to be in presenting itself to the community.

At this point I must present part of the way that my personal system of psychotherapy and judgment operates, because it becomes important when considering how I assessed my experience with Dr. Bion and the other analysts. My system has a large physiological component. Different parts of my body have appropriate pure sensation reactions in terms of the purity of the people who are presenting their state of being to me. I have had little interest in over intellectualized discussions. I am particularly sensitive to cognitive material presented in a camouflaged manner in the service of one's ego--an unintentional result of which is that the content of what is presented becomes convoluted so that the particular pathology and/or egotistical message of the presentor, therapist or analyst would overshadow the spoken message. In other words I was concerned about analysts' egos getting in the way of their Being.

I had geared my choice of therapies to those which I felt would give me the best opportunity to minimize those traits in myself-what I considered to be the more experiential therapies. I became fine tuned to the point that I can see and feel energy patterns and when I work with higher sensory perception I almost exclusively tune into my body to see if what is going on clears my system. When things clear, both sides of my head vibrate and with my eyes closed I often see what appears to be bright lights flashing. When a patient's words or actions, or just their state of being does not clear my system, I may feel pain on the sides of my head--which is usually congruent with the psychic pain experienced by the person I am working with. Or I may feel a twist in my stomach, which usually corresponds with the degree that person tortures themselves and others-usually passively. Or I may feel a pain in my heart, which corresponds to the degree people are broken hearted or living a life that does not follow the path of heart. Or I may feel a pain in the neck--which is self-explanatory.

And if I was going to pursue psychoanalysis, which I have had a notion about doing after completing my training in the other modes of therapy, I would have to be intrinsically motivated by an analyst who made me feel by the sense of his being, his cleanness about following the path of heart in his life, his having removed his ego from the content of his words, and his ability to clear my channels to the degree I was beyond the shadow of a doubt convinced such a long and expensive process would be able to benefit me at a point in my life where my abilities are already excellent at much of what I am doing in therapy and where I am at peace with myself for the most part.

The criteria I had, made it all the more shocking for me that an experience, so profound was to occur in the mere presence of Dr. Bion.

I felt inspired. My mind was clear and my soul was filled with passion.

I am going to present mixed reactions about the panelists, all of whom were well respected training analysts, so I will not mention them by their real names. I will call them Sam, Ralph and Fred. The reader must be apprised that I am making my judgments with a perfectionist zeal in the pursuit of excellence-and that my comments about these_analysts must not be viewed in any way as being derogatory because they were excellent in a variety of respects, and further along than most. Also, everything I charge them with, I too, have grappled with. So I do not criticize as an outsider. Thus, perhaps what we are going to examine are some of the differences between excellence and the pinnacle of magnificence.

Further, my judgments were based not only on the speaking, and my physiological reactions to the state of being of each of the panelists, but also to the way they interacted with each other and the kind of interpretations they made. And in my experience, people do what they do. I am further making the assumption that the kind of responses each of the panelists made and the state of being in which they presented themselves, is what they would have to offer to their patients as psychoanalysts.

The first presentor, Sam concerned himself with Dr. Bion's concept of "reverie". The essence of his verbal message was that this concept would help children to be able to think clearly. When he was talking the sides of my head became so pained that I could not think. So I began to build up energy over my heart area feeling that I would increase my empathy enough to withstand the pain in my head when he spoke. I felt I would be able to stay tuned to the intellectual and cognitive parts of what was going on no matter how painful it became, by using this method. There were times when I would also place my hands on the sides of my head to block off negative energy and protect myself. This would give my head time to clear from the bullshit that was being interweaved with the content by the speaker. SO WHILE THE SPEAKER WAS TALKING ABOUT THE PAIN THAT CHILDREN FEEL IN THEIR HEADS THAT PREVENTS THEM FROM THINKING CLEARLY, AND

THAT DR. BION HAD CONCEPTUALIZED THE PAINFUL NEGATIVITY SENT TO CHILDREN IN TERMS OF ALPHA AND BETA WAVES, WHAT THE SPEAKER WAS ACTUALLY DOING WAS SENDING OUT OPPRESSIVE AND PAINFUL DON'T THINK MESSAGES DUE TO THE STATE OF HIS OWN PAIN AND DIFFICULTY WITH THINKING IN LIFE. UNFORTUNATELY, THIS WOULD LEAVE THE CHILDREN HE SPOKE ABOUT, HAVING TO OVERCOME THE DOCTOR TO GET WELL. He made some reference that the children he worked with usually had a few clear thinking sessions near the end of his work with them.

Later on, Sam asked Dr. Bion a very together question and as a student of the master he was in a very good space with himself. He cleared all of my channels. This told me that he was capable of doing excellent work when he didn't overextend himself-pretending to be more than he is. If he remains curious, and he doesn't take the negative hypnotic suggestions that he now believes to be the truth too seriously, he will have the opportunity to approach finer and finer discriminations of truth that will leave him freer to practice what he preaches.. I had a sense that this was one of his attractions to Dr. Bion because the speaker talked about the concept of negative achievement, which I interpreted to mean negatively weeding away the cobwebs until one approached more truth in themselves. By negative hypnotic suggestions, I mean that the speaker made statements something to the effect that "children would not be able to think clearly and would have pain that prevented them from thinking clearly until the end of therapy". When such beliefs may be projected onto the patient, they can determine how the therapy or analysis will go. The children may very well be responding appropriately to the doctor's pain, lack of authenticity, and his hypnotic negative suggestions. Such suggestions may be so powerful to a child who is looking up at an authority figure, that the child would mentally "nod" out. Such children can easily grow up to be non-thinkers, dopers, alcoholics, or in any case, less than they might be! Anything to blot out the pain.

The second presentor, Ralph was described by the third presentor, Fred, as esoteric. He was very bright and enjoyed presenting the paradoxes and absurdities of Dr. Bion's work. I had a mixed reaction to him. That is, the lights I would see when I closed my eyes were going off at incredible rates of speed, and I was staying with the content of what he was presenting, so I was enjoying his brightness and in a sense got carried away by it. However, while I was experiencing the lights that usually mean my channels are being cleared, there was also a numbing heaviness. The experience didn't make sense to me at the moment, because I had only experienced such a dual effect when someone was making a transition in their life. But someone making a transition to a better place with themselves would usually effect in me a heavier experience with lights beginning to go off. This analyst's lights in my head reaction were going absolutely wild-and indeed, most people I spoke with in the audience considered him a star. Perhaps they too were swept away with the glitter. This speaker's message was of Dr. Bions's concepts of negative achievement and how that helped one come closer and closer to approximate truth. He commented that "the truth does not need to be thought-but truth is composed of thoughts without thinking." In this sense this presentor's brightness was able to_capture a major part of Dr. Bion's way of being in the world. Truth would transcend itself through thoughts without thinking. He further_stated "learning is experiencing the experience", and that "intuition is a higher form of mental thinking than is thinking". Of course, I_liked that statement because I have always relied on intuitive thinking (the converse may be that this is only a bias). To this point I had been somewhat swept away by this presentor and the importance of this reaction, which was similar to audience reaction, will be commented upon a bit later on in the chapter.

Fred referred to himself as exoteric--and after he spoke a bit I had the impression that what he meant was that he spent so much time focusing on that which was outside of himself that he didn't know what was going on within himself.

The first thing he said was that he was 'strong'. (I immediately sensed he was a driven man.) Then he dealt with Dr. Bion's work with aggression. I experienced him as not having a grip on dealing with his own aggression. My experience was feeling oppressed. My chest felt suffocated. The thought raced through my head-a disgusting liar who does not know his own lie! I had pain in the heart, severe pain, and thought I wouldn't be surprised if he were a future heart attack victim.

???

When the panel discussion started, the second presentor, Ralph, who effected me in that I experienced bright shining lights in my head, asked a rather complex question, but the question had the feel of someone saying "look how good I can masturbate". The longer he went on the more nauseous my stomach became. I didn't pay enough attention to the heaviness the first time he spoke due to the overwhelming nature of his brightness. Dr. Bion asked him to expand on what was already a very lengthy and complicated question. Dr. Bion's single question shook Ralph, as his body backed up and he looked much more humble. When he rephrased the question Dr. Bion said, "I'm afraid you asked the wrong member of the panel for the answer." While I am not sure of the order of events, Fred talked of Ralph's way of saying that Dr. Bion was so complex that practically no one understood him. It was clear to me that I ignored the heaviness I first experienced amidst the bright lights of Ralph because I was still struggling to some degree with the same blind spot--letting my ego and ability get in the way of my being. My personal struggle when writing this chapter is in working more and more from the heart and less from the head, or at least in balance between the head and the heart. It became clear to me that_Fred had an excellent eye. That is what he meant by exoteric was that he could quickly and brilliantly spot the pimple on the ass. He and I, too, had this talent and tragedy amidst our being. The talent comes in the ability to see that quickly and to know. The tragedy comes in what one has internally given up to be able to do that. I could feel the pain and appreciate the talent.

Now the analyst chairing the panel, a thoroughly enjoyable character who reminded me of a combination of George Bach, Marlon Brando and Peter Lorre all rolled into one, announced in a way that made me feel if he were treating women patients that the mere tone of his voice and manner in which he presented one interpretation would make them climax on his couch at the very first session, announced that Dr. Bion would speak.

While all the other speakers were presenting I had to keep my hand over my heart to keep the energy in my heart area to stay with the intellectual commentary they were making, and at times I would have to put fresh energy into the sides of my head to continue to be able to think clearly. While this may sound very strange, and is a system I developed through rather extensive work in higher sensory perception and its inclusion in the practice of psychotherapy and clinical hypnosis, this reaction is absolutely critical to my commentary on Dr. Bion, because it was the most rare experience I can recall since beginning to use higher sensory perception in clinical practice.

While the other members of the panel were presenting I occasionally glanced at Dr. Bion. He was very formal and somewhat Prussian looking from a distance. Nothing would shake him. He is as solid as a block of granite. A few jokes were sent his way that he didn't so much as smile at. It was extraordinary that he didn't consider it necessary to be polite or socially courteous even though these particular jokes came from the egotistical needs of the joke teller and not the heart. In other words Dr. Bion's responses prior to his speaking were impeccably true. He began by saying that after hearing all that has been said about him and his work "I can hardly wait to hear what I am going to say." <u>This humor came from the heart and the audience felt warmed by him immediately</u>. This was a bit surprising to me because he had somewhat of a foreboding look while he was listening. Who knows what was going on in him in reaction to what he was experiencing?

As soon as he began to talk I closed my eyes. Any remnants of pain immediately left my head. I saw pure <u>purple</u> (a purple rectangle with a deep purple diagonal line running from top left to bottom right.) and a <u>feeling of deep peace</u> went through me from the beginning of what he was saying right to the end. Purple was of particular significance to me because it is the color of Milton Erickson, M.D., who had a profound effect upon me in that he helped me to change my life around by coming to trust my unconscious mind and go with it until my reactions became purer and peace came into my life. Purple-Royalty/ Red-Freud oedipal-sexual Aggression. My only negative reactions were a few very slight and fleeting twinges-possibly three or four seconds during forty or more minutes of his talk. It was hard to tell how long he talked because he created such a peaceful environment that a hypnotic time distortion occurred. The thought raced through my head-MAGNIFICENT!! I GOT A THOUSAND TIMES MORE THAN A BARGAINED FOR OR EVEN EXPECTED POSSIBLE! This reaction was absolutely incredible when compared to other excellent men in the psychoanalytic_society of a very large and sophisticated city such as Los Angeles, with a very psychologically sophisticated audience-where I experienced differing levels of pain of a severe nature for extended periods of time throughout the other presentations. Actually, the painful reactions occurred nearly all of the time before Dr. Bion spoke. As he continued to talk, my imagery was a large purple rectangle with a pure purple line cutting across it diagonally.[2] I thought the rectangle stood for the formality and sophistication of Dr. Bion and the audience that was attracted to him, but within that rectangle he was absolutely magnificent. What I mean is that there was a reserve about the people and the presentors whereby it was clear you would not see them acting out a mad play as might happen in a gestalt therapy creative expression scenario. Yet, the expression was creative and unusual in that at its best Dr. Bion was able to respond so purely, combining thought with truth with the heart, and in a sense making the kind of cognitive, emotional, intuitive, and knowing statements, that would just cut through an entire lifetime in one split second. And Dr. Bion was at his best all the time. For example,_a psychiatrist asked a question from the audience and he was requested to ask his question up at the podium. He sat down and began to ask a question about a patient whose leg would move on the couch. Dr. Bion could not see what the audience was privy to, that the psychiatrist's

---

[2]\ his purple rectangle divided by a line became the bottom part of my logo. The top was red with a diagonal. This meant I built on Bion's work with underlying psychotic thinking disorders while at the same time not losing track of the fact I am Freud linking all the work up to the psychosexual connectedness of working through the oedipal situation.

leg was shaking back and forth under the table-just as his voice was shaking. Dr. Bion answered the question in a way that did both therapy and supervision with the psychiatrist asking the question. While he gave what appeared to be a cognitive answer he said that in such a case "the receptor may not be receptive" to the patient's movement. And I instantaneously knew that the psychiatrist's resistance and unfinished business prevented him from being able to move through that space with the patient. Interesting to know whose side the resistance is on. I don't remember the full answer Dr. Bion gave, but it had the same quality as his first sentence. I remember remarking to my friend that Dr. Bion should charge a consultation fee for everything he said because everything that came out of his mouth was therapeutic.

As he continued to talk at a consistent slow pace he never varied from his center-that is, the center of his being. His presence was awesome, but in a peaceful sense. His talk was pure. It felt like hearing a Stradivarius, but not a violin, cello-mother a Stradivarius cello. While he was a complex man I found his way of expressing his thinking very simple and very easy to understand. In fact, I didn't keep my hand over my heart and never had to recharge my head with pure energy. I understood every word he said-even if I did not understand the words as in the case of a few medical references he made. I felt both nourished and replenished as I was continuing to learn to think more clearly by being in his presence.

My head felt so clear I thought this is how it must be when a baby is born. But the clarity felt warm and soft and nurturing. My entire body just kept feeling fuller. To put it bluntly DR. BION'S THINKING ISN'T COMPLEX AT ALL. IN FACT, IT IS SO CLEAR AND SIMPLE THAT I BELIEVE IT IS WRONGLY MISTAKEN TO BE COMPLEX DUE TO THE CONVOLUTION AND NETWORK OF LIES EXISTING IN THE MIND OF THE LISTENER. IN FACT, IF DR. BION WERE TEACHING FIRST GRADE I SUSPECT HE WOULD HAVE AN ENTIRE CLASS OF PUPILS GETTING A GRADE OF A.

I also experienced Dr. Bion as being very existential. That is, the purity of truth with which he spoke captured one existential moment after another. I felt that while I understood what he was saying, I had no need to try and remember it, because I at some level knew it was true, and existed within me and the rest of the human race. I believe he mentioned the value of the analyst coming into each session fresh, without any remembrances from the past session to cloud the analyst's mind. This would leave the analyst's mind free to continue to experience one moment of truth upon another-and to make interpretations that have a freshness that soothes the brain instead of creating the confusion the analyst tries to analyze. In this sense Dr. Bion was doing what the first presentor spoke about-being with us in a way where our minds felt as if we were receiving a gentle massage-and then returning our capacity to once again be clear thinkers-not intellectualizers-and to have that thinking congruent with our entire being both in receiving and in responding. This is truly, in my opinion, Dr. Bion's most rare gift to humanity.

Dr. Bion made a comment that being an analyst was rough work in that "tolerating what the patient said to you is a tough assignment". His Containment of patients' emotional state for 50 years killed him. He died of a rare blood disease three days after he was diagnosed.

While I have struggled with a variety of levels of being combined with a variety of therapeutic methodologies to deal with a "tough assignment", Dr. Bion's level and quality of his own being has evolved to the degree that his technique is that of merely being present.

While Dr. Bion is in his eighties, he has a purity of skin and a clearness in his eyes that I have only noticed on one or two other occasions. Dr. Milton Erickson was one of those people. I had a feeling that living one's life with such clarity and truth would manifest itself in terms of the presence of such a person.

While Dr. Bion is a psychoanalyst, it was the quality of his being, or magnificence of his presence, that had such a profound effect on me. Just being in the audience for three hours left me thinking clearer than I ever knew I could. That is, pure thinking that is composed of cognition, emotion, intuition and deep levels of knowing in sync with a compassion for the human condition that permits injured minds to replenish themselves with a childlike sense of freedom and joy. In_fact, my friend brought his wife and five week old baby. At 11:20 p.m.

the baby's eyes were wide open with a serene and clear expression on her face. I sensed she knew she had partaken in a rare happening. I wondered what the difference would be in her life in the future in terms of an unconscious memory of this experience.

It was also interesting that at the times during the evening which I physiologically felt the most discomfort with different speakers, the baby cried or shrieked.

After the presentation I noticed Dr. Bion walking out and went up to him, telling him that "being in the audience while he was talking was like having a warm bath massage my mind." In an instant he replied, "I enjoyed myself and I always make it a point to do what I enjoy doing." We looked at each other as if we both knew we had more to say to each other, but that it wasn't right to say anymore then. What struck me about his comment is that it has been the central struggle through my entire life-that is, getting in touch with my desires and responding so I will enjoy myself and to consistently do that to add meaning to my life.

But perhaps most of all, I was taken with Dr. Bion's generosity of spirit in giving himself to the audience. His heart was as impeccable as_the rest of his being. As I told Dr. Bion, I have felt privileged to know him for even a few hours as part of a large audience.

While this chapter was not written merely to exemplify the magnificent qualities of Dr. Bion, it was meant to focus on the existential qualities that cut through both the personality of Dr. Bion_as well as his unique psychoanalytic way of working. As the method of treatment he received was psychoanalysis, I cannot help but feel if one has the desire and courage to pursue truth to the levels of purity I have described with Dr. Bion, the psychoanalytic process-by the very nature of its time, commitment, and expense, when working with an analyst who has pursued such a quality of being, can be a most effective psychotherapeutic method.

I was having lunch with a psychoanalyst who was analyzed by Bion. He told me that he would go into a session having a particular view of reality. Bion would say things that would put this man's mind into chaos. He commented, that each session his particular views of reality were shaken and he left the session with a sense of chaos. He then told me that Dr. Bion felt the analyst's mind should always be in a state of chaos, because it is in this way that both the analyst and the patient will continually be open to fresh experiences instead of boxed in stereotypes of reality. This psychoanalyst also said that Bion would say things to him that gave him a feeling that he never had been understood that well in his entire life. He said it was eerie, almost as if Bion would have to be him to understand him that well.

Again we see the paradoxical nature of Bion. Many people in the audience found him confusing. I found him to be very simple in existential terms-that is, he was manifesting close approximations to both pure being and primary process. While, I felt it would be easy to understand him at the personal level if one had unraveled many of their lies that boxed them into a fixed reality, I now saw when I began to read one of his books, about the other side of him. And the analyst who told me Bion believes that the analyst's mind must be in chaos to keep open a "state of discovery"! The comments of the authors who wrote a book introducing Bion's work! They said Bion's language contains what appears as doubts, half-truths, mysteries and uncertainties, and that to convey those aspects of his ideas was an impossible task.

With all this contradictory evidence, in addition to my personal reaction to Bion, I am making the following assumption. Bion is as simple as he is complex. At the personal level if one understands that simplicity of self then Bion would be very easy to understand. However, the consistency at which he responds at such a simple level would sooner or later blow wide open the framework of boxed in realities that most people manifest. Bion is always fresh.. He is always simple. Peoples' network of lies would be shattered as they approached more approximate levels of truth. This would leave them experiencing chaos-or the existential anxiety of not knowing. It is amidst such turmoil that people would enter a "state of discovery".

Perhaps to read Bion easily one would have to manifest similar levels of being, and a willingness to experience chaos and to live with evolving realities instead of fixed realities-and possess the same clarity of mind that comes from living so purely. Perhaps Bion's teachings can best be understood if psychoanalysts approach them in terms of his being and primary process. This may make his concepts easier to implement in practice..

My heartfelt thanks to James L. Rice, M.D., Diplomate American Board of Psychiatry And Neurology in private practice in LaJolla, California for his valuable input to parts I and II of this chapter.

From that first night on I began doing psychoanalysis. My first case came in 1979. I began seeing a plastic surgeon four times a week and being supervised one time per week on this case. I also was supervised on another case by a different psychoanalyst who had been psychoanalyzed for a second time by Bion. Both of my supervisors were analyzed by Bion as well as the person I chose as a psychoanalyst after Bion's death. However, doing everything I could do that was humanly possible and then some; as well as by and with The Grace of God, I was able to hone and fine tune my "gift of extrasensory perception" to have a full psychoanalytic practice, seeing patients three to five times a week, for from between three and seven years. As time went on they were all five times a week for about seven years. I will comment on these differences later, but for now I will move on to the second part of my writing entitled:

BETA ELEMENTS, BION AND BEYOND: THE LANGUAGE OF EXPERIENCE

1986

BETA ELEMENTS, BION AND BEYOND: THE LANGUAGE OF EXPERIENCE

by LEN BERGANTINO, ED.D., PH.D.

450 N. Bedford Drive
Ste. 300
Beverly Hills, CA 90210
Now 424293-9511 (Let it ring 7 times)

INTRODUCTION

One of Bion's analysands, a well-respected physician and training analyst in his own right, told me that Bion would make interpretations that were quite long, often times a paragraph and sometimes considerably more. This analysand would often say, "I didn't get it, or What did you say?" He went on to say that although Bion would respond in ways that were fresh as opposed to repetitive, Bion said once, and often communicated the message, "Well, I'm speaking ordinary conversational English."

Bion was speaking ordinary conversational English, however, he was speaking in the language of experience. This language is one whereby the analyst must not only be able to pay attention to the subtleties of what the patient is saying, and how the patient is saying it, as well as the quality of being manifested by the patient when it is said, but also be able to pay attention to the subtleties of what kind of language opens the mental space so experience cannot be destroyed through (K) knowledge what kind of language contacts the patient, what kind of language reaches the patient in a way that frees the patient to be in contact with oneself, what kind of language is solid in itself and evokes that solidness so the guts of the patient become more solid via the solidness of the analyst, and what kind of language that not only keeps the space open so the patient cannot either emotionally or verbally destroy the analyst's offerings, but also does so with the constant possibility of providing the patient the opportunity for the expansion of thought to infinity, while the analyst is constantly either maintaining or expanding upon the quality of his or her own being.

The problem then becomes what kind of book, and what kind of paragraphs must I write to help the reader expand their capacity to pay attention to the kind of nuances I have described, even though these paragraphs might initially be looked at as grammatically incorrect, or as run on sentences that evoke an avid desire in the reader to experience shorter sentences with more frequent periods.

Milton H. Erickson, M.D., in his last letter to me before his death wrote, “Much has been said about the solid rock of truth but little has been said about the shifting sands.”

This was a response to a tape I had sent him of my storytelling to an audience of one hundred at the Southern California Society of Clinical Hypnosis 25th anniversary birthday party at Dr. William Kroger’s home. I received a standing ovation by the hypnosis group, and an additional surprise was that two well respected psychoanalysts in the community who heard the tape saw the connection between the storytelling and psychoanalysis, and asked me to be on a program at UCLA as part of a faculty that included Bruno Bettelheim and Erik Erikson. The program was entitled “Myths and Fairytales” and I was requested to do “The Clinical Application of Storytelling”. One of the two psychoanalysts who selected me referred to the method as “reverse psychoanalysis”.

Years later another psychoanalyst said to me, “Freud said we should pay attention to the unconscious of the patient. You are saying that to the greater degree we develop the unconscious of the analyst and learn how to use that unconscious in talking to the patient, then we can bypass the resistance of the patient, and it may be as important or more important to focus on the talking of the analyst as to the priority having been given to the talking of the patient.”

Back to my first individual hour with Dr. Milton Erickson. He said, “Now what can I do for you young man?” I said, “Dr. Erickson. You are the foremost psychotherapist in the world today. When I get out of here I want to be as good as you are!”

I had trained with many excellent therapists but none had been able to help me with this problem-being gifted in what I did and being extremely competitive in ways that would either threaten the therapist father figure, bring their wrath down upon me, or see to it via countertransference problems that I didn't grow past them.

This was not the case with Dr. Erickson, and for that, I am eternally grateful. He said, in a way that surprised me, "Where do you think you stand now?" I said, "The top of the average!" I said this in a very challenging way. He said, with absolutely no bones to pick and no axe to grind, "Well, why don't you be the best top of the average you can be then, you'll never be Milton Erickson."

The way in which this interaction occurred had the outcome that I did not feel competitive with Dr. Erickson, I was open to hearing what he had to offer me, and I was left with the lifelong impression that this was how to father a son.

The reason I give this preface about Dr. Erickson's work with me is because I think the nature of it must be understood to understand the significance of his last letter to me.

After three years of intensive work with Dr. Erickson as my mentor, and after I had completed my work with him, in a prior letter he wrote, "Dear Len, Perhaps we can get together on a more casual basis." He signed it, "Milton". I was quite surprised in that early on in the work I sent him a letter and addressed it "Dear Milton," to which he responded, "Dear Dr. Bergantino:" and signed it "Milton H. Erickson, M.D." Throughout the work he kept the boundaries clear. He was the doctor, the senior colleague and the mentor. I was the patient, the junior colleague and the student. Then there was the surprise of his invitation to get together on a more casual basis, and still the surprise of the unconscious reaction of his last letter to me. Little did I realize he was going to be the reincarnated soul of my son and best friend.

Throughout those three years Dr. Erickson responded to me at the unconscious level in as full a way as he could. It often threw me into chaos and evoked a great deal of self-searching. I can now laugh about much of what he said and did when I tell the stories, but it was not quite so funny as it happened.

I responded with my best effort at the unconscious level. Mrs. Erickson years later told me that Dr. Erickson always respected my dedication to the work. Dr. Erickson and I had an intense relationship over a three year period in which we both gave it our purest effort and I learned to trust completely what that evoked in me at the unconscious level, and my own unconscious mind. This was Erickson's gift and he had passed it on to me.

Given this background, there was the second part of his last letter to me, "I can't understand why a two legged skater would want to imitate a one legged skater, anyway."

Dr. Erickson died about one month after sending me this letter. I tried several times to respond, and never could. Even in his last letter before his death, he left me in chaos. This certainly did not seem to be a cordial response to a junior colleague to whom he recently invited to get together on a more casual basis.

And yet, as time came to pass, I began to understand this comment in the fuller context of the entire relationship between us, including my initial request, "When I get out of here, I want to be as good as you are!" So here it was, what he evoked in my unconscious was the following: "Look, you have the capacity to take what I have given you about the shifting sands and you are a substantive person whose presentation was of the solid rock of truth, and teach the work of the shifting sands to psychoanalysts so they can do the complete job of an analysis by using the shifting sands to expand upon the solid rock of truth so that a patient who wants to go all the way in pursuing 'O' can be provided such an opportunity by a psychoanalyst." (This is solely what I synthesized and a major reason I wrote this book.

Was it not in this vein that Bion said to his analysand, "Well, I'm speaking ordinary conversational English." Without my prior work with Dr. Erickson I would not have been able to pay the kind of attention to the subtleties of Bion's work to realize that these two great mentors had a great deal more in common that one may realize, despite my dedication and lifelong interest in becoming 'O'.

Dr. Erickson's gift was to find out what behavior a person used against themselves and to arrange that behavior in such a way that would help the patient turn the tragic corner and become functional in his or her life. It involved a kind of psychological judo.

However, what he evoked in me was quite different in that the storytelling, which was the method by which he therapized, supervised and taught in his last years, evoked in me a method of storytelling that was as pure as I could get it at the unconscious level in that it was connected to the fullness of my being and was the thing-in-itself, thereby creating dramatic changes, many times in one session, as a result of the series of psychodynamic releases that occur via the stories and the psychophysiological state of well-being that occurred via the pacing and centeredness I utilized. In other words, I found a way to take what Dr. Erickson taught me and put it in the framework of becoming 'O'.

Thus, we have a method of shifting the sands because what was primarily thought of as sand shifting that had nothing to do with in depth long term work, now has been shifted into the context of becoming 'O'.

Margaret Mead said the only time she had experienced the pace at which Erickson told his stories was in a rare African tribe that was relatively free of dis-ease. Bion, who was born in India, and may have incorporated some of the meditative ways into his quest to become 'O' was the only other person I had ever experienced who spoke consistently at that pace.

Bion did it in a way that connected thought to the being of the person with impeccable precision. That is, he maintained that pace and the quality of his being while connected to thought in a way that facilitated an environment that left many referring to him as mystical or being a mystic. Through my experience of him, after learning what I did from Erickson, I know how Bion did this. I will do my best to convey this quality of being as connected to thought by writing about the unusual nature of my experience of Bion in his presentation to an audience of 500. I think it is the manifestation of this quality of being as connected to thought that has as much of a curative outcome upon patients (primitive insight) as insight, and I further think that insight that is not connected to the quality of being of the psychoanalyst, to the degree that it is not, limits the degree to which the analysis will be potent, both in terms of restoring and expanding upon the capacity to think and in terms of the working through of the oedipal situation.

While much of Bion's work is restorative in nature in terms of building a self that has suffered developmental gaps and expanding the capacity to think to infinity when the self is cohesive, Bion did indeed take in the work of Freud in that he personally had worked through the oedipal situation, and his work would do so, depending upon the length of time one worked with him and from whence the patient developmentally began the analysis.

I think the point that Bion was a sexual being, and his work did include this aspect, is a very important factor, because I think it is overlooked in many of those who studied with him in that from whence they began the work they did not have time for the full course of treatment and development due to his departure for London and his death which was soon to follow.

I think much of what is presented as the work of Bion, or even of Kohut when viewed from a restorative or developmental capacity, fails to take into account the working through of the oedipal situation in a way that the patient can maintain consistency of sexual beingness as connected to the fullness of being, cohesiveness of self, and capacity to expand thought to infinity. This is the key to linking Bion's work and Erickson's work to Freud—that of being psychosexually connected, where everything else works.

In a conference in 1903 Freud gave a paper to a group of colleagues. One of the brighter ones, even though Freud had written about the oedipal situation in very technical terms, was able to surmise that Freud was writing, talking and presenting about sex. He stood up, pounded his fist and screamed, "This is not a matter for a scientific meeting! It is a matter for the police!" You can imagine the courage Freud must have had to proceed with such disdain from colleagues, in such a state of isolation, except for the few that followed. Well, with all our liberation I think things are hardly much different today in terms of what psychoanalysis and what psychoanalysts actually do and transmit via the quality of the sexual being they manifest and how the quality of that being affects the quality of the interpretations made to patients, and then, not just in words, but how that patient is then affected in terms of maintaining a quality of sexual beingness-or dare that patient not travel beyond where the psychoanalyst has traveled lest he or she be murdered off and made out to be irrelevant.

Another of my primary interests in Freud had to do with the humanity in which he approached his patients. While Bruno Bettelheim was ignored by American psychoanalysts when he wrote about Freud's humanity and the problem with the dry English translations of Freud, it is only with the kind of humanity Bettelheim talked about[1], that the patient could withstand the full course of the analysis in becoming 'O', with the full sense of deprivation involved in such an analysis.

I once heard Carl Whitaker tell a joke to an audience of 500 therapists.[2] It was about a farmer and his son. The son said to the father, "Dad, I'm going over the hill to get me a wife." The father said, "Good, Son. When will you be back?" The son said, "In a couple of days." The father said, "I'll see you then." In a couple of days the son returned and the father said, "Well, son. Where is she?" The son said, "Well, Dad, I found her, but she was a virgin." The father said, "Son, you did the right thing. If she wasn't good enough for her own family, she wasn't good enough for us."

This is a very stark story to which the audience did not know how to respond. They sat there somewhat dumbfounded, and yet to be able to utilize the absurdity, the craziness and the madness of the patient in making an interpretation that invades the unconscious, the patient has to be able to tolerate such an intervention from a well-disciplined psychoanalyst. But in order to be able to tolerate interventions at the unconscious level that have such a bizarre nature, when in fact, that is what is going on with the patient, the quality of the being of the therapist must be connected to thought at both conscious and unconscious levels, and the humanity and sexual potency of the psychoanalyst must be such, that the minimum conditions of the analysis, day after day, at the most primitive levels, can be tolerated by the patient.

(Tim hug, hatred)

Knowing how to deal with the minimum conditions of psychoanalysis, and knowing how to call the first shot at the first or first several sessions, is often the lever upon which the success of the analysis rests. Bion had a particular way of doing this that was evocative in the development of my view of the conditions. Bion and Erickson, in their own very different ways, evoked in me the thought that if the psychoanalyst did not get the conditions whereby the patient's commitment to his or her life was absolutely first on the list of priorities, and if such patient was not dealt with in this manner throughout the course of the analysis, not much could be expected.

It is to these ends that I have written this book.

BION AND BEYOND: THE LANGUAGE OF EXPERIENCE LEN BERGANTINO, ED.D., PH.D. (WORKSHOP PROPOSAL) (EXPERIENTIAL)

Bion's work has been difficult to understand for psychoanalysts. Through the language of experience I am able to utilize much of what Bion viewed as the practice of psychoanalysis by demonstrating these methods, ways of thinking about phenomena, dealing with the most minute subtleties of experience and by adding a fine tuned utilization of sensory perception that was evoked in me by my work with Milton H. Erickson, M.D., that takes the psychoanalytic method beyond where Bion left it at his death-which in this practitioner's experience, was far ahead of the field in terms of providing an analysis that would be successful. This method will teach analysts how to make interventions that focus on subtle moment to moment sensory perception, while containing patient projections, which enhances evocation of thought and access to primitive preconceptions as opposed to evacuation of thought, while moment to moment detoxification occurs so patient life force and psychoanalyst well-being can be maintained throughout the entire time of work. There is a particular focus on Bion's contribution in working with underlying psychotic thought disorders; the kind of interpretations that arc madc to thc narcissistic personality disorders which contain both empathy and the kind of quality of being or sense of presence that deals with patients at primitive levels of solid and centered contact; the kind of interventions that can be utilized with borderline patients who evacuate thought and may be quite depressive; the way to take control of the session through pacing with long winded interpretations to help the obsessive compulsive and schizoid personalities come into contact with senses, emotions, feelings, containment of emotions and feelings, and evocation of thought; and what has often puzzled psychoanalysts when they referred to Bion as a mystic-the creation of a healing environment where thoughts without thinking begin to occur as if they were just floating in from somewhere. I worked with thoughts floating in midair (thoughts without a thinker) in Newcastle Australia in 1988.

Further, Bion had an unusual way to deal with the minimum conditions of analysis. In Bion's way of evoking the mind to contain contradictions he once said, "Knowing how to deal with those conditions is about all the bloody analysis one will ever need to know." I add to this viewpoint that the minimum conditions must be dealt with in ways that has the purity of the patient's life substance at the core of things, elsewise analysis cannot be done.

Freud gave us the knowledge. Bion became well through two (John Rickman and Melanie Klein) analyses and the lifelong disciplined pursuit of the quality of his own being, and he wrote about this in ways that are most likely to be comprehended only on the basis of primitive experience-knowing at that level, and being able to make interpretations whereby emotion is contained and thought evoked from the entirety of that patient's being. Further, he wrote of detoxification, however, this is for me to contribute in analytic technique what Freud created as a body of understanding and what Bion exemplified through his being and his writings, is an analytic method that detoxifies patient projective identifications & splitting during the entire fifty minutes of each session, as best one can do. It is to the degree that the analyst knows how to detoxify such experience that patients will get well and will develop the analytic tools by which they can pursue the lifelong quest of the quality of their own being, or as Bion wrote, becoming 'O'. I think that while Bion demonstrated to me through who he was that he had done this and thereby evoked the thoughts through learning from that experience whereby I could develop the analytic technique, that such technique is unknown to psychoanalysis.

Having had the opportunity to work with many of the nations' most gifted therapists to study technique, and then with gifted psychoanalysts, I know that psychoanalysis has most of the tools it needs to be the treatment that has the greatest opportunity for success with recalcitrant personality characteristics and recalcitrant personality disorders that prevent patients from turning the tragic corner in their lives and from developing the capacity to function at qualitative levels of being. Yet without knowing at the most primitive levels how to deal with both the minimum conditions of what is required to do the work with a particular patient and how to detoxify patient projections on a moment to moment basis that also softens character armor via the analytic interpretation, it is doubtful that psychoanalysis can deliver the goods. With Bion's contributions implemented in the practice of psychoanalysis, and the additional contribution of focus on subtle sensory perception as a first place from which reality and the basis of experience are cued psychoanalysis is the only method of treatment that can provide an enhancement of the quality of being, at finer and finer levels of discrimination, that will provide that patient with an opportunity for a qualitatively functional life at the multiplicity of levels of achievement to which Bion addressed himself through the language of achievement.

LEN BERGANTINO, ED.D., PH.D.
450 N. Bedford Drive, Ste. 300
Beverly Hills, CA 90210 (213) 273-8705 (1981-1991)
Current message machine 424293-9511 (Let it ring 7 times to leave a message)

WHAT ARE THESE THINGS CALLED BETA ELEMENTS?

Bion wrote about turning beta elements into alpha function. Why did he write about them as beta elements? Did they actually exist or was this a metaphorical way of thinking about things? Being a psychoanalyst Bion had a great respect for ideas and concepts. However, he did write a book that referred to both the language of experience and learning through experience. Why would he do such a thing if he did not base his work on his experience? However, given he was a psychoanalyst, and psychoanalytic education has a formal way of being presented, could Bion have been limited in the way he could actually present this learning by experience and particularly these beta elements without his colleagues thinking he was too far out to be of sound mind. Perhaps what he did was take things conceptually to the outer perimeters in creating a paradigm through which psychoanalytic technique might be rethought and perhaps retaught through the language of experience itself. Wouldn't this give one the best opportunity of becoming 'O', or give the psychoanalyst the best opportunity to continually move toward finer and finer discriminations in terms of the lifelong quest of becoming closer and closer approximations of his or her own being? Isn't this life's work? Wouldn't psychoanalysts have to be able to do this themselves in order to help their patients do it?

If these beta elements are just a conceptual way of viewing things then is Bion's work conceptual poppycock that many will not understand and even fewer will find any utility for.

On the other hand, what if these BETA ELEMENTS ACTUALLY EXIST! Then might we have the experiential elements by which to refine the psychoanalytic technique to actually do what needs to be done in a psychoanalysis?

What needs to be done in a psychoanalysis? Well, that is too broad a question to respond to right now.

However, it may not be too early to expand upon what psychoanalysis has not been able to do in that the question of these beta elements may provide the missing elements to expand the technique necessary to do those functions.

Bion concerned himself with underlying psychotic thinking disorders, even in those who were not psychotic. He dealt then primarily with primitive phenomena, did he not? He, having been analyzed by both a man, John Rickman, and a woman, Melanie Klein, might have had an unusual perspective in terms of the breadth of his understanding of both the male psyche and the female psyche, might he not? Could this be one of the reasons, as evoked by his work with Melanie Klein, that he came to realize the importance of the mother and the mothering function to the whole bloody analysis, as he might have put it?

How did he view this mothering function? He wrote about the mother having a reverie for the baby's primitive experience and being able to contain that experience. His theory about the container being important for a psychoanalyst to do with a patient, implied that if the psychoanalyst can contain the patient's feared out of control primitive experience, this detoxifies such experience for the patient and the patient becomes well, implies that the repetition compulsion is best dealt with through the discipline of this containment. YET THE TECHNICAL PROBLEM IS THIS! IF ONE IS NOT ABLE TO PICK UP THESE BETA ELEMENTS AS THEY ARE BEING SPLIT OFF FROM OR PROJECTED OUT FROM THE PATIENT ON A MOMENT TO MOMENT BASIS, WOULD NOT THE ANALYSIS BE OUT OF CONTROL DURING THE FIFTY MINUTE HOUR? WOULD THE PATIENT IN FACT NOT BE RECEIVING A CONTAINER THAT DETOXIFIED ON A MOMENT TO MOMENT BASIS, WHICH WOULD HELP THAT PATIENT DEVELOP THE DISCIPLINE OF CONTAINING THOSE FEARED AND HURTFUL PRIMITIVE PROJECTIONS THEY WANT TO GET RID OF? WOULD A CONTAINER ONLY BE PROVIDED IN THEORY AND NOT IN TECHNIQUE? IF THIS WERE THE CASE, HOW WOULD THE PATIENT'S THINKING DISORDER BE CURED BECAUSE THOUGHTS WOULD NOT BE CONNECTED TO THE BEING OF THE PERSON, IF THE PERSON WERE STILL SPLITTING OFF OR ENGAGING IN

THE PROCESS OF PROJECTIVE IDENTIFICATION? HOW COULD ANALYST OR ANALYSAND MOVE CLOSER AND CLOSER TO 'O' if the LIFE FORCE AND TECHNICAL SKILLS OF THE ANALYST DID NOT PROTECT THE PATIENT, AS ONE WOULD PROTECT THE LIFE OF A BABY, IN SEEING TO IT THAT EACH FIFTY MINUTE HOUR was dominated by Eros as opposed to Thenatos? How would the character armor or character defenses of the patient be softened in that the projective identification and splitting would still be occurring on a moment to moment basis for most of the session in cases where this mothering function of containment has been missing in patients? Well, empathy is of great help? But is it enough? Would patients as well as analysts to the degree that this function of containment and access to beta elements to develop the discipline of self where thoughts are connected to a significant degree, by becoming 'O' not be stuck in the remnants of what Melanie Klein referred to as the paranoid-schizoid position? TO the degree that analysts were stuck in the paranoid-schizoid position wouldn't their interpretations limit the enhancement of the being of the patient by the countertransferential limitations of who the analysts are as beings in the world as related to their technical capacities?

Well, of course, one might say, psychoanalysis is always dealing with the problem of transference and countertransference. There is nothing new here. But I AM WRITING AS TO THE DEGREE OF REFINEMENT OF SUBTLETY TO WHICH COUNTERTRANSFERENCE IS DIRECTLY RELATED TO LIMITATIONS IN THE DEVELOPMENT OF THERAPEUTIC USE OF SELF, WHICH IN A PROFESSION AS DIFFICULT AS PSYCHOANALYSIS, IS AN AWESOME TASK.

TO THE DEGREE THAT ONE FOLLOWS WHAT I AM GETTING AT, MIGHT IT NOT BE EASIER TO DISMISS THE POSSIBILITY OF THESE BETA ELEMENTS ACTUALLY EXISTING? ON THE ONE HAND IF ONE AT THIS POINT DISMISSES THEIR EXISTENCE THEN ONE CAN FEEL GOOD ABOUT THEMSELVES AND THEIR WORK IN THAT THEY HAVE DONE ALL THAT THEY CAN, AS FAR AS CURRENT

KNOWLEDGE GOES, AND ARE IN 'GOOD FAITH' AS CLINICIANS WHO HAVE BEEN VERY DEVOTED IN ALL THAT IT TAKES TO PRACTICE PSYCHOANALYSIS AND DEVELOP THE SELF TO BE ABLE TO DO SO.

ON THE OTHER HAND, IF ONE THINKS THAT THESE QUESTIONS THAT ARE TECHNICALLY UNANSWERED, BEAR FURTHER INVESTIGATION, THEN IT BRINGS UP THE PROBLEM OF WHAT IS INVOLVED IN LEARNING TO EXPERIENCE THESE BETA ELEMENTS, AND WHAT IS INVOLVED IN LEARNING TO APPLY THAT EXPERIENTIAL KNOWLEDGE TO PSYCHOANALYTIC TECHNIQUE.

I ASSURE YOU, THIS WILL BE NO SMALL TASK, AND PERHAPS AT LEAST AS DIFFICULT AS THE TRAINING YOU HAVE HAD TO THIS POINT.

It is my intention in writing this book to write it at a level of attention that is all that I can muster up. I think by doing so it will, in the spirit of inquiry to which Bion devoted his life, keep the space open and as much as possible prevent the destruction of the experience of being involved with the work through 'K', or what Bion referred to as 'Knowledge'.

Bion thought there were three ways to destroy the links to relationship-through love, hate and knowledge (L, H +K). The problem in learning this material through the writing of it, even though I will do my best to keep the space open, is that psychoanalytic education tends to focus on the idea or the thought of what I am writing about, and thereby RUNS THE GREAT RISK OF DESTROYING THE EXPERIENCE ITSELF, AND THAT EXPERIENCE IS THE ONLY WAY THESE BETA ELEMENTS CAN REALLY BE USED.

Further, I am writing the book in a way that is intended to expand upon or at least be difficult enough in terms of the attention or expanded attention required to read the work, to actually expand the clinicians capacity to function in terms of working with the kind of interpretations that will enable one to utilize beta elements through the medium of psychoanalytic interpretation. I learned this from Bion in that being immersed in his work was different than the reading of any other psychoanalytic material I have ever read, or any work I have ever read for that matter, in that it required an expansion in my ability to pay attention to the work that took over one and one half years to develop, at which point I read all of his work over a six month period, and had the experience of being able to apply his writing as an experience itself, in which I was both immersed and could apply in my work that very day.

I remember the frustration of not trusting that I had actually learned through the experience of reading it, and presenting a somewhat panicked question to Mrs. Francesca Bion, who has always been a soulful kindred spirit who never doubted me in my search, even when I did. I told her, "I understand it. It blows my mind. It changes my consciousness and my sense of space in terms of the space between people. But I can't recall any of it???" Francesca told me, "Don't worry about it. It's there and when you do the work it will be there." My aspirations were that this not only became true in my doing of psychoanalysis but in my writing about it. It requires a trust in your unconscious which comes from having paid your dues with a guide who has already traveled that road, a trust that you can count on knowing at the level of primitive preconceptions, in that when the quality of your being is hooked up, so to speak, between senses, feelings, depth of feelings and thoughts, that you will be as on time as the metronome of the musician. While my experience with and of Bion was seven years too short as far as I was concerned due to his death, I was fortunate enough to have had such a guide in Milton H. Erickson, M.D., over a three year period, without the evocation of whose work upon me, I would never have been able to see Bion in the fullness of who he was, experience him in that fullness, and understand the subtleties with which he practiced and wrote about psychoanalysis.

Milton H. Erickson, M.D., known as the father of modern medical hypnosis and for his uncommon methods of therapy which in brief periods of time would help patients become functional in their lives was an unlikely one to have evoked in me learnings that I think and feel are critical to the doing of psychoanalysis. I am sure Dr. Erickson would not have thought of his work in that way, but in a sense, I am not describing his work, but what he evoked in me and how that can be helpful to psychoanalytic technique.

Dr. Lawrence Kubie once said he thought Dr. Erickson had much to contribute to psychoanalysis, but Erickson was so far outside the formal system of psychoanalytic education, and equally as insulting to psychoanalysts as they were to him, that during his life only few psychoanalysts studied with him, and to my knowledge were not able to take what he offered and view it from a psychoanalytic perspective as separate from the personal power involved in how it was presented; that is, in terms of hypnotherapy and brief uncommon psychotherapy.

When I first met Dr. Erickson, his wife wheeled him into the office. He had polio, crippling arthritis, his feet were swollen like cement blocks with gout, his lips were paralyzed and his tongue was dislocated. I thought to myself, no matter how tough my job is in the world, it can't be as tough as this man's task just to get on with each day's living.

However, his physical maladies as well as his genius may have been the reason he naturally developed a pace at which he spoke, and/or worked, that permitted him to get through each day's work, given the extraordinary physical pain he had to endure each day.

When I met Dr. Erickson he was seventy seven years old. He knew he didn't have much time left and he was, in my opinion, streamlining his teaching, supervision and therapy/hypnotherapy to reach the most people with no wasted energy. He was interested in quality control. He did this through a method of storytelling, hour after hour, after hour. Sometimes he could last four and one half hours. Sometimes he could only last three hours in the last year and one half.

In one story he said that Margaret Mead told him she had only experienced the pace at which he spoke on one other occasion, in a rare African tribe that was relatively free of dis-ease. The only other time I experienced a pace like this was in Dr. Wilfred Bion, a British psychoanalyst? who had thoughts without a thinker thinking? and was as solid and centered as a person could be from what capacity I had to assess.

I began to make links between Erickson's ability to develop his own unconscious, his accessing of the patient's unconscious, the pace at which he spoke, the ability to stay centered or as Bion might have put it, "not get knocked off your seat in the line of emotional fire", the development of a solid and stable ego, and then, when steady enough, to have thoughts without thinking while keeping the mental space open as a result of being able to tolerate the chaos and anxiety of not knowing. I saw the storytelling as a precursor to the development of these psychoanalytic skills that Bion possessed, both in terms of the steady pace of a metronome and the access to the unconscious in such a certain and steady way that one could then build a conscious mind with a stable ego and enter the realm of Bion's most creative work, thoughts without thinking.

WHAT DOES ALL THIS HAVE TO DO WITH BETA ELEMENTS AND THE SENSES?

Bion was the sort of person who had a mischievous sense of humor. This must remembered throughout his writings, for he often does not spell things out, but hints at them in a way that teases those who are capable to go farther, and does not get himself killed off by those of the establishment who would find what he had to say just too threatening. For example, psychoanalytic education does not customarily focus on the utilization of the senses as a way of considering and doing the work. There is a focus upon insight and understanding in the rebuilding of the personality, but it is not really spelled out technically as to the means upon how one comes about the insight.

Again, taking a look at Bion's personality, that of a mischievous adventurer, and his view of psychoanalysis, that it was a bloody dangerous profession where one had to be on their toes not to be murdered by either patients or colleagues, it is no small wonder he utilized this quality of mischievous playfulness in his writing about the things many psychoanalysts would just as soon he not have said. After Bion's death one such psychoanalyst, who in my view was on the Thanatos side in terms of his inability to sustain his own life force, and thereby facilitate the life force of his patients per hour of work, said, "Bion was a schizophrenic fool who imposed a method of psychoanalysis upon a community who didn't want what he forced them to take. He's better off dead!" This psychoanalyst was a very famous person in his own right. But one can see how threatened even the psychoanalytic community may be at this quality of being manifested by Bion; his being described as a mystic, his thoughts without thinking, his being thought of as a man who disturbs the universe.[1] Psychoanalysis was written about by Langs[2] as a truth therapy in contrast to a lie therapy. But the problem Bion posed is that if truth were viewed as the openness to infinity, of which could never really be known in its entirety, then psychoanalysis and those who practice it would have to be able to stand being ignorant while at the same time being the doctors upon whose shoulders the responsibility for cure they had assumed and the patients looked upon them to deliver.

Bion was concerned about saturation. One psychoanalyst who was analyzed by Bion said "Every session I went in thinking I knew what reality was. Every session I left in chaos."

Another analyst described Bion as a "tank". A third said Bion would never leave him in doubt. He would help him expand his thinking in as full a way as he could to one side, and then to the other. Developmentally, Bion would treat people in terms of what they needed as individuals. For example, the man who Bion left in chaos was one I experienced as having a tendency to want to know for certain and thereby close down the space in terms of staying open to experience. The man who said Bion would never do anything like that needed more gradual building of a conscious mind and stabilization of ego function before he could get to a place of being able to tolerate infinity. So Bion was concerned with giving people the tools with which they could then learn to handle the task of becoming 'O'.

Bion was at a party and there was a very expensive painting of a well-known artist that people gathered around and talked about in a way that it is said, Bion might have viewed as a non-meeting of those gathered. When they went into another room for coffee, Bion hid the painting and then the conversation centered upon where it had gone.

When I began to read A Memoir of the Future: The Dream[3], I was dismayed, thrown off balance, and began to search throughout the book trying to put an end to the chaos that occurred when the book began with chapter eleven. That is, chapter eleven followed the prologue. Chapter seventeen followed chapter eleven. And chapter twenty five followed chapter seventeen. Well, I couldn't help but wonder where the missing chapters had gone? After several minutes of distress I looked down to the bottom of the page and noticed the details, or evidence as Bion might have put it, that the chapters were numbered according to the page numbers where the chapters would begin. Page eleven became chapter eleven and chapter seventeen was on page seventeen.

I think Freud gave us the body of understanding upon which the art and science of psychoanalysis is based. I think Bion gave us the conceptual framework from which the practice of a psychoanalysis that cures can be practiced. But the problem that remains, is that what do we make of the work both with Bion's unusual way of using his mischievous side both to educate and to prevent professional suicide, and to still be able to translate his conceptual framework into a method of psychoanalytic technique that does what his conceptual framework permits a psychoanalysis to do, to cure patients in that they will be given the tools with which to pursue the infinite being that each of us are to infinity, while remaining atop the life force in a way that our lives can qualitatively flourish.

Perhaps as close as I have seen of Bion's writings actually spelling out the point appeared in a book that was published after his death, and edited by his lovely and very dedicated wife, Francesca Bion. Bion had written of his personal analysis with Melanie Klein. He wrote, "I recovered, went back to work and my own analysis, swore' never to do it again' and, as usual, invariably did again whatever it was I had sworn not to do. I was assiduous in my psycho-analytic sessions. When I was given an interpretation I used very occasionally to feel it was correct; more usually I thought it was nonsense but hardly worth arguing about since I did not regard the interpretation as much more than the expression of one of Mrs. Klein's opinions that was unsupported by any evidence. The interpretations that I ignored or did not understand or made no response to, later seemed to have been correct. But I did not see why I regarded them as any more correct than I had thought they were when I refuted or ignored them. The most convincing were those that appeared to harmonize with what I knew, or what Mrs. Klein said, about my personality. She tried to pass on to me her interpretations of the material of which her senses made her aware. But to become efficacious her methods were dependent on my receptivity. This is in no way different from any other form of human assistance-there must be someone or something willing to receive.

"How banal is this conclusion! How obvious! And how perpetually that fact becomes clear and how frequently ignored. Yet a willing co-operation in teacher and taught is difficult to achieve when the participants are human. This banal observation seemed to be more than usually bitterly resisted when it was 'I' who had to listen to what my senses told me, even with the assistance of Melanie Klein. But as time passed I became more reconciled to the fact that not even she could be a substitute for my own senses, interpretations of what my senses told me, and choice between contradictories."[4]

So here it is. Bion spells it out clearly, that he learned to utilize his senses, and then made interpretations based upon what his senses told him, and that this was how he decided to choose between contradictories.

But the problem still remains, how do we gain access to our senses, particularly if is the foundation upon which Bion based his view of psychoanalytic technique? Then there is the problem of how to actually utilize those senses in terms of the spelling out of psychoanalytic technique, which it is my hope this book will shed light upon in pages to come.

However, the question here, is what does all this have to do with beta elements, anyway, this business about the senses? Dr. Donald Meltzer, when referring to Bion's "seven servants", wrote about the delusional system. He wrote, "if we take the delusional system in the sense of a 'place' that is located essentially 'nowhere', we imply that what goes on there has the meaning, essentially, of 'nonsense', a tissue of lies, Pandemonium."[5]

Meltzer links nonsense, as in not attendant to the senses, with a tissue of lies and Pandemonium. This further points to the problem of attempting to foster insight when such insight is not hooked up to the senses of the psychoanalyst. Might such insight only be countertransferential projective identification that limits the patient through envy, hatred and destruction to prevent the psychoanalyst's difficulty of being in the midst of a tissue of lies and personal pandemonium from becoming known to that psychoanalyst and unbeknownst to that psychoanalyst to the degree that thoughts are not connected to the full quality of being of the psychoanalyst as that being is grounded in the senses.

Meltzer wrote, "Bion has suggested that if the emotional experience, or, more correctly, the perception of the emotional experience, is not worked upon by alpha-function, its elements tend to remain as disparate bits of psychic stimulation which he has called beta-elements."[6] Would not the problem then be, if these disparate bits of psychic stimulation are actually being projected out or split off by the patient due to a lack of a mother who could provide a proper container to detoxify these disparate bits of psychic stimulation, how would the psychoanalyst be able to restore the self of the patient if the psychoanalyst could not actually sense these disparate bits of psychic stimulation as they were being split off? If the psychoanalyst could not sense these disparate bits of psychic stimulation moment to moment, focus the patient's attention upon that disparate psychic stimulation being projected off or split off from the patient due to the patient's inability to stand the internal or external psychic reality or reality at that moment and lack of cohesive self and capacity to function at such levels of refinement of the quality of being of that patient, then how could that psychoanalyst actually provide a container that would detoxify a state of dis-ease as a result of the patient's out of control manic and or dissociative ways of not being able to function? If the psychoanalyst could not sense these disparate bits of psychic stimulation from moment to moment, and sense the exact body area of the patient from which the projected disparate bits were being split off, then how could the psychoanalyst focus the patient's attention to the correct area where the split off disparate bits of psychic stimulation could then be contained? If the psychoanalyst could not focus on the exact spot in the patient where the patient is splitting off these disparate projected bits of psychic stimulation, then has Bion's conceptual view of the psychoanalytic task of providing a container stuck in quicksand in that a psychoanalytic method or technique does not currently exist with which to actually do what Bion conceptualized? For example, if the exact spot in the body could not be located, how could it be related to the thought that was being evacuated by the patient? The moment would have passed and the thought connected to the being of the patient would not have been facilitated. Let us think about the possibility that if a patient is critical of self, that the very second that self-critical thought occurs, the psychoanalyst's sensitivities are such that a pain occurs in the body of the psychoanalyst under the right ribs, or perhaps medically or organically related to the area of the gall bladder. Let us further assume that after several hundred thousand of such experiences, it becomes nearly automatic for the psychoanalyst to recognize not only the area in which the patient is splitting off the disparate bits of psychic stimulation, that being under the right ribs of the patient or the area of the gall bladder in this example, but to recognize the self-critical thought of the patient the second it occurs in that the projected disparate bits of psychic stimulation hit the body of the psychoanalyst and the psychoanalyst senses it the second it happens. If this were to occur, would the psychoanalyst now have the possibility of having a technique that could help the patient pay attention to the exact area of splitting while at the same moment making an interpretation that would facilitate self-acceptance in the patient. If this were to occur it would do several things. It would in fact substantiate the psychoanalyst as a container in that the psychoanalyst would have contained the disparate bits of psychic stimulation without being knocked off the therapeutic chair due to the intolerability of the psychic pain (not necessarily so)-the problem that mother did not know how to deal with in the first place. It would prevent the patient from engaging in a long monologue which had the appearance of expanding the functions and productions of the patient while what was occurring was that the patient was involved in sadomasochistic torture tactics in the service of expanded attention. It would help the patient contain the disparate bits of psychic stimulation while locating the thought that was then connected to the being of the patient in a natural state of existence without disparate psychic disturbance in that the bits of psychic stimulation would not only be contained by psychoanalyst and patient, but that the immediate location of thought creating the disturbance would have been released and relief would have been provided via the psychoanalytic interpretation. Could one begin to see the possibilities of the psychoanalyst being able to help patients function in such natural states of being while doing the analysis and the value of a fifty minute hour five days per week in terms of what is involved in the restoration of function in the self of the patient?

Could psychoanalysis then more accurately prevent the development of organic dis-ease from occurring. For example, if the patient, while evacuating thought millions of times in their lives are not privy to the self-critical thought that has this physiological component of creating dis-ease, and in this case, perhaps a direct correlation to the creation of a dis-eased gall bladder, might they not be able to gain enough self-control to prevent the decay of a gall bladder to the point of needing a gall bladder operation? Perhaps, perhaps not. But would the chances be significantly increased if the senses of the psychoanalyst were so fine-tuned it focused directly on the area of physical abuse of the patient related to the patient's incapacity to think clearly? Would this kind of work not help patients live in states of being that were relatively dis-ease free and would not the preventive medical and organic value of such states be invaluable to the quality of that patient's life both in terms of being able to function at levels of physical states of well-being while the mind then had the opportunity to in released states of sustained well-being with a cohesive self being sustained and stabilized, begin to function at degrees of becoming 'O' that approached infinity in terms of enhancing the capacity to have thoughts without thinking and approach the fullest and truest capacities that are in each individual, if they can be properly facilitated in their growth through the technical skills and development of the therapeutic use of self of the psychoanalyst? If viewed from that perspective we begin to see why psychoanalysis is the only method that has the possibility of curing the primitive nature of the patient that has been distorted and riddled with character defenses as related to underlying psychotic thinking disorders that concerned Bion. I say the only method because it is the only method that has the conditions available to do such work, and has the personnel as a group of practitioners who have devoted themselves through their own analysis, five times per week to be able to have such self-discipline as to be able to facilitate such self-discipline in patients who want to get well through the pursuit of their being to infinity.

I suppose in thinking about the one example of the patient with the self-critical problem, or it can also be taken the other way with a sense pain in the same spot, that is, the patient being critical of the other person, that we have a problem of too much gall and not enough bladder.

Of course, there are an infinite number of possibilities that occur during the clinical hour. For example, when a patient is angry and using the anger and sexuality as a weapon the psychoanalyst might sense pain in the right side of the genital area. The problem then is in making the kind of interpretation that will release the anger in the patient or block it. An interesting side note in developing such skills and technique is that the colloquial ways people speak are directly related to the areas where disparate bits of psychic stimulation are split off. For example, in the case of the person who is angry, and the psychoanalyst picks up the sense cue through pain on the right side of the genitals, and the patient is off center or not connected to their full sexual nature at this moment, might it not be said that they are 'pissed off'? That is, they are 'pissed off' center.

This problem of being centered I know through the experience of Bion he devoted his life to. However, he thought about it in terms of becoming 'O'. But the task of the psychoanalyst or of the psychoanalyst in terms of the functions that analyst helps the patient develop, is to be solid in self so the patient through the experience with the analyst can function in the emotional line of fire through the maintenance of a solid and centered self in the line of that emotional fire. Perhaps Bion's view of psychoanalysis was formulated on the battle field in World War I when he was a tank commander, because that is just what he had to learn to do in the face of the oncoming tanks trying to blow his head off!

Bion was as solid as a block of granite at the age of 82, and sustained this degree of solidness and centeredness in the line of emotional fire before 500 people and several colleagues who related in primitive ways that would have been enough to throw most anyone off their center spot. But Bion had the capacity not only to stay on center, but to do so while he had these thoughts without thinking and facilitated such thoughts without thinking as well as the experience of how it felt to be in the presence of someone who had developed the discipline of becoming 'O' for eighty two years, and who had done it well; among those members of the audience whose sensitivities were developed enough to know what the experience is, was and had been that was occurring and had occurred.

But to do all this one has to develop the capacity to deal at this most primitive of levels. This involves the underlying psychotic thinking disorders Bion referred to, even in those who were usually thought of in the neurotic diagnostic categories. But it also involves the development of the utilization of the senses in a way where the interpretations soften the character armor and character defenses of the patient as facilitated by the capacity to recognize the disparate bits of psychic stimulation through the developed sensitivity of the senses of the psychoanalyst. I think Wilhelm Reich had a very important idea when he wrote about character armor. Bion, through the quality of his being demonstrated the result of someone who had developed his senses in a way that had gotten through that character armor, but without all the techniques that Reich and his followers experimented with, but I think, have been unsuccessful in achieving the result of which I am writing about because they did not know how to immediately link the experience with thought.

There have been many gifted psychoanalysts who, I think have been searching for this technique because of their frustrations with the outcome of psychoanalysis, and who have become rebels, breaking away from psychoanalysis. This has been necessary, but insufficient. It has been necessary in that the areas of their exploration have evoked technical remedies that the limitations of psychoanalytic technique within the rigid confines of how psychoanalysts are educated would not permit to be developed. In fact, rather than encourage such exploration, psychoanalysts are more likely to call such explorers heretics. The problem with the heretics is that they took the small piece of the pie they developed and said it was the whole thing. This has been the tragedy in that these techniques need to become part and parcel of the psychoanalytic method if one is a patient who in good faith goes to a psychoanalyst with the notion of having the opportunity of becoming whole.

While the myriad of psychotherapeutic techniques have been thought to be so disparate from each other that psychotherapy schools can hardly talk to each other, let alone psychoanalysts, there is a common denominator that brings the entire field together and makes sense. That is, if the therapeutic use of self is developed to the degree one can actually use the senses as a base from which to operate, all the other techniques just flow from that developed therapeutic use of self within the realm of the psychoanalytic interpretation.

This is a very simple principle. However, simple must not be equated with easy. After all, most people who came into contact with Bion claim he was a genius, and he wrote of the difficulty he was having when Melanie Klein kept referring to paying attention to his senses. Further, this was Bion's second analysis, as he was previously analyzed by John Rickman. So Bion was two analyses into it and having a hard time of it.

For whatever reason the other psychotherapies that have been rebellious offshoots of psychoanalysis do not seem to be dominated by hatred and fear of each other. This has not been true of psychoanalysis, or of many of the psychoanalysts I have met. In Los Angeles there have been bitter wars between the Kleiniens and the Freudians. When speaking to one analyst and the name of another comes up, time after time, one chops off the weenie of the other with one felt swoop of the axe. No wonder Bion was careful in that he was as far outside of that system as an insider could still be.

Freudians are interested in oedipal material, or to put it more bluntly, to be hooked up to one's sexuality and genitalia on a consistent basis as a result of analyzing repressed material. Kleiniens perhaps feel that the developmental gaps that prevent wholeness need to be looked into and thinking disorders repaired before such a consistent sexual focus is taken. Reich felt the Freudians may have had the right idea but couldn't get to the life force through the analytic technique that existed in a way whereby the patient would be hooked up sexually on a consistent basis, and without such primitive connectedness, there was a deprivation of life force that accompanied the psychoanalytic experience which left its patrons less than whole, or with less than an even chance of having the tools to become 'O'.

The above are overgeneralized and simplistic interpretations just to make a point of how Freudians, Kleinians and Reichians operate.

It may not agree with how those practitioners would like to think of themselves. The problem is that they are all fighting, and I only use these three examples when it goes far beyond this to include the entire field of psychoanalysis and psychotherapy, to say that there is one true method and the others don't exist. They are both right and wrong. There is only one true method, a method that is inclusive enough to help the dedicated patient who wants to go all the way in the pursuit of becoming 'O' to actually have the opportunity to do so. I mean, what the hell, the patient comes to you for five to seven years, five times per week, shouldn't they have a crack at getting the tools to get what they came for? I only ask this question because I am seeing patients who have had seven years of analysis before coming to me and having to begin another seven. I have met many psychoanalysts, dedicated people, who are either beginning their second analysis in their late forties or early fifties, or who are in their late fifties feeling that they need more analysis, but it is too late, and they kind of missed the boat. These are dedicated people. They have worked very hard with however many years to get personal analysis four or five times per week, to get at least four years of supervision, at least four years of course work, case presentations and the rest. Why has it not worked? Most that I have met have availed themselves to continuing education in psychoanalysis. They have dedicated their lives to being responsible professionals, and I think are at the forefront as a group of those who have paid the highest dues in terms of development. Yet, the blindness prevails. The difficulty of grasping a method that facilitates whole being due to the destruction of 'O' by 'K' (Knowledge); that is, the kind of knowledge that is geared to shut down the set to learning through experience as opposed to keeping it open. There is the inherent fear that someone will see that the emperor has no clothes and that each must protect their turf, their piece of the pie. I mean, what the hell, it's how one earns one's livelihood. But I don't think one would necessarily like to think of it in these terms, that of being ruled by petty jealousies, hatred of internal and external reality that goes beyond the bounds of experience to which that practitioner has developed the therapeutic use of self. But it is this dangerous and petty nonsense that makes psychoanalysis as what Bion referred to as a dangerous profession, both in terms of the animosity it arouses in patients who may want to kill their well-intentioned analysts for having failed them after having made extreme sacrifice and extreme commitment and still not having the tools to pursue becoming 'O', and the animosity it arouses among psychoanalysts themselves, who are probably more dedicated than most, and in one way or another, at some level, conscious or unconscious, know that they must kill off the enemy whose primitive knowledge threatens their own limitations or state of being and that which their patients cannot grow beyond as a result of the countertransferential problem of hatred and fear of the patient outgrowing the psychoanalyst.

Psychoanalysts are wrong in that they have not brought the findings of their most brilliant dissidents back into the psychoanalytic education in a way that would help solve the technical difficulties involved in helping patients develop the tools to pursue becoming 'O' upon termination of the analysis.

Another example was Fritz Perls, once a psychoanalyst, who then studied with Reich, and broke off to find his own method of therapy to deal with problems of affect being hooked up to the patient's productions. He was further interested in working at the contact boundary. Perls broke away from analysis, saying the task was to 'lose your mind and come to your senses' (see Erickson-Gestalt Theory and the Problem of Thinking). This was exactly right. In fact it was what Melanie Klein was trying to teach Bion, and succeeded in doing. The problem then became that most gestaltists did not have the kind of dedicated training of psychoanalysts, so could never approach a disciplined and dedicated level of becoming 'O', to take the work of a genius such as Perls, and actually develop a method that would help the patient be one with his senses, and not in the loss of mind, but in then developing a method of having the senses help the patient develop a mind, or the capacity to think, and at the far end of the spectrum, to be able to have thoughts without thinking. Otherwise, we may have gestaltists who have not really found the method to get to their senses on the level of becoming 'O', and who therefore, have not been able to include work with thinking disorders at the underlying primitive levels as part of a therapy that is intended to help patients become whole, which is why Fritz Perls broke away from analysis in the first place. But, what if psychoanalytic education were to take into account some of the "I"-"THOU" ways of working in the present tense, of confronting as a method of interpretation when the patient's affect is not connected to the words, and then expand upon those interpretations as Bion did, in a way that dealt with the contact and the space between people, or between patient and psychoanalyst, while using the senses as a cue from which to then expand the capacity to think of the patient. Confrontations can take many forms. They can even be put into Kohutian empathic form, all in the present tense. That is, the gestalt focus on the here and now can be thought about as a way of dealing with the past, the present and the future in terms of psychoanalytic technique. On this score, I am certain that most skillful psychoanalysts practice in this way, but do not necessarily think about their work or educate junior colleagues in this way of thinking about things.

Albert Ellis, once a psychoanalyst, came up with rational-emotive therapy. This doesn't have a helluva lot to do with becoming 'O', but his methods brought into the psychoanalytic interpretation can have a lot to do with helping the patients gain the tools to becoming 'O', lest they only perpetuate their anger and lack of self-acceptance during their productions. Or perhaps these kinds of patients are thought to be unanalyzable, but the problem is never the patient's fault, only a problem in the analyst's method not being up to snuff to reach that particular patient. I am certain psychoanalysts would view Ellis' work as superficial, short term and not in-depth treatment. Yet what if it were viewed from the psychoanalytic perspective of how it could help facilitate psychoanalytic interpretation in terms of doing in-depth treatment. For example, if a psychoanalyst only took two of Ellis's tools, that of telling the patient that the patient was acceptable just because the patient was a human being, every time there was a sense perception picked up by the well-disciplined psychoanalyst under the right ribs, or in the area of the gall bladder; and, every time there was a sense perception on the right side of the genitalia that "there is no reason things must be fair and there is no reason you must get what you want, (and then I added using a series of negatives to get a positive) in order to not be angry;" then that patient would in effect be getting a cognitive restructuring of two very destructive tendencies that may actually prevent that patient from being able to tolerate psychoanalytic interpretation. Net result-the psychoanalyst could reach a greater patient population and offer those who are dedicated in this realm the opportunity of becoming 'O'.

For example, patients who continually went into self-critical or angry thinking modes would not have the capacity to tolerate interpretation, and even with an extraordinary degree of empathy and acceptance on the part of the psychoanalyst ala Kohut's work, those self critical thoughts and angry thoughts, if left unchallenged, and if the patient does not learn to challenge them, would essentially mean that such a patient would massacre himself or herself via the interpretation itself. Or, there would at the very least be a large part of the time, perhaps time in which the psychoanalyst were thinking of the patient's productions, that those productions would be at least in part torturous beyond what could humanely be done by the addition of these two principles and methods of Albert Ellis.

Martin Grotjahn, a brilliant psychoanalyst, told me that basically he gave up doing psychoanalysis because it did not work. He said psychoanalysis was a good method for education, but not for treatment. Psychoanalysis was a good method for self-knowledge, but not a method to cure people. Grotjahn developed group analysis which he found to be more effective in terms of treatment because it had a teaching function involved. But what if this teaching function could be brought into the psychoanalytic interpretation itself? Such as I have written about in terms of Ellis? Would Grotjahn still feel the same way? I think not!

While writing my first book, there was a focus on the existential moment as a linkup to potency of the therapist. In that search I was either therapized by, supervised by, trained by or taught by, through the experience itself, every master therapist I could find who I thought had a piece to add to the puzzle. The only problem, at that time, I did not know what the puzzle was. I was learning what kind of interventions would reach what kind of patients in a particular situation. But the problem with the entire situation, as I came to find out, was that each of those therapists could help cure a part of the patient in helping that patient develop a function to cure the part of the patient that could be treated by that therapist. Thus, each in itself was very limited in terms of becoming 'O', in that the method of treatment did not have the proper conditions under which 'O' could be pursued to any great degree, with the exception of Bion, both whose theory and his person were evidence that he knew about such pursuit first hand, and Milton Erickson, who had traveled a good portion of the road to infinity, but never thought about or described his work in the context of becoming 'O', which is why it is my intention to do so in this book so it can be used by psychoanalysts who have such an objective.

It is my further intention to demonstrate, in that search, what methods I find particularly useful in doing psychoanalysis that are most frequently required as a part of the psychoanalytic interpretation, and how they are all based in the recognition of the senses as a first step via the recognition of beta elements, and then how this integration can become a harmonious flow in terms of the development of the therapeutic use of self of the psychoanalyst.

I suppose Bion and Erickson stood out for me far beyond the excellence of their methods in that I experienced them as two people who could actually stand the heat of becoming 'O' to its infinite discriminations, Bion within the frame that his psychoanalytic training made available and Erickson, with no self-imposed limitations at all. It is for this pursuit of their own being, and showing me by example, that I am eternally grateful for a search I would have otherwise have remained in the dark about despite my dedication and my lifelong pursuit thereof. In other words, I actually experienced two people who did it, and I found out not only what they said they did, but what they did, and I figured out how to put it into the psychoanalytic frame, because that is the only method that has a body of colleagues who are dedicated enough, perhaps, for such a venture. To my other mentors I am very grateful for their teaching me the functions with which I think need to be reintegrated into the psychoanalytic interpretation within a situation that has the minimum conditions under which the work of becoming 'O' can actually take place. Jim Simkin, an extraordinary psychotherapist and second to Perls in the gestalt world, had the vision to understand what I was attempting to do long before I did, and gave me his full support in that task. He had the vision to know that "the existential moment was what psychoanalysts might say is the same as 'insight'"[8], long before I realized the significance of my experiential investigation to find out what the job of therapeutic treatment actually entailed, and then what means might be utilized to actually bring about those objectives. It was the link between the existential moment and Bion that led me to psychoanalysis and beta elements, which are the basis of insight that is connected the being of the person as to the degree that one dare become 'O' in that if the disparate bits of psychic stimulation are not perceived and detoxified on a moment to moment basis, in a way that contains them and sustains the life force Reich was concerned about, then the level of primitive preconceptions that are essential to the psychoanalyst and then the patient getting to know themselves as tigers know themselves in a jungle at the most primitive levels cannot occur. And if the patient cannot gain control over these primitive character defenses while having access to the primitive preconceptions as an unimpeded flow, then that patient will not only have trouble functioning in the world, but will certainly have difficulty prospering.

If one were to consider what I am describing as the capacity to maintain a cohesive self, a stable and solid self, at the most primitive levels, while having resolved both the oedipal situation in terms of the capacity having been developed for a constant sexual object without ambivalence, while having resolved the narcissistic problems in that hatred, rage and aggression are not promulgated when an avenue for self fulfillment has been reached, then the methods I am describing can be examined in such a framework.

Kohut examines psychoanalysis in such a framework in his last book[8], which interested me most among his books because it was the culmination of a lifetime effort of a worthy contributor. Kohut refers to psychoanalytic technique in writing that it is an error to guide the patient to the analysis of archaic traumata. He thought that later on in the analysis the cohesion-firming responses of the analyst and such responses as sought out by the self would provide a place where the crucial transferences of such analyses could be worked through. Kohut then referred to cure as when "an energic continuum in the center of the personality has been established and the unfolding of a productive life has thus become a realizable possibility." p. 7 The key phrase is energic continuum! This cannot be attained without the methods of which I_describe, which leads to Kohut's description of a fear worse than or equal to the fear of death, a fear he refers to as disintegration anxiety. Kohut challenged the Freudians who decree that cure rests on the analysis of the Oedipus complex, and the Kleiniens who Kohut described as stating that cure rests on the analysis of the depressions and rages of earliest infancy.

The technical problem I think he was not able to resolve was that if the quality of his being had developed to the degree of becoming 'O', that through the manifestation of that being and the vibration thereof, as connected to the full being and capacity to interpret of the psychoanalyst, he would then have been able to cut through all the methods-Fruedian, Kleinian and Kohutian, in that the method I propose provides the possibility for an analysis that maintains a cohesive self, a stable and solid self, at the most primitive levels, while having resolved both the oedipal situation in terms of the capacity having been developed in the patient for a constant sexual love object without ambivalence, while having resolved the narcissistic problems in that hatred, rage and aggression are not promulgated when an avenue for self-fulfillment in work and in love have been reached, and when the cohesive gut level solidness has even broken through the borderline psychotic defenses and permit that patient to maintain what I refer to as a constant life force, and what Kohut refers to as an energic continuum. A mere Kohut's Flicker of heart every i.e. continuum on my personal evaluation screen talent of viewed Bion = The Holy Grail.

I think the technical problem of not guiding the patient to the analysis of archaic traumata is correct, but that what needs to be done, is that through as impeccable a quality of being as the psychoanalyst is able to manifest during each session, the archaic traumata in the living here and now of the patient is to be analyzed, and passionately where necessary, in a way that gets through the defensive operations that Kohut thought could not be tolerated-particularly in borderline psychotic personality disorders. But if the quality of being of the psychoanalyst, the humanity (described Freud)[9] provided in terms of reaching man's soul (terms in which Bettelheim the technical empathy Kohut wrote about are provided in a way that reaches the deepest levels of being of that patient, they will tolerate most anything and the analysis can go to the deepest levels it needs to reach in order to constantly facilitate a life force that continues to ignite a nuclear self that has been born through the analysis and to keep it alive throughout the duration of not only the course of the analysis, but the course of every fifty minute hour, and thereby giving the patient the tools by which to do this for self upon termination of the analysis.

Re: Next Two Sections:

For those that need more of a background in Gestalt Therapy, Ericksonian Hypnosis and Transactional Analysis I refer you to my several work "Psycho Therapy, Insight and Style: The Existential Moment," now retitled and republished by Jason Aronson of Northvale, New Jersey as Making An Impact In Therapy. How Master Clinicians Intervene"

GESTALT THERAPY AND THE PROBLEM OF THINKING

This paper was written in 1985

by Len Bergantino, Ed.D., Ph.D. 10266 Kilrenney Avenue Los Angeles, CA 90064 Current Telephone 424293-9517 Let it Ring 7 Times to Leave a Message

Psychotherapy Insight & Style:
The Existential Moment is
Expected to be republished
By Workbook Press Publishing
Company shortly
After this book
Comes out. It
Was a Master Classic
in the field for
twenty years and
it became part of Jason
Aronson Publisher in Master
Classic Series

For Section-Notes On The Contributors

Len Bergantino is in the private practice of clinical psychology in Beverly Hills, California. He has received training in gestalt therapy from Jim Simkin, members of the Gestalt Therapy Institute of Los Angeles, and is a three year graduate of Erv & Miriam Polster's training program. He has authored the book Psychotherapy, Insight and Style: The Existential Moment in addition to 90 articles published in professional journals. He has been heavily influenced by the work of Wilfred Bion, his three years of training with Milton Erickson, and his training with Carl Whitaker, and has worked at both integrating and expanding upon those learnings as they might be utilized in gestalt therapy. He gives workshops in both gestalt therapy and gestalt family therapy. He has given a workshop for The Gestalt Therapy Institute of Queensland, Australia. In 1984, 1986 and 1988 was the keynote speaker presenting a workshop entitled: "The Quality of Being."

GESTALT THERAPY AND THE PROBLEM OF THINKING

Gestalt therapy is not primarily thoughts of as an insight therapy. Fritz Perls said, "Lose your mind and come to your senses". This was a proper recommendation in terms of the way most psychoanalysis was being practiced because the analysis would only perpetuate the split of mind from body, or more accurately not be able to restore thoughts that were being evacuated. So Perls was onto something big when he said, "Lose your mind and come to your senses." The problem is that gestalt therapy may have stopped there instead of viewing Perls comment as an evolutionary statement.

It is from sensory experience that thought is evoked, and without that experience you have only an excuse for a mind that vacates thought not founded in present experience. But sensory experience, when paid attention to at finer and finer levels of discrimination not only lead to having thought as it occurs, that is based in the storehouse of primitive preconceptions that have not had the opportunity to occur, but such a link between sensory experience and thought also enables the patient to begin to contain emotional experience. The containment of this emotional experience on a moment to moment basis, as it links to sensory perception and the occurrence of thought without thinking, provides the basis for "pure gestalt", or "pure being", which is what Fritz Perls wrote about. The problem is that, to this point, all the tools by which pure being can occur have not become part of the technology of the gestalt therapist. Although one never reaches pure being, one can continually move in that direction of approximation if the tools to take the journey are available.

I think what has happened is that gestalt has more generally focused on behavior and given up on the linkup of the conscious and the unconscious while the emotions, thoughts and feelings are linked up and evoked via sensory experience. So the purpose of gestalt, which is to find the "whole" cannot be achieved unless the technology is expanded so as to be able to meet the objective. I think Perls in his frustration to find this methodology, and certainly in his creation of a methodology that had the kernels of paying the kind of attention to sensory experience that may eventually evoke a fuller methodology, spoke of what he viewed as feeble attempts in language referring to those attempts at wholeness as "Chickenshit", Elephantshit", and "Bullshit".

I further contend that when the linkup on a moment to moment basis becomes consistent, Bion or when one's ability to pay attention to sensory experience which links up to emotion with internal and external experience, conscious and unconscious thoughts without thinking, the life force which Freud wrote about which is in constant conflict with the_death instinct can prevail through "good works." Good works means the work of one's life, to pay that kind of attention so that the patient has the opportunity to develop the capacity to live in "good faith", as opposed to "bad faith". That is, the patient has the opportunity through the tools given the patient in the therapeutic experience, to maintain a consistency of life force in terms of enhancing the quality of being of the patient and continuing to move in finer and finer discriminations toward becoming all that patient can be. The therapy to be in "good faith" must be able to give the patient the tools with which to carry on the work for the remainder of that patient's life. I think Perls did not see it this way due to his own frustration in achieving that kind of methodology. He spoke of responsibility as being responsible for one's work now, without much concern for what happens after. I think this was in "bad faith" by default-that is his own frustration rather than what he might have done had these linkups I write about been clear to him.

THE PROBLEM OF ANGER

For some reason unknown to me gestalt therapists rather than working on the thinking disorder aspects that lead to anger have patients, through experiment, engage in angry behavior over and over. This leads to continually and justifiably acting out psychotic bullshit! I may be overgeneralizing here, but I have had many years of gestalt training with many well respected gestalt trainers.

First I think the bottom line to angry thought, which can be picked up on a sensory perception level immediately by paying attention to what is being projected onto the therapist around the temples by a process of violent splitting in the patient, are the beliefs that "things must be fair", and "I must get what I want", which are based in what Melanie Klein referred to as the paranoid-schizoid position. This kind of self-indulgent grandiose position, if unchallenged immediately only perpetuates underlying psychotic thinking disorders. The challenging of this kind of thinking, when picked up on a sensory level, can give the patient immediate access to turning around these angry thoughts. The angry thoughts have no purpose or effect, other than to create, which also can be picked up on a sensory level, physical pains in other parts of the body. In other words there is a direct correlation between what Perls referred to as dis-ease, or the lack of oneness with the organism of the body, and the patient's splitting off from painful experience, particularly in the area of angry thought-which only exacerbates-first psychosomatic problems, and later, actual organic illness.

In addition to the two beliefs, "I must get what I want" and "things must be fair", the therapist can work with the thinking disorder by picking up the other story behind the content of what is being said. This other story is usually at the primitive level, and when dealing with anger, may be at the homicidal, suicidal, or narcissistic rage aspects of the personality. For example, the patient may make a comment about next door neighbor Joe. The therapist may notice a sudden burst of pain on the side of the right temple of the therapist's own head that wasn't there before the statement. The therapist may then make an assumption that the patient is either angry or suffering from a great increase in anxiety. The therapist may then make a statement that provides as near to the experience at the primitive level as the patient is able to experience by saying, "I wonder if you are either feeling quite angry or anxiety in regard to what you said about next door neighbor, Joe.". When patients have developed their thought capacity and are able to focus in on the sensation they are projecting off, they often say, "Yes, (pause), I notice the pain and I hadn't realized how angry I was at Joe." Or, "Every time I'm around that guy I'm nervous."

However, more than likely patients who are not able to work that close to their own experience when they arrive might think you are talking voodoo to them when you speak about experiencing pain. In such cases, or if the patient may feel guilty about giving a pain to the therapist, it is better technically to keep your access to the information private, and make the interpretation without telling them how you have arrived at your hypothesis.

When borderline or psychotic patients arrive they are usually so far removed from their primitive response that the therapist will do best technically to work from the unconscious and make the statement "I'll bet you'd like to kill that son of a bitch", in response to the rather benign statement about next door neighbor, Joe". Usually at this point, the patient will either deny being capable of such a thought, or perhaps be able to acknowledge it and move a step further. If the therapist has a good connection to self and good contact with the patient, the support and liking of the patient will permit the therapist to respond in this liberated and what may be considered somewhat outrageous way, in breaking through the concrete between the patient's ears which probably has been a way the patient and his or her family have been from generation to generation.

THE PROBLEM OF CONCRETE

While touching upon the difficulty in gaining access to an unconscious mind that has been cased in cement throughout a lifetime, in dealing with the problem of anger, there is even a more difficult problem-that is, the problem of sex and the moment to moment sexual responses of one person to another on a primitive level.

In certain families, where the bisexual feelings are terrifying, and/or homosexual feelings, concrete thinking is a way to repress what may come to the patient's mind. This may also occur in relation to the patient repressing his or her own sexuality for fear that one parent or another would murder the patient. This phenomena develops when the child is little and dependent upon the parent for life support, so they develop the concrete as a way to survive, and then respond that way to protect the archaic remnants the remainder of their lives unless the therapist has a big enough repertoire to engage the repressed sexual material on an experiential level from moment to moment. If these kinds of unconscious material are kept out of awareness, these patients may often be considered to be boring. They make statements like, “Aren’t the flowers beautiful”, or “I see you have moved the salt shaker from there to here.”.

A way to begin to work with the sexual issue is to key off of the concrete words. One patient, very worried about her self-image with underlying feelings of worthlessness that she would compensate for by inviting “All the right people” to her party, so she could be seen in the “right image”, discussed her invitation list. She said that she wasn’t sure if so and so would come, that she wasn’t really interested in any of them sexually, only to be seen. She was inviting the right number of bisexuals, homosexuals, and girlfriends some of whom were coming and some of whom she was upset were not coming. I said, “it sounds as if your party has the makings of a frustrating experience for you, in that it is likely to be a masturbatory experience.” She said, “What do you mean?” I said, “You describe a situation where no one is interested on some primitive level of ‘coming’ with each other, but they are interested in ‘coming alone’, while you try to organize this masturbatory experience without the slightest interest in whether or not you ‘come’. At this point she broke out into hysterical laughter, acknowledging that was the case. Of course, the ‘heat level’ between patient and therapist needs to be gauged on an interpersonal basis in accord with the unconscious heat level the patient is expressing. But if the patient is fearful of talking about sex, or experiencing sexuality, and the therapist is repressed in this way, you have a very boring therapy that is externally focused as if an unconscious mind did not exist.

For patients to be able to endure such work it must be perfectly clear, and often any paranoid tendencies on the part of the patient must be carefully examined, that the doctor or therapist is just that-and there is absolutely no possibility whatsoever of any sexual contact occurring between therapist and patient. Further, therapists must be aware of even the most subtle seductive maneuvers on their part to be liked, or admired sexually, or even something as innocent as a hug one would give a child, if patients are to trust the therapist with that level of work. While the therapist may feel he is giving an innocent kid a hug, the patient, who is suffering from a thinking disorder and fear of her or his own primitive impulses sexually, which may be quite out of control or feared to be out of control if the repression lifts, may view the situation quite differently and not trust the therapist. This is one reason the analytic position of technical neutrality holds up for good gestalt work to take place-that is, if the work is to move to the depth of getting as close to "pure being" of the "whole" in gestalt as possible.

THE PROBLEM OF CENTERING

On a poster on my wall there are comments by Fritz Perls. "It takes years to be centered; it takes more years to understand and to be now. Until then, beware of both extremes, perfectionism as well as instant cure, instant joy, instant sensory awareness. Until then, beware of any helpers. Helpers are conmen who promise something for nothing. They spoil you and keep you dependent and immature."

Perls outlined the problem quite well. It takes years to be centered, but how does one get centered? The development of sensory awareness is the first step. But how does one develop sensory awareness? Perls warned against those who promised instant sensory awareness. Further, Perls looked to the East in his search for his own Being. I suppose he wouldn't have looked there if he didn't sense or think there was something missing in the Western world in which we live. In Eastern cultures and religions one hears of these strange characters who meditate all day long, and of some who can project healing green lights onto sick people and heal them. How can one support a family, go to work, take care of the kids, and lead a Western culture life, while meditating all day long?

Yet there is the problem of how therapists and patients get out of touch with their own sensory perception by getting caught up in the external world to the point of losing their own internal clock. But what if a therapist were in touch with his or her internal clock, and could be as steady as a metronome (instrument musicians use to keep a steady pace) in providing a constant object to the patient hour after hour until that solid object of the therapist became internalized in the patient in accord with the patient's own internal pace. Then the patient would have the ability, and the sensory awareness, to utilize the tools of sensory awareness to keep an openness to the experience of now on a consistent basis. To be able to do this therapists would first need the kind of training where this occurred in themselves. While psychoanalysts have the frame in which to provide the consistency, and even the theory of object relations to deal with the problem, without the kind of training which Perls was about developing, and which I am attempting to extend through this writing, the job cannot be accomplished in terms of being now and doing "good gestalt therapy".

While Fritz Perls, in the comments on my poster, was privy to what patients and therapists in training needed to beware of, I think he gave a short sighted view based on where he was stuck in his own life. He warned against perfectionism. On the other hand, might it not be viewed as a proper function of gestalt to give patients the tools to move toward the "whole", or helping them close the gestalt. Of course, one never reaches the ultimate of being or the ultimate reality, but to live in "good faith", is it not the job of each person to move toward that kind of becoming if they so choose? And if it is, and they so choose by showing up in your office, then what is the responsibility of the therapist in terms of the kind of self-development necessary to be able to deliver the goods.

Perls was accurate in that there was nothing instant about the process in which he was and I am interested. He wrote, "It takes years to be centered: it takes more years to understand and to be now." I think he is right. If we might extend the thought to the practice of psychotherapy, and the training of psychotherapists, then we may see that there are at least two difficult tasks. First, is to teach, perhaps through workshops, the development of the skill of developing very fine tuned sensory perception, so that patients and therapists can continue to become more centered; and further, where Perls wrote "it takes more years to understand and to be now, might we not extrapolate and refer to his referring here to the problem of dealing with a methodology that would be effective in treating the thinking disorder aspects in patients so they could be and have the understanding to be now. Perls was trained analytically first, although I suspect his analysts and his analytic training failed him miserably on these counts, or he would not have been forced to break away and create gestalt therapy as a response to the pursuit of his own being. But he does not abandon totally the pursuits of analysis, which deal primarily with understanding. He wrote, "it takes more years to understand and to be now, and this in Perls view, was even beyond the difficulty with centering."

If one looks at the literal meaning of what Perls wrote, is he not referring to what he thinks the conditions are under what an effective therapy might entail, but saying, watch out, because to this point, the technology to deliver the goods is not available. You might say this is a far out extrapolation of what Perls wrote, but I think not. I think that Perls analysis was unsuccessful in helping him get through the grandiose paranoid-schizoid position and the technology required was not able to provide him with the substance of his life which he could trust on a consistent basis. I further think his sense of feeling hopeless about this lack of mothering function which he did not find as part of his own therapeutic experience left him putting an undue responsibility back on the patient. I am response-able for myself and you are response-able for yourself. Well, if the patient could already do that, why the hell would the patient need to see the therapist in the first place?

THE PROBLEM OF DEPENDENCY

Perls wrote "Until then, beware of any helpers." What did he mean by "until then". I think he meant until there was a methodology discovered that would help to create the kind of therapist who could meet the difficulty Perls experienced, and which made it further difficult to consistently be in touch with his own substance so that a personal abundance of life might come forth from it.

The difficulty takes the form of two nasty facts. People need to depend upon other people is the first. And the second, is that you need to find somebody who is depend-worthy. (Statement made by Wilfred Bion).

But if the therapeutic technology exists to help the therapist in training have the kind of experience where he or she becomes that kind of person, then what are the conditions under which the job can be done? That is, the job of centering and gaining the understanding to be now. I think the minimum conditions for such a job are four or five times per week for between three to seven years. In other words, I think when the job is capable of being accomplished in terms of a learning through experience that encompasses all I have written in this paper, then the conditions under which a patient can develop the capacity to utilize the tools of such a gestalt therapy to move to closer and closer approximations of being whole takes an enormous amount of practice via the sessions themselves.

Thus, we now have the problem of the gestalt psychoanalyst, who knows how to work in the here and now in ways that psychoanalysts do not, who needs to know how to pay the kind of attention to the resistance of the patient so that the gestalt psychoanalyst can do the work necessary to deliver the goods over a number of years in which the patient is going to want to terminate this arduous task of being at every available opportunity.

It is when gestalt therapists are able to work at the understanding level in the here and now, as well as the centering level, and at the constant object level, that the dependency issues can be worked through so the immature needs of the patient can be filled, and the patient need not fear dependency as a response to never having those needs met.

Learning to deal with that kind of resistance on a day to day level, and know how to deal with the frame or conditions of the therapy is a most important matter, because without knowing how to do that, the whole of the work may prematurely blow up. Perhaps Melanie Klein, when she wrote of moving from the paranoid-schizoid position to the depressive position was at least hinting at how difficult the work would be. When patients begin to become more centered in this way, they do not initially experience the experience of being centered as a satisfactory experience, but instead experience the loss of the distorted grandiose image and feelings as depressive. It is only with the ability to make interpretations that consistently help the patient contain a centered emotional experience that the patient begins to feel a wholeness that he or she begins to notice as satisfactory, and consistently filled with "life force" as opposed to an organismic deadening. It is only with the consistency of an in-depth experience that the conditions for patients to learn to utilize the tools of a gestalt psychoanalysis to maintain the consistency of a "life force" that helps the patient both notice and consistently win out over what Perls referred to as "organismic disgust" can occur. Or in Freud's terms, providing the kind of experience that helps the patient consistently win out over the "death instinct"; or as Franz Alexander might have put it, provide a "corrective emotional experience."

THE PROBLEM OF CONTAINMENT

The problem of containment might otherwise be referred to as the problem of mothering. The problem of the mother is to be able to contain the projected emotional experience of the baby, so the baby can come to tolerate the feared emotional response it has in response to that stage of life. For example, if the baby fears for its life when it is not being fed, or has feelings of wanting to kill the mother, and the mother cannot contain those feelings so the baby can then contain them as opposed to splitting off from them because they are feared to be horrible, then the baby does not develop the capacity to have access to these primitive preconceptions because they were never part of the baby's repertoire of acknowledged experience. The baby split off from them because the mother was not able to contain them. The problem that further develops is that the baby does not have access to thought that is based on the containment of emotional experience, or to sensory experience, which the baby splits off from so as not to experience pain. The problem here is the mother's ability to be able to contain what may be experienced as painful feelings, so the baby feels safe in containing them. When the baby contains them the baby has access to both emotional experience and a sensory experience which helps the baby recognize that emotional experience which then helps the baby contain it's mind as opposed to evacuate its mind. If the baby evacuates its mind because it becomes oblivious to the sensory experience that would connect to emotion and evoke thoughts, then the baby does not develop the capacity to think as thinking links up to emotional experience. Hence you have a baby who projects painful experience via a process that may be referred to as violent splitting, of which the baby is afraid, and of which the mother is incapable of containing, which leaves the baby unable to have thoughts without thinking as they are evoked from sensory experience to emotional experience to having thoughts without thinking. Thus the baby grows up without having the capacity to think in a way that is connected to experience or in a way that the baby can learn from experience. Hence we have Melanie Klein's definition of the paranoid-schizoid position from whence forth this problem can begin to be thought about.

To provide a "corrective emotional experience" in terms of providing the kind of experience that will cure the problem on a sustained basis, the problem of mothering during the initial mother-child relationship must not be perpetuated by the therapist. Otherwise the emotional experience is not corrected nor is the problem of the evacuation of thought by the adult still responding at the infant level, altered.

I can recall an instance where I failed at providing proper mothering by inappropriate acting out-as it felt as if I could not stand what the patient was projecting, and it knocked me right off my therapeutic seat. This only increased the panic of the patient. The patient, whom I was seeing four times per week for about a year at this time, projected an emotional experience that left such a heaviness in my chest I could barely breathe and in addition, felt a kind of panic like someone who was drowning. Instead of making an interpretation to the effect "I think you are trying to show me how it is to feel so deeply depressed and so panic stricken about feeling helpless to do anything about it, or even that I might not be able to tolerate the extent of it, that you feel you could jump right out of your skin." This interpretation would have demonstrated to the patient that I not only understood him, but could contain the worst of it, thereby detoxifying the fearful experience itself.

However, I was not able to respond in such a way and got up from my chair to open the window and take a breath of fresh air, as if to say, I am as panicked as you are about your situation. It is this kind of interpretation on a consistent basis, one after another in the emotional line of fire, without the therapist getting knocked off the therapeutic seat so as to intensify the fear of the patient, that makes a corrective emotional experience possible-especially with narcissistic personality disorders. Of course, therapists are going to miss some of them, but the greater the consistency, the more likely the corrective emotional experience will take place. As opposed to a response of opening the window, or a direct response such as "Whatever the hell you are doing, I can't breathe. Knock it off." This kind of interpretation brings in the aspect of empathy, which helps the narcissist feel understood and helps the pathology congruently disappear. That is, congruently disappear in conjunction with the quality of the corrective emotional experience that is being provided.

With the narcissistic patient the therapist may initially begin working at four or five times per week, and the problem of narcissism itself-the desire for the perfect image may enable the therapist to be able to set the minimum conditions of the work successfully. Further, the contact becomes solidified through successive sessions and if the work is being done correctly, the therapist has the conditions set under which the job can take place.

It is more difficult to gain conditions to do this job with the borderline patient, who has a desire to be emotionally held but is so fearful of dependence, and evacuates thought almost at the speed at which it occurs, so the accumulation of experience that is substantial remains unknown to the borderline patient for a long time into the treatment. Thus, the problem of how to set the conditions of the treatment. You need to leave it up to the patient, telling the patient "You are the boss. You can hire and fire me whenever you choose." In this way the borderline patient gets what they need in terms of the function you provide for them, but do not feel frightened by dependency, because they are in charge of frequency, and whether or not they see you at all. With these patients you may see them once per week or preferably twice per week, until or maybe not, the substance of what exists between the therapist and patient motivates deeper work. In such cases the therapist must be particularly careful to have no desire for cure beyond the desires of the patient. Otherwise patients feel entrapped and will rebel out of the therapy.

The problem of containment needs to be approached differently with the borderline. They can stand and respond to a confrontational approach that evokes and accesses primitive thoughts that occur behind the conversation or material being presented by the patient. The confrontations and solidness of the therapist are most important and need to occur with great frequency as a way to restore the minds of these patients because they have little or no access to a mindfulness that would let the substance of the therapeutic experience make impact in any other way.

With impulse disorders, or character disorders who for one reason or another have gotten to your office, the most important notion is the frame or minimum conditions itself. That is, the therapist needs to solidly set down the minimum conditions of the treatment-you come so many times per week and you pay so much money. That may be the only stabilizing force in the patient's life, and if that gets disrupted the therapy is over.

With obsessive compulsive personality disorders there is a problem of space. That is they only have tunnels between the ears, and if you say something outside of the particular tunnel they are in, they are gone mentally, or relatively unaffected by anything you say or do. The problem of empathy here is for the therapist to be able to make longwinded interpretations based on a pacing and sensory perceptive experience of the therapist that both slows down the pace of the obsessive so they cannot run over the surface of their experience and be as crazy at the end of the analysis as at the beginning of it; and further, to create a kind of space through this sensory perceptive pacing and constancy of it, that permits the feared material to gradually begin to emerge via the gestalt analytic experience and interpretation.

With the schizophrenic, empathy looks quite different in that the therapist must in addition to providing a constant and warm object, which might actually frighten the borderline patient, have to be able to interpret absurdly in sync with the patient's experience at the unconscious and primitive levels. Here is where the therapist can use the first person and say, when a patient refers to a person with whom he is having difficulty, "If it were me I would enjoy the fantasy of boiling the son of a bitch in oil!". In this way, you go first, so it becomes permissible for the schizophrenic after awhile to have the same kind of thought and enjoy it. The enjoyment removes the craziness aspect of the psychotic thinking problem, as it becomes acceptable to have the thought as a result not only of the therapist's containment of the feared emotional experience, but the therapist's actually going first. Being able to deal absurdly, crazily and paradoxically in the ongoing flow of experience is critical to not getting hung out to dry when working with the schizophrenic. On the other hand if you went first with a narcissistic personality disorder, that is sharing yourself in a way that showed vulnerability or blemish from the perfect image of narcissus, they would use it to boil you in oil. With the narcissist you must maintain your therapeutic seat, and with the borderline, of distinction between doctor and patient or therapist and patient, to an impeccable degree. Humanity comes in the form of caring enough to develop your capacities to be able to do so. Humanity with the schizophrenic is more of how humanity is ordinarily thought about in terms of utilizing self disclosure. If the cult, or the gestalt cult as it may be, does not draw clear lines between doctor and patient, the therapist is at a clear disadvantage in terms of providing a corrective emotional experience in that it is more difficult to maintain therapeutic neutrality where it is required to do the job. Particularly with the borderline, if you don't know how to use therapeutic authority in a way that commands respect, and makes the separation of generations clear, they don't take you seriously. And with the narcissist you are doing a kind of precise mental surgery that one would expect of the most talented plastic surgeon. There is little room for error, although when you do make an error, the therapeutic technique as well as the human aspect of admission of the mistake, gives the narcissist the opportunity to forgive you and you are providing a corrective emotional experience that the parent could not provide, because the parent of the narcissist could not admit to mistakes.

Then there is the patient who is so concrete, so obsessive, so depressive and so overwhelmed, that the patient projects this mass of unfortunateness upon you unrelentlessly and all at one time. With the focus, always on the quality of being of the patient and the therapist, and in maintaining the life force moment by moment in the here and now, the therapist must be able to respond with the fullness of being and with force and tenacity equal to the patient's negative force. When patients have this self-massacre tied to the failure to meet external criteria they have set up for themselves, it is important that the interpretations be made with a fullness of being that continually works on forcing a detachment of being from doing on the part of the patient. If you are tenacious with this method, you hardly ever have to use it for more than several minutes at a time because the patient feels calmed down and secure in knowing that the quality of being and life force of the therapist is stronger than the death instinct of the patient. Tenacity is the key here, particularly when what the patient projects makes you feel like giving up, because that is exactly how they feel. So the spirit of the therapist is most important in helping the therapist to interpret as fast and as ferociously as possible so the life force can be consistently maintained.

The basis for being able to do this kind of work lies in the therapist's capacity to recognize and detoxify experience that is unnatural, or experience polluted by organismic disgust, moment by moment in the here and now in an unbroken continuum of experience. It is such an experience that has the best opportunity of providing a corrective emotional experience. This requires the therapist knowing and being able to utilize as much therapeutic methodology as is possible to maintain the life force for the full fifty minute hour over a number of hours and a number of years. The key to being able to do this, as Fritz Perls began with, was being able to know what your sense experience is from moment to moment on finer and finer levels of discrimination, and realizing where these are projections of the patient that must be contained by the therapist and put back to the patient in a way that helps the patient contain the painful split off sensations, and thereby the feared emotional experience, which gives the patient access to primitive preconceptions as opposed to being stuck with a mind that evacuates thought.

My own method of sensory perception works as follows. If I experience pain on the sides of the temples I usually mention it asking the patient to focus in. Whether they notice it or not, the focusing of attention in that area usually takes away the projected splitting off of painful sensory experience. I then look for the primitive preconception, homicidal thought, or existential anxiety that created the pain. This helps the patient contain the emotion, the sensory experience, and link up with the thought that was being evacuated. If I notice stomach nausea my association, utilizing the same method to facilitate moment to moment containment by the patient, is with lying to oneself, and organismic disgust. It actually feels like the patient is projecting a slight feeling of vomitus. Pain in the center of the stomach, right around the solar plexus refers to conflict. I ask, on the one hand and then on the other, so patients contain the sensation while discussing both sides or the conflict. Also, in terms of analysts' interest in empathy, this provides the closest thing to a <u>near experience of the patient as is technically possible</u>. That is, if you are on time with this_method, you are about one second behind the thing in itself,-that is, the actual experience of the patient, and are privy to the information much before the patient is able to go through the process of reowning sensory experience, which helps to reown and contain emotional experience, which links up to having thoughts without thinking as a result of access to primitive preconceptions. So it is the highest form of empathy that is technically possible to achieve.

The extent to which you can use the method initially, or throughout the work, must take into consideration the part of the patient that wants to meet the image of what the patient thinks the therapist wants the patient to be, or take into consideration Fritz Perls comment, "Until then, beware of both extremes, perfectionism as well as instant cure". When I asked a patient who was a year into the treatment about her thoughts and feelings regarding this method she said that she felt like a catcher of sensations, and motioned as if to reach out the way one would catch flies. I asked her how that was for her. She said it was fine, and that the only thing she had to be careful about was not letting that hook into the crazy part of her. By that she meant the part that would either feel inadequate at the inability to do it perfectly, or might not please me, if that is what she was up to finding out how to do. Of course, that is somewhat of a problem with all patients and must be analyzed as it occurs so as to free the patient and be able to proceed with the work.

All the methods I have indicated in the section on containment can facilitate such freedom so the patient can work at the highest level of achievement and development as possible. I think the method I am proposing does indeed offer that possibility, and with it the capacity to restore gestalt therapy to what Fritz Perls had hoped it to be-a Whole Therapy.

In that one of the jobs I feel psychoanalysis must learn to succeed at is the "Igniting and sustaining of a nuclear self" that Kohut wrote could not be done, I am including a short section of how I used what I then referred to as hypnotic storytelling, but in retrospect may have only involved my making long winded interpretations such as Bion did both at his presentation at the Franz Alexander Memorial Award evening and in the twelve hours of tapes in which I heard him supervising Dr. Salenger. In other words the primary difference between Bion's interpretations and Ericksonian Hypnotic Storytelling was the length of the uninterrupted storytelling or interpretation. They were both made at the same s l o w pace Margaret Mead told Erickson she had only heard in a rare African tribe relatively free of disease. That is why I have included this brief section for consideration by psychoanalysts, in that those who view it from a hypnosis point of view are basically quick fixers who never would and never could develop the self-discipline to do the work. Erickson was not like this. He was as dedicated as Bion. The problem was with everyone else in hypnosis. So this is not an article for hypnotists in that it would be useless to them. It is an article for psychoanalysts to consider some possibilities of expansion of technique to expand upon their capabilities to do certain kinds of psychoanalytic jobs that cannot currently be done.

IGNITING AND SUSTAINING A NUCLEAR SELF THAT HAS THE CAPACITY TO THINK THROUGH HYPNOTIC STORYTELLING

by

LEN BERGANTINO, ED.D., PH.D.
450 N. Bedford Drive, Ste. 300
Beverly Hills, CA 90210 (1981-1991)
Private practice of clinical psychology specializing in psychoanalysis and Ericksonian hypnosis.

ABSTRACT

There are a sizeable number of patients who are dedicated people who have shown up in my office after a seven year analysis without being able to sustain an ignited nuclear self that has the capacity to think; or that have not cured the underlying psychotic thinking disorder that accompanies the borderline personality disorder. Through prior gestalt, transactional analysis and psychoanalytic exposure the issues involved in the igniting and sustaining of a nuclear self were taken into consideration in the utilization of Ericksonian hypnotic storytelling to ignite and sustain a thinking well-functioning nuclear self in a surprisingly short period of time.

In his last book before his death, Dr. Heinz Kohut, when dealing with the question, 'Does Analysis Cure?', wrote of the difficulty in treating borderline and psychotic personality disorders. Basically, he wrote that analysis did not cure because the task at hand was both to ignite and to sustain a nuclear self when the defenses of the patient were so significant that he couldn't imagine any patient that would be willing to tolerate the breaking down of those defenses even if the work could be done.[1]

Gestalt therapy has focused on the igniting and sustaining of that nuclear self with its emphasis on being and/or the enactment of being. However, the emphasis has been so one sided that gestalt therapy has done little to deal with the underlying psychotic thinking disorder that accompanies or is the consequence of a patient having a nuclear self that has never been developed, or perhaps no nuclear self at all.

Transactional Analysis attempted to deal with the thinking functions when they defined the work in terms of adult ego state, parent ego state and child ego state, whereby there would be a significant degree of work to build an adult ego state that could think. They appropriately integrated gestalt methods to focus on the being or ignition and sustenance of nuclear self. The problem is with the split loyalties to being and thinking, when TA therapists themselves were basically trying to cure others of a problem of which they had not cured themselves, the nuclear self was not sustained in a way where the core of one's being is sustained in a personally enriched way. Thus, they have begun to look for a union with James F. Masterson, M.D., who has written extensively regarding working with borderline personality disorders, and has been the guest speaker at some of the larger TA conferences.

While TA and gestalt help people become better off than they were, and perhaps psychoanalysis, too; I think Dr. Heinz Kohut put his finger very honestly on what is a nightmare for the patient psychotherapy population of our universe, that a patient, who pursues psychotherapy in good faith, has one helluva time getting cured because the state of the art has not been as such to either ignite or to sustain a nuclear self that could then think and feel as a whole person.

I had years of gestalt therapy and training and I am a clinical member of the International Transactional Analysis Association. I now practice psychoanalysis and have found methods of which I am writing which are based upon Bergantino's work that do get the job done igniting and sustaining a nuclear self that can think and feel. But the conditions for such treatment are five times per week over five to seven years, a rather lengthy and extensive undertaking. This background and my prior experience is what I think makes the report of the following unique single case so extraordinary in its results.

A woman was referred to me by an excellent psychotherapist who was stuck in his work and reported to her that he could not help her over the hump. He sent her to me with the understanding that she was still seeing him once per week, but it was alright with him if she chose to work with me exclusively, or see both of us. He said that he felt due to my wide variety of technical skills he thought I might be able to get her over the hump. (I realize this offer is fraught with many psychoanalytic problems psychotherapy may view differently albeit inadequately.

When she came in I saw a woman about fifty who looked very masculine. She was tortured and hated herself. She felt she could not succeed at anything and tortured and hated herself for failing. She had been to many therapists, all of whom had failed, she felt, because she was a hopeless case.

When I tuned into my senses there was a projected pressure on both temples that felt as if it kept crushing her head and making it impossible for her to think. I thought, it would be particularly important to hold that space open between her temples without that crushing pressure for long periods of time, in order to get a released state of being from the pressure. Further, the outcome of this pressure was that she could not think. In TA terms one might describe this psychotic or borderline situation by saying that the parent ego state, the adult ego state and the child ego state were all engulfed within a sleepy child ego state. In other words, there was not an ignited nuclear self nor a sustained one.

The method I chose was Ericksonian storytelling at a very slow pace which Margaret Mead told Dr. Milton H. Erickson, she had only experienced in a rare African tribe the was relatively free of disease. Further, I told her that I would need to see her for two hour sessions because I had an instinct that it would take at least two hours at a time of keeping that crushing pressure around her temples from destroying her to make an impact.

I knew she was going to watch and be critical of every move I made and I had a sense that she would destroy the hypnotic work in this way if the frame were not appropriately set. So I told her I wanted her to watch every move I made, that she would be somewhat anxious and uncomfortable and that she at the end of the hypnotic work would not be certain that any hypnosis at all took place, but that her unconscious mind would have understood everything I have said and begin to cooperate in ways that would make her succeed and be successful in life in all the ways she had imagined.

When she came out of trance after this first fifty minute session, she reported that she was uncomfortable, critical of herself and me, and that she didn't know whether or not she was hypnotized or if the work did any good at all. I said, "You are an excellent hypnotic subject. You have succeeded at doing exactly what I requested. In fact, you are the only person I have ever worked with who has been able to maintain such a polarization throughout the work of having your unconscious mind understand everything, without knowing that it knows, while your conscious mind was able to maintain a state of irritability at the particular pace at which I was speaking."

An honest statement of a more usual nature which I thought was 'I can't believe you didn't experience relaxation at that pace over fifty minutes in that nearly everyone I have previously worked with has done so.' So I could see why she was so concerned about failing and being hopeless because the phenomena she presented me was among the worst I had experienced. But I reframed it in a way where this tragedy was turned into a victory-a success, of what an extraordinary patient she was to be able to do that, and she was as I had never seen anyone do it quite that way before.

There were two more sessions of two hours in length where the focus was on keeping the sensory pressure off of the temples while telling stories at a slow pace that had the intended focus of building a personality through reparenting in the areas of competition, success, femininity and extending the capacity of the adult ego state to think by having her focus her attention two hours at a time (100 minutes) so as to take her out of that sleepy child ego state. So the building of an adult ego state through extended attention while the pressure was off the temples registered in her unconscious mind in a way that she could hypnotically use to recreate the psychophysiological state that existed in the office and use it by herself. Further, the connection was of such impact between us during this kind of work, that I was "counting on a subject-object merger," and that she could continue to take my voice with her and it would be there as she needed it. (Kohut had written of such a merger in "How Does Analysis Cure?"

I expected things would go well as I have confidence in my work and trust the unconscious minds of the patient implicitly in terms of the help they want, basically seeing it as a job of my creating the correct therapeutic environment in which change can take place. BUT IN ALL HONESTY IN MY WILDEST MEGALOMANIACAL THERAPEUTIC FANTASIES I WOULDN'T HAVE DREAMED IT WOULD HAVE OR COULD HAVE GONE AS WELL AS IT DID!

When she came in for her fourth session which was her third two hour session she looked very beautiful which she acknowledged was from the inside out. She felt very feminine and beautiful inside. However, I did notice that this was the state of affairs from the waist up and there was still a dead looking quality from the waist down. However, she was no longer in that sleepy child ego state. There was a functioning adult ego state, and to my surprise, she was able to sustain a nuclear self over two hours and work at a thinking capacity equal to and better than most people I was seeing five times per week. I was dumbfounded by what I was experiencing as I did not think such a radical change possible.

She described it by saying that the slow pace allowed her to slow down and wait for a thought to occur so she could begin to hear her own thoughts, and that my voice, and the pace at which I spoke went with her in a way that she could recall to ignite herself and at this slow pace of allowing the next thought to occur she could also sustain herself.

During this session, she was quite productive in an analytic sense and described her work and power as going into her art work. I told her I knew a ventriloquist who put all of his power and personality into the dummy and asked her if she had any ideas about how he might regain his power. She said, 'by destroying the dummy'. I said, 'that is what he did, but can you think of a friendlier way to do it?' For example, I said, "When Freud was at a scientific meeting in 1903 and presented a paper one of his brighter colleagues figured out what he was talking about with all this oedipal and Electra stuff, and he shouted out, "This is not a matter for a scientific convention, it is a matter for the police!" Well, things may appear to be more liberal today, but at the most primitive levels, perhaps they are not. Now how would it be instead of putting all your gut level tummy power into your art work you put only vaginas and penises into your art work". As I kept on with this she began to feel the energy of the nuclear self return to the lower half of her body and she had a sense of sexual vitality about her that she sustained for the remainder of the session, on a thinking and feeling capacity, both.

The issues we explored at that point were whether she would return to her therapist which she was going to do because she had a strong emotional relationship with him and felt she needed continued work at that level to help her with relationship problems, and whether the work here hypnotically had gotten her to a place where she was over the hump in being able to work with him, or whether she would be stuck with him and needed further analytic work with me to expand her capacities to think while sustaining a nuclear self, or whether the hypnotic hearing of my voice at a pace that let her thoughts continue to occur to her would be enough and she could legitimately fire both of us and be able to function well on her own.

I thought all her questions were good ones and do not at this time know the answer. But again, I can only say that I was most surprised and hopeful in what Ericksonian storytelling at a slow pace that extends the attention span of the adult ego state can do in both igniting and sustaining a nuclear self that has the capacity to both think and sustain feeling, in a very short period of time. The fact that I had a working knowledge of TA and had a sustained nuclear self that was ignited throughout the work are variables that I think were critical to the success of the work, in that without this prior gestalt, TA and psychoanalytic background I may not have known which corners to turn when in the storytelling and may not have been able to create the sense of a subject-object merger with someone who was already ignited and sustained for the patient.

Nevertheless, I am describing a method that if it takes what has gone before it, and the quality of being of the therapist into account, has the possibility of answering Kohut's question in the affirmative-Does Analysis Cure! And perhaps, does Hypnotic Storytelling Cure! in that a nuclear self might be both ignited and sustained in a relatively short period of time. As to whether this is all the work that is necessary, or whether it can help make successful psychoanalytic patients out of those that were thought to be hopeless, is yet unknown, but the material here certainly merits further exploration if we are to have a body of therapists who are to give the therapeutic patient population a fair crack at coming out of this alive!

REFERENCE

Kohut, H. How does analysis cure? The University of Chicago Press, Chicago, 1984, pp. 8,9.

POSTSCRIPT

Two weeks after I had last seen the patient I received a telephone call from the referring doctor telling me that their was a dramatic change in the patient and that she had mentioned that she may return in the future for she could now see a vision of what was possible.

CARL WHITAKER, M.D.'s INFLUENCE UPON ME AS I APPLIED IT TO PSYCHOANALYSIS AND THE TRAINING REQUIRED TO BECOMING 'O'.

I am going to write this intro meaning no disrespect in the spirit with which Carl Whitaker trained me. The kind of freedom I exemplify when I write is required in terms of being able to work with

1.\ Primary Process
2.\ Primitive Mental States
3.\ The Underlying Psychotic Core of the Personality That Bion's Work was concerned about.

Carl Whitaker was a crazy bastard. All the fuck he ever thought about was homicide, suicide, incest, and being boiled in oil and eaten by cannibals. He once told a story about a farmer and his son. The son said, "Dad, I'm going over the hill and get me a wife." The father said, "Good, son, how long will you be gone?" The son said, "A couple of days, dad." The father said, "Good, son, I'll see you when you return." When he returned the father said, "Well, where is she son?" The son said, "Well, Dad, I found her but she was a virgin." The father said, "Good, son. If she wasn't good enough for her own family she wasn't good enough for us!"

As crazy as Whitaker was he was convinced I was crazier than he was. I was just twice as fast. Then again, he never saw a speeding bullet before. Being trained by Whitaker reminded me of the Harold Robbins movie "The Betsy". Money, Sex, Power! Robbins had the formula to sell books and write movies. Whitaker had the formula for staying alive among barbarians. That is family members, or the nice little psychotics next door, or the narcissistic and borderline personality disorders in your practice. Most of all he loved schizophrenics. He claimed he was one and always wished he had the courage to become a homosexual every time he used that as an entree to the latent homosexuality in the family. He had a lot of balls of a sort in that he made problems bigger than they were when you got there. His idea was that you had to be able to create chaos and anxiety and make the problems bigger to get the sexual heat going. He was very Freudian in a way. That is, for a family therapy situation which is an absolute son of a bitch to mobilize and isn't long enough to work through an oedipal situation, you get pretty torrid! One time Whitaker had a male patient sit on his lap and he fed him a baby bottle with a nipple full of milk. Other times he fell asleep during a session. He worked more by organic time than a fifty minute hour. He bragged about being untrained and not contaminated by the culture bind, which I loved and hated about him because you got all the pluses and all the minuses of knowing such a character. One time he was chairman of the Department of Psychiatry at Emory University and was fired for having all the M.D. interns go through group therapy. That was 1956. People didn't know M.D.'s were nuts then. Carl became a paranoid son of a bitch after that and he was always on the lookout as to who was going to whack him. Although, as I said, He had a lot of balls. One of his patients threatened him that one of these days he was going to be standing in front of a urinal and he was going to get a shiv in his back. Whitaker bragged until the day he died about all the times he stood in front of urinals, took a piss, and never got a shiv in his back. Of course there was the time he worked with John Warkentin, M.D., at the Atlanta Psychiatric and a patient threatened to kill Whitaker. Whitaker was terrified. He got up from his session and knocked on Warkentin's door telling him it was urgent that he come to Whitaker's office, that he needed help with a patient. Warkentin was a bit annoyed at having to disrupt his own session, but he came. Warkentin said, "What's the trouble Carl?" Whitaker said, "This patient wants to kill me!" Warkentin looked away and thought for a moment, then he said, "I've often wanted to kill the son of a bitch myself." That created a release in the patient, Warkentin went back to his office, and Whitaker went back to work. The first time I met Whitaker he demonstrated his style of work and I was working on my book, "Psychotherapy, Insight and Style: The Existential Moment" for which Whitaker later wrote the foreword and one helluva pre-publication review. So I said to him, knowing that he worked with Tom Malone, M.D., at Atlanta Psychiatric, "Dr. Whitaker, you have just demonstrated your style of work and I know you worked at Atlanta Psychiatric. I wonder if you would demonstrate what Tom Malone's work was like." Whitaker looked up in the air for a moment, then said, "Tom Malone was catatonic, but I think you ought to look him up. He has something to offer you." It was one of those things that left me feeling, "What the fuck did he mean by that?" "Does he think I'm catatonic? Why the hell does he think Malone has something to offer me when he thinks Malone is catatonic?"

The first time I did co-therapy with Whitaker the process you see me writing here which is a one time through free flow of my unconscious, primitive and primal unconscious as evoked in me by working with Whitaker, was not there. I sat there like a bump on a log following the couple one step at a time. After I learned to tap in at this level, only the unconscious work of Bion and Erickson remained of interest to me of all the other kinds of training I have had. When I work this way, with I'm unique individuals when I do and did psychoanalysis, as Bion put it, "I can hardly wait to hear what I am going to say." George Bach, Ph.D. who trained me once said, "Len Bergantino, you have the most unusual talent." I said, "What's that George?" He said, "You can say the most awful things to people and get away with it!" The reason I can work this way and stay fresh and alive is that I am always in deep contact with the inner core of my being and the inner core of the patient's being if that is reachable at all. Thus, no matter what I say or do at some level they feel I am with them as no other has been before. Again, this is 1995, and some of what I have included is from 1979 and 1983-1987. Thus, all the written work is not at the same power level, but perhaps that is just as well for those who are along the road and taking the journey.

Perhaps the greatest lesson I learned from Carl Whitaker was to be paranoid in the face of my own naivety. This is the psycholitagatory 90's, where psychoanalysis as well as other sports of the Roman Coliseum are as much controlled by the attorneys as they are by our own profession, which was bad enough.

(1994) This was the last time I saw Whitaker, as he had a stroke after this and died a year later. Example, a patient calls. (This is not exact dialogue, but comes out of my unconscious as I write two years later. Conference was 1992 or???3

1st Place Call

Whitaker: Why did you call me?

Patient: A colleague told me you were good.

Whitaker: What makes you think you can trust them?

Patient: They are usually pretty reliable.

Whitaker: You know, I'm really not looking for new patients.

Patient: Dr. Whitaker, it is important that I see you.

Whitaker: I have a lot of failures and I don't know if I could take one more.

Patient: I really wouldn't be that kind of patient.

Whitaker: I have a lot of blood spilled over the years and they all said that. I don't know, maybe you ought to call somebody else.

Patient: I don't want anybody else.

Whitaker: You mean I'm stuck with you. I sure hope it's not the wrong decision. God only knows the mistakes I've made.

Whitaker worked on not being anxious to get new patients because you never know who you will get and what they might bring you (the group was discussing potential lawsuits and how to protect themselves).

This is not too dissimilar to Bion in that people had to fight their way into analysis with him. It was always Bion's view that he wondered whether or not he could afford to spend time with that particular patient. He had a set of minimum conditions under which he would do an analysis. Whitaker did that with families. The examples I gave I transposed to how he might have or would have done it with individuals. The main thing I am trying to get across is that it was from Whitaker that I freed up my trust of my primitive unconscious so that I can go with it on the spot-tolerate the chaos and anxiety-open the space (same as Bion's psychoanalytic interpretations only Bion's are more elegant in style)-and do so with tremendous speed in the moment. This gives me the capacity to not get murdered nearly all the time when doing psychoanalysis, and a good deal of the time when doing family therapy. However, families are tougher not to get murdered because you have more primitive transferences going haywire at the same time.

When I trained in the therapeutic use of self, and/or the??? Understudy at Wentworth Castle-Sheffield England 1986 Therapeutic

Wizardry of Dr. Len Bergantino, there were three parts to the training. First, was the Ericksonian Storytelling to create a transformation of being; second, the mock family therapy demonstrations as influenced in me by Whitaker for the EXPRESS PURPOSE OF SPEEDING UP THE ACCESS, LIBERATION AND RESPONSIVENESS OF THE PRIMITIVE UNCONSCIOUS; AND BECOMING 'O' with my full depth and substance and extra-sensory perception, to expand the psychoanalytic concepts of Wilfred Bion into the advancement of psychoanalytic technique at levels of discrimination that had never before been seen or experienced. WHITAKER'S MOCK FAMILY THERAPY IS A CRUCIAL SECOND STEP TO THE TRAINING OF A PSYCHOANALYST EVEN IF THEY NEVER DO FAMILY THERAPY. IT DEALS WITH THE OEDIPAL SITUATION IN VIVO AND CALLS FOR A RESPONSE IN THE MOMENT, MOMENT AFTER MOMENT, WHICH IS THE SINA QUA NON OF SUSTAINING THE EFFORT TO BECOME 'O' AND NOT HAVE THE LIFE FORCE MURDERED OFF.

The following section entitled ABSURDITY, CRAZINESS, PARADOX AND THE LIBERATION OF THE PSYCHOANALYST AND THE FAMILY THERAPIST was primarily written for family therapists. It is taken from a transcription of an audio tape of a mock family therapy session at a convention of the American Psychological Association in Toronto, Canada in 1984.

While the previous pages show the freewheeling style without academic or cognitive explanation, this section breaks up the feeling tone of the primitive unconscious flow to analyze the nature of the responses in that the reader will get an academic understanding as well as an experience of the process. Again, while this method certainly can be used to do family therapy (and by 1987 I was fast enough and powerful enough in the work that I found co-therapists a total pain in the ass to work with because they for the most part hadn't worked through the paranoid schizoid position themselves, (so I did family therapy myself), this is a critical step in the training of a psychoanalyst who hopes to make a difference in working with the underlying psychotic core of the personality as written about by Bion.

My feeling about the following session, is that it's not a bad session, and it's not a great session. However, it is a session that I have transcribed and a process of understanding is provided that I think is valuable to the book as a whole.

ABSURDITY, CRAZINESS, PARADOX AND THE LIBERATION OF THE PSYCHOANALYST AND THE FAMILY THERAPIST

written by
LEN BERGANTINO, ED.D., PH.D.
The Bergantino Institute of Family Therapy Training
10266 Kilrenney Avenue
Los Angeles, CA 90064

ABSTRACT

The purpose of this article is to both demonstrate the utilization of absurdity, craziness and paradox in the flow of family therapy dialogue and to clarify the split second thinking involved in the kind of responses made. This method provides the best opportunity to enhance the liberation of the therapist in the use of self, particularly in dealing with, metaphorically, the homicidal and suicidal nature of family interactions on a moment to moment basis. The particular value of the article is that it does much to teach a method that is quite difficult to learn.

Absurdity, craziness and paradox in the flow of dialogue prevents the life force from being murdered off in the patients as well as in the therapist. Particularly when working with families the ability or skill in doing this gives the therapist the best opportunity to be him or herself, and to reduce the chances of getting sucked into the family system of madness and increase the likelihood of escaping from the family chains when the therapist has been had. Also, when using the absurd, crazy and paradoxical way of working with a co-therapist, the ability to play off of the co-therapist and/or the ability of the co-therapists to play off of each other, further increases the chances of having an effective family therapy-that is, a family therapy where all members can be more of themselves and a spirit of liberation gets introduced into the family by the therapists that helps to create this freedom. This spirit of liberation is the only method I know about that helps families become less concrete in their way of relating, thereby creating more freedom and options for the members of the family to relate to each other in more enjoyable ways than they have presented to the family therapists at the first session.

Two things motivated me to write this article. First, nearly all of the therapists at the workshop I am going to use as an example (APA, Toronto, 1984, Division 43, Academy of Family Psychology Hospitality) said that my demonstration of this kind of work provided a spirit of liberation in themselves that left them feeling they would be better able to work in a liberated and spirited way with their patients; and second, I haven't seen many therapists who know how to do this work. Thus, the intention of this article is to take the reader through the step by step process of my responses at the workshop in order to examine the way I access my unconscious processes, the way I utilize sensory perception to enhance immediacy of response, and the importance of staying with the "I"; that is, of the therapist being able to stay in his or her own space and respond from that position as opposed to being distracted from one's own unconscious processes by the family members. If the family therapist cannot remain centered it would be very easy to get distracted and become a part of the family's madness, as opposed to being able to make clear interpretations based on the moment to moment quality of being of the family members as their sense of presence, or sensory presence as the case may be, evokes the unconscious mind of the therapist to interpret absurdly, crazily and paradoxically.

THE WORKSHOP BEGINS

I am being introduced and the description I wrote is being read to let the audience know about the experiential learning that was about to take place.

Moderator: (Alan Entin, Ph.D.-Richmond, VA, Whitehill trained him at U. of Wisconsin) And Len has presented in similar situations for the Academy in previous conventions. I'm sure it is something we will find very interesting. "Absurdity, Craziness and Paradox-Some patients are not amenable to secondary process interpretations. They are usually quite repressed, have a good deal of underlying hostility covered by 'niceness', and respond on primitive and primal levels much of the time with denial. Absurdity, paradox, and the 'craziness' of the therapist can be learned in the flow of dialogue as therapists are able to free their minds yet work in a disciplined way at these primitive and primal levels. Dr. Bergantino was mentored in this madness by Carl Whitaker-who has his utmost respect. And so we introduce the mad Dr. Bergantino-(gallows laughter) It's all yours.

My thoughts here are that the work hasn't even started, and the moderator tries to kill me on the first shot with a crazed gallows laughter as he introduces me that leaves me feeling handcuffed even before I begin. The point of the work is to get out of the handcuffs and not get murdered at all cost, otherwise both the life force of the people involved and the therapist are murdered off, and what Freud referred to as the death instinct will prevail.

Me: Well, thank you, I'll try to live up to your introduction and be as sane as I can today.

<u>My thoughts</u> are-at least I hit him back with one he didn't catch and it handcuffed him because I had the floor. It's important to win the battle for control. I'm telling him I'm going to be as sane as I can while I'm supposed to be giving a workshop on absurdity, craziness, and paradox. This is good because the audience doesn't quite know what to make of it and I have set the frame for working.

Me: I think that this technique that I was trained in all my life that Dr. Whitaker helped me along with is particularly useful when working with patients who are excellent at murdering off their own life force, and then murder yours??? (patients) off, or at least attempt to in the session. I find that when I center into my own space, tune into my own unconscious as soon as I can, and start winging it one shot after the other; it's a way to get yourselves out of the handcuffs forty nine minutes earlier. If I can stay out of the handcuffs and keep that life force consistent, the session is going to work. The family members are going to get what they need, and the individual members of the family will have the best opportunity to become free to be themselves in the family. The use of absurd, crazy and paradoxical interpretations are also quite useful when working with individuals, in particularly when you get a sense of things stagnating, or a feeling that whatever the patient may be doing has you handcuffed and you don't quite know what to make of it or what to do on a more conscious level of work. That is a sure sign that the life force is going under, and no matter what you do at the unconscious, crazy and absurd level, it will reinstate the life force of the work. Further, I have an implicit trust that once the life force is reinstated, whatever happens is going to be life enhancing. When a therapist trusts this process and makes absurd remark after absurd remark within a period of about five to ten minutes the space remains, open a characteristic trait of??? only Whitaker??? also Bion and Erickson. Also, when a patient is well defended the absurd, crazy and paradoxical interpretations in the flow of dialogue slip through the defense system and helps the patient or family system with movement. Once the interpretation slips through the defense system as "invades the unconscious" it is in there and there is no way to take it back or remove it. That is what keeps the pot boiling, increases the toleration of anxiety of the family members and creates more space for each family member to breathe and to be themselves.

Me: I would like to do a demonstration and then talk about it. (A therapist who attended the hospitality suite was getting out pots and pans, and making loud disrupting noises). (In a funny way, I tell her) DO THAT LATER! That's OK. (Group laughs) What I would like now is for a mom, a pop and two kids to get together and talk about a family dynamic and then come back as a family and let me work with you. (I am asking for volunteers who will role play a family.). We will do it experientially. Create some kind of family scenario in the next five minutes and then I will show you what I do. I think it's the best way to loosen things up.???While this is modern family-???

The Woman Who Was Banging The Pots And Pans: How heavy a problem do you want?

Me: No, yours sounds too heavy. (Group laughs) No, you could come in. (at which point another man in a stomach nauseating tone says, I'll join her.)

My thoughts are-isn't it interesting, those who are volunteering are the most difficult in the group and have the best chance to murder me off. BUT THAT'S THE SPORT OF IT, IF YOU'RE A WORKMAN! That is why I told her at the first sense that her problem was too heavy, and then invited her back in.

I thought, she already tried to kill me with the pots and pans and her next comment, 'How heavy a problem do you want'. Then the person volunteering to be the husband said, "I'll join her."

Me: That could be a problem. (My instant reaction was that he and her would mix as well as oil and water, even though it was only a demonstration with a mock family.)

My thoughts are-although I have only made a couple of responses the technique is beginning to unfold-to shoot as fast as I can from whatever goes through my unconscious mind moment to moment as it relates to the family. Two more volunteer. The girl will be called Suzy, although she is an adult therapist playing the part, as are the others. They are not leaving to rehearse.

Me: Do you want to rehearse, or do you want to take me on cold!

My thoughts are-let them know who is in charge from the start. I throw the comment out as a challenge, and also as a statement of confidence in my ability that I know what I am doing and I have enough power and skill to handle this group. Without knowing how to use this kind of authority families are likely to think the therapist is timid, and if they do, they will chew him up and spit him out.

Pop: Cold. (With a deadly coldness about him).

My thoughts are-this created so much anxiety in the group, that right from the outset the homicidal and suicidal nature of the family was being dealt with, that one of the moderators said, "How about coming closer so the tape will pick it up." He was requesting at the unconscious level, how about the family coming closer to me, or perhaps me to them, but on the other hand the fact they were willing to deal at the primitive levels showed they did have confidence in me to handle it.

Me: (to moderator) Jimmy, these people are ruthless. They're as cocky as I am.

My thoughts are-okay, I know I have issued a challenge to you to go for it at the bottom line level, and you have responded, and I accept the challenge. I think it helps in doing therapy if you have the spirit of a warrior and you love the smell of battle-the action-and if you hang in each step of the way using all the skill you have and all the cunning you have to utilize whatever resources are available where you sense strengths may be needed that you are short on at the moment, and then orchestrate a symphony that the family loves to be a part of, and if on a workshop basis, so does the audience. The payoff for the warrior is in the caring about the family, your work to become highly skilled helps them, and at the level at which you issue the challenge, and they respond, the only way you can survive is to come out a better therapist than you went in!

Me: I don't blame you. Families are crazier than therapists.

My thoughts are-I didn't know why I said this when I said it, and I didn't feel particularly solid or good about it. As I look at it in retrospect, I think I was a little taken aback, at just how bloody this whole thing might get. Now the mock family interview begins.

Me: Tell me what's happening. Why did you people come today? My thoughts are-Pop really chilled me. I referred to them as you people, and I think, unbeknownst to me at the time, I didn't like him and wished the hell someone else had volunteered. Although, I suppose I could have rejected his offer and selected someone else. But I didn't, and what is, is.

Mom: Well, I am having a lot of trouble with him. (One of the whiniest most complaining unpleasing voices I ever heard). He's been drinking again, and, I don't like the way he's treating Jeffrey, here. He really takes it out on Jeffrey. I think he is really afraid of how nice Jeffrey is growing up, (All in reference to Pop) and how good he is, and he's abusing him. And he's afraid he's losing-whatever, and I really think he's trying to kill (unfinished sentence)

Pop: How is he going to get civilized? How's he going to learn to live with the rest of us if we don't put Jeff in his place.

Mom: Jeffrey needs to feel (I cut her off)

My thoughts are-mom and pop are control mongers and they will keep control of the session and see that nothing happens as long as I let them, so the sooner I make an active intervention the sooner I will be off of my own passivity and take charge. Second, all the talk is about

Jeffrey, so he is going to get the rap for being the troubled one, or the identified patient about whom the family war would take place. Yet, Suzie didn't break into anybody's conversation. She was there looking quite depressed at the floor. Here I thought the best way to take control was to take the problem right out of their hands as they had thought about it, and Mom had used the word kill regarding Pop and Jeffrey, and then up the ante and family anxiety by expanding the problem as well as the family's ability to tolerate anxiety and chaos by bring out the family's homicidal-suicidal nature in regard to Suzie, whom they apparently were not considering. A further tipoff that I wasn't too far off was that on a sensory perception level I noticed the kind of depression that made it hard to breathe and it was coming from Suzie's direction. Always pay attention to whatever physical cues are being projected by one or many family members as being an accurate indicator of where the work should go, and then see what those sensory impressions evoke in your unconscious. For example, the sensory impression was a suffocating feeling in the chest. It was coming mostly from Suzie's direction. That sensory awareness then evoked the thoughts that it was Suzie who was suicidal, and that I could take back control of the session by going right there. Thus, I think it must be an integral part of the family therapist's training to develop this sensory awareness at very fine tuned levels, so that moment to moment, it is unlikely that the therapist will be lost for too long; and then, that the therapist will learn how to move from the reception of this external sensory perception to thought at the unconscious level, or level of primitive preconceptions, so that the family system can be dealt with through absurd interventions that create movement that permits members of that system to live, where they may be currently dying or stultified. This is different than a patient_who enters an analysis and over the course of five to seven years cures a thinking disorder at the psychotic level and has a corrective emotional experience, so that patient is no longer so personally troubled and so much trouble to everyone else. That is, providing of course, one finds an analyst who can successfully do that work. Melanie Klein referred in her writings to the paranoid-schizoid position and the work of the analysis would be to move from that grandiose position to the depressive position, which was a gradual toleration of reality, and that accounted for the feelings of accompanying depression as that reality came to be tolerated.

In family therapy it is quite a different matter. Each time the family meets it might be the therapist's last crack at them. So you don't have a group of family members who are going to work through the paranoid-schizoid position and get to the depressive position, where the feelings of homicide and suicide are much more contained and under control. You have a group of family members who are for all intent and purposes going to remain in the paranoid-schizoid position and if they are to have a family that is spirited; that is, a family that has a family spirit, can enjoy each other, and hang in together through the thick and thin of it, then they have to be able to relate to each other and deal with each other while they for the most part will continue to act out the repetition of primitive suicidal and homicidal behavior. Sartre perhaps made reference to this point when he said, "hell is others".

Thus, the point of family therapy is not to expect a family reconstruction of all the personalities in it, but a warmth with as many members of the family as possible, and a feeling of live and let live. Family members are going to have problems throughout their lives and there is no need to attempt to cure the entire situation. The critical thing is to keep the family heat or spirit going and get along with each other. Thus, it is also important to leave the family therapy door open when terminating as one would see a family doctor when needed. When reality kicks one or more family members at a later date they can always call the family doctor. Perhaps the primary job is to help reinstitute a faith in the family, and a spirit that will overcome the hopelessness that is based usually on fairly severe problems at psychotic-borderline, character disorder or schizophrenic levels. That is, how can the therapist at worst make interventions that make an unlivable situation livable for the family members, and at best relate to the family members in ways where the therapist's enjoyment of the family and it's members helps the family members learn to enjoy being with each other-for the most part, despite the lifetime characteristics of some of the members they feel have previously driven them mad. It is this type of redefining through the use of absurdity, craziness and paradox in the flow of dialogue that I think is the required skill of the family therapist to do the job.

Me: I think you two seem to be missing the main problem, though. Suzie, here, looks suicidal. How long has she wanted to kill herself.

My thoughts are-I don't ask this as a question, but make it as a statement that invades the unconscious and cannot be retracted in terms of what the family now has to deal with. It was an expansion of the problem based on my here and now experience of the family.

Mom: Well, she talks about it, but I think she talks about it because Annie in school talks about it.

Me: I don't know, it certainly looks like she could use the family juice. Jeff looks like Superman. How come he is getting it all. Poor Suzie, she's on her way out.

My thoughts are-again, to reinforce the redefinition of the problem and to expand it. Now it's a matter of where the family juice goes, referring to the family energy and caring. I'm pointing to the fact it all appears to be going to Jeff, and Suzie looks like she is emotionally starving to death.

Pop: She acts stupid, but I don't think she is suicidal.

Me: You're willing to risk it, eh. Well, it's one less mouth to feed.

My thoughts are-I'm going to make Pop take this seriously, and deal with the homicidal part of him that would not take his daughter seriously in this regard, that the family death wishes were being projected into her and she basically appeared to be defenseless against them (indicated by my comment regarding lack of juice) and offenseless in her lack of ability to dance through the minefields.

Mom: You seem very angry. I don't like the way you are talking.

Me: (Rather sarcastically) No, I'm not angry. I've got nothing better to do this hour.

Pop: You don't even know us and you are accusing us already.

Me: Accusing? (with surprise) You feel accused? Gee, I don't mean to. I was just telling you what I thought. Is that tough to say that in this family.

My thoughts are-don't take the accusation seriously. Mom and Pop tried to put me on the ropes for the knockout punch. At the time

I didn't feel any anger in myself, but I wasn't sure. But that wasn't the point. The point was, don't get killed, or the ballgame is over. In such situations I just maneuver and dance as fast as I can until I put the ball back in their court. I shifted it from their accusing me of being angry, to my accusing them of having a family where it may be impossible to say what you think. If one takes into consideration the stakes of the game here, suicide and homicide, then the only point is not to get boiled in oil so you can live to fight another fight-and continue to help the family be able to deal effectively with their suicidal-homicidal nature. Thus, when in a tight spot, the question of lying is irrelevant here. If the family accuses you of lying, just say, "I lie all the time. In fact, I hate people who tell the truth." This will give the liars in their family permission to lie, which they already do to maintain the homicidal-suicidal nature of the family, and once family members have permission to lie, it becomes easier to tell the truth. If there is confusion at this point, you can point out the difference between the truth and the lie.

Suzie: (Begins to weakly utter a few inaudible words).

Me: (Directly to Suzie) Is it tough to say what you think in the family?

Mom: (Cuts in by being concerned by smothering at the same time as if she really didn't want an answer to her question and says to Suzie) Is he telling the truth, or what?

Me: (Suzie does not respond, and I wait for a ten second pause) I probably wouldn't talk to them either.

My thoughts are-where Mom didn't know she wasn't really asking for an answer, but an agreement that this wasn't true-I said my thoughts as I experienced them which ran counter to the lack of freedom to do so in the family. This particularly gave support to Suzie.

Me: Sounds like a dangerous crew.

Jeff: They sure are. They are always fighting and forget about us. (Referring to himself and Suzie).

Me: You too.

My thoughts are-the provocation of the family members by commenting on what their existential situation appeared to be-'sounds like a dangerous crew', gives Jeff a feeling of enough support to speak.

Me: How do you see it, Jeff?

Mom: (cuts in) I'm very offended, Jeffrey. I don't want you to be like him. I want you to be different. I want you to make something of yourself.

Me: Yeah, but he might wind up like her, then.

My thoughts are-the unconscious message from Mom was I don't want you to be like him, which I thought was a seduction to be a homosexual. So I introduced the issue of homosexuality by referring to a generalized 'her' that Jeffrey might wind up like. Whether or not the family picks this up is not important here, only that when it was introduced at the unconscious level, I did not back off from it, and did slip it in unconsciously in a way that could not be retracted. It may be viewed as a territorial issue. One needs to win the battle for territory with the ground troops, to be able to carry on the battle at a later date.

Me: What's wrong with him? (Referring to Pop and saying it in a way that was friendly toward Pop.)

My thoughts are-even if you don't like somebody in the family initially, and whatever they do you feel drives you crazy, as it drives the other family members crazy, the point is not to get sucked in to responding like everybody else responds. The job of the therapist is to provide as much of a corrective emotional experience as possible. So wherever you can say something to connect, or something positive, do it. They may not take it, but do it anyway. This is also what I did when accused of being angry. Homicide and suicide are usually provocative of anger, but it is important to have a different kind of experience than what the family members hook for and usually get.

Jeff: You're always telling me what to do. I just can't take it.

Mom: Yeah, but you wouldn't be in this special school if I wasn't telling you what to do, and you wouldn't be getting such good grades either.

Jeff: You put your stock in those good grades. You don't understand me.

Me: It kind of reminds me, you know, the other day, I've got two little kids, I've got a three and one half year old son and a one and one half year old daughter and every once in awhile, you know, my wife, and she certainly has the best of intentions, and of course you know, being a mother is a very difficult job (while I am speeding the pace of my delivery up here almost in a schizoid manner). I understand that, and, eh, she wanted my son to do something and he didn't want to do it and she wanted him to do it and started trying to get him to do it, and all of a sudden it felt like gears grinding. And so he looked absolutely awful and I said to him 'Is mommy giving you a hard time again? He said, 'Yeah'. I said, 'Well, you could certainly enjoy the fantasy of stepping on her face.' And he broke out into hysterical laughter. You know, I think it's exactly what he was thinking. But he would have never said that, or had any way to free himself. But just the fantasy of it seemed to free him up. And then everything was OK between them two.

My thoughts are-where I speeded the pace up I was thinking of when I used to pitch baseball, and when you change the speed of the pitch, it throws off the timing of the batter. In this case, it is a good way to slip it through to the unconscious. I felt the best way to tell mother, that even though her intentions are good, and mothering is a difficult job, that mothers, and her in particular, can be a pain in the neck and at times induce homicidal fantasies in their offspring. Yet, I put it in a way that when the homicidal fantasies are given permission to exist, or possibly even be expressed, the basis for a reconnection has been established between mother and child. Putting it in this long winded metaphorical story has a way to handcuff the family to listen while the therapist is in control, and by the time they can figure out what to do to stop me it is already in the unconscious of the family members.

Mom: I don't really like what you are saying.

Me: I don't blame you.

Mom: You're telling him to step on my face.

Jeff: You don't like anything. Why can't you get along with people. Why can't you get along with Dad.

Mom: Because he drinks and he doesn't make enough money and I don't like what he is doing.

Jeff: You don't like anything about anybody.

Mom: That's not so, dear. I certainly like what you're doing in school and I like her. I don't know what's the matter with her. She never creates any problems. She's so quiet all the time. (Long pause)

Suzie: I really don't think Dad is so bad. Sometimes I think he drinks because it's so hectic at home; so crazy all the time (followed by anxious laughter for a moment).

My thoughts are-When mother said she didn't like what I was saying and I had already thrown in a zinger of a story, I felt it was time to kiss and make up (metaphorically speaking). So I said, 'I don't blame you.' In the meantime the family members got the unconscious message of the story and took their issues to Mom, not letting her put it back on me. The kind of responses I have been making have begun to create a liberated effect where family members, particularly those who were primarily seen and not heard from, have begun to say what was on their minds. But, you clearly don't stay at war with mom for very long, or the war is over and everyone has lost it!

Suzie: I just wish you wouldn't go out and drink. I just wish you would do something with us sometimes. (Said to Pop).

Me: Sounds like an invitation to come back in the family.

My thoughts are-wherever I see a moment of daylight, I'll take it. Family members at this stage of deterioration don't have much to build on, so wherever the therapist can find such a moment, it makes sense to go for it. You can always reverse tactics and try to focus on the hopelessness if the family members don't grab the positive and run with it, or even walk with it. But when there is a long pause, I give Pop an option to go either way by saying

Me: But I wouldn't leap into it.

My thoughts are-saying it both ways, and respecting the pause, when I say I wouldn't leap into it, he feels I understand him at this point and am respecting his position and how he feels.

Pop: They're not too much fun.

Me: No? How come?

Pop: There are always challenges like your fanny is being rubbed with sandpaper all the time. There is always irritation. From her (referring to wife)

My thoughts are Pop started to fade when speaking. There was a regressive sleepy quality, and secondly, there was some sort of a sexual vibration being projected. I felt it in my penis for just a moment. I learned to trust these moment to moment physical sensations as projected material of the patient. I thought Pop was cutting off from his sexuality by sleepy regressive feelings, so my comment, which appears to have come from out of nowhere, was based in a sensory experience that evoked these thoughts all in a moment.

Me: Sounds pretty sexy.

Pop: Not really, it's just not much fun.

My thoughts are-this guy and this relationship is even deader than I thought it was, but Pop's lack of appreciation for Mom sexually, especially when she got a rise out of him, isn't making things any better, so I'll try it again, even in the face of his hopelessness.

Me: (To Mom) It must be hard to wake him up, eh? I mean, you use sandpaper. That sounds pretty sexy, and this guy is going to sleep. (To Pop) You play enough with her.

Me: (To Jeff and Suzy) Don't you two counsel your parents about sex? How are they going to learn anything?

My thoughts are-sex is a taboo for the children to talk with the parents about, and here I have opened up another avenue. Again, once it's been said, they can't take it back. It breaks through a little bit more of the cement or concreteness.

Pop: You don't want to have sex with a rattlesnake. You never know when she is going to strike with her tongue.

Me: Gees, that sounds more exciting. (Group laughs and the environment becomes a bit warmer for a moment).

Pop: (Warm laugh) She is sexy but she is also negative (as he then turns negative again).

Me: Well, you can't have everything. You seem committed to isolation?

Mom: Yea, he is. He's left me to do the job all by myself. I don't get his help on anything.

Pop: I really get along very well with the kids when she is not around. We have our own communication. It's not as intense as we all might like, but I really am more comfortable when she is not around. With the kids, too. I believe they are, too.

Suzy: I wish Mom would go out more and do more things.

Mom: Well, I have all this housework to do.

Me: Sounds like the family wants mother to run away from home.

Jeff: Well, do something. Just stop telling me what to do all the time.

Me: She loves you. How else is she going to show it.

My thoughts are-reframe the unlikeable behavior as love, so mother can think well of herself. It is only if mother can feel good about herself that she may have the freedom and courage to do other than she is doing.

Suzy: I made a mistake about something. (Very timid voice)

Me: That's up to you, though. You're afraid to take your best shot, eh? Think she'll kill you, or what? Is she that tough, or she just intimidates you? I mean, look, she didn't like me and I got away with it. What are you guys complaining about?

My thoughts are-listen, family members, you are buying into an intimidation and protection game that isn't necessary, and I'm living proof that it isn't, because Mom didn't kill me-and she didn't like much of what I said. Again, these kind of comments are both affirmative to Mom in a backhanded way that doesn't make the other family members feel you are taking sides, even when you are. Mom doesn't know whether to be mad at you or not, and the family spirit becomes more liberated.

Jeff: You don't have to live with her.

Me: I've got enough trouble living with my own wife.

My thoughts are-this is the time for a humanistic statement to the effect that we are all in it together. "You live with your family and I'll live with mine."

Mom: I don't really think you can help us.

Me: You're probably right. You may be hopeless.

My thoughts are-no room for false sense of guilt, false sense of responsibility or false sense of power. I just put it right back in her lap.

Jeff: I don't even think you're trying. You're just sitting over there trying to make jokes out of what's happening.

Me: I don't think it's a joke. I just think you people are stuck in cement and I have a cement breaker.

Jeff: You're not even trying to help us. We came here for help.

Me: (While I was talking Jeff talked over me). You didn't hear what I said. Are you people always that deaf! I said you people are stuck in cement and I think I have a cement breaker, but I didn't think you would like it. But you know, who likes to take their medicine.

My thoughts are-my claim of having anything was a tactical error and I left myself open for trouble. I did come back in an intimidating way to them, which kept control. But then Jeff comes back at me where I left myself open.

Jeff: Well, what are you hiding it for. What's your cement breaker.

Me: Wow, he's throwing down the gauntlet.

My thoughts are-I could have come back and said the level of his stupidity or cement headedness prevented him from experiencing the cement breaker to this point, but "I can take no responsibility for blindness." However, I didn't have any spark to do it that way and felt it would turn out to be more interesting here to demonstrate how to use a co-therapist triangulate when in a tight spot. I have a particular love of playing off of a co-therapist. Now the problem was that I didn't have one and I wanted to use one, so began to talk to Jimmy as if he were one, figuring that after a bit he would either get the idea of what I was doing, or I would tell him. I had previously spoken to Jimmy twice on the telephone for about a total of five minutes, and had a sense that his heart was in the right place. Of course, this is always a chance because you never know the degree of homicidal or suicidal behavior on the part of the co-therapist selection until you are into the thick of it. So what I say about knowing him two years is an on the spot maneuver.

Me: Well, Jimmy and I have been doing co-therapy for a couple of years now. No, Jimmy, tell me, what do you think of these birds.

Mom: I don't know whether we ought to sit here while this person talks like that. I don't think he is a professional. He's not the kind of doctor I wanted to see.

Me: (Ignoring Mom, who didn't waste a moment in doing her best to go for the knockout) How do you size this situation up, Jimmy.

My thoughts are-a fresh perspective most always breaks the pattern, and if unsure about being sucked into the system at any given moment, it's much better to have access to work with a co-therapist triangulate so you can back out and have a look from the outside.

Jimmy: I think the problem you are having with this family is that you are not allowing them to do what is usual in this family. What is usual in this family is that Mama bitches about Papa, and every time she tries to bitch about Papa you interfere. When you let her bitch about Papa everything goes smooth. That's your problem. You've got a serious problem. Your problem is that you don't let Mama do her thing.

My thoughts are-I was a bit taken aback in that Jimmy went for the power right away to take a superior position over me, although I thought his comment, which they listened to, as when one therapist talks to another it is another way to slip it through to the unconscious. But, I did think Jimmy had a good heart, and if I needed to battle with him down the road I would just do it as part of the co-therapy.

Me: I see. So you think if you could help cure me with my problem, then it would get better

Jimmy: No, I don't think that. I think that what you need to do with this family, and I think you know how to do it, is to recognize how legitimate all of her complaints are. I mean here is a guy who drinks. I mean, just listen to the things she has told about him. I'll bet you that if you gave her a big sheet of paper like this and you told her to go home and let her write down all the gripes she has about this man that she is forced to live with and goes over it thoroughly and carries it with her every day before the next session so that every time that she can remember how awful he really is, she could write it down and then she could bring it in so that the whole family could see it, then maybe you'd begin to work on some of the things you need to work on.

Me: So you think she would really do that.

My thoughts are-it's clear here that Jimmy has an interesting angle, but his mistake is in trying to kill me off, so my simple question, do you think she would really do that puts him to the test. I need to use him but bump him off so my authority remains intact.

Jimmy: Ask her. You're the therapist. I'm only sitting outside looking in.

My thoughts are-Jimmy missed the point here due to his own cement headedness. The reason I wanted him was because he was outside looking in, but he didn't get it yet that I brought him in as a co-therapist. So now I may have made a bigger problem than I had with the family alone, having to deal with homicidal Jimmy, to boot.

Me: I'm asking you to be my co-therapist.

Jimmy: Yeah, well, that's the way I would do it. Don't you feel that we could really get to him and get down all the things he really needs to do to get this family going straight, then we could get somewhere.

Me: See, I don't know. I think you would still drive him out, though. (Mildly challenging tone, but subtlety forceful.)

My thoughts are-well, at least I've got it back to a conversation between two therapists about the family, which is what I wanted to do.

Jimmy: You think it would drive him out. Well, let's give him a sheet and have him do the same thing about Mama. Here, you make a list about Mama, and you make a list about Papa, and we ought to give the kids a list, too (as Jimmy hands out pieces of paper to the family members). Fill it up. The better you fill it up, the more we will have to work with.

Me: What's up Pop? You look like, another chore? What?

Pop: He's making it so hard, and it's hard enough, and he's making it harder.

Jeff: (Rethrows the gauntlet) How is this going to help.

My thoughts are-Well, Jimmy really got himself in a fix, but now I can get to see the fix from the outside as opposed to the inside. Also, I thought the family was ganging up on him because I was able to stay out of the trap longer than him and in their search for a messiah they thought I was a better bet and did not want to see me destroyed at this point. I think they were still confident I could do the job. Then, Jimmy came up with a beauty.

Jimmy: Alright, let's deal with Papa first. You find that's too hard. I'll tell you what. Why don't you also carry a second piece of paper and on the second piece of paper you put down all the things you like about your wife. (He gives Pop a tiny piece of paper, and rips another of that size for Mom. His first papers were full sheets. The group laughs). And we'll give Mama a piece of paper, and there must at least be a few things, and you bring it in for next session.

My thoughts are-Jimmy symbolically found his way through the mess by having them symbolically as a result of these small pieces of paper, and in a humorous way, realize how stingy they are with each other. This is not particularly my style, as I sensed they were a family who wouldn't carry out any such actions, but at this point I was satisfied in that Jimmy had served the function for which I wanted him, and that it demonstrated that no matter whether co-therapists styles were alike or not, it didn't make any difference in the work as long as both were consistent with themselves.

Pop: What I like about her is what I liked when I first met and married her. She is painful to be with these years.

Me: What was she like then?

My thoughts are-could be that Pops negates experience that he could build on with her.

Pop: She was warm, open, we could talk, and she gradually, after motherhood, she began so intensively controlling the world.

Me: How does she control your world?

Pop: And talking it up. There's almost no space for anybody else. By the way. She says I drink a lot. I really don't drink a lot. But I'm away a lot. That's true. But I don't drink a lot.

Mom: I have an urge to tell you why he is away a lot, but I'm not going to.

Me: (To Pop) Well, it sounds like a matter of you getting your space back instead of heading for the high hills.

My thoughts are-on a sensory perception level she actually did close down the space, but he could learn to take control over his space to open it up and make it easier for him to be with her. His passivity is doing him in. Sounds like your daughter is inviting you back in. Your son's willing to put up with you. You could try it. You know how to get your space back? With her?

Pop: Space back with who?

Me: Your wife.

Pop: Space back? I don't want it. She's not much fun to be with these days. She doesn't hear. No fun. Controlling as hell and I must admit when I have tried and I've tried often, I feel she is just too insensitive to me as a person.

Mom: Listen, I took the psychology courses and I know what I'm doing.

Pop: See, that's an example. That's an example.

Me: You could always get rid of her.

Pop: I've been thinking about it to tell you the truth. So have the kids. It's just not much fun spending time with her, being close to her, and in a sense we have been apart now for a lot of years.

Suzie: Mom tries. She works hard.

Me:: You think so? How does she work hard?

Suzie: She cleans all the time and she puts new wallpaper up and new carpet down. She tries to make nice dinners and stuff.

Me: So it sounds like you feel she loves you and cares about you and cares about the family.

<u>My thoughts are</u>-make Mom's virtues known because in a family that may miss the links to relationship and destroy them through hate, it is best to make the links obvious.

Suzie: (Laughs, as if to say, I never thought about it that way before) Her actions do, but her words don't.

Me: So then the answer is simple. Don't listen to her words and pay attention to what she does.

Mom: Haven't I given you piano lessons and haven't I taken you out to play tennis.

Jimmy: (Angrily) You're such a rotten kid, you really are, and she's such a good mother. You just don't appreciate her.

<u>My thoughts are</u>-a bit of Jimmy's own trip, and he sounded angry. Felt like he was kicking the cripple. Not a good thing to kick someone when they are down. Once you have made your point, don't rub it in.

If the patient loses face, you can expect massive retaliation along the way. Further, I was attempting to create a loving environment and he switched the game to the hostility they were already stuck in. Again, I am responsible for dealing with an additional part of the difficulty in that I spontaneously selected someone which gave me difficulties in therapeutic direction that I preferred not to have. On the other hand, if one considers the totality of the experience, I was still better off with a co-therapist because it gave me the time necessary to back out of the family system so I could return with greater impact. It is most important to be able to go in and out, and if you are working alone it is much more difficult to have or be able to manage that balance without getting sucked into the family system, no matter how fast you are or how good you are. Family therapy is best done with a co-therapist, and no matter what the effect of working with a co-therapist, if you deal with the issue of not being murdered, even in relation to the co-therapist, things will work out better than if you did family therapy alone.

Jimmy: (Gets off on his own and the same trip) Hey, does she tell you this a lot. I have a fantasy of this family's every time she has a complaint you tell her about all the good things that you do, and every time he has a complaint, you tell him about all the bad things he does. You've got to let him know all the bad things. You can't work any other way.

My thoughts are-Jimmy has gotten invested in his method and has a desire for it to work. When therapists manifest this desire, families are going to stick it right up their nose. Families have lived a certain way for hundreds of years, and it is quite pompous for any therapist to be invested in any particular way to change them. Desire must be abandoned if the family is to have the opportunity for growth. Otherwise, they will rebel against the therapist's desire and sabotage themselves.

Jimmy: You've got to straighten out. Part of the difficulty with this family is that Mama knows the rules and regulations and they won't follow it. I mean you've got a really rebellious bunch of kids on your hands. There is three rebellious kids in this family and a mother.

My thoughts are-a good comment flowed out of Jimmy here in that he backhandedly stroked mother in having to deal with three rebellious kids.

Jimmy: I think that's what you need to deal with.

My thoughts are-Jimmy is going for my jugular again.

Me: Sounds good to me.

Jimmy: Sounds the way Sue is dealing

Me: (I cut him off) Sounds like you want to change them. What the hell do you want to change them for!

Jimmy: No, I don't want to change them, but I just don't want her to commit suicide.

Me: You want to save them (with a high pitched sound of feigned surprise).

Jimmy: Do I want to save the family? Yeah.

Me: How come?!

Jimmy: I'll deal with that afterwords.

Me: No! You gotta deal with it now.

My thoughts are-Well, Jimmy, you pushed it going for my jugular. Now your ass is on the hot seat and I'm by no means going to let you go because you have been an ungracious bastard. This problem of desire you manifest, I'm going to shove it right down your throat, and I'm going to free the family while I do it. I'm going to free the family in that they will see that I have no desire whether they live or commit suicide or make something of the therapy or make nothing of it. Therapists' only compensations are the fee and that the patients leave on time. If they get into any other rewards they are setting themselves up for sabotage and setting the family up for tragedy. Further, the fight I am carrying on with Jimmy is being said in front of the family so it is something they cannot readily respond to because it is not being said to them, and yet, it removes the issue of desire of the therapists, at least for this session.

Jimmy: I have a fantasy of Suzie in the hospital after having an overdose of pills or something or maybe cutting up her wrists and then Mommy and Daddy are at the feet of the bed.

Mom: Will you stop talking like that. You are crazy. What are you giving her those ideas for?

Jimmy: There are now four kids in this family (referring to Mom).

Me: I think she's already got those ideas, but I don't understand his wanting to change things. Seems to me OK the way it is. (Emphatic)

Jeff: Well, I don't want to see my sister hurt herself.

Me: I think, Mom, you're really misunderstood, but your daughter Suzie, she really has the right answer. She said you're a loving mother, and caring, and it's just when people listen to what you say, they get all bent out of shape.

My thoughts are-I'll see if I can go back to reaffirming Mom's worth and getting the warmer environment that began to be created before Jimmy's intrusive comment's that wound up serving a purpose in terms of the confrontation to the family of a second therapist talking about suicide, although in this case it wasn't too clear if the hot potato was being passed into Suzie's guts. But if the therapist can take one step after another, effective work can be done no matter what happens in a session. It is a matter of developing the ability to work with whatever is thrown at you in the line of therapeutic fire!, AND KEEPING YOUR HEAD ON STRAIGHT, THAT IS, THINKING AND FUNCTIONING EFFECTIVELY NO MATTER WHAT YOUR GUTS ARE DOING!

Me: So if you guys just do your thing, you can come back into the family with Mom. Don't take her words so seriously.

My thoughts are-there is always a question as to whether false hope is being offered, or one ought to paint the hopeless picture. But, whenever I get a chance and I think it feels more legitimate than not I'll try to offer a bit of hope based on the moment of hopeful experience that the family can utilize if they wish. If they don't, I haven't lost very much ground and I'll just come back the other way.

Pop: When somebody is strident and knows it all and talks as much

Me: You sound like you are going to go to sleep.

Pop: Well, that's about the only way I can protect myself.

Me: Ah, you were sleepy before you met her. Don't kid me.

Pop: No. We weren't sleepy our early years.

Me: Wait a minute! Come on! You're going to sleep again! You're talking to me now!

My thoughts are-Pop was doing everything he was accusing Mom of doing in the here and now, so I decided to deal with him individually about his regressive sleepy child part of his personality. I thought he was unfairly laying blame where he couldn't cathect his own energy to move his life. In other words with that regressive sleepy quality I didn't think he could get out of his own way and hoped to provide an existential here and now experience that would wake him up NOW!

Me: You still look sleepy.

Pop: It's just the way I am.

Me: What's in it for her!

Pop: As a matter of fact we used to be very lively, and

Me: What good is that doing her now? I mean if you can't help stop her from this mouthing problem.

Pop: I tell her over and over again that she takes over and talks so loud sometimes

Me: Do you have a kingdom?

Pop: Sure, inside me.

Me: So you want to rule this as a kingdom, then.

Pop: I'm just saying sometimes it is too hard to reach her.

Me: How do you know?

Pop: I've tried hundreds of times. Hundreds of times.

Me: Do you work out?!

Pop: Yeah.

Me: Maybe you need to do more pushups, or take geritol, or vitamins. (After each recommendation Pop says)

Pop: I do. I do. I do very well when I'm away from her. That's why I am away so much.

Me: (To kids) How are you guys going to help Dad get more tenacity? He seems like he's over the hill. Mom's a forceful sort. She's right in there.

Jeff: We don't know what he wants.

Me: What difference does that make!

Jeff: Well, you said, how are we going to help him get more tenacity?

Me: Drag him by the ears.

Jeff: He says he doesn't know whether he wants to be in there or not. He's gone a lot of the time. We don't see much of him.

Me: Yeah, that has nothing to do with you guys.

My thoughts are-it is difficult to tell if Dad is wanting out because he wants out or because he has the sleepy child problem he showed us. If he is crippled and that is the reason he wants out, I am putting it in the hands of his children to drag him by the ears back into the family regardless of what he wants. Further, where Jeff makes a comment of feeling guilty for Dad staying away, I say, 'that has nothing to do with you guys" clearing the way for the two older children to use their power in helping Dad. In that way we could find out if he really wants out or if he just wants out because he is crippled. It would force his hand one way or the other in most probability in the future.

Me: He's just away. Drag him by the ears. Bring him in. You've got to bring him in.

Suzie: He saves himself but he doesn't care about us.

Me: Yeah, I know, it's tough to be your father's mother.

My thoughts are-what I am proposing is that she stop playing victim and be her father's mother and this recognition may be sufficiently embarrassing to Pop to mobilize some force in getting him off his butt.

Me: I wouldn't let him off the hook. I'd just drag him in. Have it get so bad till he can't stand it that he'll stand up and do something about it.

My thoughts are-this is worded in a way that forces Dad to either endure the children dragging him in, which he could only do if he cathected more energy, and then, to either find out if he was willing to stay, or get out, or decide to leave it at status quo. It's one of those crazy sentences that comes out naturally that has a few positives balanced off by negatives that turns out alright in terms of effectively slipping into the unconscious mind of the patient, and being responsible for movement.

Me: He's got to be able to help you out. So far he's not bringing any value to your life. That's what you're bitching about. But he's stuck. He can't bring any into his own. He needs some juice. It's a juice problem.

Mom: He's already had too much of that.

Me: Well, he's got the wrong kind of juice, though. He needs juice from whoever in the family can give it, or maybe from whoever outside the family can bring it in. So you guys are going to have to bring him in with the right kind of juice.

Mom: Listen, I think you should help him with his problem.

Me: You're right, I am. I'm telling him he's hopeless unless you bring him in.

My thoughts are agreeing with Mom but at the same time redefining it so those who can provide the help will.

Me: Don't let him escape from you.

Jeff: I don't know how to do that.

Me: Be tender, warm, as nice as you can. (I switched from a tough guy position to warm and loving in a split second, thereby modeling what Jeff wanted to know how to do.) And whenever he gets discouraged with Mom, point out whatever she does that's caring. You know, you see that.

My thoughts are-I'm giving specific direction if they want to take it. It is not always necessary to work absurdly if direct conscious communication can get the job done.

Me: She seems alright to me.

My thoughts are again reaffirming Mom and her self-esteem, which is as much a problem as Pop's lack of juice.

This is the end of the mock family therapy session, and a few comments are made after the session. One psychologist addresses the woman who played Suzie. He said, 'The family's response to Len was you stopped challenging as you got into it. You calmed down. I'm interested in your response to his style.'

Suzie: I feel like he put me into a different role. I couldn't sustain the role of the martyr. He made me laugh and I just couldn't do anything else but laugh. I felt like that was really out of character, especially in that kind of a tough situation and that was very positive for me because it let me know I had other alternatives and I wasn't going to die and mother wasn't going to kill me if I laughed (and she breaks out into laughter).

Jimmy: That was a powerful piece of work.

Me: How was it for the other family members? What was the experience like? (Tape gets really bad here and goes out altogether a little bit further.)

Jeff: You did something with my anger. I'm not quite sure, but, I tried to express my anger a number of times and finally I didn't have much left. (He begins to chuckle, as if to say I put one over on him but he was pleased that I did.

My thoughts are-patients will forgive your winning and even feel good about it as long as the outcome of your proper use of authority is in their benefit.

Jeff: It dislodged my anger and I thought that was productive. Toward the end I felt a little bit more towards Dad and that felt good (warmer).

Me: How about you, Mom?

At this point whatever electrical devices were being used in the hospitality suite made the tape recorder inoperable so I couldn't pick up any more of the discussion.

The primary feedback from the therapists present was that the style of absurdity, craziness and paradox left them feeling much freer to respond. They felt en??? looking forward to their own work. The??? these comments makes me feel that???tion of the therapist.

PREFACE TO INVADING THE UNCONSCIOUS WITH THE PATIENT'S OWN CRAZINESS TO CREATE "EXISTENTIAL SHIFTS" VOICES, SPRING, 1995

written by Dr. Len Bergantino

■■ ■

When I trained people at the international level I used Mock Family Therapy as taught to me by Carl Whitaker, M.D. of the University of Wisconsin Medical School. This method is to be used in training psychoanalysts to get their speed up in working with primitive mental states and this article demonstrates how it may be used in working with an individual and therefore belongs in the psychoanalytic book.

While this book contains many methods that I have used their sum total resulted in feedback that "Bergantino electrified the Australian Therapeutic Community and his work had lasting therapeutic results." This is quite different than Dr. Martin Grotjahn's comment that "Psychoanalysis is a good method of education but it is not a good method of therapy."

Len Bergantino, Ed.D., ABPP is in the private practice of Clinical Psychology in West Los Angeles. His book, Psychotherapy Insight and Style: The Existential Moment has been chosen among hundreds to be re-published in the Master Classic Series by Jason Aronson Publishers of Northvale, New Jersey, under a new title, Making An Impact in Therapy: How Master Clinicians Intervene. He has trained psychotherapists and family therapists internationally. At this time in his professional life, he enjoys doing family therapy and psychotherapy by invading the unconscious with the patient's own craziness to create existential shifts. Further, he is engaged in forensic consultation and expert testimony in the diagnosis and recommendations for cessation of "parental alienation syndrome", the virtual extermination by one parent and an unwitting court system of the other parent from the children's lives. He was trained by Carl Whitaker, M.D. and Milton Erickson, M.D.

Three master clinicians have trained me in terms of making an impact in psychotherapy and family therapy by "doing it to patients" much as a Zen master would do. There is no value given to patient awareness, patient insight, or understanding of the process by the patient. In this way the results of the therapy cannot be destroyed by education. These master clinicians who trained me were Milton Erickson, now deceased; Carl Whitaker, who has recently suffered a serious stroke; and Walter Kempler, who retired recently. Thus, in the spirit of Bruno Bettelheim, when asked in 1983 why he wrote Freud and Man's Soul said, "Because I am the only one left who could do it!" I have written this article to illustrate working at a level Milton Erickson referred to as Occam's Razor—"Multiplicity ought not be posited without necessity."

When Erickson, Whitaker and Kempler trained me they didn't explain much of anything. Everything was an experience so I actually had the chance to learn to do what I was being shown because it was done to me. Of all that I learned, what I enjoy most is "invading the unconscious with the patient's or family's own craziness to create existential shifts."

However, if I were to explain what I did and why I did it, the flavor of giving you the kind of experience I had in learning would significantly be diminished by what Wilfred Bion, the great British psychoanalyst, might refer to as the destruction of experience and learning through knowledge by a saturation of the space. And of course one should realize when having had a week's workshop with Jim Simkin, who was like a bulldog at your pant leg with his tenacity, that one could never again make the mistake of working with "unconditional positive disregard!"

When discussing the kinds of interventions therapists made, Simkin was telling me of Rogerian kinds of responses where the therapist's own reaction to the client, if it were negative, would not be shared. Simkin referred to what was known as "unconditional positive regard" as really being "unconditional positive disregard" in that the therapist's self was missing from the response. Thus, I have attempted to write a psychotherapy article much as Mickey Spillane might have written about Mike Hammer.

THE PATIENT CALLED

I hadn't seen Joey in ten years. He called very disturbed and said he had an urgent situation; his sister had been alcoholic for twenty years and when her husband recently left her, she tried to kill herself. I said, "Come in at 3 p.m." He said, "that will be fine."

We were glad to see each other with a feeling of affection after all these years. He began by sounding guilty. I let it pass for the moment. He said, "My sister tried to kill herself three times." I said, "How come she is so incompetent!" He said, "she was smarter than anyone back on the East Coast. They put her in a hospital with 24 hour security and she walked out. She was pissed because they didn't have a mirror where she could put her makeup on." I said, "I guess she wanted to look good in the coffin." There was a long pause. I said, "what the hell are you guilty about?" He said, "I left her and I left my family twenty years ago." I said, "you said that the last time I saw you, and you're still guilty?" I paused, then asked, "are you still a lawyer?" He said, "I am in another kind of business." I said, "no wonder she is pissed at you. She had all the brains and you went to law school!" He said, "you haven't gotten any nicer." I said, "Thank you. Coming from you that's a compliment!"

He gave me a reasonable sounding diagnosis a psychologist who was a self respecting lawyer with a criminal's mind might have given. He then went on to expound and even pontificate about what he should tell her about taking responsibility for herself. It was all too pat.

I told him a story about Sal Maglie, the ex-Giant-Dodger great, and Jim Bouton, the ex-Yankee pitcher when Bouton was all washed up and pitching for Seattle in the minor league. I said, "Bouton had the bases loaded and nobody out. Sal Maglie came to the mound." Sal said, "Jim, I want you to throw him two high hard ones on the inside corner and then book him low and away on the outside corner." Jim looked at Sal and said, "Sal, if I could do that, what the hell would I need you for?" (A question all therapists ought to ask themselves.)

The patient told me, "Her two sons moved out here and my wife hates my sister." Remembering his wife, I knew full well what hatred was and thought for an instant, against my better judgement, that making an offer to have her in family therapy was the coefficient of adversity beyond which I dare not tread. I thought, "maybe he'll leave now." He went on by saying in reference to his sister, "Her husband had left her but was too much a gentleman to just walk away." I thought, but didn't say, "Maybe he has the same wish for me." He said, "my sister described her husband as a nice man who was always helpful and thought the world of her without ever raising his voice. He just got his own apartment but was too much a gentleman to just walk away from her." (The second time he said the same thing.) I said, "what she meant was that his pastime was letting her cut off his penis and he was useless to her." (If someone is in a relationship he or she can either bring value to the other person's life or he or she cannot!)

He then talked about his mother coming out here from New York to visit, staying two months and now deciding to move out here. I said, (thinking of the mirror and the makeup story.) "Mirror mirror on the wall, who is the fairest child of all?"

I said, "look, I don't know what is going on with them and your sister but I am pretty confident in my own responses. If you want to have coast-to-coast sessions with them I am willing to do that." He thought it was a good idea (working by conference call. Carl Whitaker, M.D., trained me to do that kind of work three generational.) I said, "let me see, who are the players?" He said, "I don't know about her husband." I said, "I don't trust you. I want him in just because you don't. I'll teach him to put his penis back on! No wonder your ex-wife wants to kill your sister (he is still married but emotionally I sensed he was married to his sister); you're married to your sister!" I said, "get your sister, her daughter and her husband who moved out back there; bring your mother, yourself, your wife, and her (his sister's) two sons out here.

I looked at my watch. A fifty minute session had been scheduled. 35 minutes had gone by since he walked in. I said, "we're done." In full acknowledgement that the existential facts had been dealt with, he said, "we're done." I said, "you must trust me a lot." He said, "you did it last time!" He hugged me with a sigh of relief. He said, "how much do I owe you? What's your current fare?" I said, "It's $200 for 50 minutes."

I heard from him about a week and a half later. He called to tell me the check had been returned in that he must have written the wrong address. He mailed it back to me and somehow he had written the correct address and it had been returned to him with a "return to sender" stamped on it. It then hit me that he made the check out for $200. I called him back and said, "I am returning the check. Scale it down to 35 minutes and make it $140." He said, "My sister's in an alcohol rehab unit back there. The whole family is doing better as a result of what you did with me. I feel much better. I thought it was worth $200! Keep it!" I said, "I thought so, too! You got my best shot!"

Foreword

Len Bergantino, Ed.D., Ph.D.

Making an Impact in Therapy:

How Master Clinicians Intervene

JASON ARONSON INC.
Northvale, New Jersey
London

The plethora of how-to books is increasing. This is not one of those. Barbara Betz stated that the dynamics of psychotherapy is in the person of the therapist. Abraham Maslow stated that the peak experience lasts two weeks. Winicott insisted that if you haven't been hated by your psychotherapist you have been cheated. Erenwald has stated that psychotherapy is the effort to evolve an existential shift.

Len Bergantino is trying to expand this operational territory by stretching the psychotherapeutic geology. He succeeds. Describing the therapist as a person of liberated wisdom, he dares to the chaos and anxiety of not knowing; he opens a gate to see and make the impact of psychotherapy more clearly. His description of beingness as a process is reminiscent of Paul Tillich. His grasp of responsible involvement with the patient as a discipline of self shows his own search for creative options. He makes no pretense of camouflaging the psychotherapist as a wounded healer. Furthermore, Len makes crucial the pattern of the therapist's search for his own healing and successfully validates the authentic trickery of the psychotherapist as a liberated spirit. The approach to his own craziness, the freedom from the culture bind, and the discipline of self each emerged as obtainable goals of that professional parent we call the psychotherapist.

Further evidence of his own search is illustrated by his impersonalized impressionistic response to the other searchers he uses as models.

Simply reading his book leaves me feeling it would be meaningful to join in his search for his beingness. Though he would be enjoying himself and enjoying me as a patient, he would not be doing things to keep from being himself and thus I could be more fully myself.

Carl A. Whitaker, M.D.
Professor of Psychiatry
School of Medicine
University of Wisconsin

What the Reviewers Say:

Psychotherapy, Insight and Style

The Existential Moment

by Len Bergantino, Ed. D., ABPP

The book sells for $26.95 / Send check to . 1215 Brockton Ave. #104, Los Angeles, Ca 90025

Interested? Contact Dr.Bergantino / (310) 207-8818

Dr. Carl A. Whitaker, M.D. Professor of Psychiatry / School of Medicine, University of Wisconsin

"The plethora of how-to books is increasing. Barbara Betz stated that the dynamics of psychotherapy is in the person of the therapist. Abraham Maslow stated the the peak experience lasts two weeks. Winicott insisted that if you haven't been hated by your psychotherapist you have been cheated. Erenwald has stated that psychotherapy is the effort to evolve an existential shift.

Len Bergantino is trying to expand this operational territory by streching the psychotherapeutic geology He succeeds. Describing the therapist as a person of liberated wisdom, he dares to the chaos and anxiety of not knowing; he opens a gate to see and make the impact of psychotherapy more clearly. His description of beingness as a process is reminiscent of Paul Tillich. His grasp of responsible involvement with the patient as a discipline of self shows his own search for creative options. He makes no pretense of camouflaging the psychotherapist as a wounded healer. Furthermore, Len makes crucial the pattern of the therapist's search for his own healing and successfully validates the authentic trickery of the psychotherapist as a liberated spirit. The approach to his own craziness, the freedom from the culture bind, and the discipline of self each emerged as obtainable goals of that professional parent we call the psychotherapist.

Further evidence of his own search is illustrated by his impersonalized impressionistic response to the other searchers he uses as models. Simply reading his book leaves me feeling it would be meaningful to join in his search for his beingness. Though he would be enjoying himself and enjoying me as a patient, he would not be doing things to keep from being himself and thus I could be more fully myself."

Dr. Donald Rinsley, M.D., F. R.S.H. Fellow, American College of Psychoanalysts in his review of Dr. Bergantino's book published in Bulletin of the Menninger Clinic, Vol. 47, No. 5, September, 1983 wrote:

"The book reflects the personal odyssey of a trained, disciplined yet openminded professional psychologist who has drunk at the wells of a number of acknowledged healer-therapists whose work he has carefully studied and evaluated, among them, Viktor Frankl, Wilfred Bion, the Gouldings, Frederick Perls, Milton Erickson and Carl Whitaker. A unique feature of Dr. Bergantino's presentation is his detailed accounts of these therapists' hour-to-hour work, drawn from his own personal experience and from verbatim descriptions provided by their students and analysands, offering fascinating and instructive insights into the therapeutic labors of admittedly gifted treaters."

Dr. Martin Grotjahn, M.D., Training and Supervising Analyst Emeritus, Southern California Psychoanalytic Institute, in a pre-publication review wrote:

"Dr. Bergantino is obviously a gifted therapist ...Most cases as reported in the literature describe the patient's associations and productions while the therapist remains hidden in the mystery of darkness unrevealed. Dr. B is an exception: the great advantage of his work is the openess and frankness with which the author reveals his experiences when treating patients or when accepting himself as a patient of another therapist.

Dr. Walter Kempler, M.D. The Kempler Institute - Costa Mesa, CA

"Len's writing is intelligent and lucid...engrossing.....

I think his book is valuable...an interesting and propelling work...His ideas ride the crest of current thought in the field, provides clean reviews of popular modes, formulates in the popular jargon of the day using traditional interpretions and terminology. His personal touch is enchancing."

Dr. James S. Simkin, Ph.D. American Board of Examiners in Professional Psychology - Big Sur, CA

"Professionals could benefit directly from this book in that Bergantino describes how it is possible to integrate a variety of psychotherapeutic approaches."

Dr. Ernest Lawrence Rossi, Ph.D. Diplomate in Clinical Psychology - Los Angeles, CA

"A deeply moving flood of insights and approaches to becoming oneself as a psychotherapist.....It is a highly readable record of (Bergantino's) development as a therapist via his personal contacts and training with a variety of current-day psychotherapists....a new understanding of what it means to be a creative therapist continually living in the present's potential for change and transformation...

.....focuses on the precise and often provocative and shocking techniques that are useful in helping patients break out of their learned limitations to realize their potentials for creative change."

***This book is being republished by Jason Aronson Publishers Inc. as part of The Master Classic Series under a new title, Moments of Impact in Psychotherapy: How The Masters Intervene**

LEN BERGANTINO Ed. D., ABPP

In-Depth Family Therapy • Ericksonian Hypnosis

Mental Health Professionals
Education and Training
Psychological Testing/Evaluation
Mental Health & Social Services
Organizations Centers & Institutes
Mental Health & Psychology News
Job Search Mental Health Jobs

***I WILL PAY FOR THE TELEPHONE CALL. YOU PAY FOR THE SPEAKERPHONE AND THE TWO OR THREE GENERATIONAL FAMILY THERAPY. GRANDPARENTS CAN BE PLAYED IN FROM STATES OTHER THAN CA, AZ, HI!

Directory Search
Find
Advanced Search
Psychology Psychiatry Psychoanalysis Psychotherapy
Directory Index > Mental Health Professionals > Psychology > Psychologists

THREE GENERATIONAL INTERSTATE TELEPHONIC FAMILY THERAPY / TRAINING / SUPERVISION-DR. LEN BERGANTINO

Name/Company: **THREE GENERATIONAL INTERSTATE TELEPHONIC FAMILY THERAPY / TRAINING / SUPERVISION-DR. LEN BERGANTINO** premium member

Description:
DR. BERGANTINO – A LICENSED PSYCHOLOGIST IN CA, AZ & HI
DIPLOMATE IN FAMILY PSYCHOLOGY – AMERICAN BOARD OF PROFESSIONAL PSYCHOLOGY
THREE GENERATIONAL INTERSTATE TELEPHONIC FAMILY THERAPY WAS TAUGHT TO ME BY WORLD RENOWN PIONEER CARL WHITAKER, M.D.
IDENTIFIED PATIENT MUST RESIDE IN CA, AZ OR HI, BUT OTHER COLLATERAL FAMILY MEMBERS CAN BE IN ANY STATE OF THE FIFTY
THIS KIND OF FAMILY THERAPY HAS A CHANCE TO:
1. Create a shift so that what does not work in a family now works (sometimes in 1 session)
2. Evoke a psychosexual heat among the married couple in the nuclear family
3. Teach each family member what his/her value is to the family as a whole-as in gestalt family therapy the whole is greater than the sum of its parts
4. Give grandparents a way to contribute to the family's well-being without being a burden and to die with a clean slate between them and their children
5. Utilize the spontaneity of the grandchildren to bring value to the entire family
CALL AT 310-207-5397

Country: United States
State: California
City: West Los Angeles, CA
ZIP / Postal Code: 90025
Phone: 310-207-5397
Contact Person: Dr. Len Bergantino
Map / route: View map / route
E-Mail Address: Send message
URL / Website: http://n2.webstarts.com/lenbergantino/

Classification(s):

- Mental Health Professionals | Psychology / Psychologists
- Mental Health Professionals | Psychotherapy / Psychotherapists
- Mental Health Professionals | Psychotherapy / Other

From Beverly Hills Psychologist-Psychoanalyst TO PSYCHOLOGIST ACTIVIST IN A STATE PRISON

By Len Bergantino, Ed.D., ABPP
Los Angeles, CA

I practiced psychoanalysis in Beverly Hills from 1979 through 1999 and found the work very interesting and personally rewarding. I retired fairly well off but lost 40% of the value of my annuities, so I found work as an independent contractor in a state prison. As much as I enjoyed my private practice, I never really got to use certain skills that I brought to my work with the prison inmates. I had trained with Milton Erickson and Carl Whitaker, two pioneers who helped me create a style of work that I referred to as "existential shift," where I had a chance to make a difference in a person's life each and every time I saw him, no matter how short the session.

I have always held the existential viewpoint that one's decisions in the world should be in good faith and that ethical decisions need to take into account a) oneself; b) significant others; and c) all other people in the world. My training analysis, with an analyst who was himself trained by Bion, gave me the strength to be "a solid rock of truth" in a system that hardly ever treats inmates in a humane way.

Bion once said that the entire psychoanalytic library was good for about the first hour and a half of an analysis, and that after that you needed to know what to say to the patient. It was like that, working in the prison.

I had about 100 inmates in my caseload in the Administrative Segregation section of the prison ("the hole"), which was reserved for "lifers," mostly men who were in for one or multiple murders. The state had decreed that 70% of the inmate population needed to be seen one time per week for a five minute session of psychotherapy or the prison would be closed down. Inmates did not want to be seen for five minutes of psychotherapy because they felt there was nothing in it for them. Further, they had to be brought from their cells in hand and leg chains and put in a cage (like Hannibal Lechter in the movie) by two correctional officers. The inmates hated the chains and the cages.

My treatment approach was simple. I was straight with the inmates. I did not lie to them, because they could smell it a mile away. I was asked to do cell-to-cell canvassing to recruit inmates to attend sessions. One inmate asked me, "Why should I come out to see you for five minutes, to be dragged down in chains and put in a cage?" I was straight with him. I said, " Because I need a favor. If I don't get 70% of you guys to come out every week, they are going to fire me!" He shocked me when he replied, "You are a holy man! You can make a difference around here!"

> *I have always held the existential viewpoint that one's decisions in the world should be in good faith and that ethical decisions need to take into account a) oneself; b) significant others; and c) all other people in the world.*

My job was to keep inmates' spirits up and stop them from committing suicide, an understandable temptation when you are 30 years old and have two life sentences plus eighty years ahead of you. I used the psychoanalytic principle of maintaining a non-judgmental attitude of fairness toward the inmates, regardless of the crime they were in for. I treated them as tabula rasa, as if I knew nothing of their histories, nor did I really care; it had little to do with what I was hired to do.

A few clinical vignettes

A senior correction officer, one of the "good guys," said, "You'd better see Mr. Smith in Cell X; he tried to kill himself last night. They brought the man to the cage and he was drooling saliva, his head downcast, he looked totally dispirited. He had tattoos all over his body and rings coming out of his nose, bellybutton, ears, etc. He was a big, bulky tough guy you would not want pissed off at you. His projective identification, as received via my countertransference, showed me how to intervene. Looking at him in the most scolding way I could, I said, "What the fuck are you still doing here?" That pulled him out of his stupor, as what I said to him had been totally unexpected. "What do you mean? he asked. I responded, "I thought you would have escaped by now!" He beamed from ear to ear, having heard me tell him I had enough confidence in him that I believed he could escape from an impossible situation. All I needed was five minutes. One comment was the psychotherapy that day, and I reached him at a very deep level.

The administration never knew what I said to inmates in their sessions but in general they did not trust me as one of their own.

For group psychotherapy, six cages, one for each inmate, were arranged in a semicircle. Guys dressed like Darth Vader sporting black machine guns were on hand to monitor the session. Sometimes I found myself wondering, since all the inmates were locked up in cages, who were they planning to shoot? One little fellow seemed to have little contact with reality that day and shouted wildly at me, "What are you, one of those correction officers?" I had been taking notes throughout the session (mandatory in prison psychotherapy), and told him "I'll get to you next." Finishing my notes, I shouted at him, "What the fuck makes you think I am one of them?" The inmate looked up at the guards and said to me, "I don't trust them." I leaned over and whispered to him through the cage, "I don't trust the sons of bitches myself." He trusted me implicitly after that session, and that one sentence laid the groundwork for the therapy that followed. ❑

approach. I guess that visceral reaction may be genetically determined, according to the research I've just mentioned, as the serotonin coursing through my brain leads me to reasonable consideration of Gracey's feelings. And Gracey's mom is certain and immovable as to her extremist approach, as the dopamine in her system demands a certain degree of personal control in her experience of life. What's clear is that neither of us is likely to move from our respective positions, despite the eloquence of experts to the contrary.

Meanwhile, Gracey continues to deal with her parents' differing views, enjoying her casual and humor-tinged approach to life, until she's reminded by the harsh criticisms of her mother that it's time to get back to work.

DAVID RYBACK is the author of ConnectAbility: 8 Keys to Building Strong Partnerships with Your Colleagues and Your Customers (McGraw-Hill) and heads EQ Associates International in Atlanta. He can be reached at 404/377–3588.

GRACEY RYBACK is in her last year of middle school and contributing author of this, the first English publication in her young life.

A Case Against Self-Assisted Suicide

— Len Bergantino

One of my skills as a clinical psychologist is to get deeper quicker and get to the rock bottom heart of the matter while doing so.

Somewhere between 1993 and 1999 I consulted at a nursing home with the elderly who were disabled enough that they weren't coming back to any degree of normalcy.

My job was to knock on the room door and introduce myself and do one hour of psychotherapy per week with them, albeit I only stayed two weeks.

On the first week, I knocked on an African-American woman's door and opened the door while saying, "I am Dr. Bergantino. I am your new psychologist." Immediately, as she had had a stroke, with a dislocated tongue, she said, very, very slowly and with great difficulty, "I want to kill myself!" I said, "Let me try this one more time," and I went outside the room and knocked again on the door and while entering said "I am Dr. Bergantino, your new psychologist." Again, she said in exactly the same manner, "I want to kill myself!"

I sat down beside her on the bed and said, "Lady, if you to kill yourself, you have come to the right guy! Jack Kevorkian is a personal friend of mine. All I have to do is spin twenty cents in that telephone and you are dead. (This was prior to Kevorkian's incarceration.) She said, "What's your hurry?"

The thing is, a less-skilled clinician might have felt she really wanted to kill herself, and yet when I pushed her to the wall (even with no apparent reason to me as an outsider why someone in her condition would want to live) there it was at the deep levels after her first two demands of me were to help her kill herself—when I pressed her to the limit, she wanted to live!

Further, a medical doctor not trained by such people as I was (Milton Erickson, Carl Whitaker, or Jim Simkin) with somewhat unusual and bizarre responses, might have felt they had made a "good faith effort" and think the woman actually wanted to commit suicide. Therefore, this small sample statistic of one on its face justifies the law being rather safe than sorry, as even the best clinicians cannot say for certain that they know a person wants out.

LEN BERGANTINO, ED.D., ABPP is in the private practice of clinical psychology specializing in telephone psychotherapy or supervision. He is a diplomate of the American Board of Professional Psychology and a licensed psychologist in the states of Arizona, California, and Hawaii, and he can work with those who call from one of those three states or internationally (1/310-207-9397). He resides in West Los Angeles, California. In addition to being trained by Milton Erickson, M.D., and Carl Whitaker, M.D., and other world-renowned therapists, he has authored 80 publications and the book ***Psychotherapy Insight and Style: The Existential Moment****, 1981, Allyn & Bacon, Boston.*

PUBLISHED IN SOUTHERN CALIFORNIA PSYCHIATRIST
VOL. 46 NO. 4, DECEMBER, 1997

Guest Book Review

by: Scott Carder, M.D.

Making an Impact in Therapy: How Master Clinicians Intervene

by: Len Bergantino, Ed.D., Ph.D., ABPP. *This first soft cover edition was published in 1993 by Jason Aronson*

The book is a new release of a 1981 edition that was originally entitled, Psychotherapy, Insight, and Style: The Existential Moment. As a psychoanalyst I usually read and review almost exclusively psychoanalytic psychotherapy material. I was surprised to find my positive reaction to reading this "moveable feast" where Dr. Bergantino very openly and artistically describes his experiences with some of the top psychotherapists of different theoretical schools. The reader is first prepared to understand Dr. Bergantino's approach and purpose, and then accompanies him as he and sometimes his wife, Barbara, participate in a wide range of psychotherapy techniques. As an eclectic psychoanalyst, it was refreshing to read about the good learning experiences of Dr. Bergantino in other than psychoanalytic therapeutic modalities. My psychoanalytic work, especially my application of object relations theory, has been constructively enhanced by reading this text.

There are two sections to this book: the first relates the author's view of how he developed an existential perspective of psychotherapy and how he found the pursuit of emotionally impacting events which he calls "existential moments" as a foundation to effective process oriented psychotherapy. Part two is a detailed discussion of his exploration and understanding of different therapeutic experiences. It begins with his psychoanalytic exposure and continues through a wide range of transactional, gestalt, behavioral, somatic, hypnotic, confrontational, and family therapy experiences.

Only recently has the field of psychoanalysis discussed theoretical ideas concerning the intersubjective aspects of our work. This study of intersubjectivity more openly focuses on the influence of the psychoanalyst's beliefs and style on the treatment process. Over fifteen years ago, Dr. Bergantino made the attention to the therapist's style or his unique treatment enhancing qualities, the subject of this book. The author attempts to define and demonstrate existential moments that impact both patient and therapist. He also focuses on the liberation of the therapist: his effort to free himself to use the full range of his personality to constructively influence the patient.

The author's clear writing style makes it easy to understand the different therapeutic modalities and to experience the many clinical examples as if we were actual participants. The self-disclosure in the process of relating his efforts to become a more liberated therapist gives the book a real human feeling.

Of course from a psychoanalytic view, the best of the book is his fourth chapter, "Psychoanalysis and the Existential Moment" in which he describes his and other people's experiences with Wilfred Bion. It did appear to me that Dr. Bergantino, himself, had an unconscious idealizing transference to Dr. Bion since after only minimal personal contact he speaks in somewhat grand terms of the influence of Bion's personal presence. However, Dr. Bergantino was able to very clearly present a number of Bion's ideas such as the importance of language, of a clear mind, of a state of discovery, and of the ability to tolerate pain. In the subsequent pages, Dr. Bergantino marvelously edits material from several analysts who had intimate contact with Bion in Los Angeles. It was a special treat to read how psychoanalysts such as Richard Edeleman, James Grotstein, Lars Lofgren and Michael Paul experienced personal psychoanalysis and supervision from Bion.

Dr. Bergantino skillfully clarifies Bion's understanding of Melanie Klein's contributions. Using Dr. Grotstein's thinking on Bion and Klein, the author clarifies many good ideas that were Bion's particular focus as an extension of Klein's ideas. For instance: he explains Bion's "selected fact" concept; his use of deprivation and interpretation of projective identification in analysis to help the patient experience their own human richness; and Bion's emphasis on attention in the here and now of the analysis. I was especially appreciative of Dr. Bergantino's clarity in explaining many concepts of Bion's.

After this review of Bion's ideas, the reader is given a unique opportunity to experience the process of Bion's supervision of Stephen Salenger, M.D., who was at that time a clinical associate from the Los Angeles Psychoanalytic Institute. It is the only published process material of Bion doing supervision.

The remaining one third of this book has many refreshing comments as Dr. Bergantino relates his experiences with the styles of therapy of such non-analytic greats as: Albert Ellis on behavior modification,

(Continued on page 15)

Selegiline
(continued from page 6)

measures negative symptoms but rather neurocognitive deficits). On other scales, improvements were seen in withdrawal/retardation symptoms, lethargy, and psychomotor retardation. No change in positive symptoms were seen. Of note, the subgroup of patients on clozapine showed similar benefit compared to those on conventional neuroleptics. One patient became more psychotic during the trial, while another had the emergence of panic attacks. No hypertensive episodes were seen in this (or the previous) study, as expected, given the low doses of selegiline used.

Both studies can be criticized by their obvious design flaws—the total number of patients treated was small and the treatment was uncontrolled. Nevertheless, the results of the two studies were similar and are consistent with our emerging understanding of dopamine's role in negative symptoms.

It seems unlikely that selegiline is acting as an antidepressant; depression ratings were relatively low at baseline in the second study (not reported in the first) and did not change with treatment. Additionally, other studies and general clinical experience suggest that selegiline 10-15 mg is an insufficient dose for antidepressant efficacy.

At this point, one cannot recommend the general clinical use of selegiline to treat negative symptoms. The results just described are too preliminary and the risk of untoward effects associated with schizophrenic patients taking an MAO-B inhibitor are still unclear. Whether the emergence of panic attacks and one psychotic exacerbation seen in the second study are rare phenomena or not, is not yet known. Nonetheless, these studies indicate a potential treatment for some selected patients and even more, point the way towards further research into the treatment of negative symptoms with dopamine agonists that do not exacerbate psychotic symptoms.

Book Review
(Continued from page 11)

Milton Erickson on hypnotherapy, and Carl Whitaker on family interviewing. Dr. Bergantino looks for and underscores the existential moments as he saw and experienced them in his work with transactional analysis, analytic group therapy, Tavistock group experiences, Gestalt treatment, somatic therapy and direct confrontation of seriously disturbed psychotics. The book has many enlightening clinical examples, many of which are very personal as Dr. Bergantino and his wife Barbara traverse this therapeutic terrain.

I can heartily recommend this book as a learning experience to all psychotherapy clinicians and especially to psychoanalysts who would like a clear view of Wilfred Bion and his application of some of Melanie Klein's concepts.

To purchase book, send check for $35.00 to Dr. Len Bergantino, 1215 Brockton Ave., #104, L.A., CA 90025

The SCPS Editorial Committee and Staff

Wishes You a Happy Holiday Season and a Healthy and Prosperous New Year

NOVEMBER 19, 2012

TO WHOM IT MAY CONCERN RE:
AUTHORITY AND LEADERSHIP

DECLARATION OF DR. LEN BERGANTINO

I, DR. LEN BERGANTINO, DECLARE:
Around 1994 3 STAR GENERAL HOWARD GRAVES, SUPERINTENDENT AT THE U.S. MILITARY ACADEMY AT WEST POINT WAS THE GUEST SPEAKER AT TOWN HALL IN LOS ANGELES. I GOT THERE EARLY AND GENERAL GRAVES AND THREE OF HIS MILITARY ASSISTANTS WERE IN THE ROOM ALONE.

I WONDERED, HOW IS IT I COULD RELATE TO A GENERAL? WHAT WOULD I SAY TO HIM? I had the thought when I was in grammar school I always wanted to be a general. I bent over and pointed at him and like a little kid began to say in a voice much younger than my current age, "YOU MUST BE THE GENERAL!" He called me over and said, "Yes, how did you know?" I began pointing at the others saying "Look at the way you stand! And look at the way they stand! (Absolutely straight as opposed to curved spine and slightly hunched). He said, "Would you like me to teach you how to stand that way?" I said (enthusiastically) "YES!" GENERAL GRAVES SPENT THE NEXT HALF HOUR TELLING ME WHAT WAS REQUIRED TO BE ABLE TO STAND LIKE HIM!!! (IT WAS A FULL TIME JOB!)

WE CORRESPONDED BY MAIL SEVERAL TIMES AND HE INVITED ME TO TRAIN CADETS IN "AUTHORITY AND LEADERSHIP!" LATER HE BECAME CHANCELLOR AT TEXAS A&M UNTIL HIS DEATH IN 2003!

I declare under penalty of perjury that the foregoing is true and correct.

The Professional School for Humanistic Studies
420 Ash Street, San Diego, CA 92101 (714) 232-3171

June 24, 1981

Dr. Len Bergantino
415 North Camden - Suite 202
Beverly Hills, California 90210

Dear Len,

Many thanks for the copy of your book. I was delighted and surprised that you did include your excellent summary of the workshop and the case, after all.

The publisher did an excellent job and there are some lovely quotes. If you need any more you can use the following paragraph.

Many have written about the science of psycho-therapy, but it has remained for Dr. Bergantino to describe and illustrate the art of psychotherapy with such elegant impact.

Sincerely,

Harold Greenwald, Ph.D.
President

HG:cd

Len Bergantino
WARUM HEILT PSYCHOTHERAPIE?
Der existentielle Augenblick
Mit einem Vorwort von Carl A. Whitaker
EHP

»Nach der Lektüre dieses Buches wurde mir klar, wie sinnvoll es sein könnte, sich an Bergantinos Suche nach dem eigenen Sein zu beteiligen.«

Carl A. Whitaker

Warum heilt Psychotherapie?

Existentielle Augenblicke mit

Sigmund Freud	George Bach
Wilfred R. Bion	Albert Ellis
Robert und Mary Goulding	Harald Greenwald
Miriam und Erving Polster	Milton H. Erickson
Jim Simkin	Jack Rosberg
Stanley Keleman	Carl A. Whitaker

ISBN 3-926176-45-8

DR. LEN BERGANTINO, Ed.D. (USC), Ph.D., A.B.P.P.
Diplomate-American Board of Professional Psychology

**TELEPHONIC CREATIVE AGGRESSION THERAPY
FOR INDIVIDUALS, FAMILIES AND GROUPS**

Clinical Psychologist and Director of the
INSTITUTE FOR SANCTIMONIOUS
PSYCHO PROTOCTOLOGICAL INVASION

If you have failed with your Proctologist, *don't call me.*
"AGGRESSION TURNED INWARD IS THE WAY PEOPLE SHORTCHANGE THEMSELVES!!!" *(QUOTE OF DR. LEN BERGANTINO)*

**Licensed Psychologist in
CA (3837), AZ (266) & HI (990)** **Call 310.207.9397**

WHEN YOU CHEAT YOU NEVER KNOW WHEN THE DEVIL IS GOING TO MOVE THE FENCE

SUBMITTED BY LEN BERGANTINO,
ED.D., PH.D., A.B.P.P.
PSYCHOANALYST-CLINICAL PSYCHOLOGIST

■■ ■

In CIVILIZATION AND ITS DISCONTENTS FREUD saw society as a downward spiraling situation. Psychoanalysts are among the privileged in terms of both training, what they can do in terms of treatment, and having had the financial wherewithal to get to this stage of achievement. THUS, IT IS A PSYCHOANALYST'S RESPONSIBILITY TO INTERVENE AT EACH AND EVERY POINT THEY THINK AND FEEL THEY CAN MAKE A DIFFERENCE WHERE THEY HAVE AN ORGANIC INTEREST AND PERHAPS EVEN PASSION FOR A SITUATION THAT WILL ENABLE THEM TO DO WHATEVER IT TAKES TO GET THE JOB DONE AND MOVE A SITUATION THAT MIGHT OTHERWISE BE CONSIDERED HOPELESS AND PERMANENTLY ABUSIVE TO A MINORITY POPULATION, EVEN IF THAT POPULATION IS NOT NECESSARILY CONSIDERED A MINORITY POPULATION ACCORDING TO PRIVILEGE AND WEALTH.

I have been trained by the best of Wilfred Bion's M.D. analysands as well as Martin Grotjahn, M.D. in psychoanalysis; and by Milton H. Erickson, M.D. in terms of setting strategic double binds among other things and by Carl Whitaker, M.D. in terms of invading the primitive unconscious and expanding the number of family therapy participants to include all remnants of three generations.

I have read Machiavelli, Sun Tzu's The Art of War, Erwin Rommel and Heinz Guderian's works on being a tank commander, and many books that one way or another deal with the psychology of evil.

Bruno Bettelheim, Ph.D. was my friend and my supervisor, and he told me "THE AMERICANS WILL NEVER UNDERSTAND ANALYSIS BECAUSE THEY DO NOT UNDERSTAND THAT ANALYSIS IS THE FIGHT FOR MAN'S SOUL." BETTELHEIM WAS TRAINED BY FREUD IN HIS ORIGINAL TRAINING GROUP AND FREUD TOLD HIM THAT VIA PERSONAL COMMUNICATION.

The reason I mention all this is because if you are going to make an intervention it is important that your skill set be such that you can give your opponent a go for his money and that you be willing to do so in the face of great personal risk, because NO ONE WILL BACK YOU UP ON IT. THE ONLY REASON YOU ARE DOING IT IS THAT YOU, AND MAYBE YOU ALONE, ARE BOTHERED ENOUGH BY THE SITUATION, THAT YOU ARE WILLING TO RISK IT ALL! DO NOT LET THIS STOP YOU! PERSISTENCE IS OMNIPOTENT! JUST KEEP IN MIND THAT THE SITUATION WOULD NOT BE BOTHERING YOU IF IT WAS NOT EVIL YOU WERE STARING SQUARE IN THE FACE, AND MOST OF THE BIG MONEY IS BET ON EVIL THESE DAYS!

I am a virtuoso mandolin player having made a cd you can purchase on the internet on AMAZON.COM via Orchard Records.com where I made a cd with world renown guitarist Joe Diorio playing Italian-American Old Standards, you know, actual songs. People no longer write songs. (Misty, I'm In The Mood For Love, etc.) Mandolin is the same as bandolim in Brazil where bandolim is used as a lead instrument in Choro music. So I went to Rio to study with the masters of bandolim players who play Choro. That week there were 136 murders in Sao Paulo. In Rio after hearing Choro players in LAPPA DISTRICT, getting out about 1 a.m. I was told the safest place to walk was in the middle of the street, not on the sidewalk where I would be mugged for certain. Cars did not stop at stoplights after six p.m. because people would walk up to your car window with a gun, put a bullet in your head and take your car. I was congratulated on my intuition for having picked Rio that week instead of Sao Paulo in that the murders might just as easily have been in Rio.

There was a delightful woman at my hotel who spoke English and Portuguese and set up all of my bandolim lessons and concerts. I asked her "Why don't You Do Something About This Situation?" She said, "I wake up in the morning. I hope for the best. I do my best to enjoy each day. BUT THE DOWNWARD SPIRALING SOCIETY IS SO FAR GONE THAT THERE IS NO WAY BACK!"

THIS IS WHY PSYCHOANALYSTS, EACH AND EVERY ONE OF YOU, MUST BECOME ACTIVISTS, BECAUSE WE ARE THE ONLY ONES WHO ARE SOLID ENOUGH IN OURSELVES AS A WHOLE TO EVEN CONTEMPLATE TAKING THE DEVIL HEAD ON ALL BY OURSELVES!. THIS IS WHY I SAY, IT BETTER BE SOMETHING YOU ARE ORGANISMICALLY REGULATED SO YOU CARE ENOUGH TO BE WILLING TO GO THE DISTANCE, AS IT CAN BE A FINANCIALLY RISKY AS WELL AS POSSIBLE PHYSICAL HARM TO YOUR BODILY PARTS!

I AM SIXTY SEVEN YEARS OLD AND SOME EXAMPLES THROUGHOUT MY LIFE AND THINGS I HAVE DONE ARE GIVEN AS EXAMPLES IN CASE YOU HAVE THE COURAGE TO READ FURTHER:

1. In 1972 I got transferred, before I was licensed as a psychologist to a VA Outpatient Clinic in San Diego which was under a flight pattern where planes came over the clinic while you were doing psychotherapy at 120 decibels. I was having a loss of hearing. The VA Doc told me "That was the price of working at the VA. Everybody was losing their hearing working there!" I said, "It may be the price you are willing to pay, but I am out of here!" I went on leave without pay, passed the licensing exam, was the first white colla??? professional to become President of The American Federation of Government Employees, and defended blue collar workers against the Hospital Administrators who crippled such people for life. I terrified them!

On top of this, I was on the phone every day with Cecil Peck, Ph.D Head of Psychology Service for the VA in Washington, D.C., Senator Tunney's office (more receptive than Senator Cranston's office). Although I had all the facts on my side, suing the King in the King's Court did not provide any short term solution as they left me on leave without pay until hell froze over. So I was a rookie psychologist in Paradise (San Diego) attempting to convince people that I was competent A few Protestant Ministers gave me a chance and I backed up my claim that I was the best they had ever seen and I had a $48,000 practice in six months which at that time was the highest amount of money paid to any psychologist-1972. About three years later one of my patients walked into the office and said "I read in the paper that you lost a case with the VA Hospital". They never informed me directly. Later I found out they moved the entire clinic from 2131 Third Avenue to somewhere in Mission Valley, way out of the fly zone landing patterns. So my ACTIVISM BENEFITED OTHERS IN THE LONG RUN AND NOT ME PERSONALLY, AS I LOST A JOB PAYING ME ABOUT $14,000 a YEAR AND ENTERED THE WORLD OF PRIVATE PRACTICE PAYING ME $48,000 A YEAR. I WAS A POLITICAL SCIENCE MAJOR AT THE UNIVERSITY OF CONNECTICUT AND THE ONLY THING I REMEMBER WAS PLAYING IN ALL NIGHT CARD GAMES WITH THE SON OF A MAFIA WARLORD AS MY PARTNER AND EVERY TIME THERE WAS A CRITICAL CALL HE WOULD SPIN THE CARD UP IN THE AIR AND SAY "NB, NBC-NO BALLS, NO BLUE CHIPS!" Frankly, throughout my sixty seven years, I think that was all I really needed to remember from my political science days at UCONN!

It is public Policy that there is gender bias in the Courts in California in favor of women. They make calls even the worst of umpires would not dare make if the ballgame was fixed. I had a personal interest in this matter in that I have paranormal abilities, extrasensory perception, and was able to be trained to pick up pathological projective identifications the second they occurred and detoxify them, which left me seeing patients five days a week for seven years at a crack, paying me $625 a week in 1983 to hold the time open for six months while a movie was being made so I would not fill the time, all of which was prior to Welch vs. The American Psychoanalytic. I just said I could prove what I could do in public demonstrations and no one else could. This was a kind of activism that led to Welch vs. The American Psychoanalytic and subsequent occurrences.

Then I became an expert witness in "parental alienation syndrome and had my own radio show where I took on crooked judicial officers who made deals with organized crime which lead to a full scale encounter with the United States Government that lasted 22 years. To this point it is a tie which to my knowledge only Mohammed Ali and Che Guevarra have accomplished against the United States government in being a "freedom fighter" for the U.S. Constitution and the Democratic Way of Life as Benjamin Franklin and Our Forefather??? had envisioned it!.

It is my opinion that the United States Government is well on it's way to becoming what the woman in Brazil described as "TOO FAR GONE TOCOMEBACK!"WHICHINTURNWILLLEADTO"THERISE AND FALL OF THE UNITED STATES GOVERNMENT. THE UNITED STATES GOVERNMENT DOES NOT ENCOURAGE DISSENT IN RESPECT OF THE FIRST AMENDMENT AND WILL EVEN PUNISH YOU AND BOTTLE YOU UP IF YOU GET "TOO CLOSE TO DISTURBING THE UNIVERSE" (a book edited by James Grotstein, M.D. about the work of Wilfred Bion by contributors who were analyzed and supervised by him.

Mort Sahl heard my radio show. I worked with a woman and did a Carl Whitaker like jiu jitsu move where she was in place a and within seconds moved to place b. This was not the kind of sequential step by step work that a David Viscott, M.D. did and the next caller said "Dr. Bergantino, My opinion is!" I said, in an outrage, "What the hell makes you think you are entitled to an opinion!" and I slammed the phone down and took out my mandolin and played "Sorrento". Mort Sahl called me the next day and said "Where the hell did you get a style like that!" I said "I was born with it!" We became friends for about ten years. IT WAS MORT SAHL WHO FIRST TOLD ME "IT ONLY TAKES ONE GOOD PERSON TO STAND UP!"

Mort backed Garrison in New Orleans against the Warren Report during the Kennedy Assassination. He was making two million a year at the time as the leading political satirist in the United States. The United States Government banned him from appearing and his salary dropped to $19,000 a year. I was told by his best friend at the Polo Lounge in Beverly Hills, Bobby Kaufman, who produced "Love At First Bite" a movie starring George Hamilton, that the United States Government gave him a stipend from the middle of nowhere for $30,000 a year-and Bobby said, Mort was too proud to ever admit to this. He further said that a C.I.A. owned cable company made one show a year featuring Mort and then put it in a can and never let it be shown, although he was paid for it. I was at one such show and Mort Sahl was as funny as ever!

Dr. Bettelheim told me that "Wilhelm Reich was Freud's most gifted training analyst!" Wilhelm Reich said, "If you can't do politics, you can't do analysis!"

Some of my current interest include Musician's Union politics and their relationship with the Dept. of Labor, having policies that are detrimental to the majority of musician's throughout the United States, and organized college athletics in terms of evoking a situation where college athletes are paid what they are worth instead of African Americans like Reggie Bush being targeted for helping his parents get a home worth living in, and Terrell Pryor having to sell his championship ring for pocket change. Now you may not care at all about my personal interests unless you happen to be a professional musician or a lifelong sports fan who has a good deal of knowledge about the ins and outs of higher education from his doctoral work at The University of Southern California. The important thing is that I am willing to go to the mat on these issues, and I expect no help from you whatsoever! Pick your own issues organically, as I have shown you here!

The other great feat of my life is that I tried the case that Mesmer and Wilhelm Reich lost pro per with paranormal phenomena in the Superior Court of California and came out a tie with the United States Government! That is the greatest accomplishment of my professional life!

BOOK PROPOSAL OR QUERY LETTER TO PUBLISHERS FOR A PROFESSIONAL BOOK ON PSYCHOANALYSIS

THERE ARE SEVERAL WORKING TITLES THAT WOULD FIT THIS 400+ page manuscript.

They are:

1.\ Psychoanalysis and the Development and Use of Extra Sensory Perception Within The Psychoanalytic Frame
2.\ Psychoanalysis and The Development of a Therapeutic Use of Self.
3.\ From Psychoanalysis to Infinity
4.\ BECOMING "O" (A reference to Wilfred Bion's view that the purpose of an analysis is to give one the tools to pursue pure being, and the work takes the analysand to closer and closer approximations of Becoming "O" while "O" is unattainable.

I.\ The psychoanalyst can only be as curative as his or her quality of being has become enhanced whereby that psychoanalyst

1.\ Does not put severe pathological projective identifications into the patient rather than know how to analyze and detoxify them at their most primitive levels.
2.\ Does not turn his or her aggression inward as in "aggression castration" therefore leaving patients who turn their aggression inward and bringing the rath of hell down upon themselves as in holocaust.
3.\ Has learned to make sufficient progress in working with countertransference as a therapeutic tool when working with the underlying psychotic core of the personality as described in Bion's works.
4.\ Has made significant inroads in enhancing the quality of one's own being by working through the analyst's own severe

character armor which would impede the depth of contact the psychoanalyst is able to make with the patient. In other words, if the psychoanalysts' depth of contact level is impeded-the patient may attend sessions five days a week for seven years and the analyst's interpretations may be at a level of depth similar to the first session. In such a situation the psychoanalyst cannot treat the underlying psychotic core of the personality even in normal neurotics, narcissistic and borderline personality disorders and obsessive compulsive disorders, let alone those who are actually psychotic.

II.\ DEVELOPMENT OF THERAPEUTIC SKILL SET

1.\ Developing access to the unconscious mind.

The transition from conscious awareness most utilized in gestalt??? therapy for example, to the unconscious mind is best done by the use of a term coined by Los Angeles Psychoanalyst James S. Grotstein, MD, called "REVERSE PSYCHOANALYSIS"

Reverse psychoanalysis has many components to it.

a)\ Bion used to make long winded interpretations several paragraphs long and Milton H. Erickson, M.D. known for his psychiatric genius in other areas used to tell stories 4 and one half hours at a time at a pace Margaret Mead told him she had only heard in a rare African tribe relatively free of disease. Fritz Perls, M.D., Ph.D., had the notion that dis-ease led to disease.

b)\ Both Erickson and Bion made interpretations or told stories at the same pace. At a time when I was trained by nearly all of the best clinicians alive, these two stood out heads and shoulders above all others in their healing qualities as clinicians. They would have had a lot more in common with each other than Bion with other psychoanalysts and Erickson with other psychiatrists had they known each other. They were the most disciplined clinicians I ever met.

c)\ The greatest compliments I ever received given where they came from were from Bion who wrote that my writings to him were both “evocative and stimulating,” and Erickson who stated he “respected my dedication to the work.”

THESE SLOW PACED INTERPRETATIONS OR REVERSE STORYTELLING INITIALLY MAKES THE CONSCIOUSLY CONTROLLED ANALYST BORED AS REALITY IN THE WESTERN WORLD AT LEAST MOVES AT A MUCH DIFFERENT PACE; THEN THE ANALYTIC CANDIDATE WILL BEGIN TO DRIFT OUT FOR LONGER AND LONGER PERIODS OF TIME. DURING THOSE PERIODS OF MENTAL DRIFTING IN AND OUT THE ANALYTIC CANDIDATE WILL NOTICE TWO THINGS BEGINNING TO HAPPEN:

1.\ A kinesthetic development of sense perception which when trained takes the analytic candidate at the moment of perception to the exact spot in the patient’s body from which the severe pathological projective identifications are occurring, and after much experience at recognizing patterns of splitting experientially the analytic candidate will be able to identify the psychological issue as in “repetition compulsion” immediately, thereby enhancing the analytic candidate’s capacity to enhance closer and closer approximations of pure being in the patient.

2.\ A mental precision whereby after a lot of practice the analyst’s mind will develop an unimpeded flow of his or her own unconscious mind as picks up and deals with the pathological projective identifications the patient.

3.\ The experience will be that of developing an unimpeded flow moment to moment (the existential moment et. al Bergantino) from conscious thought or awareness, to sense perception, to the unconscious in a mind in a general sense, to pinpoint accuracy of the unconscious, to feeling to depth of feeling, in a way that the psychoanalyst "knows" with PRIMITIVE CERTAINTY as would a tiger in a jungle making a psychoanalytic interpretation to a patient.

4.\ Developing a "freedom from the culture bind" where the analyst takes the freedom necessary to make interpretations based on the "craziness" of the patient that may either be projected or split off from the patient during the transference ala severe pathological projective identification (as written about by Melanie Klein and as broken into finer particles to work with via Wilfred Bion's conceptual use of beta elements. Dr. Bergantino found out these beta elements, thought by psychoanalysts to be conceptual are existent in reality and in fact on occasion Dr. Bergantino has been able to analyze these split off beta elements in midair as the fragments of thought written about by Bion in his book "Second Thoughts".

III.\THE DEVELOPMENT AND USE OF EXTRASENSORY PERCEPTION IN WORKING WITH BETA ELEMENTS TO WORK WITH

a)\ primitive mental states

b)\ underlying psychotic thinking disorders

c)\ analyzing thought and even fragments of thought as they are split off into mid air.

d)\ analyzing the body part at the exact moment the splitting occurs to see where the painful severe pathological identification comes from; what part of the body it repeatedly comes from (as in repetition compulsion and then help psychoanalytic researchers find the links between repetitive psychoanalytic severe pathological projective identifications and the development of specific medical diseases as related to that specific psychophysiological repetition compulsion.

d1)\The place to begin here is in working with dis-ease and finding out how dis-ease leads to disease and then what specific repetition compulsions lead to what specific diseases when repeated millions of times over the course of a lifetime.

d2)\In one of her more frustrating moments a patient yelled out to me "Working with you is like trying to catch Mercury!" Again, as Bion put it "One never fully becomes "O", but moves toward finer and finer discriminations of pure being "O", and the closer they come the less disease currently worked with on a psychotherapeutic level will manifest itself in disease that kills people in the end of life.

d3)\In other words with an effective analysis you have a lot better chance of dying from natural causes than from debilitating and painful disease. That in itself, might be worth the cost of the analysis.

IV.\While I had extensive training with Milton H. Erickson, M.D. and some personal experience and exposure to Wilfred R. Bion, MRCS (Medical Royal College of Surgeons) and the greatest psychoanalytic thinker of his time-these two giants had more in common with each other than they had with those in their own sub specialties of psychiatry.

Erickson used to tell stories hour after hour-nonstop at a <u>s-l-o-w</u> pace that Margaret Mead told him she had only heard in a "rare African tribe relatively free of disease." For purposes of this book we will look at both the words disease and dis-ease and how the treatment of one may lead to the cure of the other.

<u>Bion used to make paragraph long interpretations at exactly the same slow pace at which Erickson told his stories. This is the key to the entire process of developing a therapeutic use of self that functions on a different clock than the one the rest of the world ticks at</u>. IT IS SIMPLE, IN FACT SO SIMPLE A BABY IS TUNED THE SAME WAY WHICH IS WHY PEOPLE ARE NATURALLY ATTRACTED TO BABIES. THE PROBLEM IS THAT WHILE IT IS SIMPLE, IT IS NOT EASY TO DEVELOP AND TAKES A DEDICATION OF MANY HOURS A DAY

FOR ABOUT ONE AND ONE HALF YEARS TO RETRAIN ONE'S BODY TO FUNCTION ON THE NEW TIME CLOCK!

V.\ It was Dr. Len Bergantino who made the link in developing his therapeutic and psychoanalytic use of self in a very disciplined manner, that if the psychoanalyst controlled the psychoanalytic environment with LONG WINDED INTERPRETATIONS AT THE SLOW PACE EXEMPLIFIED BY BOTH BION AND ERICKSON AND IDENTIFIED BY MARGARET MEAD, THAT A PSYCHOANALYTIC ENVIRONMENT WHICH PROVIDED "A GOOD ENOUGH MOTHER" (Bruno Bettelheim, Ph.D.) and a deepening of feeling allowing PRIMITIVE CERTAINTY TO DEVELOP IN THE PSYCHOANALYST WOULD ALSO PERMIT THE PSYCHOANALYST TO ENGAGE THE PATIENT AT DEEP ENOUGH LEVELS WHERE AS BETTELHEIM WROTE IN "FREUD AND MAN'S SOUL" BOTH THE ANALYSTS AND THE PATIENTS WOULD UNDERSTAND THE NATURE OF THE STAKES FOR WHICH THEY WERE PLAYING-MAN'S SOUL!

VI.\FREUD AND MAN'S SOUL Freud is known to have stated that the best an analysis could do "was give one the tools with which to carry on the work." While this is a lot if one approaches the level of work of which I am writing about in addition "an analysis offers the opportunity to develop the tools to "SAVE MAN'S SOUL AS ONE APPROACHES FINER AND FINER DISCRIMINATIONS OF BECOMING "O", and depending upon the exemplary quality of life the patient lives as a result of that analysis, perhaps the souls of significant others with whom that patient comes into deep and meaningful contact (more than superficial acquaintances) and in some cases such analysands may have the capacity to make and stand behind such political decisions such as to enhance the capacity for many to save their own souls. This would in effect change Freud's currently accurate viewpoint that mankind is suffering from a downward spiraling society that is in fact incurable in that too few are analyzed, and of those that are analyzed too few analysands and their analysts have developed a quality of being that would make much different at all in reversing the equation of a downward spiraling society. It is primarily in this manner that psychoanalytic decisions can be in existential balance-that is a harmony among a) Being for one self, b) Being for a significant other and c) being for all other people in the world. Without psychoanalysis making this kind of impact the downward spiraling society Freud referred to is a guarantee and there is no other vehicle other than the kind of psychoanalysis I write about that has a chance to turn the downward spiral into an upward spiral!

VI A.\Wilfred Bion was 3rd in a line of creative and impactful psychoanalytic thinkers-Freud was first or we all would have been plumbers and carpenters. His work was primarily geared to working with neurosis.

VI B.\Melanie Klein developed analytic concepts and technique to work with psychoses at deeper primitive levels.

VI C.\Wilfred Bion-analyzed by Melanie Klein-and is thought to have written complex mathematical theories and abstract concepts such as beta elements in writing about psychoanalytic that dealt with underlying psychotic thinking disorders as well as narcissistic and borderline psychotic disorders.

VI D.\I believe this book is the next breakthrough in that it makes one realize that the development of the psychoanalyst's therapeutic use of self as a discipline can take what was thought to be Wilfred Bion's conceptual work and actually put them into the practice of psychoanalysis on a daily basis to actually effect and affect primitive cures that will not only benefit the patient at hand, but have a spin off effect in having a reversal of the downward spiraling society Freud wrote about and change will have an opportunity to occur at the deepest primitive levels.

Bion had an amazing effect on a person's mind, in that after being in his presence, with the discipline of self of who he was, at the dis-ease free pace Margaret Mead spoke about, I experienced a happening such as a light bulb went off in my head with "a clear mind and a state of discovery" and wrote a 37 page paper in one night about Bion's presentation and what I thought and what I discovered, and sent it to him. It was then that he wrote back "Your work is evocative and stimulating." Coming from the greatest psychoanalytic thinker of our time I was most proud of that comment among all others. Some of Bion's works were actually entitled "A Clear Mind And A State of Discovery", but the experience itself of what he meant was beyond imagination. It felt as if you were a baby and your mind had never been interfered with and instead of people in the world who took care of you interfering with your development it felt as if someone was pumping your body up to be as full and as big and as solid (as in solid sense of self) beyond imagination and then the thoughts would flow because your level of attention was far beyond what it had ever been before.

I read all of Bion's books. They were not books about a subject. They were written as "the thing-in-itself" as Sartre might put it, or as close to pure being as one might ever write a book. My level of development was that of having been trained by many world renown psychiatrists and psychologists prior to my meeting him, and having written all but the section on his work in my book PSYCHOTHERAPY, INSIGHT AND STYLE: THE EXISTENTIAL MOMENT, ALLYN AND BACON, BOSTON, 1981, 288 pages. So my level of attention was pretty good, yet when I started to read Bion's THE SEVEN SERVANTS I could not read more than 3 pages at a time before it required such a level of attention that it exhausted me and I would have to go to bed whether it be day or night. WHEN MY LEVEL OF ATTENTION (another of his writings) was built up I was able to read all of Bion's work in 6 months. Reading Bion's work at that level of attention was similar to being in psychoanalysis with him. You were reading "Pure Being" or as close to it as you would ever see in a lifetime and be lucky you ever saw it once and you came out different and forever altered, in time and in tune with the harmony of the universe but not necessarily going along to get along with anyone else in the universe Dr. James Grotstein who was analyzed and supervised by Bion and is loyal to his legacy put together a compilation of psychoanalytic writings of a number of authors in a book entitled "DO I DARE DISTURB THE UNIVERSE!" In other words, if Bion's written work was experienced as he meant it to be, it would in fact disturb the downward spiraling society Freud wrote about and there is the real link between the two; Bion carrying on Freud's work!.

DEDICATION TO THE WORK

Milton Erickson said of me that he "respected my dedication to the work." Coming from Erickson this, along with Bion's comment, were the two highest compliments ever paid to me.

Erickson as a younger man worked as a psychiatrist at Wayne State Hospital. He had a patient who spoke in word salads that none of the other psychiatrists could communicate with. The man used to sit every afternoon on the park bench at the Hospital grounds. Every afternoon for two and one half weeks Erickson went out to the park bench to speak with the patient and took down every word the man said in writing. That evening Erickson would go home after work and spend many hours each evening writing a word salad that was in response to the man's word salad and the next day for 7 and 1/2 hours Erickson would read to the man the very precise word salad that he wrote. After two and one half weeks of this the man said "Erickson, you are the only damn guy in this place that can speak English! Why don't we go down your office and talk!"

Bion's dedication was geared toward 'Becoming "O" and he went farther along those lines that any human from any walk of life I have ever had the good fortune to meet.

Stephen Salenger, M.D. was supervised by Bion and he made audio tapes of those supervision sessions, which he permitted me to copy and write about in Psychotherapy Insight and Style: The Existential Moment, where I also had editorial and clinical help in the writing from Bion's analysands James Grotstein, M.D. and Michael Paul, M.D.

as well as some supervisory work from Richard Alexander, M.D. My analyst in Bion's methods shall remain confidential.

Bion in 1979 gave the Franz Alexander Memorial presentation at Rodeo Junior High School in Beverly Hills, California. That is the evening that evoked in me for the first time in my life at the level of which I write and speak, A CLEAR MIND AND A STATE OF DISCOVERY. I can remember a few other things about this night. A psychiatrist friend whose eyes were kind of lifeless and his wife who was overweight with the same detached quality brought their baby along. The baby's eyes were at half mast at about 8 p.m. Bion finished about 11:30 p.m. and the baby's entire sense of presence had changed to alive, eyes wide open, with a very alert look. I remember having the thought, "I wish I had Bion for a first grade teacher. My entire life would have been different!

Of the 16 other world famous clinicians who had trained me at the time, my own discipline and development of therapeutic use of self on all the levels I write about, permitted me to see Bion for who he was. There was another young lady and psychotherapist who said about two weeks later, "I saw you at the Bion presentation. That was the most boring old man I have ever seen in my life."

Years later after I had learned how to use the gift of extra sensory perception within the psychoanalytic frame actually doing what Bion wrote about that other analysts thought he only meant conceptually, at the same presentation a woman psychiatrist said to me "Dr. Bergantino. What you do is marvelous, even spectacular. However, I would have to devote my whole life to developing that kind of ability in myself. I am not willing to do that." Another clinician yelled out "Bergantino, when the fuck are you going to teach something somebody can learn?!"

What I am attempting to do here is write the experience itself so there will be a book for the ages until someone comes along and develops more. This book can be read and appreciated along a continuum, perhaps with some only attaining little bits of skill from it depending upon what kind of life they are willing to lead and what kind of dedication they bring to the psychoanalytic table.

THE BIGGEST PROBLEM-OPENING UP THE SPACE

Bion wrote that there were three ways to destroy the links to relationship. Through love, hatred and knowledge.

Psychoanalysts destroy Bion's work through attempting to understand it as one would any other book they have read or any other course they have taken in college, with their conscious mind. Bion's work or what I am writing about here cannot be learned other than "learning through experience", and to do this THE TRAINER, PSYCHOANALYST WHO TEACHES OTHERS, MUST BE ABLE TO KEEP THE SPACE OPEN. Of the seventeen world renown psychiatrists and psychologists I wrote of in PSYCHOTHERAPY INSIGHT AND STYLE: THE EXISTENTIAL MOMENT, ONLY WILFRED BION, MILTON ERICKSON AND CARL WHITAKER HAD CLINICAL TECHNIQUES TO OPEN UP THE SPACE WHERE ONE COULD ACTUALLY LEARN THROUGH EXPERIENCE.

The more brilliant the analysand or the patient, the more skillful at opening up the space so an experience could actually happen, is required. Richard Edelman, M.D. who received some analysis from Bion told me "Every time I would go into a session I thought I had a lock on reality; and every session I would come out of there with my worldview being turned upside down." Then Dr. Edelman would chuckle as if to say, "How the hell did Bion do it?"

OPENING UP THE SPACE MEANS THE CLINICIAN HAS TO FIND A WAY EVEN WITH THE MOST CONSCIOUSLY CONTROLLED AND OVERCONTROLLED MINDS TO INTERVENE IN WAYS THAT LEAVE THE ANALYTIC CANDIDATES OR ANALYSANDS IN A STATE OF HAVING TO DEAL WITH THE CHAOS AND ANXIETY OF NOT KNOWING. This is why Freud thought Ph.D.'s in some cases would make better psychoanalysts than MD'S, because they were less consciously controlled and in many cases, less brilliant, but still "good enough" to get the job done.

The ultimate goal of this book is that it gets into the hands of the most gifted and most disciplined, who learn how to open up the space, so they can open up the space for the most patients over a clinical lifetime, and those patients will have the opportunity to respond to the world in ways that can make it an upward spiraling society.

Bion was invited to a party in Beverly Hills. All of those at the party were engaged in what he referred to as a non-meeting; that is, small talk, chit chat about the weather, etc. When all the guests were in one room he removed an expensive painting from the wall and hid it and the party turned into an event where people really got to talk with and know each other. Or as Milton Erickson used to say, "Surprised can be pleasant, too!"

REVERSE PSYCHOANALYSIS

Reverse Psychoanalysis is a term coined by James Grotstein, M.D.-psychoanalyst to describe some of my writings of a process of non-stop storytelling whereby the psychoanalyst taps into his own unconscious mind and tells stories to the patient in front of him based on the projective identifications of that patient, at a very slow pace Margaret Mead stated she had only heard in a rare African tribe relatively free of dis-ease. (disease)

Milton Erickson, M.D. who was known as the father of modern medical hypnosis used to tell stories like this from his own life experience for 4 and 1/2 hours at a time at that very slow pace. Margaret Mead stated she had only heard in a rare African tribe relatively free of disease.

When I told Erickson that his stories had pinpoint accuracy he said to me, "Oh, No. I am just an old man who tells stories. It is your unconscious mind that has the pinpoint accuracy." He was correct. I began telling stories at that slow pace about 20 hours a week in my private practice and it got so I could tap in within three to four minutes so accurately I would sometimes get what I refer to as an existential shift in a lifelong personality characteristic in that one session.

What happens during the first one and one half hours at that slow pace is that the patient or psychoanalyst with rigid conscious controls begins to drift out there and not care so much about being in conscious control.

THIS OPENS UP THE SPACE, AND INSIGHTS BEGIN TO OCCUR FROM THE UNCONSCIOUS MIND OF THE ANALYST TO THE UNCONSCIOUS MIND OF THE PATIENT WHILE BOTH ARE NOT UNDER THE CONTROL OF THEIR CONSCIOUS MINDS. IN OTHER WORDS THIS METHOD BEGINS TO OPEN UP THE SPACE.

THE PROBLEM IF THE SPACE IS NOT OPEN IS THAT NO ONE CAN LEARN FROM EXPERIENCE, (ONE OF BION'S BOOKS) AND NO MATTER HOW HARD THEY TRY THEY WILL DESTROY WHAT BION MEANT TO CONVEY THROUGH EDUCATION (THAT IS CONSCIOUS MIND PRESENTATIONS OF AN ACADEMIC NATURE) To this point all psychoanalysts I have seen present Bion's work have destroyed his work through education-that is consciously controlled academic presentations, where the better and the brighter the analyst thinks he is, the more destructive he is to the 'actual learning through experience' that Bion was getting at. In fact, Bion wrote his books at a level where if you can pry open the oyster shell (the consciously and rigidly overcontrolled mind) all his books are actually written so the experience itself is the way you learn what is in them. Having attempted to do it before I reached this state of existence when reading his work was like taking knock out drops in that I could read about 3 pages and I was exhausted and went to sleep. On the other hand, when I had fortunately learned to open the space in my work with Milton Erickson, Carl Whitaker and one of Bion's analysands in Los Angeles, I read his entire works in 6 months. I have never had to go back and make reference to any of these works as they became part and parcel of my own being, (the thing in itself-Becoming 'O'), and therefore became an automatic part of either my technique of the technique I developed from having had that experience with Bion. In other words, I am telling you Bion was full of tricks, and the trick he played on psychoanalysts was that rather than present material that would create "more heat than light" he wrote in a way that could not be understood at the conscious level in terms of the multitude of meanings with which he wrote, and if a person had a DISCIPLINE OF SELF IN APPROACHING ALL

THAT HE WROTE, IT WAS ALMOST AS IF BION ANALYZED YOU AND YOU CAME OUT DIFFERENT AND YOU NEVER FORGOT WHAT BION WROTE IN TERMS OF YOU GOT WHAT YOU COULD FROM IT AND IT BECAME PART AND PARCEL OF YOUR OWN BEING AND PSYCHOANALYTIC USE OF SELF. I AM ATTEMPTING TO WRITE IN THIS MANNER BUT I AM NO BION, AND THIS IS WHY I WAS IN AWE OF HIS EFFORTS IN ADDITION TO A ONCE IN A LIFETIME PERSONAL EXPERIENCE OF SOMEONE WHO HAD TRAVELED THAT FAR ALONG THE ROAD TO HIS OWN BEING AND BECOMING AS TO BE DESCRIBED AS "MAGNIFICENT". WHAT CAN BE SAID OF ME AT THAT TIME IS THAT I TRAVELED FAR ENOUGH ALONG THE ROAD NOT TO MISS HIM, THAT IS TO EXPERIENCE THE FULLEST OF WHO HE WAS AND WHAT HE DID IN A MANNER THAT FOREVER ALTERED MY PERSONAL AND PROFESSIONAL LIFE. I NEVER SAW ANYONE EVEN RESEMBLING WHAT I HAVE DESCRIBED ABOUT BION BEFORE HIM AND NEVER ANYONE AFTER HIM. HE DIED IN NOVEMBER, 1979 and I am writing this section in 2009. I have developed myself enough to use extra sensory perception within the confines of the psychoanalytic frame and would certainly have noticed if anyone had come along who even resembled of what I am writing. Bion did the work necessary to be what I have written about. I did the personal work necessary to receive him. He wrote:

Ernest Rossi, Ph.D. wrote an article I hope to include in the book in its entirety about "ultradian cycles." He refers to Erickson working longer than the fifty minute hour and that the "existential shift" as I have described it occurred after what Rossi wrote was a kind of "letting go in the patient" that occurred as a result of the extended period of time past the fifty minute hour.

When I trained psychotherapists at the international level the first thing I did was Ericksonian storytelling and it was usually a couple of hours, although one day I wanted to test myself to see how long I could tell stories non-stop and I actually lasted six hours.

SO THE FIRST JOB WAS TO OPEN THE SPACE AND THE FIRST METHOD I USED WAS STORYTELLING. I WAS A LOT YOUNGER THEN AND MY REPERTOIRE WAS BUILT UPON STORIES MILTON ERICKSON HAD TOLD ME WHEN HE TRAINED ME. However, as this reader will not have that privilege any stories from your unconscious mind to the unconscious mind of the patient will do, as long as it is at that s l o w pace Margaret Mead told Erickson she had only experienced in a rare African tribe relatively free of disease.

SECOND METHOD OF OPENING THE SPACE IS MOCK FAMILY THERAPY VIA THE METHODS TAUGHT TO ME BY CARL WHITAKER (TO HELP OPEN THE SPACE OF THE PSYCHOANALYST AND GIVE THE ANALYST MOMENT OT MOMENT ACCESS TO THE PRIMITIVE AND PRIMORDIAL UNCONSCIOUS MIND OF THE PATIENT.

CARL WHITAKER, M.D. known for his seminal work called "The Roots of Psychotherapy" co-authored with Tom Malone, M.D., Ph.D. (Atlanta Psychiatric-6363 Roswell Road) said the craziest sounding shit in public of anyone-psychiatrist or psychologist-that I had ever met.

The first time I met him was at the Biltmore Hotel in 1979 in Los Angeles where he was presenting a one day all day Saturday workshop of about eight hours. He gave an example of his work by saying "The patient said-------and then I said-----and on and on for about five minutes. At the break I told him I met Tom Malone but had no idea of his working style/ Whitaker always looked upward a bit so as not to be as Bion wrote seduced to lose his unconscious mind through human contact said, "Tom Malone is catatonic, but you ought to look him up. He may have something for you." Then I wrote to him and asked him to write the foreword to my book "Psychotherapy, Insight and Style: The Existential Moment", Allyn & Bacon, Boston, 1981, 288 pp. which he did.

Then I met Whitaker again at the first Ericksonian Evolution of Psychotherapy Conference after Erickson's death on March 3, 1980-around December, 1980. I said, "Hey Carl, do you supervise family therapy?" He said "Yes" I said, "Only two problems-I live in Los Angeles" and he blurted out "Get a speakerphone" and I said "There are no families in Los Angeles" (a psychoanalytic stronghold along with New York City). He said, "Maybe God will be good to you!" Two weeks later two families came into my Beverly Hills practice-almost unheard of in Los Angeles.

He began to supervise me on a weekly basis, but kept saying "How can I take you seriously that you want to learn family when you don't have your own family in family therapy!" I was the moving force that made it happen so my parent were on the phone from Connecticut, Whitaker was on from Wisconsin Medical School, and my wife at the time, her parents, her brother and his future wife were all in three generational family therapy with Carl Whitaker. I remember on one occasion my mother shit all over him in a manner that she used to do to me that drove me up the walls. I said, "Hey Carl, what are you doing with that one?" He said, "Enjoying the taste!"

The chapter I wrote using a mock family therapy demonstration gives a good idea of the off the wall kinds of interventions that are totally unexpected by patients and therefore open up the space where psychotherapeutic intervention may actually sneak through the cracks.

THE LAST TIME I SAW WHITAKER PRESENT A WORKSHOP WAS IN SANTA BARBARA IN ABOUT 1994 shortly before he got a stroke. He said it wasn't the work that was hard, it was the justification. In other words, lawyers, licensing boards have forced psychoanalysts and psychotherapists to make everything explainable by the left brain, which severely reduces the likelihood that psychoanalysts would spend years of work on themselves to develop the capacity to do their best work when they are likely to be persecuted for that work which is correct at the unconscious level-or as Bion referred to it "LEARNING THROUGH EXPERIENCE", opening up the psychological space for learning through experience to actually occur. The older you get the less you want to explain yourself to legal authorities who have crippled the profession to this point in any case.

I sought out the best in the world to be trained by and of those only four knew how to keep the space open so the patient could and would learn from the experience itself. They were Milton Erickson, Carl Whitaker, Wilfred Bion and my analyst who shall remain anonymous.

THUS, WHEN I GAVE WORKSHOPS AT THE INTERNATIONAL LEVEL MY FIRST TASKS WERE TO: (OPEN THE SPACE SO ONE COULD "LEARN THROUGH EXPERIENCE" AS BION WROTE WAS THE PRIMARY WAY PSYCHOANALYSIS COULD BE EFFECTIVE!)

1.\ CREATEATHERAPEUTICENVIRONMENTWHEREBY THE PSYCHOLOGICAL SPACE WAS OPEN SO THAT TRAINEES COULD LEARN EXPERIENTIALLY AS THIS WAS A KIND OF LEARNING THEY WOULD NEVER FORGET AND BE ABLE TO UTILIZE IN THEIR OWN PERSONAL LIVES AS WELL AS THEIR PRIVATE PRACTICE. THE METHODS I USED TO BEGIN EACH WORKSHOP WERE

1.\ Ericksonian Storytelling where I told stories at the pace Margaret Mead told Milton Erickson she had only heard in a rare African tribe relatively free of disease for between one and one half and six hours (ultradian cycles as written about by Ernest Rossi, Ph.D.) which on many occasions had pinpoint accuracy in reaching the followed by unconscious minds of the trainees, followed by

2.\ Mock Family Therapy Demonstrations with volunteers from the workshop role playing mother, father, daughter and son, or additional family members the audience members may wish to create-dealt with in the free wheeling use of the absurdity and craziness of the role players (pathological projective identifications), at a speed of intervention that taught the trainees to give the responses of their unconscious minds prior to destroying the experience itself through left brain knowledge.

AT THIS POINT THE GROUP WAS IN A DIFFERENT STATE OF CONSCIOUSNESS WHERE THERE WAS THE TIME OF A DIFFERENT DRUMMER AND WHICH PSYCHOANALYTIC INTERPRETATIONS ALA BION COULD BE MADE IN A VERY LONGWINDEDMANNERCONTROLLINGTHEPACEASONE DID IN THE ERICKSONIAN STORYTELLING AND THEREBY CREATING "DISEASE FREE STATES OF BEING" IN WHICH THE PSYCHOANALYSIS WAS BEING DONE. THE REASON THAT BION'S WORK CANNOT BE CURRENTLY TAUGHT OR PRACTICED IS BECAUSE THOSE HAVING LEARNED IT AT THE LEFT BRAIN LEVEL DO NOT PRACTICE IT

Milton Erickson wrote of me that he "Respected my dedication to the work."-another of the greatest compliments ever paid me in that if Erickson didn't think you were a serious conscientious person he was just as likely to say to you "I never want to see your face again as long as I live!"

Donald Rinsley, M.D., Fellow, American College of Psychoanalysts stated that my having been trained by 17 world renown gifted "treaters" left me being able to do psychoanalytic work that was both "HEALING AND CURATIVE" and that he kept my book "Psychotherapy, Insight and Style: The Existential Moment" under his pillow at night." This was in an era prior to 1987 Welch vs. The American Psychoanalytic-where MD's had relatively little to do with clinical psychologists, who were viewed more as poachers on medical terrain.

Psychotherapy, Insight & Style: The Existential Moment, Allyn & Bacon, Boston, 1981, 288 pp. by Bergantino, L. is still of great value to psychoanalysts as it has verbatim excerpts from Bion actually supervising Stephen Salenger, M.D. psychoanalyst and a chapter on Bion's work where I had editorial help from James Grotstein, M.D., Michael Paul, M.D. and feedback from Richard Alexander, M.D. and Richard Edelman, M.D. all were Bion's analysands and had fascinating commentaries about their second training analysis with him when he came to Los Angeles from 1967-1979 from Sao Paulo Brazil.

VII.\ STATEMENT OF THE PROBLEM-DEDICATION

Erickson said he respected my "dedication to the work". This was the key element because without it little of what I wrote about in this book can be accomplished. To give an example in 1987 I was president of the Southern California Society of Clinical Hypnosis-a branch of The American Society of Clinical Hypnosis and at the time composed of medical doctors, dentists and psychologists. Many of the MD's were psychoanalysts as well and one of the presentations I gave was on working with "beta elements" that Bion wrote about within a psychoanalytic frame.

AT ONE OF THESE MEETINGS:

a)\ One woman psychologist yelled out, "Hey, Bergantino, when the fuck are you going to teach something somebody can learn!" (Blaming me-saying it was my fault she had no chance to profit from anything I said or did.

b)\ At the same meeting a woman psychiatrist said, "Dr. Bergantino, your work is marvelous, however, to achieve that kind of skill I would have to devote my entire life to doing clinical work. I use hypnosis to give a few suggestions so a person can lose weight or stop smoking, and then I go home and enjoy my husband and my children. I am not willing to devote my entire life to developing the clinical skills necessary to do what you do."

c)\ My experience of the psychiatrist was that she was fully appreciative of what I accomplished; and very honest about what sacrifices she would or would not make in terms of what she was or was not willing to do to develop her "THERAPEUTIC USE OF SELF" in terms of what I had shown her to be possible! This is perfectly alright. The mark of a good clinician is someone who knows his or her clinical limitations.

VIII.\ SCOPE OF THE BOOK

I lived a devoted almost monastic kind of life-almost like a Buddhist Monk-and the result was that an extrasensory perception became part of my personhood-from which I then had to learn where it could best be utilized-which was within the psychoanalytic frame of seeing patients 5 days a week (not 4) for fifty minute hours (not 45) for between 3 and 7 years per patient.

As only a few will take this book and its work as far as I did, and only a few will surpass it, the book provides a roadmap to psychoanalytic infinity which as Rod Serling used to say leaves students and practitioners of psychoanalysis with a viable option of how far they dare to travel along the road to "THE TWILIGHT ZONE."

IX.\DON'TTHROWOUTTHEBABYWITHTHEBATHWATER.

There have been many gifted treaters whose work I have relied on that for one reason or another, their work never became part and parcel of the development of a psychoanalytic use of self when it could have been instrumental in helping psychoanalysts turn certain tragic corners that otherwise may remain out of the clinician's reach and therefore never benefit patients particularly in treating the psychotic core of the personality and the underlying psychotic thinking disorders that Bion's work targets. Some of these whose work should have been included were

1.\ John Rosen, M.D.-a character disordered fellow as rumor has it who was thrown out of the American Psychiatric Association because he physically beat up some patients and he had sex with others. It is my understanding via hearsay that he lost his medical license.

Nevertheless, if you read Rosen's work on Direct Analysis in the 1950's, his work is both brilliant and seminal in knowing how to treat character disorders.

Rosen figured out in severely character disordered people that unless the clinician "cuts out the character disorder" as in psychoanalytic surgery; the analysis is little more than a masturbatory exercise in which the character disordered patient only becomes more proficient at manipulation.

As Woody Allen quoted Attila The Hun having said "Violence is justified when in the service of mankind", so went John Rosen.

Martin Grotjahn, M.D.-training analyst-Southern California Psychoanalytic Institute and Society-told me he was in Rosen's farmhouse in Doylestown, Pennsylvania, watching him work with a schizophrenic who got up from his chair and kicked Rosen right in the generals as hard as he could. Grotjahn said "When Rosen recovered he leaped out of his chair, got the man on the floor, and choked him within an inch of his life until he was blue in the face." Grotjahn, who was solely accustomed to psychoanalytic interpretation via words then said, while shrugging his shoulders with a feeling of helplessness, "What could I do? It was the man's method of treatment!" Then in an admiring way he laughed liked hell!

Carl Whitaker, M.D., another pioneer in the treatment of schizophrenia, told me he and Rosen were doing group analysis with a group of schizophrenics around 1956, and Rosen said, to a dissatisfied patient who had gone from therapist to therapist, "So here with me you are finding the golden breast milk in my interpretations that you have been searching for"; and the patient said, "Yes, yes" "You are providing the golden breast milk I have been looking for." Whitaker, then, tongue in cheek, as with Grotjahn, wishing they had the courage to do it themselves, said, "I could never forgive Rosen for what he did next. Right in the middle of the group (one hour into it) Rosen said, "Hey, Carl, let's go play golf! and both Whitaker and Rosen walked out right after the golden breast milk comment-another version of "I never promised you a rose garden."

2.\ Milton H. Erickson, M.D. told stories over 4 1/2 hours to six hours at a time at a pace Margaret Mead said she had only heard in a rare African tribe-"relatively free of disease". Dr. Ernest Rossi's article on ultradian cycles shows that the break time where patient resistance wears out and the patient becomes open to experience is about one and one half hours. I have had

> those break points at one and one half hours most of the time although in my workshops sometimes I told stories for either 4 and 1/2 or six straight hours at that very s l o w p a c e Margaret Mead told Erickson was relatively free of disease. Fritz Perls, the co-founder of gestalt therapy, wrote of working with people to reduce the state of dis-ease in helping patients move toward becoming all they could be.

At the pace Erickson told stories, and that Bion made long winded psychoanalytic interpretations, it is my gift to the profession to have made the connection that they both spoke at the same pace Margaret Mead told Erickson was "relatively free of disease" and I have connected that to what Perls wrote about reducing dis-ease in patients.

With the extra-sensory perception this book is intended to help you develop it is also my strongest hypothesis that psychoanalytic interpretation can deal with the "repetition compulsion" on a moment to moment basis "the existential moment-Bergantino, 1981" whereby such moment to moment psychophysiological knowledge can give the patient the tools with which to alter millions of repetitions that would otherwise later in life cause FATAL DISEASE FROM THE WEARING OUT OF BODILY ORGANS VIA THE REPETITION COMPULSION.

REVERSE PSYCHOANALYSIS-a term coined by James S. Grotstein, M.D. Training Analyst-Los Angeles Psychoanalytic Society and Institute, is where these non-stop stories are told while the analyst is paying attention to "minimal cues" which evoke in his or her unconscious mind to tell and weave together a series of stories from the psychoanalyst's own life which have PINPOINT ACCURACY IN EVOKING AN EXISTENTIAL SHIFT IN A LIFE LONG PERSONALITY CHARACTERISTIC THAT IS DESTRUCTIVE TO THE PATIENT. On occasion I have accomplished this in one session, while I continued afterwords to tell the stories to establish the disease free pace, and then shifted over to the long winded psychoanalytic interpretations as Bion used to make. (I actually have 12 hours of Bion actually supervising Stephen Salenger, M.D. where you hear the kind of interpretations of which I write. I have never heard them before or since Bion and his work cannot be accomplished without a working knowledge of his technique. As to whether these tapes could ever be published along with the book, or perhaps a video I made in Australia in 1988 where by work was described as "a mental precision that electrified the Australian therapeutic community." The use of extrasensory perception once developed can be utilized within the psychoanalytic frame to facilitate this kind of work.

THE DEDICATION OF THE PATIENT

I wrote of the dedication required of the psychoanalyst, but it takes just as much on the part of the patient to tolerate this kind of work.

One woman, in a moment of low frustration tolerance yelled at me, "Working with you is like trying to catch mercury!" Nevertheless, after two psychoanalyses and years of psychotherapy without her primitive mental states being helped (20 years of therapies) she was willing to do anything to get better. And with what I was doing she was experiencing progress. I respected each of these patients with whom I did this kind of work as much as I respected myself, my own gifts and abilities. They were extraordinary human beings.

3.\ CARL WHITAKER, M.D. = MOCK FAMILY THERAPY Mock family therapy is role playing where workshop trainees for example play the roles of mother, father brother and sister, and maybe add grandmothers and grandfathers, and the therapist increases his or her speed at trusting whatever goes through his or her unconscious mind in relation to that family, or mock family, as being relevant to doing the therapy even though it may sound totally crazy even to the therapist..

These crazy thoughts that go through the unconscious mind of the person role playing the therapist are actually in psychoanalytic terms severe pathological projective identifications that patients split off from because they are too painful to tolerate in oneself. While I use methods taught to me by Carl Whitaker, M.D., Carl often bragged that he was untrained and therefore unspoiled by psychotherapeutic and psychoanalytic education. This was a good point as far as it went but he never met or fully understood Bion's work and therefore as he said to me in our last meeting in Santa Barbara, CA in 1993 or 4-about six months prior to his stroke, he stated "the work wasn't the problem, but the justification". In other words he knew he was right and experience proved that to be true but onlookers thought he was a crazy son of a bitch and kept asking him to explain why he said as many crazy sounding things as he did.

However, if you look at saying the crazy pathological projective identifications of family members within the family system and even make systemic interpretations along the line of Tavistock with the madness being put into the group, the psychoanalyst significantly ups his or her speed of recognition of primitive unconscious material which is necessary in the psychoanalyst's development of psychoanalytic use of self to be able to move from sense perception, to depth of feeling as related to projected madness or craziness unique to that particular family or even the unconscious minds of its individual family members. This is why Whitaker had trouble with the justification. He did not understand severe pathological projective identification as a working concept while he indeed had the skills to pick up the phenomena better than any psychoanalyst I met other than Bion himself, and perhaps one or two others whom I shall leave unnamed for the moment.

By doing mock family therapy as part of the training of a psychoanalyst and responding to the patients' craziness with the craziness they evoke in the unconscious mind of the psychoanalyst much powerful work can be done by the psychoanalyst's manifestation of COURAGE in EXTENDING AND EXPANDING HIM OR HERSELF BEYOND THE CULTURE BIND.

4.\ Jean Paul Sartre and his work *Being and Nothingness* was the basis from which I began to do and consider humanistic existential psychotherapy between 1968 and 1971 in my doctoral work at the University of Southern California. The professor that taught this philosophical approach to experience was William Ofman, Ph.D. and he was brilliant. Psychotherapy wise I never had much interest in psychoanalysis until May, 1979 when I experienced and met Wilfred Bion, M.R.C.S. (Medical Royal College of Surgeons). For years I had read in existential and gestalt arenas, that the goal was "TO BE" "TO BECOME ALL THAT YOU COULD" and some patients and some therapists looked a little better or a little worse on that level, but basically they all put their pants on one leg at a time and there was no one whose "quality of being" really stood out as if to say, "OK, I read Sartre's Being and Nothingness and I have taken a path that has helped me evolve to the levels Sartre wrote about.

This was not so with Bion. He was magnificent! I have never seen or experienced anyone like him prior to meeting him, nor since I have met him, and the only thing that compels me to want to get this book out for all time, is that being a technical wizard of the psychotherapeutic arts, I figured out how to do it. Not everyone may want to do it, but in case they do they should not have to reinvent the wheel. I gave workshops in the mid-eighties entitled "THE THERAPEUTIC WIZARDRY OF DR. LEN BERGANTINO" The problem is that when psychoanalysts and psychotherapists understand what I am writing, they fear for their own livelihood because they are not that far along the journey. They should not be ruled by this fear, but by the opportunity to move farther along the continuum to as Bion wrote "BECOMING 'O'" Bion thought it was each person's job in life to devote his or her efforts to becoming all that they could (Sartre), but more specifically to devote their life to "Becoming 'O'" although one never reaches 'O' (pure being), one moves toward finer and finer discriminations of Becoming 'O'.

Bion wrote in this obliquely because during his lifetime it was bad enough he was considered from the Kleinien School, and the devout Freudians who misunderstood the Soul of Freud would have unmercifully persecuted him, so he wrote things in mathematical sequencing when referring to psychoanalysis, and most analysts didn't know what the hell he was talking about, but had to acknowledge he was brilliant. If he did not take the oblique approach his work would have been destroyed en toto, and analysts would have figured out Bion's work could cost them a lot of money if they really understood it.

5.\ Fritz Perls, M.D., Ph.D., who responded as best he could as the thing-in-itself, was the co-founder of gestalt therapy. For example, gestalt therapy has as an objective "aware process". However, Perls was known in the vignettes about him more by how he was in the world than "aware process." Perls was more than the sum of his gestalt parts-he responded in as full a way most of the time as his awareness and being permitted. Fritz did his most dramatic work in gestalt therapy training groups in Vancouver, Canada prior to his death in 1970. I was a doctoral students at USC from 1968-1971. I came from Connecticut where people customarily wore jackets and ties to everything and for the most part looked and felt like they fell off of a wedding cake. In Los Angeles, few people wore jackets and ties and even the jazz musicians were affected by "The Cool Era". But Fritz wore a "Red Robe" when he worked. I mean, a "Red Robe" and he was gifted. You just had to take this guy seriously!

Story has it that in one of these training groups a man got so angry with Perls that he wanted to kill him. He went to where Fritz was doing therapy and put his hands around Fritz's throat and began to choke him with the intent to kill him. Fritz said and meant every word of the following "KILL ME! I HAVE LED A FULL LIFE AND I AM READY TO DIE!" This was different than doing psychotherapy or doing gestalt therapy. This was BEING THE THING IN ITSELF AND IT SO MOVED THE MAN STRANGLING FRITZ THAT HE BEGAN TO WEEP. THERE WAS NO MANIPULATION IN THIS. IT WAS "PURE BEING"

Gestalt therapy gives the greatest degrees of latitude for this kind of response and it would probably fall under and understated category of creative process.

Another not so dramatic story was that in a group training session Fritz gave a patient-trainee an assignment to interrupt him every so many minutes-as a method of treatment for the man's withdrawn and reticent nature. Finally, after several interruptions Fritz yelled at the man to stop interrupting him! The patient-trainee responded "But Fritz! This was what you assigned me to do in the group!

Now, we come to the pure being part. Fritz was a very sophisticated psychotherapist and a trained psychoanalyst prior to his creation of gestalt therapy along with Paul Goodman. Yet, there is part of every person's personality that is a total jerk at times, and Fritz used this "Total Jerk Pure Being Part of His Personality" to do the therapy when he retorted "Yes, but I didn't say that I would like it!" That is the kind of thing therapists are customarily trained not to do or say and here it made the most sense to break the culture bind and intervene in this childish manner.

CONCLUSION

This is a book for all time. As I had extrasensory perception to help me find out things on a primitive level and depth with an ability to pick-up split off severe pathological projective identifications moment to moment, in an era when psychologists were only permitted to be research psychoanalysts by the American Psychoanalytic Association (but tightly controlled where that research was going that in many way nullified it as true psychoanalytic research, I have presented you a book that might at that time have been considered "wild psychoanalysis" and have shown you how "extrasensory perception can be developed and utilized by the therapeutic use of self within the psychoanalytic frame in ways that can enhance the treatment of borderline, narcissistic, obsessive compulsive, schizophrenic and other diagnoses as well as help pinpoint psychophysiological awareness which through the repetition compulsion can prevent dis-ease which will circumvent disease in later life . This kind of psychoanalysis will go a long way in preventing the next holocaust!

Dr. Bergantino and his two children were sent back on a karmic mission to complete the work. Dr. Bergantino is the reincarnated soul of Sigmund Freud and Julius Caesar. Those skill sets were required to complete this project. His children are Wilfred Bion and Milton Erickson. They taught Dr. Bergantino how to use paranormal abilities. We are all off the karmic wheel and WE WIL NOT BE BACK!!! GOODBYE!!!

[illegible] West Los Angeles • DR. LEN BERGANTINO (SPECIALTY: BETRA... Page 1 of 2

PsychDirectory. About Us | Basic Listing | Sponsored Listings | Contact Us

Mental Health > Psychology > Psychologist in West Los Angeles

Home Page Psychology Psychiatry Psychoanalysis Psychotherapy

Directory Index | Mental Health Professionals | Psychology | Psychologists

» Submit New Listing
» Psych User Login

Mental Health Professionals
Education and Training
Psychological Testing/Evaluation
Mental Health & Social Services
Organizations Centers & Institutes
Mental Health & Psychology News
Job Search Mental Health Jobs

Directory Search

Psychology Psychiatry Psychoanalysis Psychotherapy
Directory Index > Mental Health Professionals > Psychology > Psychologists

DR. LEN BERGANTINO (SPECIALTY: BETRAYAL MANAGEMENT)

Name/Company: **DR. LEN BERGANTINO (SPECIALTY: BETRAYAL MANAGEMENT)** [illegible]

Description:

"I AM FREUD! I AM CAESAR!"

FREUD: "THE PURPOSE OF AN ANALYSIS IS TO SAVE MAN'S SOUL."

EVIDENCE: WHEN MY FATHER DIED ON NOVEMBER 11, 1983, I SAW HIS SOUL LEAVE HIS BODY! DO YOU HAVE ONE!

CURRENT JOB: "SAVING MAN'S SOUL!"

"ET TU BRUTUS!"

"GIVE TO CAESAR WHAT IS CAESARS!"

Licensed Psychologist (CA 3517)

Diplomate in Family Psychology

American Board of Professional Psychology

CALL 310-207 9197

CORDIALLY,

CAESAR

Former Employment: EMPEROR OF ROME!

P.S. FLORAL SHILLS WELCOME

Current levels of interest:

1) Center for Kinetic Rehabilitation

2) Center for Megalomaniacal Studies

Country: United States
State: California
City: West Los Angeles, CA
ZIP / Postal Code: 90025
Phone: 310-207-9197
Contact Person: Dr. Len Bergantino
Map / route: View map / route
E-Mail Address: Send message
URL / Website: http://[illegible].com/lenbergantino

Classification(s):

Mental Health Professionals / Psychology / Psychologists
Mental Health Professionals / Psychotherapy / Psychotherapists

http://www.psychdirectory.com/directory/Mental_Health_Professionals/Psychology/Psyc... 12/21/2010